SALVATION CREEK

An Unexpected Life

SALVATION CREEK

An Unexpected Life

SUSAN DUNCAN

BANTAM

SYDNEY AUCKLAND TORONTO NEW YORK LONDON

Note: Some of the names of people in this book have been changed to protect their privacy.

SALVATION CREEK
A BANTAM BOOK

First published in Australia and New Zealand in 2006 by Bantam
This edition published in Australia and New Zealand in 2007 by Bantam

Copyright © Susan Duncan, 2006

Duncan, Susan (Susan Elizabeth).
    Salvation Creek: an unexpected life.

    ISBN 978 1 86325 638 4.

    1. Duncan, Susan (Susan Elizabeth). I. Title.

920.72

Transworld Publishers,
a division of Random House Australia Pty Ltd
Level 3, 100 Pacific Highway
North Sydney, NSW 2060
http://www.randomhouse.com.au

Random House New Zealand Limited
18 Poland Road, Glenfield, Auckland

Transworld Publishers,
a division of The Random House Group Ltd
61–63 Uxbridge Road, Ealing, London W5 5SA

Random House Inc
1745 Broadway, New York, New York 10036

Cover painting 'Church Point' by John Lovett
Chapter openers feature linocuts by Katie Clemson, from the series
'Pittwater Boatsheds', 2003.
Cover and text design by Nanette Backhouse/Saso Content and Design
Typeset by Midland Typesetters, Australia
Printed and bound by Griffin Press, South Australia

10 9 8 7 6

For my brother, John

PROLOGUE

THERE IS A HOUSE on a high, rough hill that overlooks the tawny green waters of Lovett Bay. It is pale yellow, with three chimneys and a red tiled roof splattered with lichen. An elegant verandah, with stately columns and polished wooden floors, stretches from end to end and on a still, summer evening it is quite magical to dine there, watching the light fade and birds fly home.

The house is reached by a winding stairway that begins at the shore and seems to meander on and on to nowhere. Sometimes, if it is early enough in the morning, or late enough in the afternoon, swamp wallabies pause on the pathway and stare with big, uncertain eyes before suddenly taking fright and thumping off into the bush. In summer, the path is flecked with mint coloured moss, the same shade of green as the blotches on the smooth trunks of the spotted gums that form a towering canopy in front of the sky. It is a mysterious pathway that seems to lead perhaps to the heavens themselves. The climb is steep and yet if you take it slowly and pause to look at Lovett Bay, there is no need to feel tired or breathless.

Many boats are moored in the bay, some big and immaculately maintained, with tall masts that seagulls or cormorants cling to, scanning the waters for their next feed. Others are the dreams, perhaps broken, of people who have seen beauty in an old wreck and who plan, one day, to restore it to former glory. Many of these wrecks have sat for years and I have never seen anyone go near them. Sometimes, the Water Police do a tour of the bay in one of their orange and white motorboats and from time to time, one or two of the rottenest vessels are towed somewhere else or taken out to sea and sunk.

It is more than six years now since I first started trekking up these steps and when I reach the fork in the pathway near the top, I still can't decide which way is preferable. The right fork is steep and leads to a vast, spongy lawn which is a stark contrast to the muted, scraggy bush. It isolates the house, like an emerald lake, from the spotted gums that soar like straight-backed, silent sentries. There are a few brooding ironbarks too, that are sometimes twisted, like wounded warhorses. The other pathway is a gentle ascent but it veers slightly away from the house. The temptation is to go for the direct route even if it makes calf muscles ache and the blood rush to your head. But the better choice, I think, is the milder access even though it appears to lead to an old, wooden workshed that lacks even a hint of the grandeur of the main house.

The house is called *Tarrangaua* which is an Aboriginal word meaning, I am told, *high, rough hill*. But I cannot find the word in any Aboriginal dictionary. The woman who named the house was a famous Australian poet, Dorothea Mackellar. She died in 1968 so I cannot ask her how the name came about. Perhaps she sat around the dinner table with a group of guests one night in the beautifully proportioned main sitting room and they played a game to invent the best title. The name is certainly grand, and so was she.

She would arrive at Church Point in a chauffeur driven yellow Rolls Royce where her caretaker would wait for her with the launch. Lovett Bay, you see, is accessible only by boat – unless you want to walk five kilometres along the escarpment then down into the valleys of the Ku-ring-gai Chase National Park. It is a sensational walk that takes about an hour and a half but it is tough in parts, with steep rocky tracks where you can easily lose your footing. In contrast, the boat trip is five minutes of pure pleasure as you cut past McCarrs Creek, then Elvina Bay and finally swing west into Lovett, with the wind blowing in your face and the snap of salt air in your lungs.

At the time the house was built for Dorothea Mackellar in 1925, she was wealthy, single, forty years old and already involved in a love affair with the brandy bottle. But I knew nothing of all this when I first made my way past the house and into Lovett Bay. I was a messy, jangly forty-eight year old struggling to find a place to belong. I'd watched two of the most important people in my life slide slowly and painfully into death and the horror of it snatched away lightheartedness, stubbed out hope. Blotted out my idea of where I fitted in. I'd been spinning in a career for more years than I cared to remember, where the days had become a blur of office politics and office pressures, where I felt only a rising sense of detachment from one week to the next. I had no idea what I was looking for to give my life new purpose, only that when I found this intangible, wraithlike *something*, I would be able to still the restlessness. Begin again.

As I bumped across the water in a leaky tin dinghy to see a property for sale in Lovett Bay, I did not know that the journey had begun. That *Tarrangaua*, the pale yellow house with the corridor of columns and the long verandah on the high, rough hill, would hold the key to it all.

1

ONE MORNING, FOR NO reason at all, I cannot find the strength to get out of bed. It's mid-winter in Melbourne. Trees are naked under a dirty brown sky. A few dead leaves skitter joylessly in an irritable wind. The alarm clock went off an hour ago. The dog hasn't been walked. I haven't showered, dressed or left for the office. The thought of throwing back the covers and putting my feet on the floor fills me with terror. I lie there, squeezing my eyes shut. Descending slowly into a deep, dark hole that I welcome. I want oblivion so badly I can think of nothing else.

When I look at the clock again, two hours have evaporated. I reach for the phone and call the doctor.

'I can't make the decision to get out of bed.'

'Stay there, then. Stay there for as long as you want. You're ill.'

I put the phone back in its cradle, look around an anonymous mustard bedroom in my rented house. Mirrored closet doors reflect a haggard old woman. I turn away and face the window, counting on my fingers. Eighteen. Eighteen months since my brother, John, and my husband, Paul, died. For a second only, I squint into the future. The vacant spaces are unbearable.

The crying starts in silence. Tears wetting the pillow, dampening the collar of my pyjamas. Through the day it builds, until swollen eyes reduce the world to a narrow slit and my dog, Sweetie, climbs on the bed for the first time in her life to press her warm, black body close. When the maelstrom ends two days later, nothing has changed. My brother is still dead. And so is my husband.

My brother battled cancer for five years. They say a heart attack killed him. But it was exhaustion. I sat, the night before he died, on a white chair on white carpet in his white bedroom. He lay on a white bed under white sheets, so thin, frail and white himself, he barely existed. He breathed in quick little sips, the tumours in his lungs wider than his arms. They squeaked like an old flywire door when you rubbed them. As I'd done in the past to relieve a smidgin of his pain. On this night, he moved a finger. No rub. Thank you. One eye open, the other closed. Already nearly dead.

'Shall I hold your hand?'

The finger again. No.

My brother never showed fear. A lifetime on the racetrack taught him to disguise his emotions. Win? Lose? He never changed. Perhaps a deeper tinge of pink in his cheeks if the win was big, a white band around his mouth if the loss hit hard. The only time I saw a hint of dread was the day we watched the races on television – he in bed, me propped against pillows alongside. I knew he'd had a big bet and nerves got the better of me.

'I'll just go and make a cup of tea,' I said, getting up.

'Not yet,' he said. 'Don't leave the room yet.'

So I sat, truly frightened for the first time. As stupid as I know this is, my brother had been ill for so long I thought he would just stay ill. I refused to accept that he would die. Not the handsome, blonde, blue-eyed big brother who built a billycart so his irritating little sister could be dragged along behind when he went out double-dink riding with his friend. Not the brother who got his girlfriends to make his sister's clothes because he thought her mother had lousy ideas about what suited her. Not the brother she had loved without question all her life. Larrikin, gambler, beautiful dresser, generous spirit, comfort and support. Not her big, invincible brother.

As a child, John was wise and compassionate. Almost five years older than me, he steadied the impact of rocky episodes in my parents' marriage, dragged me along in his older life. Sometimes, at the height of my parents' disappointment with each other, they would turn to us children standing white-faced and trembling and demand we choose between them.

'Choose no-one,' my brother would whisper in my ear, his arm protectively around my shoulders.

'But I want Mummy.'

'Choose no-one and they will have to stay together.'

My brother recognised early the power of emotion. He quickly learned the power of money. When he was barely ten years old, he set up a soft drink counter at the local tennis club. On days thick with bush flies and corrugated heat, profits soared. When frost crunched underfoot and our hands turned blue waiting for the school bus, he kept profits flowing by scrounging empty bottles from the local tip. Worth threepence each, he filled the billycart he towed behind his horse over and over until the tip was cleared. He amassed enough cash to buy a big, boxy blonde stereo on tiny, tapered legs that seemed to glow and throb in our sombre sitting room where we played *South Pacific* on wet winter nights until the record wore out.

Once, my mother hit him. I can still smell that cold, damp morning when my father's belt came out and she wrapped it around John's legs as he marched barefoot down the path in front of the hydrangeas. He was about eight years old, blue-eyed, hair so white we nicknamed him Snow. Tall for his age but all bones.

'You are *not* going to school without your shoes!' she snapped.

'I told you. I can't find them!'

'Get back inside and have another look!'

'No!'

Whip. A red streak on white legs. My mother sitting abruptly on the concrete pathway. Crying with shock and remorse. She had never raised a hand to either of us before.

John squatted beside her and pulled her head to his chicken

chest. Holding her until she calmed. 'Please, Mum. Don't hit me again. It upsets you too much.' He'd always been unbeatable.

My husband's illness, like my brother's, came out of nowhere. His sneezing woke me at about 2 am.

'Get a tissue, for heaven's sake.'

The sneezing continued. Seriously cranky, I turned on the light. His eyes were open but unseeing. Please, God, please. Not both my boys. Please. I promised a God I thought I didn't believe in obeisance forever in return for Paul's life.

He was still breathing when they lifted him into the ambulance, the seizures settling into a steady pattern. I climbed into the seat beside the driver, a calm young woman with an open face.

'This is going to sound bizarre,' I babbled, talking fast and intimately to try to hold back panic.

'Tell me anyway.'

'Two Sundays ago, Paul dreamed his friend, Terry, who is dead, landed in a plane and tried to convince Paul to join him on a trip. Exactly a week later, Paul dreamed his mother, who died before Terry, was combing his hair and asking him to follow her.'

The driver said nothing as she eased the ambulance through the empty streets in the last hour before dawn.

'So I guess what I want to know . . . want to ask . . . Is my husband dying back there?'

'It doesn't look good,' she said, gently.

She was brave in many ways, that smiley young driver, but especially courageous to tell me the truth. She could have lied. It would have been so much easier on her.

A few hours later, when the drugs kicked in and the seizures finally abated, when life and understanding filled Paul's eyes again, one of the doctors asked him a question: 'Who is the Queen of Australia?'

'I suppose you mean that bloody Elizabeth,' he grumbled.

I laughed with relief. This was the Paul I knew so well.

Irreverent. Pig-headed. Caustic. Unswervingly true to his Irish political heritage despite never having set foot on the velvety green land of his ancestors. Thank you, God. I owe you.

Days later, after tests and then more tests, the tidy, cleanly shaven neurosurgeon with thinning hair pulled the flimsy curtain around Paul's hospital bed. 'There's a tumour at the front of your brain. It's the size of a small apple.'

Paul smiled. As though he'd known all along. He looked almost uncaring, dissociated. But I thought I might faint. For a moment the room lurched. Then settled. I felt the blood drain from my face as though a plug had been pulled.

Paul kept smiling to himself, withdrawn into his own space. So I did all the talking. 'You can operate, can't you?' I asked.

'We'll have to. The tumour is putting pressure on the brain.'

'Well, it could be all right, couldn't it?'

'We won't know until we've done a biopsy.'

'Can you guess?'

'Why don't we wait and see?'

Three days later the worst possible news. Glioblastoma. A quick growing, aggressive son-of-a-bitch that could not be stopped. A death sentence. I didn't owe God at all.

When my brother first became ill, I'd traipsed the dusty roads of Mexico after hearing about a miracle clinic. On the way through poverty stricken villages, along a road more potholed than whole, my cab broke down. The driver, too drunk on tequila to be able to even lift the bonnet, sank to the ground on the shady side of the car and told me to keep walking. I'd get there eventually. An hour later I staggered into a clinic set in a flaking 1950s motel with blood red carpet, vinyl chairs and saggy wooden beds. People queued at a box-office window that used to be the motel reception desk, squandering their last few dollars on hope.

One man, tall, thin and dark with desperation, argued with the nurse on the other side of the glass partition: 'The money will come through. I've arranged to mortgage the house. Give me the medication. Please.'

He didn't get his pills that day, that young Englishman who would probably die in Mexico. But I took my brother there anyway. Try anything. That's how I saw it. There was nothing to lose. John walked away.

I made other calls to obscure clinics in Europe and America, some in Australia, and felt surges of hope when friendly voices asked for medical details but then, quick as a flash, came back with fantastic fees for treatment. I'm not sure exactly when I understood it was all a sales pitch, selling guilt to the healthy, hope to those without hope. Maybe it was when a clinic in California asked for a list of financial assets to be faxed before it asked what disease needed to be treated. I decided, quickly, that I would not go down that path with Paul.

The tumour gobbled everything. His brilliant intellect. Laconic humour. Razor sharp wit. Once a voracious reader, he would lie in bed, book in hand, giving the impression his mind still kicked over. But he seldom turned the page. I stopped by the hospice every morning on my way to work as the editor of a national women's magazine. On my way home, I called in to see my brother, then drove another two suburbs to visit Paul again. To sit alongside his bed until he drifted into sleep. Which meant getting home late. Wondering when to fit in a load of washing. When to clean the house. Whether it was selfish and irresponsible to steal an hour for a hot bath. Whether I could find enough strength and energy for the day ahead. It was like being on a hurdy-gurdy. Not enough time. Ever. Nothing done properly.

Occasionally, Paul would suddenly become lucid again, in a way that was as cruel as it could be because it made me think – hope – that the experts were wrong and he would beat the odds: 'What's on the cover of the magazine this week?'

Halfway through my answer, he'd drift off again into a strange world where thoughts were tangled and friends, many long dead, flickered in and out of his mind: 'Must look up Don in Hong Kong next time.'

'Yes. Great idea.' But Don had succumbed to alcoholism a decade earlier.

My brother died as the sun came up on a Wednesday morning. His flame-haired, sharp-tongued wife, Jan, whom we call Dolly, steadfastly by his side as she had been throughout their lives together. I set aside Saturday morning to write his eulogy so when the phone rang, I flew into a rage at the interruption.

'What!'

'It's the hospice. Can you come and see Paul?'

I wanted to scream 'No!' Wanted to yell at everyone to leave me alone, to give me a break, just a tiny break, so I could write my brother's life in a way that did him justice.

'What's the matter?'

'Nothing. Nothing. Well, he's had a bit of a fall. Can you get here? Quickly? He's asking for you.'

In his room with its views across monochrome Melbourne suburbs, Paul lay on a mattress on the floor. Another, empty mattress had been placed next to him. So I knew he was dying. The empty mattress was for me. Late one night when I was sitting with him, a nurse had told me that when death approached, a second bed appeared for families to lie close and hold tightly for the last time.

I crawled onto the mattress beside him and cradled his head in my arms. 'I love you more than anyone in the world,' I whispered.

He lifted his hand with its beautiful long fingers – like a surgeon's, his mother used to say proudly – and pointed to where his heart was fading away.

'More,' he said. He smiled wonderfully.

The fall, I discovered, had been caused by a heart attack. And that's what killed him. Not the tumour at all. So we had two funerals in a week. My brother's in Melbourne. Paul's in Sydney, his hometown.

A few days after Paul's funeral, when it was Monday again, I zipped on my work face, climbed into my high heels and returned to my office to sit behind my desk. I locked loss in a hollow space and, fortified with my good old Melbourne public school upbringing that hammered home the maxim that the best way to get over a problem was to get on with it, I goosestepped onwards.

Until the day I couldn't get out of bed.

2

I LAY UNDER THE DOONA in my manky blue-checked cotton pyjamas, staring at those mustard walls, confusing day and night, for five days. I suppose I must have fed the dog and I have a vague memory of the phone ringing. I also recall opening a can of tomato soup and eating it with buttered toast. Which is what my mother gave me when I was a little girl and my tummy felt bad. Tomato soup or rice pudding. But I didn't have any rice pudding.

On the sixth day I finally get up, walk the dog, shower, dress, turn the key in the ignition and swing carefully into peak-hour traffic. I pick up coffee from the corner shop. Hang my coat behind the office door. I sit behind my huge, ugly desk with its desolate views of West Melbourne and wish every celebrity to hell, every whining bad luck story to the same place.

When colleagues look enquiringly at me, I smile. 'Better?' they ask.

'Yup. Virus or something. Fill me in.'

Covers to choose. Stories to chase. Staff to manage. Crying often, but pretending it's over a reader's heartbreaking story. I alone know I don't really give a stuff about the readers any more.

Sometimes, when the cover lines won't gel, I daydream about being dead. Escaping the whole shit bundle of grief in a single bound.

But then I hear my brother's words: 'All those people who kill themselves and I lie here fighting to live another minute.'

Paul's words: 'Live for the quicksilver moments of happiness. Recognise and absorb them. They are rare and precious.'

I have long given up the search for happiness, though. What I want now is peace. No Friday morning envelope with disappointing circulation figures. No shrinking budgets, no being beaten by the opposition. No stress. No responsibility beyond my front door. Work, a career, the media — it is all a silly game, anyway, when death is inevitable and it's simply a question of when.

During those awful first months after the boys die, a routine begins with my stepdaughter, Suzi. We meet on Friday nights for dinner at a casual pub restaurant in St Kilda. Suzi, the actor. Big-eyed and skinny in her fashionably frayed op shop clothes. Suzi, who was there when her father died. Who sat with him each afternoon. Who loved him unconditionally. Which was the only way with Paul. I tell myself I am helping her to talk through the loss of a parent at our regular dinners. But she gives me far more than I am able to give her. She listens and listens and is the only one who lets me drop the façade of coping.

I call her around six thirty every Friday night. 'Let's meet early. I'm buggered.'

'Great. I'll catch the tram now. See ya there.' Her actress-trained voice carries far beyond the phone.

We never alter the routine. I order the same main course every week. So does Suzi. Lamb for me, steak for her. And the same wine. I ask for the same table, and when it's not available, I feel a sudden lurch of fear, as though I am plunging unprepared into the unknown. Death has snatched away any illusion of control and only dogged routine gives me a semblance of stability.

White napkins are swished into our laps, wine ordered, the buttery smell of baking pastry fills the room. Waiters, black clad stick figures balancing plates and human nature with equal skill, take our orders and give us respite from our everyday world. When Suzi and I cry, as we often do, they look the other way, those waiters. Or bring a glass of water and no words. Or a sinful pastry. The kindness of strangers. It is overwhelming.

One night, when it is nearly midnight and I've drunk too much, and the world has shrunk to the table where we sit, wine blots out my last vestige of emotional reserve.

'You know, you're a gift, Suzi. A gift in my life. If I'd had a child I would have wished for you.'

She shrugs as though it's no big deal. 'You have me,' she says.

And for a moment I feel as though I belong somewhere. But it has been a habit, for most of my life, to need others to tell me where I fit. So I back away from the impulse to make Suzi an anchor. Anchors, anyway, if they do not come from within yourself, can die on you. Or move on. Or turn out to be just plain unreliable.

There are moments, though, when my breath comes in short gasps and a single word or sound, such as my brother's name or an ambulance siren, can trigger waves of panic that make me want to jump up and flee. Or lean over and vomit. Just the sight of an ambulance leaves me shaky and distraught, unable to continue on my way for a small passage of time.

I discover quickly that there is no such thing as an ordinary moment any more. Too many ordinary moments have ended in disaster. Like going to bed one nondescript night and waking up to a husband with a brain tumour. Like listening to my brother's light cough and then getting a phone call to say it's a rare kind of cancer. I begin to assume the worst outcomes from the most trivial events. If Suzi is late for our dinner, it's a crash, not heavy traffic. If the phone rings late at night, it's a death, not a friend touching base. No. Nothing can be trusted to be ordinary any more.

At the office, I sometimes find myself sitting and staring at nothing, playing little mind games. I ask myself one question after another, but they are all the same in the end. What I ask myself in a dozen different forms is, if I die tomorrow, who will miss me? Will there be any regrets?

Answering the *regrets* part is easy. I've danced at the White House with tall, handsome young soldiers in crisp dress uniform. Driven around Somalia with men carrying machine guns perched on the roof of the car. Talked to Demi Moore about sex over a cup of coffee and watched her push a half-eaten chocolate petit four around her plate, too disciplined to swallow the final, tiny mouthful. I've jumped icefloes in Newfoundland to photograph helpless baby harp seals being clubbed to death while nearby their mothers wailed pitifully as the floating, white wastelands turned red with the blood of their young.

I've been blasted by the foul stench of a polar bear's breath while he was being airlifted from a tiny town called Churchill, in Canada, to an isolated, snowy place where there were no humans to feel threatened, no rubbish bins to ransack. I've wandered through Imelda Marcos's vast, stuffed closets in Malacanang Palace, in the Philippines, counting her shoes and fur coats. Hitchhiked from Cape Town to Windhoek, sleeping by the side of roads so isolated only a car a day passed by. Spent an afternoon with a sober Richard Burton in his movie set trailer, lulled by his seductive voice and charmed by his earthy humour. Heaps of assignments, miles of travel, mostly at someone else's expense. An interesting, privileged, capricious journalist's life.

No. No regrets. I'll die without feeling there is still much to do. But the other question, the one about *who will miss me*, I find difficult to confront. Because no-one will, not for long anyway. Transitory lives like mine touch many surfaces but rarely leave a mark. So when an old skin cancer on my top lip returns, I merely shrug.

'How much of the lip will go?' I ask the doctor.

'Nearly all of it.'

He reaches for my hand but I move it away, pretend I don't see his gesture of compassion.

12

'That's ok. I'm ok with that. It's not like I'm a young girl with her life ahead of her.'

But what I mean is that if death is the final outcome of life, what does it matter whether you have a top lip or not?

'When do you want to do this?' I ask.

He is struggling with my off-handedness and looks puzzled, as though there's some part of an equation that's missing.

'I can book you into a hospital or you can have it done at the clinic,' he says.

'What do you suggest?'

'Well, if we do it at the clinic, I'll do the lip reconstruction myself. In hospital, you can use a plastic surgeon of your choice. Do you want to think about –?'

'The clinic will be fine. Thanks.'

That night I call in, as I do at least twice a week, to have dinner with my brother's wife, Dolly. Of the fire engine red hair. The routine suits us. She cooks, I eat. For her, the routine of two at dinner continues and she doesn't have to wrestle with what quantities to cook for one. The following morning, she does the dishes while I grind my way to the office.

She's chopping onions when I mention I need to have a little surgery on my lip.

'I'll drive you to the clinic,' she says.

'Nah, I'll take a cab. It's no big deal.'

She looks at me sharply. Then changes the subject. 'They call us the Black Widows, you know,' she says.

'You're kidding!'

'Sounds a bit glamorous, doesn't it.'

We are both flippant about death in those early days after the boys are buried. Flippant in a way that shocks some friends, relieves others, but ultimately allows us to publicly acknowledge their absence without being shattered by it.

'Jesus, Dolly. Remember Paul's funeral? Remember dear old

13

Keith, coming up to us? We were standing in the middle of the room like a couple of crows in a paddock. "*Don't stand too close*, you said. *We're on a roll!*"'

Dolly laughs, throws the onions into a frying pan, and wipes tears from her eyes. Onion tears? We fill our glasses with more wine.

'The poor bastard took off like a rabbit. Come to think of it, he didn't look too flash himself, did he?'

'What about Taronga Zoo?' she asks, still laughing.

It was the day after Paul's funeral. I'd drunk a barrel of wine at the wake and, later, even more at dinner. I had a drilling headache. Burning, roiling stomach. A paralysing hangover. All I wanted to do was lie still.

Dolly and my brother's best friend, James, were taking the ferry from Circular Quay to Taronga Zoo to fill in time before our flight to Melbourne. She insisted I join them.

Somehow, I controlled my churning, poisoned stomach on the ferry trip. From the wharf, we climbed a narrow, dizzying spiral walkway to catch a cable car to the zoo. At the summit, I turned to look at the hordes of cheerful, chatting families in a snaking line behind us, waiting their turn. Just as we were about to climb into the cable car, I felt nausea rise in a sudden, dreadful, uncontrollable wave. There was nowhere to run, nowhere to hide.

I leaned over the fence and, in front of hundreds of people, vomited copiously.

'Had the cable car all to ourselves. Three empty seats!' Dolly says, giggling.

Wine flows again. Dolly brings our plates to the table. Huge steaks with a mushroom and onion sauce, a fresh green salad with lots of chopped parsley, the same as her mother makes. Mashed potatoes whipped with more butter than milk.

'So do you want me to drive you to the clinic on Monday?' she asks again, sitting down to eat.

'No thanks. It's easier to grab a cab.'

'Right. Well. Do you want me to pick you up?'

'Nope. I'll grab a cab.'

Dolly looks at me hard. Torn between respect and concern.

'I'll be fine. Prefer to go alone, then I don't have to worry about keeping anyone waiting.'

'Should we open another bottle?' she asks.

We are still drinking from my brother's cellar which he made sure was stocked for Dolly's future. Along with the wine, he left a detailed letter telling her when to sell certain wines at auction, when to make sure the whites were drunk. Taking care of her from the grave.

'Yeah, why not? It's Saturday.'

3

THE FOLLOWING MONDAY, I call a cab to take me to the clinic. I arrive on schedule to find a yellow room full of anxious, mostly middle-aged people. There will be a long wait, the receptionist tells me. One by one, as names are called, people disappear and return a while later with red-rimmed eyes and thick bandages over ears, arms, noses, foreheads. They look hangdog, like casualties of war, as they sit and wait for pathology results and permission to go home.

Then it's my turn. I lie in a chair like a dentist's and place my mind in another world. I am in Maine. It is autumn. There's a field full of pumpkins, golden in the evening light. The trees are red, orange and yellow and the purple sky is filled with Canadian geese flying in perfect formation, going south for the winter.

I count pumpkins in my imaginary field, a field I once saw driving back from Newport, Rhode Island, when, too sleepy to continue, I pulled off the highway onto a narrow dirt track. It was after reporting the America's Cup. Not the time Alan Bond won it and made Australians proud. The time before, in 1980. The pumpkin field was so quietly exquisite, I have never forgotten it and I conjure the image often, when I need to escape moments that might otherwise be unbearable. Like losing most of your top lip to a sneaky little cancer.

The knife cut feels like a gentle tug and most of my top lip is flicked into a shiny kidney-shaped stainless steel dish. Wads of white bandages are pressed hard on the wound and the tinny scent of blood fills the room. After a while, when the blood flow

17

eases and the pathology results confirm all the cancerous skin has been cut away, the specialist begins to rebuild my lip, taking flesh from inside my mouth and pulling it forward to drag it up over the missing bit. He hums through his work and the nurses chat casually about their holiday plans as they hand him instruments.

Then he leans across me and it is the first time I've felt a body closely since I crawled onto the mattress beside my dying husband. It is strange how I can lose a lip, deny pain, smell my own blood and remain detached. Yet the casual touch of another human being almost brings me undone.

After eight hours, I leave the clinic with a brick of bandage balanced on a tender new lip like some kind of primitive tribal decoration. I am told to avoid hot food, drink through a straw, stay quiet.

At the house, my mother waits with every kind of liquid food lined up on the kitchen bench. I'd tried to stop her coming from her home at the foot of the Blue Mountains but seeing her face is unexpectedly comforting. She hands me a drink with a straw and sends me to bed like a little girl. She resists turning it into her own tragedy. At least for a while.

I am supposed to spend a week convalescing, but two days later I drive to the office and tiptoe up the back stairs to my desk to avoid having to explain what's happened. I look bizarre, but the office offers routine and I grab it like a lifeline. At home, there's too much time to think. There is a tight band of pain around my chest, though, and I begin to wonder if I am on the edge of a heart attack or just slowly going mad. I do not care much, either way.

Suzi senses my detachment from my own welfare and insists on making an appointment with a shrink. I keep the date although I am ashamed Suzi thinks I need psychiatric help. In the shrink's dimly lit office, I act weird, as though we're chatting informally at a cocktail party. I interview her, push away a loathsome box of tissues on the table next to my slippery leather chair and try to give the impression that all is well and I am tough. Shrinks, I think as I sit there, are for wimps.

'Thought you'd have a couch or something. Not just a chair.'

'That's only in movies.'

'Right.'

'So tell me why you're here.'

'Well, my brother and husband died within three days of each other. About nineteen months ago. And I still feel a bit sad sometimes. So I need some tools. To cope with grief. Give me the tools. I'll do the rest.'

She looks at me over her glasses, that kind and clever shrink, and suggests I start right back at the beginning, before the boys were even ill, and that we worry about *grief coping skills* a little later.

I tell her in a flat, off-hand way about my brother and my husband, trying to rush her to the bit where she gives me the key to escaping sorrow. But she slows the narrative down with questions and forces me to backtrack when I try to skip over the worst parts. By the third session, when I arrive with my own box of tissues, there is very little she doesn't know.

She explains that most people feel guilty for being the one still living. She teaches me to focus on the great times, not the moments I let slip past unnoticed. She brings me to understand that grief goes on for a long time, perhaps forever, but it's possible to live with it. Not for it.

Then, one day not long after she says it is time for me to move on from her, I reach the real turning point. Tired of the stress, the chest pains, the feeling that until I can sort out my head I have no right to be behind a desk making big decisions, I decide that I hate my job and a big, fat salary can't paper over the cracks any more.

I can't remember the last time I sat in the bath with a glass of white wine and a plateful of cheese and biscuits and sang my lungs out. I can't remember the last time I approached a ringing phone without fearing what I'll be told. I can't remember the last time I woke up and looked at the day ahead with enthusiasm.

The concept of jumping from a career into nothing is frightening. All my life I've never leapt until I had somewhere to land. Always the job, then the life. That's how I've lived. Now I am turning all that around. Life first. How utterly terrifying. Because by taking the life option I am once again opening myself to feeling, to being vulnerable, to taking emotional risks, to hurting. But I understand the victory in realising that hurting is one way of knowing you are alive. And I, of all people, know that time does not stretch on forever.

I join the ranks of the unemployed a little less than two years after the boys die, selling the monster white house with its lacy gazebo overlooking the Nepean River in NSW where Paul and I based ourselves. Although we never spent much time there. We flitted off to Los Angeles for a while and when we returned, used it more as a weekender, renting space in the city because the each-way 90-minute car and train commute was exhausting.

Earlier in the year I bought an apartment in Melbourne as an investment, which will provide an adequate rental income, and I have enough money to live on, if I'm careful, for the rest of my life. My plan now is to search the countryside for a new, cheap house, in a new town, where I plan to make new friends and take up a worthy cause. I am going to reinvent myself and leave loss packed in a tightly shut corner of my mind.

I have three months before the new owners take possession of the big white house. It's not much time to find a new home and I begin the search immediately.

The company car with bucket seats and cruise control is back with the company. I now have a high-slung, big-wheeled, grunty second-hand ute that can claw through creek beds and scale mountains. Its name is Fearless Fred. My dog, Sweetie, too old to jump, puts her front paws on the edge of the truck tray and I heave her in. With a sniff and a scratch, she settles next to an icebox filled with cans of dog food, tea, milk and biscuits, as though she's been a ute dog all her life.

'Forward ho, huh, old girl?' I say, slamming the tailgate. Fred slips easily into gear and the countryside beckons like the pages of a good book. I point south, perhaps because it is familiar territory.

On our first night a motel refuses to allow my gentle Rottweiler to spend the night with me so I storm into a shop, buy a foam mattress and a sleeping bag and throw them in beside Sweetie. A few kilometres further along, I swing off the highway onto a dirt track. Just before sunset, I kill the engine under a few straggly gum trees near a dry creek bed and let the dog out for a wander. Sweetie and I picnic – me, on the meatloaf sandwich I meant to have for lunch and she on a can of dog food. When it is dark, I lift her into the tray and climb alongside her to sleep on my new mattress, like a tramp under the stars. She is warm and smells like freshly baked bread. I feel safe with her.

Halfway through the night her quiet breathing slips into a grinding snore and I wake to find myself pressed uncomfortably against the wheel hub while she stretches out luxuriously.

'Move over, you great big bloody dog!'

She opens an eye, sighs deeply and doesn't budge an inch.

That lovely, placid animal and I travel through towns too small to support a local bakery. Towns where the only restaurant is a laminated annexe off the rusty, local service station. Towns where every menu is either fried, deep-fried or canned. Bacon and eggs, hamburgers, steak sandwiches. Chips, calamari, potato scallops or chicken nuggets. Baked beans, spaghetti or tomatoes on toast. In bigger towns, where there are coffee shops and at least one chemist, fresh fruit gets piled into the icebox and I drift along, apple in hand, assuming my new home will suddenly appear to me in a flash of recognition. I imagine its discovery will be akin to an epiphany and I will march onwards knowing I have done what will turn out to be for the best.

After trudging around a few properties described glowingly in real estate advertisements, I break the property description code. 'Charming country cottage' means a white ant infested ruin with a sagging verandah. 'Acreage with beautiful views' means the soil is so poor you couldn't grow a weed. No photo of the house is just plain scary. Don't go there.

'Why are these people selling?' I ask one agent after another.

There is a tragic sameness to the answers: 'Couldn't make a go of it.'

It forces me, eventually, to think beyond the romantic notion of plunging starry-eyed and reckless into a new environment and to look, instead, at the details. Who will be my friends in this town where I know no-one? Who will I talk to? What will I fill my days with? How can I learn the history of a town and people before I buy? Can I tell, by watching faces or eavesdropping on conversations, whether this is a happy or desperate place? Whether I have anything in common with even a single person?

Pulling the plug on one life and launching another is, I am beginning to understand, fraught with risk. But I struggle on, hoping fate will lend a hand. That some tiny corner of a house or garden – an old fireplace, a bed of old-fashioned roses – will strike a chord and give me the courage to commit. I see mudbrick houses, pole houses, log houses, iron houses, stone houses and even a house with a thatched roof and a herb garden that nearly seduces me. But it is in a cold, cold valley where the sun only lingers for an hour or two through winter and I know eventually it will be depressing, not quaint. On all these forays, Sweetie, loyal, patient, soft-eyed and trusting, never strays from my side. She is the best dog.

The journey leads me to my cousin in Wangaratta where she and her husband, Edward, and her father, my Uncle Frank, grow luscious peaches and nectarines. Sweetie and I arrive late on a hot summer night, so I park the ute under a row of peach trees near the house and sleep there soundly. In the very early morning, Jayne, one month older than me, peers into the back, wondering what on earth has pitched up in her orchard. Some itinerant picker looking for work, she thinks.

'It's you!' she shrieks.

'Yeah. Got here late last night.'

'Why didn't you knock, you silly old cow? Could've slept under a roof like normal people.'

'Used to sleeping out now. Do it two nights out of three. Actually, I quite like it. It's sort of liberating.'

'Daft. You've gone daft. Well, you better get up and come in. We're having breakfast and we're busy. It's picking time.'

She marches off to the house. Turns back with a grin. 'And don't pinch any fruit off the trees!'

The branches around me bend with plump, golden peaches. These are the family trees, where fruit is left to ripen on the boughs. I stretch and snap one off, pressing my nose to furry skin that smells like a lazy summer. I bite into it and juice trickles down my chin. When it's finished, I pick another.

As little kids, Jayne and I spent hours searching for delicate spider orchids in the bush around her house. If ever I wanted to pick one of the wonderful, bright green and red flowers, she would look me sternly in the eye and explain that they were rare and precious and had to be left alone to bloom again the following year. That land is now a suburb covered in houses with lots of glass windows and concrete driveways.

I'm not sure when I realise the tight band squeezing my chest isn't there any more. Perhaps it is on the second, absurdly magical, moonlit night at Jayne's home, when I sit on the porch in a tattered chair sipping a frigidly cold beer with my Uncle Frank. In the distance, peach trees – their lush, musky scent drifting on the warm night air – stretch like ghostly armies towards the magnificent Victorian Alps.

'How'd you cope, Frank, when Belle died?' I ask him.

'Didn't do too good at first.'

She was barely middle-aged, Frank's beautiful, busy wife, when her car ran off the road and smashed into a tree.

'Depressed?'

'Yep. So I'd have a few drinks, and that'd help for a minute. But after a while, booze just made it worse. Found that out.'

'What? So you stopped drinking?'

'Yeah, which wasn't that easy. Plays dirty tricks on you, your noodle. If you don't watch it. Always wants to push you down the wrong road. One drink, I'd think. It'll help. But it didn't. Biggest battle was getting my noodle sorted.'

'Frank?'

'Yes, love?'

'I can't seem to settle. Can't find my feet somehow.'

'Yeah. It's a bugger that. But you'll come good.'

We sit silently and my mind fills with memories of the boys. Instead of shutting them down, I let them swirl and take shape. How lucky I am to have known two such wonderful men. Odd, to call my husband wonderful, though. In reality, we fought, ploughed through hurts and angers and often went our separate ways. He was difficult, fascinating, volatile, infuriating, vibrant and never, ever dull. A blue-eyed bull of a man with tight, curly blonde hair who always had a dream that only he thought was possible. But somehow, through even the worst times, we never lost sight of the fact that we cared for each other.

After nearly a week trawling the area with real estate agents, Sweetie and I drive on, looking at a few more houses for sale as we make our way back to the white elephant on the Nepean River. Time is running out. The new owners of the house are due to move in and I have to move on. Desperate for somewhere to land while I search for the dream house, I decide to make the Melbourne apartment a temporary base. Temporary because I need the income from the rent if I am to avoid dipping into capital. Spending capital was my father's greatest no-no. It was a rule he drummed in to me from the day, as a five-year-old, I bought my first shares with the two pounds I'd reluctantly saved from the ten shillings my godmother sent every birthday and Christmas. The money always arrived by post wrapped in an embroidered white handkerchief and enclosed in a flowery, lavender-scented card.

From the apartment I will search, once again, for a piece of earth where I will plant a lemon tree and a herb garden. The lemon tree is for my father. To him, a house didn't become a home until there was a lemon tree. He wasn't strong on herbs. He liked parsley in rissoles or in a white sauce over lamb shanks but mostly stuck to salt and pepper. A herb garden fills me with contentment, though. All those flavours. All that healing. The thrill of picking and eating what you have grown. It is the most basic instinct.

Back at the sold house, the slow, sorry business of reducing two lives to one begins. Here, Paul and I dumped stuff accumulated from the last assignment so we could travel light to the next one. It was the *home* we kept intact and ready to flee to if all else fell apart.

It is crammed with the confetti of our irregular lives. Unwanted birthday presents. Acres of books. Clothes long out of date or in a size long gone. Thousands of unedited photographs. Newspaper clippings that might be worth following up in a year or two. Choosing what to keep and what to discard is an awful process.

Every so often, a stack of Paul's old notebooks, filled with his spidery writing, turns up. I read them at first, to feel close to him, but soon it is as though I am opening someone's mail, prying into a private part of a life. I put the notebooks aside, unable to bring myself to toss them in the bin. Later, I pick them up again and read on. I want to know whether, if I'd looked at him more closely instead of rushing back and forward to the office, I would have seen an early sign of the problems to come. His words, though, are clean, precise reminder notes, sensible and perfectly spelled. There is nothing that even hints at failing faculties. Not a suggestion of confusion.

At his clothes closet, I open and close the door quickly. Here, more than anywhere, Paul comes alive. Corduroy trousers in neutral colours, heavy cotton shirts, soft pink, baby blue and cream; shoes the size of canoes. A black leather jacket and a fine wool herringbone blazer, a navy blue double-breasted cardigan, and a cream, cable knit sweater. The clothes seem to wait for Paul to fill them and for a blinding moment I think he might walk out of the shower, still damp, with a towel around his waist, saying, as he always did: 'Baby, where's my . . .?' In the end, I pack the clothes and take them with me. To this day, I do not really understand why.

The removalists arrive with a semitrailer big enough to live in. Eighteen years of memories are crammed into the long dark space and the past is closed down. I take the ride-on mower because who knows where I may end up? Fred is loaded to bursting point with Sweetie, my old Burmese cat, Banana, brooms, mops, pot plants and suitcases. The house is clean and empty, ready to be infused with a new personality.

Dearest Pat, a friend of my mother's who looked after the house and animals for six years while Paul and I roamed, stands in the driveway. Next to her, my mother looks abandoned. She moved from Melbourne to the foot of the Blue Mountains in 1989, to be near me when her relationship with my brother's wife failed to thrive. Now her son is dead and her daughter on the move. Paul's death changed both our lives.

I climb behind the wheel. The cat is stuffed with Valium and sleeps on my lap, Sweetie is confused by all the gear in her space in the ute and it's a stinking, stinking hot day. The bitumen shimmers with heat and the smell of hot tar rises under our wheels. I do not look back. Cannot. By mid-afternoon we swing off local roads and onto the Hume Highway, with a long, numbing drive ahead. It will be the early hours of the morning before I put the key in the lock in Melbourne.

Around Tarcutta, halfway to Melbourne, the cat fights his way out of his Valium fog and pees in my lap, then staggers off me like a chronic drunk and scratches blearily in a pot plant on the floor beside the driver's seat. He pees again. By the time I stop for food and coffee, I smell like a public lavatory and the cat is wide awake.

I fill the tank and order cold sausages for the dog and a steak sandwich for me.

'Make that two steak sandwiches. One for the dog, too.'

The girl behind the counter looks out the window to where Sweetie sits straight and expectant, her eyes glued to the door through which I disappeared.

'Oh, and some raw steak. For the cat. He's inside the car.'

She nods and grins, and walks into a giant fridge. When she emerges, she's giggling uncontrollably, her chef's hat quivering.

'What's up?'

'Now I know why I can smell cat pee!'

She wraps the raw meat and puts it in a white paper bag before passing it across the counter. 'There you go. On the house. Good luck.'

Do I look like I need luck? How wonderful, though, that kindness of strangers.

At 3 am we cruise into the outskirts of Seymour. The animals are frazzled and I'm almost sick with exhaustion. The cat is clawing at windows, mewling hysterically. He's only moved house once before and it took him four days to climb down from the highest shelf in the laundry. This is a nightmare for him. Sweetie looks at me accusingly. She wants a good long walk, time to sniff around, but we've still got three hours' driving ahead. She gets a pee stop and that's it.

I fill the tank with petrol and go to pay. A middle-aged woman is propped behind a cash register in a neon lit box. It's a time of night when only desperate travellers still roam the roads. She eyes me suspiciously for a moment then smiles.

'You look knackered, love.'

'Close to.'

'Behind you. Coffee. No need to pay for it.' Her compassion is easy, instinctive.

'Thanks. Thanks very much.'

I fly down the final stretch of highway, warmed once again by the kindness of strangers, and pull into the driveway of my temporary home. Sweetie gets a walk around the block, the cat gets dinner. I make up a mattress on the floor and sleep until 10 am.

No matter where it might lead, I've made the leap. No job to give structure to the days. No-one to take into account. There's only me. Essentially, I can do what I damn well please. I thought it would feel like freedom but it feels more like entering a dark tunnel. It is just three months since I left the office behind.

4

THE APARTMENT IS ONE of two in a sombre, 1930s liver-brick building on a large block of land in a trendy suburb. The ground floor includes three bedrooms, two bathrooms, a kitchen and a long, open-plan room with areas for eating and sitting. French doors open from the bedroom and lounge room onto a small private courtyard with a low-maintenance garden. It is in perfect order. Luxurious. But it feels like a genteel prison. Because there is nowhere to go each morning after I've showered and dressed. No agenda to keep. The days loom vacantly.

After a month, the gloomy green pittosporums that block the afternoon sun are depressing so I dig them out. They are mature trees and it takes a long time but I am fueled by the energy of the righteous. I am making *improvements!* Improvements mean I can ask for higher rent! *Clever girl!* When they are gone, I order a truckload of chocolate soil that I barrow in from the nature strip over a three-day period. At night, physical exhaustion sends me to sleep and I dream of brightly coloured flowers and bountiful peach trees espaliered along the sunniest of the garden walls.

When the courtyard is planned and planted, which doesn't take long because it is small and I have plenty of time, I decide to paint the bedroom walls and get new curtains measured. Often, I move furniture here, there and everywhere. At whim. And then move it back to its original position. *Decisions. Decisions.*

I discover old fireplaces concealed behind gyprock walls in nearly every room. Four in all. Which is exciting because the apartment has just a single gas heater and there is not enough room under the floor to install central heating. *Time to get practical!* I will have a fireplace in the bedroom and another in the sitting room and I will fill the old, asbestos-lined wood room out the back next to the communal storeroom with twisted mallee roots that will burn long and slow and keep me warm when winter comes. I am being *constructive!* By the time I organise a builder to install floor to ceiling bookcases on either side of both fireplaces, I have filled in three months. *Busy! Busy! Busy!*

Now what? Back to perusing the real estate ads in the Saturday paper, making appointments and wandering the countryside. The dream house/life *must* exist somewhere.

Retiring is not easy. A lifetime of strong work ethics, schedules and routines – the fabric of my daily existence – suddenly becomes meaningless. Even if you hate what your work has come to mean to you, as I have, it still provides a daily goal. Now there is nothing to focus on except myself. Which I thought would be a relief. Only it isn't. Depression switches on and off. Not the illness kind. The ordinary kind. When you feel worthless and just plain blue. I start to play silly little games. If I do the right thing (ring my mother, take Suzi to dinner, help an old lady) three times today, tomorrow will be better. If I see a sign that says Susan twice, the future is rosy. The blunt reality, though, is that I am forty-four years old, overweight, with a self-image that's shot to hell and that even regular hairdressing appointments can't fix.

I develop an obsession with cleanliness. If even a speck of dirt appears on the white carpet, I bring in the cleaners. I polish kitchen counters until they glow, rearrange closets and iron sheets. I sponge light switches to shiny whiteness and wash skirting boards until the paint threatens to flake. I tell myself it is a luxury to be able to take the time to clean properly. But it is only while I scrub away that I am replete with the illusion of busyness.

My Friday night dinners with my stepdaughter, Suzi, continue, and sometimes, on a Sunday afternoon, I join her, her partner and friends at a gig in a pub somewhere, listening to music that seems to come from another planet. I end up drinking too much and getting home when most people are leaving for work. I am too old for this, I realise, and it makes me feel seedy. And yet I do not want to think I have begun the long slide into old age and oblivion with nothing to show for it except a *bit* of a career and a *bit* of money in the bank. There has to be more. There has to be some secret trapdoor waiting for me to find the key to open it. I will fall down the ladder and wake up in the rabbit hole where the jigsaw will finally fall into place and all the dreams and wishes of a lifetime will suddenly come true.

But what are the dreams? What are the vague but nagging yearnings that invade my mind every evening as I sit in front of the fire, the dog at my feet, a glass of wine in my hand, a book face down on the coffee table, obsessing over whether a painting is hung too high or too low? Is *it* all over? How much of our self-image is tied up with what we do and when we cease to do it, we wonder if we have somehow passed our use-by date and have nothing left to offer, personally or professionally? Five phone calls to become a volunteer worker for everyone and anyone result in rejection. Not even licking envelopes for the Cancer Foundation. The Foundation is overflowing with envelope lickers, apparently. My loose ends feel like they are trickling into infinity.

I don't consider finding another partner. If my mind drifts in that direction for a moment, I yank it back: 'Too fat, too old, too independent . . . too hard!' Looking back, too scared is closer to the truth. After eighteen years in a rigorously faithful relationship, the idea of sex with anyone else is terrifying. Stripping in front of someone new is quite simply horrifying. I have no concept of how the rules are played any more. And also, if I'm being strictly honest, I don't trust my judgement. What if I end up taking an axe murderer home for the night, if you know what I mean?

Then one morning the cat leaps out of his basket next to the heater and drops dead. He lies in a heap, like an old moth-eaten fur collar, and the sight wrecks me. After sitting next to him for an hour or two on the floor, the grief of the past few years eventually settles back into its closed niche and I call my brother's friend James, who is now like a brother to me, to ask in a thick voice if I can dig a hole somewhere on his property. There's no room in my little courtyard, and anyway, Banana always preferred wide open spaces.

'Plenty of land here,' he says. 'We'll find a top spot for him.'

'Thanks. I'll be there this afternoon.'

'They get to you, don't they?'

'Sorry. Don't mean to sound all sobby. How's Cliffy?' Cliffy is his ancient border collie, a dog as grand as Sweetie.

'He's right. Now you just get in the car and bring Banana here. We'll sort it out.'

All I can think as I drive along, glancing at the little body lying stiff-legged in his basket, is that it's another bloody death. Another empty compartment. I begin to wonder if I attract it.

Two hours later James' partner, Polly, draws me into the house.

'James is out on the tractor. Let's have a gin and tonic. Then we'll work out where to dig a hole.'

After the second gin, I am maudlin drunk. By the time we've finished half a bottle, I've forgotten the cat and we're both laughing at stuff that, sober, would not have been the least bit funny. We spin around guiltily when we hear James come through the kitchen door.

'So where'd you put Banana?' he asks, shuffling towards us in his socks and sinking into his favourite chair by the fire, the one where there's a photograph of my brother close by.

Polly and I look at each other. Aghast.

'Oh God! The cat! We forgot about him!'

I stumble outside where he's baked in the sun through the car window all afternoon, apologising as though he can hear and understand every word. But he doesn't move. Dead is forever.

'I've got a tree to put on top of him,' Polly says, holding a pot plant and a spade and looking over my shoulder at the body. She is unperturbed. Farmers are familiar with death.

At the back door, James wriggles his gammy left ankle until his foot slips into his work boot. He pulls the second boot on easily and follows us up the path.

'Give me that.'

He grabs the shovel from Polly and ducks under the clothes-line and around the outside laundry to the front lawn. We follow him in a line like little ducklings.

'Where do you reckon, Polly?'

After half an hour of putting the pot plant in twenty different positions, the decision is made. James sends me inside while he fetches Banana from the car and buries him three feet deep with a baby oak tree to mark his life.

Not long after moving to Melbourne, the phone rings at about 10 pm. It's Pat. 'Your mother is in intensive care,' she explains in a quiet and calm voice.

'What's wrong?'

'Heart attack. An ambulance took her off about an hour ago.'

Because it is Pat on the phone, I ask no questions. Just throw the bewildered dog in the back of the ute and drive all night to Sydney.

I have always had an uneasy relationship with my mother. We love each other, of course, but sometimes I want to throttle her. And she, me. I wonder if her ambition for her only daughter was blighted early. Born with a lazy eye, a strawberry mark down my face and not enough chin, a glamorous marriage was out of the question.

An operation fixed the lazy eye and the strawberry mark turned out to be from pressure in the womb and faded in a few months. But it was not enough to transform me into *pretty*. By then, anyway, my face had turned freckly and I was showing every sign of growing as tall as my father, who was six feet five inches. Hard to place a big woman in days when *petite* was considered an asset. No. There wouldn't be any successful marriage that would liberate my mother from her working class shackles and catapult her into the glittering social world she craved.

There was also the problem of my disposition. As a teenager, I was a judgemental little prig. And what I hated, above all, was alcohol. My attitude made life a bit strained, considering my parents bought a country pub after my father retired from his job in the public service at Bonegilla migrant camp, near the Albury–Wodonga border.

Twelve hours later, when I reach the hospital where my mother is allegedly lying close to death, I circle the crowded car park three times, then yank the ute into a no standing zone in frustration. I'm as frazzled as the dog and seesawing between thinking 'She'll be right' and 'Oh, Jesus, don't let it be too terrible.'

The front desk sits in an acre of empty space and when the receptionist cannot find my mother listed in intensive care, I think for a suffocating moment that she must be dead.

'Ah, here she is.'

Relief pounds through my body. 'What ward is that?'

'Ward C, Room 14.'

'I mean, is that the cardiac ward?'

'Oh, no. It's where they put people with problems they can't identify.'

A roaring red rage consumes me, driven by my mother's self-ishness and my own stupidity. Not getting enough attention? Fake an illness. The more drastic the better. In the elevator the walls close in and the desire to smack my mother with a loud, crunching punch swims in my head for a few moments. After a lifetime of creative illnesses, mostly with the prospect of imminent death or, at the very least, paralysis, I should have known better.

When I find her room, she sits in bed perky and pink, eating chocolates.

'You seem well for a woman who had a heart attack yesterday,' I remark.

She looks me in the eye without a tremor of unease. 'I've had three more this morning. Two mild, one big.'

She is so convincing that for a second I believe her. But her pale blue nightie falls neatly from its embroidered yoke. No tubes or wires there. The only blemish on her wrist is an identity tag. She is snappy, alert and healthy. Then my anger at being manipulated deflates. She is my mother. The loss of my brother, her adored only son, made her mad with grief. Perhaps this is her way of focusing on a situation that hurts her less. I turn and walk out.

The nurses say there is nothing wrong but my mother appears to be in pain. I tell them about the last *heart attack* and how, when I called the specialist, he told me her problem was depression. 'Not depression,' I replied. 'Lack of attention.' But it was probably both.

A few years later my mother confesses her *heart attack* had, in fact, been hemorrhoids.

'Why did you tell everyone it was a heart attack?'

'Nobody mentions hemorrhoids!'

'Why didn't you say you had the flu?'

She's dismissive. 'They don't put you in hospital for the flu any more.'

'So did you get your hemorrhoids fixed?'

'I couldn't talk about them! I told you that!'

'But I could have been killed driving all night. With no sleep.'

'Rubbish! I didn't get a proper night's sleep for years after you and your brother were born.'

I give up. My mother is who she is. In a way, her weakness has become my strength. I never expect sympathy, do not seek coddling. I learned very early that to look for sympathy from my mother was to invite a ticking off. 'Pull yourself together,' she'd say.

'Don't make a fool of yourself. Not in public.' Another era. A different generation. Mostly, she is just as tough with herself in a real crisis.

When she is in her early eighties and falls, breaking a wrist, she shrugs off the discomfort and manages on her own at home. 'A nuisance, that's all it is,' she says when I ask if she wants to come and stay for a while. 'I'll be right. I'm like an old dog. Prefer to lie in a corner on my own until I'm better.'

How did she fasten her bra, though? How did she open a can of baked beans? Button up her shirt? I didn't even think to ask.

When she flies headfirst down some stone steps not long after her wrist heals, she laughs at the absurdity of her large breasts finally being useful. 'Might've broken a few ribs if they hadn't cushioned the fall,' she jokes. Not a single tear escapes as she waits to be lifted from her rocky landing. And it must've hurt like hell. Sometimes, it's impossible not to feel proud of her.

Two weeks after we bury Banana, I teeter towards buying a rickety weatherboard house in the coldest part of Victoria. All because I like the look of the old, collapsed bluestone barn. But a couple with a new baby and the future scribbled all over their eager faces outbids me. Thank God. What would I do out there where I know no-one and I have no need of a barn anyway?

5

A PHONE CALL COMES mid-morning in early July as I'm wandering the Melbourne apartment looking for something to polish. My feet are freezing. The dog is groaning with arthritic pain. The cold is tangible and hateful. I want to lie in the tropical sun sipping daiquiris but I have rarely taken holidays. They always seemed a waste of money to someone who travelled everywhere and rarely had to pick up the bill.

'It's Fleury's birthday. Come to Pittwater for the weekend.'

'Stewart! How are you? What are you up to?'

I have known Stewart for twenty-five years or more. We trekked the sidewalks of Manhattan at the same time, calling ourselves foreign correspondents. Our lives crisscrossed on assignments, in bars, at Australian functions. Stewart and my husband were great friends and I tagged along until the friendship became mine as well.

'Good. I'm good. Can you make it?' he asks.

'When?'

'July twenty-three.'

I hesitate.

'Be great if you could help with the cooking. And Sophia needs a lift.'

The clinchers. I'm needed. Can't say no to all that. Especially the cooking. I love it. Passionately. Have no idea why. Even alone, I cook dinner with the care of a chef. Set a polished table with silver and crystal. Have a cloth napkin. Always a glass of wine. Or two. My mother once told me that opening a cupboard full of glittering crystal made her feel rich. A civilised dinner does that for me. Alone, or with twenty guests – it doesn't matter.

Stewart waits for an answer. Then adds: 'You're going to be the surprise guests. You and Sophia.'

Part of me wants to stay safely at home. Another part says get a life. 'Great. I'll be there. Get Sophia to call me.'

'Don't say a word to Fleury!'

I have not met Sophia yet, know her only as Stewart's and Fleury's friend who writes a column for a Melbourne newspaper. She is a Buddhist, lots of fun apparently, and very clever.

That night, I undress for bed. Look in the mirror. The sight is shocking. How long is it since I looked at myself without clothes? About a millennium. I ate everything as a teenager and stayed pencil slim. Thought I'd be one of those people who never gained weight. Dream on. Wonder if I can still cancel. Being a fat boss is fine. Being a single, unemployed, overweight woman in her mid-forties makes me want to hide in a closet.

I pull on pyjamas quickly and slide into bed. Turn out the light. The fire blazes and orange gremlins leap all over the walls. Good idea resurrecting the fireplace in the bedroom. But I can't see the flames if I lie down. It's too early to sleep anyway. The light goes back on. I sit up and grab a book. Some mawkish instinct has made me put a couple of my husband's favourite poetry books on the bedside table. I put down my trashy novel and pick up Emily Dickinson. When the phone rings, I'm pathetically thrilled. I've never grocked poetry.

'Susan?' Deep and drawn out.

'Yeee-s,' I say tentatively, not recognising the voice.

'It's So-fi-ah.'

Rack my brains to think of someone called So-fi-ah. Come up blank.

'Stewart tells me you're going to give me a lift to Pittwater.'

Each word is carefully enunciated. As though my English, or my hearing, is dodgy.

'Oh, *Sophia*. Yes. Glad you called.'

'Does it suit you?'

'Yes, of course. Great to have company on the drive. Hope you don't mind utes?'

'Love 'em. Grew up on a property.' Tension drops out of her voice. 'What are you going to get Fleury for her birthday?' she asks.

'Dunno. She's got just about everything.'

'Yeah. It's hard. If you come up with any bright ideas, yell out.'

We meet for the first time on a cold, bleak morning two weeks later. Sophia parks her ancient orange Volvo off-street, behind the apartment. Locks the doors one by one, testing the handle each time.

'We won't get there before dark,' I say, anxious about our late departure.

Sophia is dismissive. 'Of course we will. We'll be in Sydney by lunchtime at the latest.'

'It's an eleven-hour drive! It's nearly nine o'clock now!'

'You weren't planning to do the trip in *one day*, were you?' Sophia, rugged up in a navy cashmere sweater, orange trousers, a windcheater, her white hair spronging in all directions, looks terrified.

'I always do it in one day.'

She seems stricken. 'It's not safe to drive for more than six hours in a day, even with ten minute breaks every two hours.' Her tone is schoolteacherish.

'Who told you that?'

'The driving safety manual.'

'Driving safety manual! I've never even seen one of those.'

'They're given to you when you sit for your driver's licence.'

'Sophia, I got my licence nearly thirty years ago.'

'Well, I got mine a year ago. I've read the book.'

'Ok, we can stop somewhere if you're tired. But if we both feel ok, we'll go on. Yeah?'

Air drizzles out of her in relief.

I drop the apartment keys with the missionaries who live next door so they can feed Sweetie. I give the dog a hug. 'Be back in a couple of days, Sweetie. Stewart has a dog that doesn't like other dogs. Sorry.'

She gives me a heartcracker of a look. Who says dogs can't speak?

Sophia and I begin our drive under a leaden sky, feeling each other out. She is bright and funny, well-read, informed, articulate. And the first Buddhist I've met.

'Why Buddhism?'

'Only philosophy that makes sense to me.'

'Were you Church of England?'

'No. Catholic.'

'Jesus. Big swing. Parents freak?'

'Not for long.'

As we drive, the sky drifts from black to grey to hot blue. Golden wattle fluffs alongside the highway making it feel like spring and we discover we were born in the same hospital in a small country town on the border of Victoria and New South Wales. Our parents might even have known each other.

'Heard your brother died. And your husband.'

'Yeah.'

'My mother and sister, too. Six months between them. Nursed them both.'

'Hard, huh?'

'What about you? How're you doing?'

'Good, yeah, really good,' I lie. 'Don't understand this dying shit though. I mean, what's the point of it all?'

'The Buddhists understand it. Only ones who do.'

'What's their take on it?'

'Well, years ago, when I was in my
I was in Katmandu when I got th
shocking relationship but I was com
know why. Why him? Why at that partic
went to see a monk at a monastery. Know wha

I shake my head.

'Everything that is born must die.'

Everything that is born must die. So simple. Utterly inevitable.
Accept it.

'Once you understand that, you should try to look for the gift
in the death of your husband and brother.'

'Gift! Are you mad? What kind of gift is it to have half your
family die?'

Sophia smiles smugly and doesn't answer. The highway
switches from dual to single lanes and the speed limit drops. I need
to concentrate so I don't kill us both. Half an hour or so later, my
anger has flattened and the highway has switched back to dual
carriageway.

'So what was the gift *you* got out of the death of your mother
and sister?' I am aggressive with her. I want to put her on the spot.

'Oh, that's easy,' she says. 'I learned anything can happen to
anyone at any time and you must live each day the best way you
can.'

'Do good, do you mean?'

'Oh yeah. But be the best person you can, too. You know,
nothing gives wisdom faster than a good attitude to death.'

We are silent again, for a while.

'So just how *do* you pronounce your name?' I ask eventually.

'Oh, I dunno. Never been able to get it right.'

'But is it So-fi-ah or Sofee-a?'

'Depends what school you went to.'

We burst out laughing. We both went to schools where snob-

mpant and thumbed our noses at it. Anyway, my family,
ers with fluctuating fortunes, didn't have the money to
any kind of snobbery. When school fee time came around,
sometimes had to ask an old uncle – who came for a holiday
then lived with us until he died nineteen years later – to dive
to his old boot for a fistful of pound notes. He'd push aside the
cheese he matured in the dark recesses of the toe and hand over
the required amount. The money always stank like dead rats but
no-one ever refused to take it.

By mid-afternoon we cross the long straight bridge that spans
the Murrumbidgee River and the lush river flats where fat cattle
graze in the thin, sharp winter light. We know, by now, we will be
lifelong friends. We bypass the little black dog on the tuckerbox at
Gundagai, and whip Fearless Fred up gut-busting hills of shale to
the edge of the icy, treeless Southern Tablelands, the colour of
taupe in mid-winter. An hour later we cross the Yass River into a
wide main street speckled with solid old buildings that date back
to the days when a good wool season turned struggling farmers
into instant millionaires.

I itch to continue. So near. Just a little longer. Three or four
hours, tops. But Sophia is firm. She won't push the limits.

'There'll be a lu-verly motel here.'

She grins. I give in.

'We'll find the cheapest. All we're gonna do is sleep there.
They're all the same in the dark,' she adds.

The motels look like clones. Low slung brick buildings,
flashing neon lights saying *Vacancy*. We scope a Chinese restaurant where we agree to eat. A little further on, we check into a
tired motel where the beds have faded orange chenille covers
and the rooms smell used. Dingy lace curtains frame the
window and the brown carpet is worn through at the door. I
get twitchy. Worry about clean sheets. Other people's detritus.
Sophia is pragmatic. Pulls incense out of her handbag. Lights it.

Sandalwood. Knocks out even the scent of cheap air freshener from the bathroom.

'I've stayed in places fleas have rejected,' she says.

'Oh.'

'In India.'

'Oh.'

'This is five star compared to them. You take the double bed. I'm used to a single.'

I go out to the ute and bring in our bags. Dump them on the brown carpet. We fiddle around until it's time to go to dinner, finding pyjamas, our novels.

'Oh shit. I left my new shirt at home,' I moan, 'Bought it for the party. Bugger.'

'Got anything else?'

'Yeah, but this was one of those big flowing things. Supposed to hide the rolls.'

'Just have to let 'em hang out.'

Pride and ego are big no-nos in Buddhism. Vanity is right up there with them.

We go out to dinner. Two beers each. The food is sugary with a sticky coating on the beef. We chew it slowly, under the dazzling red and gold flocked wallpaper, delaying our return to the motel.

'What's the plan tomorrow?' Sophia asks.

'Get up and go. But we've gotta find a present for Fleury. What about flowers? Heaps of them. From the wholesale markets. We drive past them on the way into Sydney.'

'Fill the house with them.'

'Look great for the party.'

We beam at each other.

Back at the motel, Sophia climbs into her pyjamas and mumbles some prayers, doing a series of prostrations on the worn carpet.

'Shouldn't you have a prayer rug or something? For that?' I'm worried she'll pick up some awful infection.

She doesn't answer. Ten minutes later, she slides under the orange chenille covers, flicks off her light and falls asleep.

I sit in bed, wide-eyed, with a book. The sheets are thin and clean but the bedspread smells of other people, not soap. If I had a mattress, the dog and it wasn't two degrees outside, I would have retired to the back of the ute and the comfort of my own smells. I try to read in a little pool of weak, blue fluorescent light to wind down from the long drive. But I can't concentrate on the words. My head spins with recipes for possible party dishes. Lots of people. Keep it simple. One dish lunch. Plenty of nibbles and a huge dessert. Think about the practical. Put off the personal. *Busy. Busy. Busy.*

I turn out my light. Run through the possible guest list. There'll be lots of old friends. Will they care how fat I am? Can't believe I'm finally going to Pittwater. Fleury has tried to lure me there for years, stepping up the pressure after the boys died.

'There's a guest cottage behind the house,' she told me after Paul's funeral. 'Use it.' Fleury is the kind of woman who stays in touch whether you've become a star or a drunk.

'I'll think about it.'

But I never did.

In the morning, the cold makes our noses dribble. The heating in the room doesn't help much. We have a quick cup of tea and eat the two little complimentary biscuits in a plastic rack next to the tea bags and kettle. That's breakfast done. Neither of us talks. Thank God.

Cold water on the windscreen cracks and melts the frost. Start the engine, switch on the heater. Duck the first cold blast of air. Silently urge the heating to kick in quickly. My hands are blue on the steering wheel. Our breath erupts in clouds.

Sophia belts up carefully, folds her hands in her lap. Glances at me almost regally and indicates with a slight incline of her head that she is ready to move. I slide into gear and pull out of the motel.

'I'm not sure but I reckon we'll miss the market. Closes around eight and I don't think we'll get there until after nine,' I say.

'Let's give it a go anyway.'

'Check out the directions in the street directory. I don't know my way around that part of the world. Are you a good navigator?'

'Excellent.'

'Great. Because my marriage nearly ended every time I did the navigation.'

On the radio, regional news floods the car. Cattle prices are recited so quickly it sounds like an auction. The value of lamb is down. A detailed weather report warns of a cold front coming through. There's a stock alert. Sophia listens as though she has a flock of newborn lambs at risk. Once a country girl, always a country girl.

Turn down the heater a little as the sun beats in the windows. But the glass is still icy. We make our way through folding blue hills along a highway edged with twisted silver gums. The road hums an endless single note. Signs tell us which radio station to tune in to. A small white truck is for sale in the middle of nowhere. Light rain falls and we're going so fast it tadpoles up the windscreen.

It's nearly 10 am when we veer off the Hume Highway to go to the Flemington markets where there's acres of cold, concrete emptiness except for one bloke with a few buckets of pink tulips. We scoot over to him. Settle into bargaining mode. But he's our only chance and he knows it. The price doesn't drop much. Sophia, a seasoned negotiator from years of travelling in India and Nepal, tries to get him to throw in a bucket to hold the flowers but he won't do it.

'Bastard,' she mutters, not used to defeat.

'Very un-Buddhist of you.'

She grins.

We lay armloads of tulips, deliciously pink and feminine and still in tight buds, gently on the back seat. They remind me of ballet dancers, sitting with heads bowed, fingers touching their toes. I turn off the heating. Don't want them to burst open before we get there.

Sophia grabs the street directory. 'Right. Now let's see. Where are we meeting Stewart?'

'Somewhere around Surry Hills. He's going to call us.'

Sophia gets us out of the market and onto the highway without mishap. I'm impressed. I just don't get map reading. Even holding the book upside down.

We weave through awful city traffic. Sydney roads don't work. It's a city that grew out of cart tracks and a convict population that probably believed it would go home to England one day. Not much planning needed for a short-lived convict colony.

Stewart rings when we're still twenty minutes from the city centre. 'Where are you?'

I pass the mobile to Sophia. He asks her the same question. She turns to me. 'Where are we?'

'About half an hour away.'

'Stewart, we'll be there in half an hour,' she shouts. She scratches an address and directions on the inside flap of the novel she's reading. 'Right,' she tells him.

She turns to me. 'What do I do with this thing now? How do I turn it off?'

Mobile phones are irrelevant in her ordered life and she has resisted the trend to own one. I grab it and show her the button to press, one eye on the traffic. She holds the dashboard like the handlebar on a roller coaster.

'Would you *please* keep your eyes on the road!'

46

Stewart waits in his car outside his office in Surry Hills with his highly strung German shepherd–cattle dog cross, Gus, beside him in the front passenger seat.

We wave madly and stick our heads out the car windows, yelling happily. 'We're here! Gidday.'

'Follow me,' he shouts, pulling in front of us.

Everywhere I look I see places where Paul and I once ate or drank. When we drive past his favourite pub I half expect him to step a little unsteadily out of the doorway, his face moony with contentment. Paul always loved a *jar* with his mates. Every Friday afternoon he held court in a favourite corner of the bar and relived old scoops and glorious moments and argued too, about Hemingway, Fitzgerald and Vonnegut. He charmed and entertained, stimulated and provoked. His mind moved like mercury but not much held his interest for too long.

We met in New York when I was twenty-six and he was thirty-nine. At least that's what he told me. Three years later, when he was still having a thirty-ninth birthday, I tackled him. He cheerfully explained that like W.C. Fields, he intended to remain thirty-nine forever. He must have been forty-one or even forty-two when we met and I wonder, now, if he wasn't already disappointed with the way his life had turned out. Everything came so easily to him when he was young that when his luck dried up, as it always does for a while, he couldn't handle it. Or maybe, like me, he'd reached the age when the seedy side of journalism wore out his hubris.

When we returned to Australia from New York a few years later, after filthy streets, decrepit subways and lunatics on the loose lost their charm for us, we bought our first house in inner city Sydney. My mother always referred to it as the Kowloon Slum. It was small – eleven feet wide – and the only renovated terrace in a truly depressing street of decaying, cockroach infested houses with garbage-tip backyards. But it fulfilled our criteria: we could afford it without borrowing too much. It was within easy walking distance to the city. It was close to the pubs where journos hung out. And the neighbourhood, after living in New York city, was tame.

We sold it about three years later for almost triple what we paid, when plans were announced to rebuild Darling Harbour on our doorstep. That's when we bought the big white elephant on the Nepean River where Paul intended to write books and screenplays.

'To be a good journalist you need an interest I no longer have,' he told me. For him, journalism had become the same old story over and over again. After a while it's impossible to hose down your cynicism.

The door of his favourite old pub stays shut as we drive past, though, and we claw through the clogged city to sort out the jumbled lanes of the Harbour Bridge and then cruise through suburbia.

Stewart is covered in dog hair when he gets out of the car in the vast open air car park of the supermarket in Mona Vale. He tolerates a hug and shouts at Gus to *shut up* at the same time. Gus keeps barking. Like us, he's excited.

Sophia looks sideways at Stewart, smiles. 'Helloooo, Stewart.' She kisses his cheek and the three of us – greyer, fatter, slower and less sparkling than we remember ourselves – go shopping.

'Does Fleury know we're here?' Sophia asks.

'Nope. It's still a surprise.'

'When's she coming to Pittwater?'

The party is a Saturday lunch. It is Thursday.

'Tomorrow night.'

'But the surprise will be ruined! Can't you make her stay in town until Saturday lunchtime?'

Stewart is agonising over the different types of mustard. 'No-one makes Fleury do anything. What do you reckon? Hot English and French. Is that enough?'

Sophia says we only need one kind. Hot English.

I say get both. And seeded mustard. And the honey mustard sounds good, too.

When we've filled three trolleys with everything from fillets of beef to chicken wings (hot English and seeded mustard only) Stewart pays the bill. There's enough food to feed an army for a week. We load the shopping into Stewart' dog-hair encrusted car and follow him to Church Point.

We scoot past million dollar houses, a few rackety old holiday shacks from the fifties that haven't succumbed to property developers, and a couple of swank marinas. Where the sea tickles the roadside, a few mangroves cling to muddy flats and further on, little dinghies bob up and down on lazy waves. Yachts crowd coves like floating car parks and people in shorts and T-shirts pound along the waterfront track with tongue-lolling, tail-wagging mutts and combed designer dogs. It is a sparkling, summery, seaside day and the gloom of Melbourne fades into a shadowy memory.

Just past a bucolic general store, ferry wharf and a motel and restaurant that looks as though they've seen more halcyon days, Stewart turns into Mitchell's Marina where he keeps a boat, because the only way to get where we're going is across the water. There's a chaotic collection of long, slender yachts loaded with tackle, glamorous motor cruisers, and bare-boned runabouts with outboard motors. At the end of the jetty, a tanned boy in navy shorts, navy polo shirt and navy boat shoes fills the tanks of a three storey motorboat from a rusty old petrol bowser. The skipper, all in white, leans back in his cosy captain's chair as though he's king.

'What's that worth, the boat at the end?' I ask Stewart.

Stewart squints into the distance. 'Few million.'

'Jesus.'

'You know what's worse? Most of these boats don't get used. They just sit here and rot.'

Halfway along the jetty, Stewart's bright yellow commuter boat is already loaded with six cases of wine, delivered earlier and left unattended.

'Don't you worry stuff will get stolen?' I ask, unable to believe you can just leave wine out in the open for a few hours and it will still be there when you return.

'Stuff gets knocked off from time to time but everyone knows who's done it and the word goes around,' he says.

As commuter boats go, the *Yellow Peril*, as I'm later told it's nicknamed, is a Rolls Royce. Padded seats. A canopy for shelter from the rain. A steering wheel instead of a tiller. Ignition, not a pull start. But to me it looks small and bouncy. I wonder, not for the first time, about the mysterious physics that make boats float when by rights they should sink to the bottom.

Gus jumps aboard without being told to. He lands with an easy balance and scrambles into the front passenger seat.

'Yeah. Good dog, Gus. Good dog,' Stewart says.

Gus turns his long speckled snout forward and stares ahead, front paws at attention. Like he's on the bridge of a naval ship with a very serious job to do. Sophia and I are told later that they're known throughout the community as the General and his loyal lieutenant.

Stewart follows Gus into the boat. We hand him bag after bag of shopping. Then our baggage. Then the flowers. Sophia and I fossick for a seat. We are clumsy and flat-footed in the confined, unsteady space. Neither of us likes boats much. Only the whimsical, fictional romance of them. Stewart offers to move Gus but they look too content and comfortable together.

'So *this* is Pittwater,' I say.

'Yep. It's been home to smugglers, convicts, fishermen, farmers, layabouts, entrepreneurs, brothel owners, artists, writers and, until the last few years when real estate prices surged, the odd bloke who was doing it a bit hard,' Stewart says.

Sophia shuts her eyes, raises her face to the sun. A closed smile creeps into her lips.

'They reckon if you stay two years, you never leave,' Stewart adds.

'That's a long time to take to settle in.'

'Ah, don't be seduced by the sea and sun. Living here full time takes stamina.'

Stewart turns the key and the engine kicks into life with a cough. We cruise sedately through a maze of boats rolling gently on their moorings, bows pointing into the wind. Long, sleek, short, fat, top-heavy, newly painted or green with the slime of neglect. We're moving at a snail's pace, which I assume is Stewart's way of giving us a guided tour.

'Nah. You can't speed through the moored boats,' he explains when I thank him. 'It's against the law. Too many kids and a few blokes have gone overboard when they've been hit by a big wake.'

At the end of the go slow zone, where the waterway opens up and there are no boats on moorings, Stewart pushes forward the throttle. Tulips scatter everywhere. Sophia and I lunge to grab them, rocking the boat dangerously, losing our balance.

'Slow down, Stewart!' Sophia shouts.

He doesn't hear her and we look at each other and laugh, falling back into our seats and letting a few tulips become offerings to the sea. We feel as uninhibited and abandoned as the frothing white wake behind us. Like kids on school holidays.

'This is too good,' Sophia says. 'Too damn good.'

We pass a lovely white wooden cottage at the water's edge, another that is built on pylons so it hovers over the water. Just beyond a plain grey boathouse there's a wind-beaten finger of land Stewart tells us is called Woody Point.

'This is Towlers Bay,' he yells, swinging past a shallow water marker at Woody Point. 'We're nearly there.'

'What's that?' I ask, touching Stewart on the shoulder to get his attention and feeling like a tourist at the edge of a city where I once lived for more than a decade.

'Sea eagle.'

Stewart turns the boat to follow the bird as it glides in to land on a tree near the water's edge.

'Not often you get a chance to see one so close,' he says, his hand on Gus to keep the dog quiet.

When we are about twenty feet away, he cuts the engine. The big, white breasted bird with silvery grey wings stares casually over his hooked beak. He looks pure and elegant although he is, by nature, a scavenger as well as a hunter, scouring beaches for carrion washed in by the tides.

'There are usually two of them,' Stewart says quietly. 'A male and a female. But the female doesn't seem to be around. Probably nesting.'

A light breeze nudges us away from the eagle surprisingly fast and Stewart starts the engine to continue. An eclectic mix of houses with jetties and boatsheds beads the coastline on the southern side of the bay. Some are grand, with curved roofs and acres of glass, some simple, with fibro walls and sagging decks. The northern side is thick with rugged bushland and near the escarpment, ochre rocks with almost human features hang precariously. There's a beautiful, sheltered, quarter-moon beach and behind it, dense, dark rainforest trees loom out of a damp gully. Stewart's house is located towards the end of Towlers Bay, where a freshwater creek runs from the escarpment to the tidal flats. There's a shelf, or drop-off, and the water changes from the blue of the deep to sandy turquoise. It's like a tropical paradise.

When Stewart pulls into his dock, Gus gets overexcited and rudely dashes past Sophia and me, knocking us sideways. He leaps off the boat before it's stopped moving and nearly goes paws first into the water.

'Gus has no manners, Stewart.'

Stewart doesn't answer. To him, Gus is faultless.

'What do you want us to do?' Sophia asks. She means, is there a boat protocol? Are there rules to be learned? Is there a right or wrong way to behave?

'Jump off,' he says.

Sophia and I look at each other. Ok, we nod. We can do that.

Stewart slides his arm through the edge of the awning and holds the boat firmly against the pontoon as we scramble off. He passes me a rope.

'Hold this. Don't let it go.'

He and Sophia unload the shopping carefully. If anything drops it will sink to the bottom and stay there. Soon the pontoon looks like a garbage dump. There are boxes and shopping bags everywhere. A massive amount of food and drink. I know there's a party on but it still seems excessive.

'Once you're here that's it,' Stewart says. 'If you run out of anything, you can't just dash to the corner store to pick it up. So we go for plenty. To be sure.'

I glance along the weathered grey planks of the jetty to steps that climb to a brown timber house above us with a deck covered in a rampant vine.

'How do we get the shopping up there?'

'We carry it,' Stewart replies.

'Oh.'

There are six cases of wine, forty or so shopping bags. Luggage. For a moment my holiday spirit falters. Five trips at least. Each.

Stewart takes the rope and secures the boat. He lifts two cases of wine and sets off. Sophia sighs and gathers two thick handfuls of shopping bags. I look for the ice-cream, milk, butter and cream – and follow the leader. At the top of the stairs, hot and sweating, I strip off my sweater. Sophia is already in the kitchen, swilling a glass of water. Stewart is filling a glass for himself.

'Are you sure this is winter?' I ask, wiping my face with my arm.

'Yup,' Stewart says, turning to do a return trip to collect the next load.

'You stay here,' I tell Sophia. 'We need someone to unpack the shopping as we bring it up.'

She has an arm that is weak from a car accident some years ago. I have always been as strong as an ox. Healthy as a buffalo, I always say, when anyone asks me how I am.

It takes four trips to clear the dock. By then the fridge is full to busting point and most of the non-perishables are stacked in the laundry. We're pretty pleased with ourselves and to celebrate we crack open some icy cold beers. It's nowhere near 6 pm, the usual time to open the batting, but hey, this is Pittwater where the living is easy. Booze is always the signal for celebration, right?

Sophia and I sit on the deck and absorb the view while Stewart fiddles with a build-it-yourself wine rack. It's a collection of bits which he looks at intently, piece by piece. Eventually he sighs loudly and goes over to the phone on the kitchen bench.

'Col? Stewart. Mate, I need a hand. Can you come over?'

'He's on his way,' Stewart tells us when he hangs up.

'Is it that simple around here? Tradesmen come to your door by boat? Whenever you want them to?'

'Col's a mate!'

As if that explains it all.

We can hear Col approaching as we're on our second beer, his tinny thumping across the waves like slow clapping hands.

'Gidday,' Col says to Sophia and me. I nod. Sophia inclines her head ever so slightly. He's tall and handsome, with a wicked sparkle in his blue eyes that give you a hint that this is a bloke who knows how to have a good time without losing his good manners.

'Great to see you, mate,' Stewart says. 'Come and take a look at this.'

They disappear inside and we follow to watch Col, who moves with the slowness of the tides, assemble the wine rack. He makes it look as easy as plaiting a rope. When it's done, he casually slips bottles into their allotted spaces. Neat and tidy. No fuss. My husband would have bought two books at vast expense, consulted them for at least two weeks, looked at the job for another week, then called a carpenter.

'Beer?' Stewart asks Col.

'Oh yeah. Wouldn't say no.' Col's words rise and fall with the rhythm of a song. Always ending on a high note. He slugs back his beer. 'Just call Cher. Let her know I'll be a while.'

The echo of his wife slamming down the phone bounces around the room. Col looks at us, genuinely surprised. 'Don't think Cher's happy,' he says.

'Might as well eat here then,' Stewart suggests, helpfully.

'Nah. Better go.'

He stays for one more beer, takes another in case he gets thirsty on the boat ride home. No-one seems to rush about much, here on Pittwater.

After he's gone, darkness falls in quickly, quietly. Stewart gets the fire going in a wood burning stove and the room turns toasty. The evening is clear, the stars luminous. Later, a huge, almost full moon creeps silently above the horizon, coating the bay in a pale, shivery light. The night is filled with good friends, good wine. Dinner is one of Stewart's famously hot curries and the smell of spices drifts tantalisingly through the house.

Every so often, I wander onto the deck to listen to the gentle swish of sighing waves dropping onto the beach at the bottom of the garden. There's an occasional hoot of an owl. A rustling of leaves. A pink-nosed possum walks along the handrail of the deck looking for food. It eyes me suspiciously and imploringly at the same time. I go inside and cut up an apple. But when Gus sees the possum he goes berserk and tries to sool him up. The possum rips up a tree and I eat the apple, leaving the core for him if he returns.

It is the stuff of romance and, for a long while, I put aside loss.

Friday is a frenzy of preparation. Salad greens are washed and dried and then stored in plastic containers with dampened paper towels to keep the leaves fresh. We all huddle around a cookbook to read how to poach the glistening, giant salmon Stewart bought at the Sydney fish market at dawn the day before.

'I've never cooked one,' I tell Stewart.

'Well, I have, but not this size.'

'There has to be a weight/time chart in a book somewhere.'

Sophia, a vegetarian, mutters a prayer and pats the 'poor little creature' on the head. Then she returns to washing watercress, sprig by sprig, in the laundry sink.

We can't find any cooking instructions so we decide to throw in about six bottles of white wine with a few bay leaves, some onions, carrots and celery, and put the lid on top. Basic French cooking rites that never fail.

'We'll open it up at the fattest point and test it after about twenty-five minutes. It can't take too long,' I say.

We slather a whole fillet of beef in crushed garlic and sit it on a bed of thyme to rest overnight. By the afternoon, most of the work is done and we mooch around feeling clever and competent.

Stewart is in the shower when the phone rings, and he yells to us to pick it up. He's waiting to hear whether the banjo player can make it to the party. Fleury's always loved the banjo. No-one has the faintest idea why.

'Hi, Fleury!' I gush, without thinking. Oh shit.

Sophia looks at me. Speechless. Stewart, wrapped in a towel, takes the phone. Game over.

Fleury arrives late Friday afternoon to our cries of 'surprise', even though it isn't any more, and we crowd around the table for dinner. We sit down to bowls of minestrone thick with vegetables and grated parmesan, with lots of sourdough bread to mop our bowls. We wash down camembert and quince paste, which is like eating strawberries and cream, with red wine, and rehash old times. We toast absent friends and family, wiping tears, more aware than ever that we, too, are creeping closer and closer to the finishing line, and fall into bed.

In the early hours of Saturday morning, long before any of us wake, low clouds drift in bringing drizzling rain. By the time we gather around the breakfast table, holding steaming cups of tea and pounding heads, the damp, grey weather looks entrenched.

'It *will* clear,' Stewart insists, used to getting his own way.

But as the clock hands move towards noon, the drizzle has developed into steady rain and there's no way it's going to fine up. Tables are moved inside, the fire re-lit, food planned to be hot instead of room temperature. In that peculiar way of Sydney weather, though, the day is still soft enough to leave open the glass doors and let the clean smell of newly damp soil and eucalyptus leaves waft through the house.

Guests arrive on the local pink water taxi and trickle up to the house under the shelter of umbrellas, smelling of damp wool and wet leather shoes. So I don't see his face until he walks into the sitting room. He is, to me, quite beautiful and I am drawn to him. It is an impulse without reason.

There are crises in the kitchen. The salmon poacher is too big for the stove and I can't get the liquid to reach boiling point. The frying pan is too small to sear the beef before putting it in the oven. It feels like chaos, which in a kitchen makes me want to cry. I slug down a few glasses of white wine and begin to loathe the banjo player.

When I look around, everyone is having a great time. They don't care that the sauce béarnaise for the beef is curdled and I'm worried the salmon will give everyone food poisoning. After a couple more glasses of wine, neither do I.

At one stage I become drunkenly fixated on something Sophia said on the drive to Sydney. I seek her out, drag her away from the people she's talking to. Too smashed to care.

'Got a question.'

'Yeah?'

'Remember you said I should look for the gift?'

Sophia hasn't a clue what I'm talking about.

'You know, the gift. The gift in death. The gift the boys left.'

'Oh yeah, yeah, yeah.'

'Well, I thought about that a lot. I think I know.'

'Yeah?'

'It's learning to live in the moment, right? Not to let life thunder past while you fight change? Right?'

'Can we talk about this tomorrow?'

'Yeah. But it's ok. I've worked it out.'

She pats me and wanders off.

By the time the banjo player has long gone (moments before I whack him on the head with a wooden spoon) and the music is pure sixties, I am ready for bed. I slink off, unnoticed. The pace is too hectic.

6

THE NEXT DAY THE party splits up. Sophia leaves for the airport, nearly everyone heads back to town.

'Back to bloody Melbourne,' I whinge. 'Cold feet and dark days.'

The sun has returned to Pittwater and the world is a sparkling blue.

'Why don't you stay on for a while?'

Fleury is packing one of about eight bags that are schlepped in full of provisions then carried out to be filled again the following weekend.

'Nah, got to get back.'

'What for?'

I stop and think. Nothing urgent. Only the dog. But she's in good hands with the next door neighbours. They adore Sweetie.

'Yeah, could stay on then. If it suits you.'

'Great! Enjoy. That's what Pittwater is all about.'

'Just until the weather turns.'

Which I expect will be the following day. Only it's two weeks later. Because that night, when I am finally alone at the house, the phone rings.

'Would you like to have dinner?' he asks.

'When?'

'Tonight?'

'Sure. But I don't know how to use local transport. If you can find your way back here from Church Point, I'll cook. There are plenty of leftovers.'

And when, a few bottles of wine later, on a deck dappled by the shadows of the bush at night and looking at a moon so big and yellow it seems larger than the earth itself, he says, 'Let's go to bed,' I nod easily.

It is no big deal, after all, to cast aside inhibition when desire drowns the rational mind. 'One night,' I think. 'It can't hurt. And tomorrow I will be gone. Where is the harm? Only he and I will know.'

But it opens a floodgate and the harm is done. It isn't the sex. It is the light, cool touch of skin on skin, the whispered words late into the night, intimacy much more compelling in the dark when eyes cannot be read, expressions fathomed. It is rolling over and, still half asleep, feeling the warmth of another body alongside. It is understanding that some little corner of yourself you'd thought long dead has merely been lying in wait.

When he gets up to return to the city not long before dawn turns the bay into a pool of shining light, I feel reborn and Pittwater seduces me. After two intense weeks, I return to Melbourne to pack. I plan to lease out my Melbourne apartment and rent a house on Pittwater. I tell myself it is because I have fallen in love with the sea and the sun. I tell myself that perhaps I have found a place where I can settle. I tell myself that Pittwater is paradise and everything that I tell myself is true.

But it is also true this fling, or affair, or whatever it is, has scooped me out of a life that is dull and drab and pointless. It is fun. It is light-hearted. It dissolves the brick of despair. It makes it easy to jump quickly from the old life to the new. Easy to discount the difficulties of Pittwater living. Easy to be reckless and thoughtless.

The apartment in Melbourne is packed away into a garage in less than two weeks. A real estate agent quickly finds a tenant, and I am ready to swan into a grand new scheme on Pittwater. I am full of plans to find a beautiful house with magical views and immerse myself in Pittwater life and culture. Fleury offers the Towlers Bay house as a temporary base and Sweetie is delivered into my mother's care while I search for a property to rent.

Moving to Pittwater is like waking up one morning to find yourself on a new planet. It is a place where the rhythm of the sun and tide set schedules. Wake at dawn. Kayak at high tide. Eat when you're hungry. Sleep when it is dark. There are no cars, no street-lights, neither buses nor trains. No crowds, no pavements, no sooty residues at the end of the day.

Here, the backyard is the rugged bush and soaring escarpments of the Ku-ring-gai Chase National Park. The front yard is the bay, where stingrays glide along the sandy bottom like satellites and armies of soldier crabs, blue as the sky with purple striped legs, march across the tidal flats in perfect battle formation.

As I knew it would, the affair continues. Hormones I'd forgotten existed suddenly leap into gear. I feel sixteen again on a first date, only this time the restaurants are expensive, weekends away five star, and the whole dissolute business is kicked along by a sense of the illicit. Because he is, of course, married.

It's easy, at first, to shove that thought somewhere into the dark recesses of my mind. I have never met his wife. I tell myself I am not hurting anyone. I am clear this is a fling and will wear itself out in a very short time. There is an urgency that is not just to do with being a woman in her mid-forties who feels there are only dimin-ishing possibilities ahead – although that is a big part of the way I am thinking. It is also like living in a war zone. Everything could end in a second. There is nothing like that sense of *maybe there's no tomorrow* to make you shrug aside caution.

After all those years of work, the years of grief, the years of feeling lost, suddenly I am catapulted into a world where the only responsibility is pleasure. There are no commitments, no expectations, no demands. Unencumbered romance at a time of life when I thought it would never happen again. I defy any woman to turn her back on it.

The lover and I discover we have similar backgrounds. He grew up in a country pub. So did I. He enjoys thoroughbred racing. It was my brother's lifeblood. He worked as a journalist around the world. Me too. We wonder why our paths never crossed in London, New York, Cape Town, anywhere. And then we realise we did meet once, in New York, at a journalist's bar. Why didn't we click then? 'The time just wasn't right,' we agree, blithely ignoring the fact that he is married and the time is still decidedly not right.

I know, from the first, that this is not a man you would want forever and for a while I stop and start the liaison. But when he says, one day, that we are in a relationship, not an affair, I stop thinking about ending it and instead slide easily into the role of mistress. For a while, it gives me the illusion of belonging some-where. But there is never contentment, only gut-gnawing anxiety because he does not come home to me each night and he is mercurial and women are drawn to him. I cannot be sure he always turns away from their invitations. Yet every time there are hints that he is a compulsive womaniser, I become an old lady who sees and hears only what she wants. I am selectively blind and deaf to all the signs that this is a man who can never be faithful, not even to his mistress.

On days when I don't race to the city to meet him, I take long, solitary walks through the Ku-ring-gai Chase National Park, trying to switch off the monkey that spins in my mind in never-ending loops. Will he call today? Will I see him tomorrow? Is it over already and I don't know it? I stride, hatless under the sun, from waterfront to escarpment, counting the steps, willing myself to be slim and fit. Often almost fainting with heat and fatigue.

Sometimes, when he lightly refers to a cyclonic week at home, firecrackers of hope explode wildly and brightly and I, the mistress without any legal or emotional rights, think, oh, the marriage must be coming to an end. But it isn't. And anyway, if hazy dreams of a future together even nibble at the edge of my mind, all I can see, rearing in anger and hurt, are the faces of children. So I switch off the most natural desire in the world, the desire to share and be with someone you love and respect. I settle for crumbs and tell myself each crumb is worth more than a whole cake with anyone else. But really, it isn't.

I walk so long and often, my weight loss is dramatic, and friends look confused when I say hello. As though they have a lingering memory of someone who looks like me that they can't quite place.

I preen. I like the new persona. The one that's ditched the apologetic insecurity of the overweight and unfit. Old clothes are flung into the charity bin at Church Point and my new wardrobe is fresh and sexy. Short skirts, tight trousers, stretchy fabrics become sudden favourites. I splurge on clingy little sweaters in the softest wool, buy toe-peeper shoes and get my toenails painted. I book a regular leg wax, change the colour of my hair and do not understand that I am reinventing myself until much later. My confidence blossoms. For the first time in my life I feel beautiful and clever, which means people react to me differently. And that reinforces my new, burgeoning sense of self.

'How did you do it?' people gush.

I do not, cannot, mention the lover. So instead, I talk about my exercise regime. I do not say that, often, tears mingle with sweat as I tramp the chalky pink and white tracks through the bush. Because up high on the escarpment where the world is pure, I see clearly the affair that has begun to rule every waking moment can never offer anything of value. Beneath the surface of stolen afternoons, devious weekends and quick snatches of time together are lies, deceit, a duplicity I never dreamed I could embrace, and a deepening distaste for the person I am becoming. I tell myself it is living but it is a slow dissembling.

Sometimes as I trudge along, I wave my arms angrily, demanding answers from a cosmos I think should arrange itself more tidily. 'What is right? What is wrong? What lies ahead?' I want to know. But the landscape is mute, the isolation intense. The sharp-edged, prickly bush, as ancient as the rusty pink sandstone it grows on, offers neither comfort nor peace.

There is a cave – actually, more of a rock overhang – a little beyond where the Towlers Bay track eases into the national park, and every three days or so someone places a fresh flower in it. The flowers aren't native, none can be plucked from the side of the track. Once it is a rose, once a gladioli, once a lily. There must be young lovers, I think as I march past, and this is how they arrange to meet. I find the ritual charming on some days and spooky on others. Then one day there are no more fresh flowers in the little cave and the last offering, a yellow lily, just fades into nothing. Has someone died? Is the affair over? I never discover what it is all about.

Mostly I am alone on my walks, except for the canting in my head. But often, I spin and look behind me, prickled by the sensation that the eyes of long dead generations are drilling into my back.

Once, this was a place where young Aboriginal boys were tapped on the shoulder as they slept near their mothers. The boys, about twelve years old, were silently beckoned to follow their elders higher and higher through the moonlit scrub to the sacred sites at the top of the escarpment, to be initiated – with the pull of a tooth – into manhood. When I walk to these ancient sacred sites that date back ten thousand years, there are never many people gathered around them. Perhaps because they have neither the glamour of grand architecture nor rooms filled with golden treasure.

There is an immense spirituality here, where Aborigines once used flat sandstone outcrops as sites for their rock engravings of fish, whales, echidnas, emus, goannas and wallabies. The engravings, smooth with time, simple and evocative, are etched on charcoal-grey tessellated rocks where, when it rains steadily but not too heavily, little rivulets run rampant in the grooves, crisscrossing busily. The fish engravings seem to swim and it suddenly becomes clear why, thousands of years ago, it must have seemed a good idea to carve fish so far above the waters of the bays.

In one area, there's an etching of a half-man, half-animal that I learn the Aborigines called Daramulan. Today, his significance is guessed at by experts because the Garigal tribe, who carved his image on the rocks and who lived here unmolested for thousands of years, was wiped out when European settlers brought smallpox and venereal diseases.

In summer, the low buzz of insects provides a backdrop sonata to the random crackles and crunch of the bush. Then, just when it seems at its most still as I trudge, sometimes with a mantra running through my head exhorting myself to be happy and content, the silence is shattered by the raging screeches of sulphur-crested cockatoos. Huge, clumsy white birds that fly as gracelessly as old, fat-bellied seaplanes. The noise is deafening. Somewhere out of sight, a hunt is on.

To me, reaching the escarpment is like stepping into my own, private ancient art gallery where the walls are textured by needle bush, tea tree and dwarf apples; where the silver trunks of young scribbly gums glitter starkly against the bright blue sky. Where hundreds of shades of green are broken every so often by a strike of blood red from a rogue eucalyptus leaf. Where leaves are spiky, sharp, serrated, tapering, elegant, tufted, or rounded. Where the sky, its own ever-changing canvas, provides a dome for a gallery of subtle, timeless beauty.

On a day of misty rain, so gentle it seems to hang like a sigh before wafting to the ground, the achy smell of damp, charred black trees, the remnants of the 1994 bushfires, ignites pangs of undefined yearning so intense I double over. Up here on the escarpment, where my lies to myself sit like lead in my mind, I know the affair is wrecking me. It will leave me altered and stunted, like the burned-out stumps around me.

'Were you here, Stewart, when the bushfires roared through in ninety-four?' I ask one Friday not long after I move into the Towlers Bay house while I search for one of my own to rent.

'Yeah. You could say that.'

'Jesus,' Fleury says. 'That was a time I'll never forget. We'd just bought the place.'

It was a week when the hot summer westerly winds sucked the last drop of moisture out of the air and the atmosphere felt like a powder keg waiting for a match.

'We'd just returned to Australia from the US and everything we owned was barged in,' Stewart says. 'Never forget what one of the removal blokes said. "Knowledge is heavy, mate. Knowledge is heavy." He was carrying the books. Boxes and boxes of them. Up the steps. Heavy as hell. A poet, in his way.'

Two days after the last box was unpacked, fire exploded all around them. The family agonised in a rush about what to save, what mattered most. The paintings? The furniture? Clothes? It was a big decision. They didn't have insurance. While they sat by the radio, waiting to hear whether their luck was running hot – or running out – they put the family photograph albums in the boat before anything else.

'Family history,' Fleury says. 'Everything else could be replaced.'

Firemen and police swarmed in as the fire raced closer.

'Forced us to leave,' Stewart says. 'Threw handcuffs on people who refused to go.'

Stewart took Fleury and their two daughters to safety and then returned to watch from the middle of the bay as flames tongued their back door. When there seemed no way the house would survive, he felt the wind swing around to the south east. And in a click of the fingers, it was spared. His luck, that day, was running hot.

'Do you worry there will be another fire like that?'

'You don't *worry* about it. But you know it can happen,' Stewart says.

7

By Christmas, I still haven't found a house to rent. And it's summer, the high season, when rents soar and houses that lie vacant most of the year suddenly roar to life. I cannot abuse hospitality any longer. The lover, anyway, has always refused to commute here and I am afraid our meetings in the city will eventually be discovered. I need a place of my own. In the end, the beauty of Pittwater fails to diminish the power of the lover and for a while, it becomes just another lightly touched location in a lifetime of them.

In Sydney I look for a house to share with a long-time friend, Pia, and my husband's youngest daughter, Lulu, who's in her twenties. I tell real estate agents that Pia is divorced. I am a widow. Lulu is my stepdaughter. I'm concerned about appearances. I'm not sure why.

While I worry they'll think we're an odd collection, they actually wonder if we're planning to run a brothel. Why else would three single women need a six-bedroom house? But Pia and I are new to sharing and we want various rooms where we can disappear. Lulu simply wants a roof over her head. She's just split with her boyfriend. When we find a house with three levels (one each), we cautiously move in.

To our surprise, we three dispossessed women have a grand time living together and evolve into a peculiar sort of family unit. Pia and I wave Lulu to work then sit down to a breakfast of tea and toast while we read our daily star signs in the paper. She tells me how to keep white clothes white and I tell her how to grow hydrangeas from cuttings. She likes to be lyrical in her appreciation of food while I enjoy cooking it. I mow the lawn. She polishes the kitchen. It's an ego-less relationship that revels in the mundane. We throw lots of boozy dinner parties but stay within strict budgets by cooking trays of grilled polenta and buckets of spaghetti bolognese. Lulu puts up with both of us but watches a lot of television after dinner in her own sitting room.

At weekends Pia and I join an old friend, Tony, a wonderfully wicked theatrical and literary agent, at his shack at Little Gairie Beach, in the Royal National Park. The shack, a relic from the Depression, is less than basic. No running water. No electricity. The loo is a plastic bucket under a toilet seat in an outdoor cupboard. It is Tony's job to dig a hole somewhere in the hills to empty the bucket but often he puts it off for too long. I learn to pee behind trees or I grab a shovel and head into the hills.

Whenever we take off, I load a thermos of soup, cooked legs of lamb, jars of gravy and mint sauce, kilos of sausages and large cakes, into a huge backpack so heavy it takes two people to lift it onto my back. 'This is Susan, our *packhorse*,' Tony says, making introductions to the shack community.

Tony, in his late fifties, is a sixty ciggies a day man, so he can't carry much of a load. And he loves a drink. Although to look at him, you would never know. His excesses leave no visible marks. He is slim as an athlete. Handsome, too, in the way that turns people's heads. And he could charm the balls off a brass monkey – as he was fond of saying.

Pia carries her share but has a bad back to protect. I relish my own strength and tell people with pride that I am *strong as an ox, healthy as a buffalo*. I lug our three days' worth of supplies a couple of kilometres from the car park along a goat track cut into the side of the cliff. The track ends where there is a two foot drop to a ledge of slippery, emerald green rocks. Stepping onto the rocks is precarious enough with a forty kilo load on your back. It's just plain life-threatening on an incoming tide with waves breaking only a few feet away.

'You'll be fine,' Tony yells one day, even though the surf looks treacherous. It's raining and he is impatient to get to shelter. He is way ahead, already past the green rocks and safely on the beach.

'Ok,' we shout.

But I pause. Some instinct holds me back. Pia, who is also wary, stands next to me.

'Do we go?' she asks.

'Nuh. Not yet.'

A moment later a huge, rogue wave comes out of nowhere and crashes at our feet. If we'd stepped from the track, it would have snatched and dragged us along the rocks to the ocean. Damaging us badly or even killing us. But it didn't.

Pia and I look at each other and laugh. 'Jesus!'

'Not meant to cark it yet,' Pia says. And we laugh and laugh.

When we reach Tony a few minutes later, the cigarette in his hand is shaking. 'Ker-rist,' he says.

'Tone, you nearly lost your shack sheilas!'

Our laughter calms him.

'I don't suppose,' he says, 'that you feel like a drink?'

'Do we ever!'

And we follow him up the hill to the shabby shack with its peeling paint, crooked windows and holey flyscreen door. We're still laughing as we shoo a herd of feral but friendly deer away and search for the door key. Joyful, I suppose, with relief.

Tony's routine when we arrive at the shack is always the same. He immediately lights the old kerosene fridge that takes about six hours to work up a decent chill. Then he shoves ice trays in the freezer so he'll have cubes for his late morning gin and tonic ('with lime, dear, not lemon, if you don't mind'), and assembles the bar (rum, gin, whisky, wine).

His shack, with its 1950s kerosene heater and ragged linoleum floor, is fitted out with flotsam and jetsam thrown out by other households. Multicoloured crockery, mismatched cutlery, a wobbly kitchen table and a laminex-topped dining table that resides in a spot that looks out on a glorious view of the surging surf. It's like the tatty holiday shacks of my childhood where the roof leaked and the boards rattled when the wind blew, and where you were allowed to run riot and if anything got damaged no-one yelled.

At Little Gairie Beach, Pia and I sleep in an alcove separated from the living room by long strands of beads hanging in the doorway. It has two bunk beds, one above the other, covered with brightly coloured, crocheted Afghan blankets. Tony sleeps in the kitchen-cum-sitting room on a blinding orange divan, also a refugee from the fifties. Every night he coughs in violent, racking spasms. When they finally abate and we call out to make sure he is still alive, he's immediately cranky.

'Whadya wake me for?' he grumbles.

In the mornings, we urge him to quit smoking.

'Why?'

'Because you cough all night!'

'What rot!' he says.

In less than a year, the landlord turfs us out of the three level home we share so happily because she wants to move in. So we set off again, this time to a big white house on a main road that overlooks a park. Here, there are no places to escape from each other and bathrooms are communal. For me, the move is disturbing, almost disorienting. A reminder that I have no roots. No place where I belong. I am still floating aimlessly and it's scarier than ever.

The affair has long passed the point of being thrilling. Putting yourself last in the queue for attention creates anger and resentment. Too often, now, the euphoria couples with depression. What good, after all, can come from any course that is taken without care for the damage it may do to others? Yet every time I feel I can no longer continue, the dark spectre of loneliness smothers my shaky shreds of courage and I stay on and on.

Pia, who knows about the affair, watches the highs and lows with disbelief. 'Have you always been like this in a relationship?' she asks one night as we dine together. I pick listlessly at food, my stomach roiling with anxiety, the greatest appetite depressant in the world.

'Never,' I reply.

And because it is the truth, I excuse the madness by telling myself this is a *grand passion*, the one we all seek, believe we are entitled to, dream about.

Much later, a woman tells me: 'I had an affair outside my marriage and sometimes I wished my husband and children dead so I could be free. It was madness. And yet the thought was there. Lust is not rational.' Nor can it satisfy beyond the moment.

I begin going out with other men but it feels like an even bigger duplicity and I badly hurt an old friend whom I allow to misinterpret the time we spend together. To blur the edges of a useless, careless life, I party harder.

When I'm offered a job two years after my bid at 'retirement', I grab it like it will save me and give me stability, as it did for more than twenty-five years. The work is the stuff of dreams. Travel editor for a national women's magazine. I sail on the luxurious *Queen Elizabeth 2* and watch rich, lonely old women in couture ball gowns snapping at each other jealously over the attentions of the *paid gentlemen* who are there to be dancing partners. Do we ever lose the desire for romance, I wonder? No matter how foolish it sometimes makes us look?

I snorkel amongst the teeming coral reefs of Fiji with the son of Jacques Cousteau, touching a turtle for a cosmic moment before it shrugs me aside and wings on its way. I sleep on the ground at Palm Valley in Finke Gorge National Park and wake drenched with dew to find a kangaroo staring intently at me, as though he is deciding whether to tick me off for invading his patch. In the early morning light, the ancient fissured gorge is on fire. It is a privileged job and lifestyle but I move through it all like a sleepwalker. Some inner core is wearing out and I know it.

I have turned myself inside out to be all things to the lover, my mother's words ringing in my head: 'No-one will love you unless . . .' Words I heard *her* mother use one cold, rainy day when we warmed ourselves near the wood burning stove in the rammed earth kitchen of my grandparents' rough slab, bush house. Nan's kitchen always smelled of wood dust, baking scones, kerosene lamps and tea leaves, which she scattered on the dirt floor when she swept it.

'Now, Esther Jean,' Nan said, 'no-one will love you if you act like that . . .'

My mother, married with children of her own, fuming because the men were late home and would probably be tipsy when they arrived, turned away before she said something she might regret.

Nan gave my brother and me a Bible one Christmas and told us to read it because it contained a few useful tips on how to lead a good life. Nan always said that *as you make your bed, you must sleep on it*. For years, I had no idea what she meant.

I drive to the office towards the end of spring. In the traffic, people with mouths turned down or phones crammed to their ears rage silently. Looking at them, I wonder what the hell I think I am doing. I am back on the treadmill with an increasing leaning towards all the gods I know are ultimately unsatisfying. Ambition, success, material gratification. None of that made a squit of difference when the boys died. No need to think it will now.

On the car radio, the news is all bad, as it tends to be. And, to me, irrelevant. I could *not* listen to the news, *not* read a newspaper, *not* watch a television report for a year, I think, and nothing would change, I would *not* miss anything.

I quiz myself: 'If I could do whatever I want, what would it be?'

The answer rockets back: 'Return to Pittwater.'

The idea swirls and eddies. There are many reasons *not* to go there, all practical. There's the commute to work by ferry and car. And boats! What do I know about boats? If I buy one, how will it be to set off alone across dark waters when I come home late at night? There's the relentless schlepping of the groceries. Every package is handled five times before it lands inside the door. Shop to car to dock to boat to dock to house. At the end of a day when you are tired before you begin, it wears down even the most dedicated offshore residents and I am too weary to be thrilled by daily physical challenges.

And there is the lover, who would find it inconvenient. He neither enjoys nor understands the peace of Pittwater. Racetracks are more appealing to him.

The radio hammers on. Fast paced voices, fast paced news, in a rhythm that describes a fatal accident on the M4 in the same honeyed tones as the weather. New South Head Road is a stalled, sinuous queue of cars shitting exhaust and going nowhere. Doesn't matter if you're stuck in a BMW or a dented thirty-year-old Datsun, we're all marking time in the same foul air. Stuck is stuck.

Will moving unstick the lover? Maybe. Hopefully.

Our Sydney lease is due for renewal and we three women at *Virgins' Perch*, as Tony dubbed our home, are wondering whether to continue or go our separate ways. After two years, we have begun to grate on each other at odd moments and as this is not a marriage, we are not compelled to smooth over the rough bits. We are beginning to niggle over whose turn it is to vacuum, unload the dishwasher, sweep the backyard, when once we did it cheerfully because we felt like it.

When I finally get to the office, semi-dazed people are girding for another day of going through the motions. Or that's how I see it this morning. After a few *giddays*, I sit at my desk eating toasted banana bread and drinking a bucket of super strong coffee for the kick start. Even my bones feel worn out and brittle these days.

My contact book, filled with phone numbers collected during a lifetime in journalism, lies neatly on the desk. I idly flick the pages until I reach the Rs. The number for the real estate agent at Church Point is still there. Written in a red felt tip pen more than two years earlier. Before I have time to think about it, I punch in the numbers. The phone is picked up by a different agent, a woman I've never met.

'Do you know the area?' she asks.

'Yes. A little. I once spent a bit of time at Towlers Bay.'

'So you know the houses are all water access, that you have to take a ferry or use a boat?'

'Yeah.'

'I have to ask. Most people have no idea how life is lived here. They lob up all excited to see a waterfront house and then cancel when they find they'll need a boat to get to it. Wastes a lot of time.'

'That's ok. So what have you got?'

'A fabulous house came on the market this morning. Sounds like it could be what you're looking for.'

I don't get excited. They all say that.

'Waterfront?'

'Yep.'

'Deep waterfront?'

'Yep.'

'Where?'

'Scotland Island.'

'Oh.'

Deep waterfront is good, it means boat access during the lowest tides. But I don't want to live on Scotland Island. When I looked at houses there on my first attempt at Pittwater living a millennium ago, it seemed as crowded as suburbia. There were holiday shacks made from scraps glued together in the forties and fifties. Fading hippie houses with psychedelic walls and stained loos from the sixties and seventies. Basic family homes from the eighties when land was comparatively cheap because *water access only* was seen as a handicap, not an asset. There were comfortable family homes and grand and beautiful estates with manicured gardens and saltwater swimming pools but they rarely came on the rental market. Out of my price range anyway.

Back then, I decided great views couldn't compensate for the crowding and I was looking more for comfort than a community. But that was two years ago.

'Just come and look,' says the agent. 'If you don't like it, don't take it!'

It is impossible to guess what I will be seeing. I know, at least, that it isn't perched at the top of the island. Which is a good thing. At the rate I go through wine, the shorter the lugging distance, the better.

'I'll drive up this afternoon. See you around four thirty, ok?'

'Great.'

But I put down the phone, collect my bag, return to the car and drive immediately to Church Point, leaving work untouched, phone calls unreturned, telling no-one where I have gone. Forty-five minutes later, I stand in the scrappy little Church Point real estate office with its map of Pittwater pinned to the wall, still not quite sure what I am doing but in a rush anyway.

'I'm Susan. Come to see the house on Scotland Island.'

'You weren't supposed to be here until this afternoon!'

'Yeah, I know. Sorry. Does it matter?'

The real estate agent, casual in jeans and a white T-shirt with a faint coffee stain, flaps around making phone calls, checking the timing is ok with the owners, grabbing the file on the house.

'Keys?' I suggest, trying to be helpful.

'No. Don't need keys.'

'Doesn't the place lock up?'

'Oh yeah, but people around here don't bother. If anything goes missing, nearly everyone knows where it is and who's borrowed it.'

She calls the pink water taxi while I check out properties for sale on the noticeboard. I didn't use water taxis much when I lived at Towlers Bay. Made the walk to Halls Wharf to catch the ferry. Forgot the car keys once. You only ever do that once. But I always thought the colour of the water taxi boats was silly. Baby pink. For some reason, whenever I saw them dashing around the bays, I wanted to laugh. They looked ridiculously out of place. Girlish instead of tough.

'Let's head off!'

'That's the house. Over there,' she says from the end of the Church Point ferry wharf.

It's a pleasant, low-slung wooden house that seems to overhang the shoreline. So far, so good.

'Gidday,' the driver says. 'Where to?'

'Mottles' house, thanks.'

'Right.'

No street numbers here.

The water taxi drops us at a jetty that leads straight to the front door. Level access, easy schlepping, a prize on Pittwater. It's the beginning of the seduction.

'Does the water wash inside at high tide?' I ask, not altogether jokingly.

The agent grins. 'You might want to roll up your rugs during a *king* tide.'

The house has the feel of a sprawling boatshed. It is shacky and casual but properly built. Not tacked together. The kitchen, which has a polished wooden bench with a stove in the corner, is part of a long, T-shaped room that includes a dining, sitting and entrance area. There's a study space with views to Church Point. The main bedroom, once a separate boatshed, is connected to the house by a back porch or French doors that open onto the front deck. I visualise rolling out of bed on a hot summer night when the heat feels like a fur-lined glove and splashing into the water. The house faces west, so there is afternoon sun. A plus in winter. A negative in summer. It will broil. But there are double doors everywhere so it opens up to let the sea breezes flow through. A positive.

There are angles and corners, lots of conjoining roof lines and an upstairs bedroom that is like a ship's cabin, high above the sea. On odd walls, the owner has papered beautiful bark drawings. When I meet him briefly a couple of weeks later to haggle over the rent and seal the deal, he tells me he collected them when he sailed in the Solomon Islands.

'Is everyone around here a sailor?' I ask him.

He looks at me as though I am dimwitted. 'Of course. Otherwise we wouldn't need the water.'

'Not even to look at?'

'Well, not for long.'

We settle on a date for me to move in, two weeks later.

'You won't regret it,' says the agent.

Friends have a different view. 'Don't!' they scream. 'It's ok for weekends, but don't live there if you want a life.'

I think of them running in and out of meetings, playing politics, looking harassed and stressed and complaining bitterly about the rat race.

'The deal is done, the lease signed. Cheques handed over,' I reply.

They shake their heads in concern, convinced I have been both reckless and stupid. That I will live to regret this latest, mad whim.

They do not see, perhaps, the courage it takes to walk away and embrace change. And yet without change, without taking risks, where is growth to come from? At this stage of my life, the growth I want has nothing to do with the material. I know that money in the bank may make you feel less vulnerable and open up choices, but it doesn't guarantee happiness. How I wish I'd known that years ago when chasing the dollar seemed worthy. Or perhaps time alters our perspective and what is compelling at one age becomes worthless at another?

I want to know about the mind and spirit now. I want to understand why some people wake up joyful each day and others struggle out of bed. Why some people see good in the most devastating situations and others see the bad in the best. Why do some people die too young? Why does success fall at someone's feet while others slog and get nowhere? Are there heroes – or are we all flawed? Is it luck? Is it timing? Why do some people get on a plane that is doomed to crash and others wait for the next flight? My friends might shake their heads but at least I am having a go, giving myself a chance, chasing life instead of hoping it will find me. I guess I am finally taking responsibility for my own happiness and not looking for it through anyone else.

Dismantling my city life is easy. A huge garage sale. Two-thirds of the furniture to auction, including the dreaded ride-on mower that's been in storage for years. Whatever is left I give to a bloke who says he's from the Maroubra Boy Scouts, but he's probably a dealer. He squishes the scrag ends of the sale into a dusty station wagon and drives away looking very pleased with himself.

By Sunday night, the rental house is empty except for Sweetie, a few pieces of furniture such as the bed, and stuff that evokes cherished memories. Pia and Lulu have already moved to separate inner city apartments. They say Scotland Island is too far and too hard. But I suspect they think I've lost the plot good and proper this time.

8

MOVING DAY IS BRIGHT AND sunny but I feel like shit. Can't rev up energy or enthusiasm. It seems like a hundred years since the prospect of change made me sparkly-eyed, since I believed new horizons led to growth and knowledge. Today I just feel shattered. I am aware I've frittered away the opportunities of so many new starts. It's hard to believe this move is going to be any different. The view is just better.

Everything that is small enough is packed into brown cardboard boxes with their contents neatly labelled on the sides. Instant necessities – teapot, kettle, milk, beer, wine, bread, butter and a selection of cold meats and cheese – are packed into two clothes baskets to take in the car. The rest will go in a truck with the removalists. I have become expert at moving.

In the backyard, Sweetie lingers in her kennel.

'Come on, old girl. Time to get up.'

Her pretty head is resting on her front paws, and she doesn't raise it when she lifts her eyes to look at me.

'Are you ok?'

I kneel and ruffle her fur.

'Come on, Sweetie. It's moving day. Let's go.'

She looks away and groans.

She is thirteen years old and, according to the vet, four years past her use-by date. I have a sickly feeling this is the end but I go to the kitchen and grab a piece of cold meat from the *instant necessities* basket, hoping she has an upset tummy and nothing more sinister.

I wave the food and her lovely brown eyes follow my hand. But she doesn't move. Then she looks at me as though I can save her. We're mates, right? I'll fix everything, right? Her once glossy black fur is faded into brown and grey and everything that is born must die. Right? Yeah. Bloody damn right.

When the removalists arrive they help me to pick her up and put her in the car to take to the vet, who explains she has a tumour that's ruptured her spleen.

'We can do some tests to verify it, if you like,' he says, kindly.

'Will it make a difference?'

'Not really. No.'

'Is there anything we can do?'

'Well, she'll probably live a couple more days but all we can do is dose her with painkillers. That's about it.'

'What would you do if it was your dog?'

'I'd put her down.'

I crouch on the floor with my faithful old dog, cradling her head in my lap, stroking her gently. She knows what is ahead, in the way animals always do, and struggles briefly when the needle goes into her thigh. But she doesn't take her eyes off me.

'Oh, Sweetie. What a great dog. What a good dog.'

And she is dead. Closed down and gone.

I have nowhere to bury her, no nearby friend with a farm, no plot of land in my own backyard.

'She's not going on any bloody garbage dump,' I tell the vet. 'I'll bury her some place great, even if I have to drive a hundred miles.'

'She can be cremated, if you like. Her ashes will come back here for you to pick up.'

I nod because I cannot speak and the vet lifts Sweetie and she is gone.

I make a vow to bury the box when I find a home where I will spend the rest of my life. Until then, the box will come with me.

No matter how many times I move, no matter how long it takes to find somewhere to belong.

I write out a cheque and leave, anger quickly pushing aside grief. Another bloody loss. Everything that is born must die. The line spins in my head and I hate the truth of it.

I slam the car into gear, shout at a woman who takes too long to cross the road at the lights: 'What are you on? A bloody picnic!'

She gives me the finger. I want to smash her face. The lights change and I move on. Driving recklessly.

At the house, the removal van is loaded, the boys waiting for directions. Another move, another house, another journey leading to what? I mentally add up my home bases over the past decade and stop when I reach seventeen. New houses, new jobs, new countries, new clothes. None of it seems very glamorous any more. More like sad.

The lover calls as we set off. I don't mention Sweetie. Fake breeziness. This is not a man who likes to share the downside.

'How's it going?'

'We're just heading to Pittwater now.'

'When can I see this fabulous house?'

Never! 'Whenever you like.'

And the one piece of baggage I should have dumped before all else slides effortlessly along with me.

Three young men and a dog wait at Cargo Wharf, where any large scale loading or unloading takes place in this part of Pittwater. Two are obviously brothers. Small boned, sinewy, dead straight jet black hair, tanned in the deep, even way of people who spend most of the day outdoors. It's the tail end of spring but they wear shorts, scruffy T-shirts and bare feet. The third man is taller, bulkier, with tightly curled black hair and a winter pallor. He is dressed in jeans.

There's a T-shirt under a checked flannel shirt. He wears socks and boots on his feet. I suss already that he is newly a local.

The dog is a beautiful, glossy black labrador in his prime. Focus on the job, I quickly tell myself. Put Sweetie into a faraway corner of your head.

Cargo Wharf, a little beyond Church Point ferry wharf, is wide enough for a couple of trucks side by side so I drive right to the edge of the wharf. Wind down the window. 'Gidday.'

The boys straggle to their feet. Smiles everywhere. Jump off their rusted old barge onto solid ground.

'Yeah. You'd be Susan, then?'

'Yeah. Going to Scotland Island. Mottles' old house.'

'Oh, right. George's place. Know where you mean, now. Anyway, I'm Andrew. This is my brother Chris. And he's Paul.'

'What's the dog's name?'

'Bosun.'

'He's beautiful.'

'Yeah. He's a good dog.'

'No sign of the truck?'

'No. Not yet.'

'Don't know where they've got to. I left about half an hour after them.'

'Might be lost.'

Less charitably, I figure they're pushing the number of hours to do the job as high as they can. 'Could be. So you put everything on this barge?'

'Uh-huh.'

It's long and flat. Cracked with random holes in the deck. Looks like an overcooked biscuit. There are no side rails. Nothing to stop everything falling off.

'Ah, how does all the stuff stay on?'

Andrew grins. 'Don't worry, we haven't lost anything yet.'

'Oh. Good.'

There's no sign of the truck and it's nearly lunchtime.

'I'll just park and get a sandwich. Can I dump the stuff from the car with you now?'

'No worries.'

'Anybody want anything to eat?'

The boys shake their heads.

Andrew looks at his watch. 'Those blokes know where to come, don't they?'

'Yeah, I gave them all the landmarks. Drew a map.'

'Bit worried about the tide, that's all. If it gets much later, by the time we load and get there, it'll be low tide. Makes the job a lot harder.'

'How much leeway have we got?'

'From now? About half an hour.'

'Even if they're later, we'll still be able to unload, right?'

'Yeah. But it means a lot of lifting. Much trickier.'

Shit. Where are those blokes?

Half an hour later they casually roll onto Cargo Wharf, hands filled with sandwiches. Passively aggressive. They throw open the doors of the truck and settle to eat, and watch the Pittwater boys do the work.

Andrew shrugs. Jumps lightly into the truck. Starts work. Polite. Laidback. No drama. The city men are shamed, look sheepish. Bolt their food and pitch in. Hard to hold on to the upper hand when there's no contest.

Sofas, a couple of armchairs, a couple of tables, dining room chairs, sideboard, coffee table and two beds. Four lamps. Paintings. Books. Clothes. Kitchen equipment and crockery. Minimum of bed linen and towels. Tubs of Iceberg roses and herbs. That's it. I still have too much kitchen stuff but some things will never change. No dog. No kennel. Slam the door shut on that one. No tears please.

It all gets piled onto the barge which has old tyres tied around the sides like bows on a banquet table. My belongings are layered and braced against each other. Hard to believe it will all stay steady.

Nothing is tied. The boys ride the rock and roll of the barge like horsemen.

'Can I get a lift to the house with you guys?'

'Yeah, sure. Climb on.'

'Where's the engine? How do you steer this thing?'

Andrew points at a battered old tinny, which is what aluminium dinghies are called in this part of the world. It's tied alongside and he jumps into it. Light as a dancer. The boat barely shifts balance.

'The tinny does the steering by pushing the barge.'

He yanks the engine cord. After a couple of coughs it kicks into life. The Sydney blokes lean against the truck, ankles crossed, and watch. They're waiting for disaster.

We pull slowly away from the wharf. That tiny little tinny with its twenty-five horsepower, two stroke motor carefully pilots us to Scotland Island. We ride the wakes from passing boats and not a stick of furniture moves. Only the skirt of one of the sofas gets a little damp when water slops over the side. Who cares?

'Can there be a better way to travel?'

Paul laughs. 'I haven't lived here too long,' he says, 'but I don't think I'll ever leave.'

We dock about five feet from the front door.

'If we'd caught the tide at exactly the right time, we'd just slide stuff off the barge onto the deck and into the house,' Andrew says.

The drop from the jetty and deck to the barge is now about two feet. Doesn't sound like much, but when you're lifting heavy furniture from an unstable base, any advantage counts.

'What a bugger.'

He smiles. 'It's not too bad. Would have been worse in another hour.'

Doesn't anyone whinge around here?

The empty house smells of wood and polished floorboards. And the sea. Dust motes frolic in shards of sunlight. Nothing is locked.

I've been given keys but they don't work anyway. I throw open all the doors and look up McCarrs Creek, across to Elvina Bay. Church Point is a good swim away. Water traffic buzzes by. Tinnies. Cabin cruisers. A beautiful wooden rowboat with a man in a wide brimmed hat. And silent yachts under sail in a light breeze.

A tight little band of anxiety loosens around my chest. It's too beautiful, too bloody exquisite not to feel a touch of joy. Sweetie would have loved it. Bad timing, old girl. But when is death ever good timing?

'Where do you want the pot plants?'

Paul is holding the rosemary. Looking around, there is only deck space. The ultimate waterfront house.

'Put it alongside the bedroom. Full sun, there.'

'So what do you reckon? Is rosemary the top herb? Or would you go for basil?' he asks.

Paul envies me the rosemary. Explains he's a passionate cook. There's not enough sun to grow rosemary successfully where he lives on the north side of Elvina in an old sandstone boatshed.

'The thing about rosemary is that it can be delicate or strong,' he continues. 'It's good dried or fresh. A leg of lamb without rosemary is almost naked. A bit of a waste. And it doesn't have seasons. Basil is strictly summer.'

'Not true! Just because basil is a summer crop doesn't mean you can't freeze it and put it in sauces and dressings, in curries and stews.'

'On a boat, I reckon curry's the go,' Andrew says, lining up the sofas perfectly. Chris piles boxes in the middle of the floor.

The brothers stand next to each and look at the barge, the falling tide. 'Better move her. She'll be aground soon.' They walk lightly out the front door.

'Curry isn't a herb! It's a whole lot of spices,' Paul calls after them.

The last few boxes and a bed are carried up the steps from the end of the jetty. Where my own tinny might go one day. If I buy one. If I stay.

The final box joins the stack inside. A weekend of unpacking lies ahead. Oh happy days. Not.

'I've put cold beers in the fridge. How about it?'

'That'd go down ok.'

The boys sit on the jetty. Legs hanging over. Feet above the water. The bay picks up the pink of a sunset sky and life feels soft.

'So you boys do this all the time?'

'Nope.' They all say it at once.

Andrew and Chris like to sail.

'See that black boat over there? The ketch?' Andrew asks, pointing with his finger.

I turn around, look south. I have no idea what a ketch is but there's only one black boat. 'Yeah. Got it.'

'I'm restoring it.' Andrew turns and faces north west again. Sunlight fills his face. 'Then I'm going to sail it. Maybe around the islands. Maybe around the world one day.' Chris has the same dream.

'Moving business is a way to get the money together.'

Paul is qualified to skipper a water taxi, a ferry, and a charter yacht. 'Not sure what I really want to do yet. I'm looking around. Testing a few things. So what brought *you* here?' he adds.

'Felt like a change.'

'Helluva change.'

'Yeah, well sometimes you need a helluva change. Might buy a house here. If all goes well. Not sure yet. See how I go.'

'If you last two years here, you hang on for life,' Andrew says.

'That's the golden rule, is it? I've heard someone say that before.'

'I move people in, I move people out. Some hate it from day one, can't cop boats, weather, rough days. Others settle here so easily, it'd take a bomb to shift them.' Andrew finishes his beer. Gets up.

'Another beer?'

'No thanks. Gotta get going.'

'Can you pick the ones who will last?'

'Mostly.'

'I'm here for the long term. That's the plan.'

'Wait and see.'

Chris, the quiet one, stands alongside his brother. 'You never know how it's gonna go. Wait and see,' he says.

Paul hesitates over another beer, then declines. He'll be stranded or have to take the ferry from Bells Wharf if he stays on.

I watch them walk down the jetty. Andrew whistles to Bosun, who appears out of nowhere and gallops after him. A floppy, loose-lipped, doggy kind of smile all over his happy face. The boys untie and cast off. Chris pushes the barge away from the jetty with a foot and then leaps for the deck. No chance he will miss. He stands as though there's an invisible yarn knitting water, barge and man into a single unit.

It's dark enough to turn on lights in the house. But I hesitate. Don't want to disrupt the outside light. The softness. The rosy satin smoothness of a day that doesn't seem quite as terrible as it was earlier.

I leave the bedroom doors open on my first night in the little boat-shed bedroom alongside the main house, the floor only inches higher than the water when the tide is in. From my bed, I see stars in a black sky. And a few lights. An insomniac perhaps, or a forgotten porch light, somewhere along McCarrs Creek.

There's a wondrous peace without the absolute emptiness a city needs to be quiet. I cannot sleep, though. And counting stars doesn't help. I throw back the doona and wander out to the edge of the silvery deck. There are no handrails here and the tide is out, exposing a little beach about eight feet below, sharp with rocks and broken oyster shells. *Don't leap into the water before checking first*, a little inner voice cautions.

It is a cold bright night, but the chill is clean so I sit at the end of the jetty where the bottom steps, exposed by the low tide, are covered in green slime. *Watch out for those. Could slip and crack your head open in a flash*, the voice continues.

What am I looking for, I ask myself? What can I do to ensure this change is different from all the others? Can the angry-faced jeering little monkey in my head – or 'noodle', as my Uncle Frank would say – be silenced?

You? Change? You can't do it! And what's the point? Death is inevitable. It's too late to make the big changes now. You're too old! Too tired!

When the cold is intolerable, I shuffle back to bed, my pyjamas smelling as salty as the sea. Much later, when I am still awake and raw with thoughts of Sweetie, water flip-flops like the sound of loose sandals. I understand already that the tide is lapping in again.

Dampness rolls off the sea and settles on the doona, pillows and bedside table like a layer of sweat. Just before dawn, when the light is still grey and the water flat as a table, I fall asleep.

Sharp knocking wakes me. It's a blinding blue day.

'Susan, is it?'

I lift my head and look at a cheery, open face, blonde hair hanging to her shoulders, a couple of kids leaning on either side of her, gathered into her skirt. They are standing on the deck outside my bedroom, beaming politely, not quite leaning into the bedroom, but almost.

'They told you this is public land, didn't they? That's it's a public thoroughfare?'

I struggle to get a grip on consciousness. I am in bed. Having a conversation with a total stranger. Who knows my name.

'It's the only way to get to the ferry at Bells Wharf from our house,' she adds.

'Oh.'

'Well, see ya, then. Thanks a lot.'

I fall back on the pillows. The whole of Scotland Island can, if it wants, wander past my bedroom doors – French doors, mostly glass. Jeez. Bugger. Typical bloody Pittwater. There's always a twist. Wonder briefly if this means I have to make the bed every day.

Get up. Open a can of Coke. Begin unpacking. Find the box marked 'Kitchen Essentials'. Pull out knives and forks and a chopping board. Two plates, two mugs. Jar of loose tea. Frying pan. Olive oil. Spatula. Toaster. Kettle. Yep, you get good at moving when you do it often enough. What's with the two of everything, though? Old habits? Hope? Put on the kettle. Bung some bread into the toaster. Find butter and Vegemite in the fridge. Feels like home to me.

Lunchtime and I'm still in pyjamas. Everything is in place. Have discovered a fantastic, huge cupboard big enough to turn into an office if I want to. Fabulous shelving, like a boat. Maybe I'll start a new project. Write a book.

There's a loft area, too, with a bunk bed. I remember vaguely that the real estate agent called it a third bedroom. Yeah, right. Toeholds cut into the wall for ascent and descent. No good to anyone except twelve year olds and orang-utans.

I set up the ironing board where I can look at the passing parade of boats. I feel invisible, as you do when you are inside and everyone else is outside. But occasionally someone waves from his tinny as he passes. I return the salute and feel a bit like a fish in an aquarium. Conclude the only real privacy is the upstairs bedroom.

A man wearing blue jeans and an old white business shirt rows closer and closer. When he reaches the deck that embraces the front and sides of the house, about eight feet from where I'm ironing, he waves and I open the window because I don't want to go outside in my pyjamas.

'Heard you'd moved in.' His hat is askew. Grey hair flowing. I know him from dinner parties at Towlers Bay.

'Yeah. Yesterday. How you doing?'

'Saw you ironing.' He holds the edge of the deck to stop the boat from drifting away.

'Uh-huh.'

'Lovely sight, a woman ironing. Makes me nostalgic. Don't see it often, any more.'

He looks comfortable. As though it's the most natural thing in the world to pull up in a rowboat and talk to a woman through a window while she's doing her ironing in her pyjamas. He looks settled, as though he plans to stay awhile.

'Want a cup of tea?'

'Lovely. Got a biscuit to go with it?'

He stays in the boat and I pass him tea and a slice of toast. With jam.

'Haven't got any biscuits. You ok with the toast?'

'Wonderful.'

The day is sunny and warm. He pulls off his hat and closes his eyes, raising his face to the sun. So many people do that here. As though it's life-giving.

And we talk for a while, about sea eagles and fishing, and the day feels full.

9

HOW TO DESCRIBE MY FIRST Monday morning as a commuting resident of Scotland Island? Picking around the crumpled shoreline in air tangy with brine and the weedy smell of wet sand. Hills gum leaf green and feathered with mist. The serenity of a soughing sea. Waiting in the crooked wooden shelter shed at the end of Bells Wharf for the ferry. Watching the fuzzy dawn world sharpen with the rising light. It is a caress of the senses. It feels like a prayer.

Within a week, my routine is established. Rise at 6.15 am, make tea and toast, shower, dress and walk to Bells Wharf to catch the older of the two ferries, the *Curlew*, on her 6.50 am run.

At high tide, when water slops over the goat track that leads from the house to Bells Wharf, I put on rubber boots. Eventually, I learn to leave a pair of office shoes in the car.

There's a dog gate at the start of the jetty. I am told it must be firmly closed at all times. 'Dogs love ferries,' someone explains. 'Ride 'em all day if they can. It's a bugger, though, if they jump off in one of the bays. Means you've gotta go and pick 'em up after work.'

Every morning, though, hopeful dogs hippetty-hop after their owners.

'No, you can't come, mate. Not today. It's a work day,' they explain, resisting the pleading eyes of mutts who are used to being part of the action.

'They're persistent, aren't they?' says one bloke who sends his brindle mutt home every morning, Monday to Friday. 'She reckons I might forget one day and let her come.'

I laugh.

'Pleading eyes get to you, though,' he adds. 'So she might be right.'

It is amazing, at first, to see that Lenny, the early morning ferry driver, is greeted like a close family member by commuters, although he never says much. Only *gidday* if you insist. Some mornings, if a regular is missing, Lenny looks up the stairway that climbs in terraces nearly to the top of the island. If Bob or Bill or Maude or Mavis is in sight, he holds the ferry. An extra moment or two on the water, the same kind of moment that on the road makes drivers foam at the mouth, costs nothing here.

Lenny has been at the helm of the old *Curlew* – a beautiful, low-tummied, navy and white wooden ferry built in the 1920s – for the past thirty years. He's a little bloke with big, work-cracked hands and a weather-beaten face that looks sour a lot of the time. But he's soft as a fresh lemon cake under the crust and has never been known to turn his back to avoid doing a favour. On Pittwater, he is a legend. He is in his late sixties when I first start taking the ferry and he moves around the vessel as though he is part of the deck. If you need him earlier than the scheduled first run, you let him know and he's there. Doesn't matter whether it's still the dead of night.

Many friendships, which begin easily here anyway, are initiated on the ferry. Over-riding the casual friendliness, though, is a cast iron respect for privacy. Gossip, the kind that picks away until it creates a sore, is an absolute no-no. It's ok to look through a window by mistake, but don't talk about what you see. Live and let live prevails here.

When the sun shines and we passengers sit in the open air on the rear deck, a simple 'Good morning' turns into an exchange of local information. For me, on those early trips, it is about garbage collection days, how to get newspapers delivered, where to find someone to clean the roof and gutters – essential when you gather water from the rain run-off for your tanks. There is the same relaxed familiarity as in a small country town, and like a country town, we are all bonded by location. Eventually you meet everyone.

The ferry ride takes about five minutes and at Church Point, commuters scatter in all directions. Some catch a connecting bus to the city, some car pool. Some walk to the public car park and drive to work, which is what I do. Church Point is like a town square in an old village. It's our *piazza*, if you like. The hub or nerve centre of our offshore neighbourhood. Just to arrive here is to be enfolded in the warmth of a vibrant community, to feel as though you belong somewhere.

There are a few tables with bench seats, a scattering of shade trees and a bottle shop. A noticeboard flutters with announcements for everything from home help to having a dock sale (no garages here!). Significant community events are chalked up on a nearby blackboard – events such as the Scotland Island Fair, the ANZAC Day ceremony, the Scotland Island Players' new theatrical production, the local yacht club's upcoming series and an occasional wake if money needs to be raised to pay for the funeral.

On the opposite side of the square from the bottle shop there's a restaurant and takeaway food bar, post office and convenience store where most of us pick up the newspapers and the milk. During summer, the back deck is crammed with tourists eating hamburgers and drinking coffee. They sit for hours watching ferries come and go, seeing how people cope when they can't drive home in a car. Envying just a little, I like to think, the bare feet and sarongs, the easy familiarity amongst people in a unique place. At the end of the day, Paul, the accidental removalist, is sometimes at Church Point which I soon learn is known locally as The Point, and we talk food until the ferry leaves. The herb debate rages intermittently until we both decide that garlic is probably king.

As the weather warms up, the evening crowd lingers at The

Point until the last ferry at 7.25 pm. Sometimes tinnies are tied three deep and there are kids, dogs, youngies and oldies gathered together in chaotic cheer because the twilight is just too damn gorgeous to rush through. Kids strip off to their undies and take running, skinny-legged leaps into the water. Excited, bright-eyed dogs chase sticks or balls. Kids drip water. Dogs shake rain all over you. Everyone's wet. Everyone's feeling fine. It's Rafferty's rules, exuberance is unrestrained and there's a rare kind of freedom. The kind that comes from feeling secure in your environment.

Over the next weeks my spirit soars when I drive around the last bend from Mona Vale to Church Point. Past the old boatsheds, little beaches and mangroves. When the water is high, dinghies bob and weave on their moorings, busily going nowhere. At low tide, they lean in the sand, resting. As I pass them, they signal whether the tide is high or low or somewhere in between. Rubber boots or no rubber boots. There's a constant, reliable simplicity to this physical world. It is paradise but not the lazy, languid, tropical, pina colada sort. The lushness here comes from the musky smell of the sea and early morning mists that leave damp trails in their wake. From evenings when the sun drops behind the hills of Elvina Bay and night fans out under a hailstorm of stars. It comes from sudden squalls with flashes of lightning that fire up the bays, from pounding rain so thick you can't see through it, or hear your own voice.

And when an antarctic wind occasionally races in from the pole, it whips the sea so hard that, for a while, it can't be trusted. The water taxi cancels services. Tinnies can sink and when the storm tires or moves on, they are raised from their watery rest, bailed out and restored to working order. The moon, whether a sliver or fat and golden, has new significance here, where there are no streetlights. Its pale, silvery glow silently guides late night commuter boats safely around moorings and illuminates dusky bays when the last familiar house light is turned off and it's hard to get your bearings.

Commuter traffic, which means mostly open tinnies, battered and banged up, with outboard engines hanging off the back, beats past my window. Some boats race to The Point, lifting into the air like flying fish, only to come crashing down again. Others chug slowly, enjoying the lull before joining the rushing throngs. Elegant cruising yachts glide past under sail. Cargo boats loaded with building materials churn along. Kids are taught to drive tinnies on their parents' knees, learning early to think for themselves, to make their own decisions. Always a new sight, new action, a new event that engages you. Makes you wonder what is going on. Which in turn helps you to feel part of a bigger picture.

But friends are cautionary. At the office, colleagues are full of advice. Nodding their heads, shaking their fingers.

'The novelty will wear off.'

'Maybe.'

But you have to have a go, don't you? Change is what you make of it, isn't it? Who said the greatest risk in life is not to take a risk?

It is impossible to resist entertaining prodigiously in the first euphoric flush of this return to Pittwater. I host lunches and dinners outside on the deck. When it's too hot to sit in direct sunlight, the umbrellas go up and the marble bedside table is moved to the doorway of the bedroom to be converted to a serving table and bar because it's closer than the kitchen. The tide comes and goes. The wine flows recklessly. Sometimes the wind from the south west plays havoc but we don't slow down. Not even when a rogue gust flips the umbrellas into the water and a guest dives in after them to return wet and triumphant with one in each hand. They dry quickly in the sun. So does the guest.

I want everyone – the naggers and the pessimistic – to see what they're missing by holding safely to their suburban lives. Which is a bit show off-y. But I give in to the impulse. I also want to share the whole, amazing experience of offshore living. It seems selfish to make a secret of this extraordinary environment where each day unfolds with a fresh, exhilarating newness. Where the community becomes a huge, extended family with the bonus that you don't have to tolerate anyone if you don't want to. And they don't have to tolerate you.

Naturally, not everyone agrees I have found nirvana. Lots of friends arrive and feel stranded on the island, made anxious by the giant moat that separates them from their familiar shackles. But it is the sea, or the moat, that gives me the sense of being separated from a pressured world.

Cooking becomes an even greater passion here. Why dredge through traffic to trendy restaurants when you can sit and eat on a sunstruck deck? Why sit straight-backed waiting for the next course when you can doze on a deck chair and follow your own metabolic clock? Why cross your legs tidily under the table when you could be hanging them over the side of the jetty, splashing hot feet in cool water, a glass of wine in your hand? Surrounded by a languid, instead of a rushing, world.

On a good day, when the water is smooth and the tides right, a couple of quacking penguins might cavort in front of us, ducking and diving in a comic performance that brings a smile to even the most harassed city faces. Sometimes, a kookaburra swoops and snatches a chicken fillet from a plate without disturbing the salad. It is a performance so precise we clap and do not begrudge him the food.

In summer, when there is rarely any wind at dawn, the kayakers go out, gliding soundlessly through the water. Some canoes are wooden and sanded and varnished to an elegant toffee glow. Most are multicoloured, vibrant slashes on glassy water. Boats on their moorings sit almost still just before the sun rises, and the light is gentle enough to make even neglected vessels, festooned with grunge, look loved.

When the rain falls heavily, long plastic raincoats, jackets and waterproof overalls, known by sailors as *wet weather gear*, are hauled off hooks and pulled over working clothes. High heels are carried in shopping bags, briefcases wrapped in garbage bags. Little kids waddle under a bulk of plastic. Under their hoods, faces are criss-crossed with emotion. Gleeful. Glum. Resolute. Martyred. Others walk by with eyes cast downwards, shoulders hunched, dragging reluctant feet, their backpacks drooping.

Why would they want to leave this freedom for a sardine-tinned classroom? No matter what the weather?

In a big wind, tree tops bow and rain blows in horizontal sheets. The water taxis raft up to their houseboat base and hunker down, the door pulled tight when, mostly, it is left wide open. No-one goes out unless there's absolutely no choice. There are horror stories, rarely told but never forgotten, that linger in the lore of the area. The huge motor cruiser blindly crunching over a little tinny in the murky twilight and killing the driver. A boat coming home on a moonless night, slamming into a barge moored just that day in its new position – a mother and her months old baby left to fend for themselves. A toddler slipping silently overboard in a fierce storm, his father jumping in to save him and both drowning. The body of the toddler never found.

Like any paradise, you cannot take it too lightly.

We rely on tank water on Scotland Island, which means that if you are not frugal and there's no rain for a long time, you run out. I hate being short of anything, even gherkins, so I install my own, idiosyncratic systems to use as little water as possible and still stay within the boundaries of hygiene.

Showers are three minutes long and there's an eggtimer in the bathroom that rings when the time is up.

Boys don't use the loo to pee. They go to the far end of the deck around the corner of the house and out of sight from luncheon guests, where they pee in the water. Women may pee in the loo but it's only flushed every five pees unless it's urgent. There are five seashells beside the loo and each person moves one to indicate they've used the loo. When there's five in the flush basket, the next person to pee moves all the shells back to the start basket and the routine begins again. The directions hang on a hook from the window. Some guests never make sense of it. Or just can't bring themselves to leave a loo without flushing it. Once, it would have shocked me.

Clothes washing is done in one big load once a week. All vegetable washing water is recycled to water the pot plants (unbelievably, the Iceberg roses in pots on the deck are thriving in the salt, sun and wind). Dirty dishes are scraped as clean as possible, first with a spatula and then with a paper towel, before being washed up.

Guests get into the swing of it with good humoured energy. Or they don't bother coming back.

Summer is consuming. There's always a party. A weekend sail. A time to jump in someone's boat to find a secluded little beach for a swim and a picnic. Time for a walk through the national park. Time to simply lie on a deck chair and read a book, falling asleep, usually, before the end of the first page.

Parties spring up out of nowhere – not the budget-breaking city kind where you supply all the wine and food. On Pittwater, parties blow in on the evening breeze when a neighbour comes home with a boatload of freshly caught fish and, as he passes, yells that dinner is at his house. Bring your own booze. Or when you wave from your deck as someone goes by and he turns his tinny in to your dock to say hello and then stays to dinner.

There is no rush, no timetable. Here, it is PT – Pittwater Time – all the time.

In the lead up to Christmas, the island pops with exploding champagne corks. There's the sound of laughter, of people congregating. Smoke rising from barbecues, the spicy smell of sausages cooking. It's cocktail hour on demand. There's always something to celebrate. Even if it's just another sunny day.

Blokes and their dogs suddenly start appearing at the water's edge, throwing sticks, balls, anything to get their pups to swim further and further, faster and faster.

'You in training or something?' I ask different folks from time to time.

'Yeah, mate.'

And because it's said with such wryness, I don't even think to ask what for.

There are dogs all over Pittwater. Big, little, perfectly bred, ill-bred, good-tempered, bad-tempered, long-haired, short-haired, black, brown, spotty, even striped. Ones that lick you and drop a stick in your lap. Others that don't even raise an eyelid when you accidentally tread on them. They ride the bows of tinnies like magnificent figureheads, they lollop around the *piazza* as though it's *their* party and everyone is their new best friend. They are as much a part of life here as the water. If you can't quite remember some fella's name, the penny drops when his dog is described:

'You know Mick?'

'Well . . .'

'He owns the Jack Russell on steroids!'

'Ah, right. Got him!'

It's quite normal to sit down at a dinner party with four or five dogs underfoot. No-one takes a blind bit of notice of them unless they fight or make so much noise we can't hear ourselves speak. Of course not *everyone* loves dogs but most people tolerate them.

About a month before Christmas, when Marie, my next door neighbour, and her two boys take a twilight swim, the family dog, a desert red kelpie with yellow eyes called Mabo, paddles after a tennis ball as though his life depends on it.

'Mabo in training too?' I ask when I wander onto the deck to say hello, a sarong around my waist, no shoes and a stained old T-shirt.

'Nah. He's too old to race,' Marie says.

'Race?'

'Yeah.'

'What race?'

'The dog race.'

'What dog race?'

Marie turns to look at me, her lovely blue eyes wide with surprise.

'You don't know about the *dog* race?'

'Nope.'

'Ah well,' she says, wading out of the shallows to join me on the deck, 'it's a rare cultural event here.'

Sensing a deliciously long explanation, I wander inside to open a bottle of white wine and throw some water on the stove for pasta. Her husband is away sailing in some big yacht race somewhere in the world, as he often does, so I know she'll welcome company.

'Every Christmas Eve,' Marie begins, 'we all gather at The Point for the Scotland Island Dog Race. Anyone can enter, he or she just has to pay the entry fee of a long nose bottle of beer and a can of dog food. Winner takes all. The race starts around six o'clock but we usually get there an hour or so earlier for a few drinks. It's a festive kind of time. Just about the whole of Pittwater turns up. You can take a bit of a picnic if you feel like it. Sit by the waterside, wish everyone Merry Christmas.'

'So where do the dogs race to and from?'

'From Scotland Island, just near Bells Wharf, to Church Point.'

'How long has this been going on?'

'Years and years.'

'How's it organised?'

'Well, I wouldn't say it's *organised*. It sort of falls into place. Like most stuff on Pittwater.'

'What are the rules?' I ask.

'Rules? Well, I don't know about *rules*. First dog on the beach wins. That's about it.'

When dinner is ready, Marie calls her two boys from the water. It's an evening thick with heat so we're eating outside on the deck with the sun dropping behind the hills of McCarrs Creek, making the bay shoot orange sparks. Mabo, wet and stinky, collapses under the table with a loud grunt and snoozes noisily while we eat spaghetti swizzled in roasted garlic, olive oil, bacon and parmesan. The boys pick out the bacon and leave most of the pasta. They look at the salad as though it's poison.

The toddler falls asleep on Marie's lap, his long eyelashes casting a shadow on his cheeks. Matthew, the elder son, just old enough to be in his first year of school, his hair a drift of cornsilk, goes inside to watch television. It's the first time the television set has been turned on since I moved here. Matthew's legs are long and thin like those of his father, who is always described as Zap, the bloke who ate a dozen eggs for breakfast in the middle of a yacht race during a shocker of a storm.

I push my chair back to clear the dishes and cannot resist running a hand over the downy head of the child sleeping in Marie's lap. He doesn't stir and the night feels as gentle as a baby's breath.

'How do you do it all?' I ask, gathering plates. 'How do you do the schlepping, the boats, the life, *and* little kids?'

'There's no choice so you don't think about it.'

'Your little bloke's a terror on the jetty, though.'

'Yeah, thinks it's a personal racetrack.'

She laughs, but I've seen her white-faced with fear when he's suddenly dashed along the jetty in a fit of sheer devilment. Seen her grab her bumble-footed, tippy little boy so tight he's yelped.

I have also seen Marie dock and tie her boat in a body-bending gale with her toddler, Oliver, strapped to her back, Matthew ordered to sit still in his life jacket until she gives the word to move. The boat surges, dives, bangs and teeters. The wind is stronger than ten men pulling in the wrong direction. The pontoon churns. Nothing is stable. She braces with legs astride, the kid on her back weighing her down like a sack of potatoes. Then when boat and dock rise in unison, she grabs Matthew's hand and shouts *now!* They leap. Steady themselves for a moment on the pontoon. Then, heads bent against the wind, clothes swaddling their limbs, they make their way along the jetty to the shore. It is a terrifying but regular event, one that young mothers all over Pittwater think of little note.

'Ever get you down? Wear you out?'

'Nah. Love it. Kids grow up fast here, but the right way. They learn about swimming, fishing, boats and exploring before shopping malls and video games.'

'Don't you ever long to be able to drive the shopping to your front door?'

'Well, if I could do that, I probably wouldn't have a beach at the bottom of the garden, where the kids can swim all summer. I wouldn't live on an island where they can run wild. I'd rather have the beach and the freedom.'

After Marie's gone home with the boys, I call my mother, who is coming soon for her regular two week stay with me at Christmas.

'Do you want to bring Wally?' I ask.

Wally, her big, amiable, slobbery Rottweiler who prefers to lean on people than stand on his own four paws, loves a swim, even in the dead of winter.

'Is there somewhere you can put him?' she asks. She hasn't seen the house yet. Has no idea what to expect.

'Oh yeah. He'll be fine.'

What I'm really thinking, though, is that we might have our own entrant in the dog race. Not exactly a thoroughbred horse race, but a race nonetheless. My brother would like that.

'Still likes a swim, does he?' I ask, innocently.

'Mad about it. He's in the river every chance he gets.'

Right!

'Are you entering Gus?' I ask Stewart a couple of weeks before Christmas.

'Nah. He's too old.'

'Do you think your girls would like to swim with my mother's dog, Wally?'

I have learned that owners either swim with their dogs or kayak or row alongside. No boats with engines are allowed.

'Sure,' he says. 'I'll ask them.'

When my brother, John, was alive, Christmas was an event. We all trooped to Melbourne every second year for a sumptuous feast that he planned with the precision of a major military campaign. John loved food and wine. Loved, even more, sitting around a table and sharing with friends. In fact, the only successful gift I ever gave him was a copy of *Larousse Gastronomique* when it was first translated into English.

'Possie,' he said one day when we were teenagers and doing the dishes after a family Sunday roast, 'do you wash a floury bowl in hot or cold water?'

I didn't have a clue but figured if he'd asked, it had to be cold, because hot is normal.

'Cold!'

'Right! Now tell me why.'

'Bugger!' I said, and we laughed because we both knew I was guessing.

'Because,' he explained, 'hot water cooks flour and turns it into a gooey paste.'

I have no idea where his passion for food came from. But I feel as though it was there from the earliest times I can remember. He was always adventurous with it. Loved oysters at an age when most of us retched at the sight of them.

On school holidays at my grandparents' home, we'd be sent off to the dam (to get us out of the way) to catch yabbies by dangling a piece of raw meat from a string. When we felt a tug, we'd wait for a few more tugs, which meant the yabbie was firmly latched onto the meat, then we'd pull in the string. Not many yabbies ever let go once they've got a taste of raw, red meat.

When our buckets overflowed, one of us would run back to the house to fetch our mother. She'd light a campfire on the bank of the dam and boil a billy until steam filled the air. Then she'd grab those snapping, angry crustaceans behind the neck so they couldn't bite her and chuck them in the hot water. When the yabbies turned from muddy brown to raging red, she tipped out the water and showed my brother how to rip off their tails and suck out the meat in noisy slurps. They'd eat their way through a bucket load. Then she'd fire up another billy and start again.

They ate about fifty yabbies at a time, and when they were full, they'd chuck the live ones back in the dam for another day. I remember my mother sitting on the cracked clay dam bank, her wide floral skirt floating around her, hair bright blonde in the sun, teeth flashing white, with my brother crouched next to her. Both of them golden, somehow, and incredibly beautiful.

I watched their abandoned gluttony enviously but couldn't bring myself to taste even a morsel of the muddy white flesh. In those days, I wasn't game enough to go beyond lamb chops. Hell, I wouldn't even eat fish when my father, trying to make amends after losing heavily at the racetrack, would come home with deep fried flake and vinegar soaked chips. My mother and brother loved fish, a rare treat in those landlocked days when we lived at Bonegilla migrant camp, where Dad worked after he quit the army and before he bought the pub.

At heart, my father and I preferred rissoles – minced meat made with chopped onions, parsley and loads of salt and pepper, with a bit of egg and bread to bind it. He'd eat them for breakfast, lunch and dinner and if my mother didn't make them regularly enough, he'd shuffle into the kitchen and make them himself.

'Got to loathe the smell of them,' my mother told me years later. 'It's all he ever wanted to eat. Rissoles . . . and mushrooms.'

Come to think of it, my father was a good plain cook. When he prepared the Sunday roast, which he did often, he was painstaking and patient. He even made cheese sauce for the cauliflower. And he cleaned up as he went along. My mother was a much more impatient cook. She'd turn the heat up to the max and burn the bums out of saucepans and leave the kitchen looking like a war zone. But there wasn't much she wasn't game to try – snails, frog's legs, lamb's brains, and fish eyes. Though even my brother reared back from fish eyes.

When we were little kids, my mother and I went mushrooming while my father taught my brother how to load a rifle and hit a target which he thought would *make a man of him*. My brother didn't enjoy it much, but he became a crack shot. After a bit of practice myself, I wasn't too bad either. Dad needn't have worried about my brother's courage, though. He had it in spades.

My father was passionate about mushrooms. Every autumn, the whole family trekked through soggy paddocks in cheek whipping winds, picking everything from tiny, shiny white buttons to field mushrooms the size of dinner plates. When the car was so crammed with boxes that the only place my brother and I could sit was on each side of my mother's lap, we drove home to peel, clean, cook and bottle. My father's technique was to sauté the mushrooms in butter, add a bit of milk and thicken the juices with cornflour. Then they were poured into Fowler's Vacola preserving jars and pulled down from the shelves reverently each morning to be warmed and piled on toast for breakfast. He ate mushrooms for breakfast until supplies ran out.

I was always terrified a poisonous mushie or two must surely have found their way into the pot. I knew about poisoned mushrooms. They grew under the pine trees near the block where we lived and were brilliant red with white spots. Fairytale style mushrooms. Deadly, my mother told me. Not even safe to touch. And there were puff balls that looked so similar to button mushrooms I was sure one would sneak into the mix. So I'd beg my father not to eat them, and when he just smiled and loaded up his plate, I watched and waited for him to suddenly retch and gag, to go purple and then die. I was an adult before I felt safe eating mushrooms.

One Christmas, my mother experimented with the stuffing for the Christmas bird, adding a can of chopped water chestnuts, crystallised ginger and plenty of orange rind to the mix. It really wasn't bad, but my father and I looked at each other and pushed it aside. We didn't like surprises in our food. My passion, if I even had one in those days, was for *good* food. Quality but predictable ingredients cooked with respect.

Mum made that ritzy stuffing the first Christmas after the pub was sold and my parents moved us into the brick veneer wastelands of outer Melbourne suburbia. Our new house was a spit from where my mother was raised and I couldn't help wondering whether we moved there because it felt more like home to her than anywhere else did. Does it always feel safer when we go back to our roots?

'Used to be cherry orchards here,' she told me soon after the family moved in. 'My sisters and I would steal in at night and eat them until we turned purple. Then we'd go home and face a belting.'

And she looked wistfully across the jam-packed houses from the window of her split-level home – the best she and my father could manage financially. Not exactly her retirement dream of a grand house with soaring columns at the front entrance and a sweeping staircase. But the split level gave her four steps and she contented herself with those.

'You'll just have to sweep down *slowly* in your gowns,' she told me. 'Make the most of it.'

For whom? For what? I asked myself. It was her dream of grandeur, not mine. The grinding reality was, my parents were better off than many, with enough to see them through to the end of their lives, but only if they were careful and lived with constraint. There weren't enough resources after the pub was sold, for my mother's legendary wild flings (flying lessons when she turned forty), her lavish entertaining and her dream of becoming a flirty, middle-aged jetsetter. Anyway, by then Dad had a rotting liver from too many brandy heart-starters for breakfast, and lungs choking with nicotine.

You've got to do what you enjoy, I thought at the time, because there's no telling how it's going to end up. But I forgot all that as the years marched on. By the time my parents relocated to suburbia, my brother had ditched law for the racetrack and turned into a charming but wild larrikin. Every now and again, a debt collector would knock at the door and my father would pay up. Debt, to my father, was the greatest of all shames. Thank God he lived long enough to see my brother triumph.

I'd dropped out of university for a career in journalism instead of focusing on making a successful marriage. My mother didn't seem to understand that no matter how many times she ironed my clothes and tweaked pink into my cheeks, I was never going to turn into the powerful beauty she'd been in her youth. She'd been a knockout, apparently. Her waist a man's hand span, her eyes bluer than sapphires.

'Engaged twenty-two times,' she told me as I grew taller and taller, all arms and legs with a rather large nose she referred to as my *peckin' thing* because it looked like a beak. 'Used to write their names on the kitchen door and cross them out one by one as I called off each engagement. Nan thought someone would shoot me one day. But they never did,' she added.

Looking back, the move to the brick vanilla, as we called the new house, was not one of the glossier times of my mother's life and she was riddled with disappointments. But she took up tennis again, and played nearly five days a week. And it diverted her mind from unpleasant details. It was her own style of coping. Of being tough. Of not letting life get her down.

That first Christmas when we struggled to embrace the barren confines of suburbia after being sprawling country kids all our lives was a shocker. The temperature hovered around 103 degrees, the light twanged and the bare asphalt street in front of the house pooled with mirages. The bank of white petunias in the neighbour's yard across the road sagged, and there were no trees on a street that was eerily quiet. You could've launched a missile and not hit a living soul that Christmas Day. Where were they all? Hunkered indoors, hiding from the heat? Or gone back for the day, to the cramped family homes they thought they were escaping when they were first seduced by the scent of fresh paint and the dream of a second bathroom?

It felt hotter than an oven indoors so we set the table on the concrete slab we called the patio, on the shady side of the house. There were plans to plant a garden but my father had no interest and my mother didn't know where to begin. We'd always had spec-tacular gardens but that was because we'd always had gardeners. Those days were over. We'd all thought it would be a relief to be together for a quiet family Christmas instead of dishing up roast turkey and ham for a hundred guests at the pub.

But it was a limp kind of day as we sat there with the hose running over our feet to cool us down. Without a crowd, it didn't feel like Christmas.

After that year, my brother, in his early twenties, took over the Christmas celebrations. And as his fortunes improved, the event grew.

After he married Dolly, they became extravaganzas. In their big sitting room, sofas and armchairs were shoved against the walls to make way for thirty feet of trestle tables. People contributed their own specialties – fresh lobsters from the bloke who lived near the fishing boats, a giant pudding from the best cake cook amongst us, seafood mousses from the person who lived closest, champagne or wine if that suited you better. Outside the laundry door, plastic garbage cans were filled with ice and loaded with enough beer and wine to sustain thirty or so guests through a five-hour lunch and a late supper of leftover turkey and ham sandwiches. When we were tipsy enough, we sang Christmas carols then turned up the music and danced until we ran out of puff.

But my brother is dead. And Christmas since his death has been more of an ordeal than a celebration. However, this first Pittwater Christmas, when I live in the wooden house set at the water's edge, I am determined to get organised in a way that my brother would have approved, revive the Duncan family tradition. I want it to be a grand time for the fourteen people who will gather around the table on the deck at about noon. My goal is to restore, if I can, a little of the old *joie*.

I begin making the pudding only a week before Christmas Day. Which is a bit scary because it's a three-day process. First, double the recipe. Then candy the orange and lemon peel and soak the raisins, sultanas, dates and currants in four times the suggested amount of brandy, letting the fruit sit for a couple of days. Stir (by turning over, not mashing!) every time you go past the bowl and make a wish. Invite everyone who passes to stir and make a wish. Watch them succumb to the sweet, dizzying brandy fragrance. See them close their eyes, breathe deep and hold their breath. Then wish.

'Never heard of this tradition,' Marie notes, wielding the thick wooden spoon. 'But it's a great way to get your pudding mixed!'

For a moment I wonder if it's a tradition I invented myself. Then I remember Christmas at the pub. A local woman, famous for her puddings, soaked bucket loads of dried fruit in rough-as-guts brandy for a day or two in an old tin baby's bathtub in the pub's concrete-floored laundry. A barrel of batter, made from butter, eggs, dark brown sugar, ginger and flour, was poured on top, bringing the mixture to almost the rim of the tub. It was too huge and heavy for one pair of hands to mix, so the tub was ceremoniously dumped in the public bar for a couple of hours and everyone asked to have a stir and make a wish. By the time the bar closed at six o'clock, the batter had been turned over hundreds of times and the fruit was well and truly mixed in. A bit of cigarette ash and a slop or two of beer as well, I suspect.

After mixing, the batter was divided up and wrapped in steaming, floured calico, to be dumped in the copper boiler where the sheets and towels were washed on Monday mornings. The puddings were tied to a stick so they didn't sink and fill up with water, and they bobbed on the surface like giant dumplings for about six hours. Then they were pulled out and hung from an indoor clothesline to cool down. I like to think now that those puddings were filled with the wishes of decent but reticent country blokes who would never dare say them out loud. As I recall, they were loaded with threepences and sixpences, which we warned guests about every year after one bloke swallowed a sixpence and nearly choked.

On Scotland Island, when I finally assemble the pudding mixture about three days before we're due to eat it, I'm anchored to the house for the next six hours, topping up the water in the pot. It's a broiling job but easily bearable. When the heat feels over-powering and sweat rolls down the valley in my back, I walk out the door and fall into the sea. Nice life, huh?

In that final week of Christmas frenzy, I drive two hours to pick up my mother and Wally. I install her in my bedroom, Wally on the back porch, and put myself on the silly bunk bed accessible only by the neck-breaking toeholds.

The evening before Christmas Eve, my mother polishes silver cutlery at the dining table while I make jugs of brandy sauce and a hard sauce and assemble the dry ingredients for the turkey stuffing. This year, I'm trying ground hazelnuts and grated orange and lemon peel in sourdough breadcrumbs. There's more of her in me than I like to think, sometimes.

The fridge is bursting with smoked salmon, smoked trout, ham and turkey, all the sauces and as much booze as we can fit in. The rest will go into iceboxes in the morning. There's potatoes galore. A salute of sorts to my husband, who was so genuinely shocked the first time I suggested a cold, casual Christmas lunch instead of the traditional whirlpool that he had to sit down.

'You'd at least have roast potatoes, wouldn't you?' he asked, holding his chest as though he had a cramp.

'Well, no, not really. Not with prawns.'

'Suppose you mean there'd be lots of rabbit food, instead?' His face turned pink.

'What's wrong with salads?'

'Nothing. If you're a rabbit.'

I went back to cooking a turkey on what is usually one of the hottest days of the year.

First thing in the morning on Christmas Eve, I make up the bed in the top bedroom – the captain's cabin for Pia – my old housemate from Sydney. She's due around lunchtime. I've convinced her to get here in time for the dog race. 'Bit of local culture,' I'd told her.

'Do *local* and *culture* go together out there?' She laughed because she loves the place as much as I do, but I felt oddly affronted, as though she'd called my new baby ugly.

The house gets a final dust and mop and just as I put on the kettle, Bomber and Bea, two recent friends, wave from their barge. I rush out on the deck.

'Come on in. Just put the kettle on.'

Bomber and Bea run a mooring service from an emerald and white working boat called the *Trump* – the only emerald boat I have ever seen. She's shaped like a boot, long in the front with a turned up toe, tall in the back with a bit of a heel. She's a common and cheery sight on Pittwater, scuttling from bay to bay, lifting and repairing moorings. Bomber, a tall, handsome man with a permanent tan and smile, has a big heart and a generosity of spirit that is legendary. Need a hand? Bomber is there. Need rescuing? Bomber is there. He is a backbone in Pittwater community life. His partner, Bea, is tough on the outside but mush on the inside. She has laughing blue eyes and, like Bomber, a kind streak a mile wide. She has a wicked sense of humour, too, and when she makes you a friend, the friendship is forever.

Most days, at the end of work, they motor past my front door to their anchorage in Bayview, Bea at the helm, Bomber coiling ropes and chains. If I am home and they have time, they tie up at the end of the jetty and come in for a cup of tea or a beer, depending on their mood. So do their dogs. Jessie is a soft-eyed mutt with a bit of labrador who looks like a big brown grizzly bear. Marley, a highly strung, yapping black kelpie with quizzical blonde eyebrows, has more bravado than brain and drives Bea to distraction. Old Pitey, a tan sausage dog, loves everyone and likes to sleep on your feet. Which is great in winter.

Bea sticks her head out of the cabin when I call. Marley streaks up and down the deck, barking her head off.

'Can't come in. Too busy,' she yells. 'Shut up, Marley!'

'See you at the dog race?'

'Shut up, Marley! Yeah. See ya. Shut up, you stupid brainless idiot bloody dog!'

And they wave as the emerald boot chugs on, Marley's hysterical barking fading in the distance.

When I try to pin down details about entering the dog race, though, people look at me blankly.

'I told you. The race just happens,' Marie says when I call her for more information. 'Everyone knows it's on Christmas Eve and if you want to be in it, get to The Point with your dog around five o'clock.'

Right!

Wally's been in full training with Stewart's and Fleury's daughters, and he looks sleek as a seal. His muscles ripple in the sunlight and he won't come out of the water even when you call him for dinner. Which is historic. Wally's never intentionally missed or been late for a meal in his life.

My stepdaughter, Lulu, arrives mid-afternoon with Bella, her border collie, and we decide Bella should enter the race too. She's the kind of dog who loves swimming even more than running. Drops twigs in your lap all day, mutely begging you to throw them. Which gets a bit wearing after a couple of hours. For us, not her. I've never seen that dog tire.

'The team's looking pretty good,' I announce happily. 'Might just have to have a small bet on them both.'

And for a moment, I am overwhelmed with memories of my gorgeous gambling brother and I miss him so badly I want to cry or break something.

In her corner, where she sits under a mass of white gladioli spilling from a grey pottery vase, my mother is suddenly still and silent, her face turning as grey as the vase.

'John would have loved a day like today,' I say, to let her know I understand what she's feeling.

And she nods, because she cannot speak.

For the next hour or so, we four women of varying generations dangle our legs over the edge of the deck, cooling our feet in the water. We are all without partners. My mother is a widow, Pia is divorced and her ex-husband is remarried. Lulu has mended from her split with her boyfriend but is unwilling to expose herself to new risk. I am a widow with a married lover, which is the same, really, as being single. He is away with his family, holed up in five star accommodation somewhere exotic. I cannot expect even a hurried phone call to say 'Merry Christmas'. Of us all, I think to myself, my mother has handled her emotional circumstances the most effectively. Perhaps she is right. Stiff upper lip and get on with it. That's the most useful way to behave. The least risky way to survive. But is hers a life with richness and colour? Or merely an existence?

At 5 pm Stewart swings past in his boat and picks us up, dogs and all. He drops us at Church Point and goes back to collect the team from his house.

There's already a crowd at The Point. Women in sarongs and bikini tops or T-shirts. Kids either naked or wearing swimsuits, men in shorts and shirts that sometimes look as though they've just left off cleaning the barbecue. And dogs. Dogs everywhere. Sniffing, piddling, farting, sitting, running, rutting, swimming, shaking and generally as happy as . . . well, dogs who live in a doggies' paradise.

Everyone's holding a beer or glass of wine. Sweet and gentle. Big Dave from Scotland Island has set up a table and chairs at the finishing line so his mother and a couple of other grannies have a comfy top spot. He offers everyone who passes cheese and bikkies.

But there's no sign of a race headquarters, a place to drop your beer and dog food and sign up.

'What's the drill?' I ask over and over again.

People shrug and smile. 'Relax. Have a beer. It'll happen.'

The crowd and all the other dogs overwhelm Wally. He keeps dodging feet and kids. But he's not under any stress. He finally sinks to the ground at my feet like a camel bedding down for the night and closes his eyes.

Bella, who is a tad neurotic, plunges into the water. Returns with a twig the size of a toothpick and a look on her face that says *throw it or I'll have a tantrum*.

Lulu gives in to the pressure. 'But don't wear yourself out, Bella,' she scolds, as though the dog is her child.

'That dog won't wear out until she drops dead,' Pia says out of the corner of her mouth. Bella's plonked one too many twigs in her lap in the last few hours.

As the race time gets closer, a fleet of tinnies and one or two posher commuter boats (which means they're fibreglass instead of aluminium) gather offshore like a ragtag navy. Excitement fills the air. Someone starts a book on the race, odds are chalked up. Diesel, a lanky black, ferociously loyal dog, is favourite. In the pre-race doggy frolicking, Diesel tries to steal a ball. Which starts a fight. Mothers grab toddlers, blokes momentarily abandon iceboxes. The grannies don't move from their table, though. Perhaps they think age gives them divine protection.

'Get out of it, ya bloody mutt!'

The scrapping dogs are pulled apart. Diesel sulks. People return to their positions, curse loudly when they see a pongy yellow stain on the corner of their icebox: 'Bastards!' But no-one really cares. It's a sunny, mellow late afternoon and tomorrow's Christmas Day.

The story of how the race originated is murky. The most reliable source says that when there were two ferry services competing hotly for local business (a co-op formed by residents tired of feeling hostage to a single service, and a privately owned service), both drivers had a dog. In a heated argument one evening, one driver threw down the gauntlet: 'My dog could wear lead boots and still beat your bloody mutt.' Or words to that effect.

The ferry captains agreed to a dog race from Scotland Island to Church Point. When locals heard about it, everyone with a dog that could swim naturally wanted to be in the race, which has now been going for about thirty years. But that's open to debate, too. Memories are hazy and everyone has a different version of events.

When we're all primed with enough drinks, and before the sun gets too low, an anonymous voice yells for everyone to get their dogs on Bomber's barge, the *Trump*, or into their own boats to be shipped to the starting point. Which is Matty's barge. Unnamed. It floats a little offshore from Bells Wharf.

'Wally! Bella! We're off,' I call.

Both dogs happily jump onto the *Trump*. Wally loves boats. Bella's a bit more wary, probably from the time she tried to catch the wake from Stewart's boat one day and, to her enormous surprise, went flying overboard. We dragged her out of the water by her collar and she lay soggy and subdued for the rest of the trip.

The dogs jump from the *Trump* to Matty's barge, ready for the race start. All of them a bit bemused but caught up in the excitement.

There are three fights before the gun is fired. To break them up, owners shove their dogs overboard and then haul them out of the water again. When the starting shot rings out, every dog jumps and starts swimming – except Wally. He stands and looks around.

'Swim, Wally, swim!' I shout, standing behind him and urging him on.

He wags his stumpy tail and doesn't move.

In the end, I push him off the barge and he sinks, his brown eyes wide open under the water, blinking in bewilderment, and for a moment I think I've killed him. Then he rises, paddling happily. I jump back on the *Trump*. Then turn to watch Wally's progress. He's still paddling happily. In a circle. Round and round. Going nowhere.

'Think that dog needs rescuing,' Bomber says after a while.

I strip down to my underwear. Why is it you're always wearing cottontails when you'd rather be seen in lace?

'No, love,' Bomber says. 'No need for that. We'll get him in the rowboat.'

Meanwhile, Bella is swimming magnificently with Stewart's daughters kayaking behind her. So once Wally's been pulled into a rowboat and delivered back to the *Trump*, we head to Church Point to see the end.

Bella is brilliant. Coming third. We're all there to cheer her madly. She reaches the beach. Shakes herself. Wags her tail. We're hysterical with success.

'That's not Bella,' Lulu says flatly. She points out to sea. '*That's* Bella.'

Bella, the girls tell us later, followed a floating stick. She came in second last. With the stick, though. Which was a triumph of sorts.

After the race, Lulu grabs Bella and returns to Sydney for Christmas with her father's side of the family. Pia, Wally and I hitch a lift on a boat and return to Scotland Island, where my mother waits for news of Wally's epic swim. She's at the end of the jetty as we arrive.

'Well?'

'We-e-ll . . .'

'Well, how did my Wally do? Did he win?'

Pia and I look at each other and crack up.

'Not exactly,' Pia says, hiccuping in an effort to control herself.

'Had to be rescued,' I add.

'Rescued!'

'No, no, he was fine. He just kept swimming around in the

same circle. Lost his bearings, I think. We had to pull him onto the *Trump* or he'd still be swimming in the same spot. But he made history.'

My mother smiles, waiting for the good news.

'He's the only dog who's ever had to be rescued since the race began!'

Wally, who senses we're talking about him, looks at us in turn. His stubby tail wagging madly, making his rump vibrate.

'C'mon, Wally,' my mother says, dismissing Pia and me. 'Let's go and get you a good dinner.'

At the magic word, Wally's eyes light up and he licks his lips. He prances after her along the jetty to the house.

Pia and I sit on the steps and look across the water. We'd both like another glass of wine but neither of us feels like going to get it.

'Oi!'

My mother appears around the corner from the doorway of the house. 'What?'

'Don't feel like pouring a couple of tired old tarts a vino, do you?'

She turns back into the house and emerges a few minutes later with a bottle, a corkscrew, two wineglasses and a whisky. The whisky is for her.

'Mind if I join you?'

She sits on the top step in her cream cotton dress with navy blue diamonds that my brother bought her for Christmas about ten years earlier, and sips her whisky. I know she will never throw that dress out. I wonder if every time she wears it, she feels closer to her son. A physical link when there can never be the touch of his hand or the sound of his voice.

≋

On Christmas Day, nursing hangovers, we set up an icebox at the end of the jetty and fill it with champagne. We pull red and green reindeer antlers made from sponge onto our heads. They wilt at about the same rate we do. The table is set in front of the French doors from the bedroom and when the wind whips around from the nor' east, we jump into the water to retrieve table napkins.

Pia lays out smoked salmon and smoked trout. She readies a metal bucket for the prawns Marty and Witch are bringing, and sets the sauce alongside. There's another bucket filled with fresh water and slices of lemon for washing hands but if the tide's right, we'll lean over the edge of the deck and wash our hands in sea water.

The turkey is in the oven, the potatoes are almost done, and the ham was glazed and baked first thing in the morning. It does, indeed, look like a feast. *Saluté, my brother John!*

Pia's dad arrives in a water taxi with his brother and sister-in-law visiting from Belgium. We hand them champagne as they get off the boat and their faces suddenly fill with excitement. The atmosphere and casual physical beauty lull even Pia's dad, with whom she has a lightly combative relationship.

Friends roll in. By the time we've had a few glasses of champagne and finished the seafood, a high, fine layer of cloud has filtered the sun and the wind has dropped to a tickle. It's a perfect day for sitting on the deck wearing reindeer hats, in full view of a passing world that waves and shouts 'Merry Christmas' and 'You all look ridiculous', or drops in for a quick drink before heading to their own celebrations.

After the pudding, Pia's uncle sings 'The First Nöel' in French and we join in the chorus in English. He has a beautiful tenor voice that drifts across the silken water and we beg him to keep singing, which he does until long after the moon comes up and he goes hoarse.

'C'est magnifique,' he says, waving his arm at the surroundings.

It is about 10 pm and the water taxi is waiting to take them back to shore.

He slips his arm around his wife's waist and then says formally to me: 'Thank you. This is a Christmas to be memorable.'

10

As SUMMER ROLLS INTO autumn and the days become shorter, the evenings crisp, I am lying in my room, doors open to the water. It is about 3 am and I am awake. I still don't have a home to call my own and often on sleepless nights, I roll over and silently ask the boys to help. To tell me where to go, what to do. I want a sign from them, I suspect, that will give me the confidence to believe whatever I do next will be for the best.

It is the weekend and Pia is asleep upstairs in the captain's cabin. We've got a team coming for Sunday lunch and I'm fretting because I can't sleep. Exhaustion is becoming a constant condition and I wonder if it is age or lifestyle. Probably both.

Music filters through to me, the tinny electronic kind of music you hear from musical Christmas cards or mobile phones. I ignore it for a while, but then I realise it is coming from the kitchen. I get up and walk along the back porch, the music getting louder all the time. When I go into the kitchen, it seems to be coming from the cupboards under the sink. I lean down and search for the source. But my heart is racing.

When my husband died and I went back to our Nepean home to sell it, the microwave, at various and very odd times, would suddenly erupt into the same kind of music. When I mentioned this rather strange phenomenon to Pat, who looked after the house while Paul and I travelled, she kindly refrained from saying I'd gone nuts. But one night when Pat and I were sitting at dinner with the handyman who'd come to fix up the house before I sold it, the microwave burst forth with a loud rendition of 'Danny Boy', Paul's favourite song. Pat and the handyman jumped up and ransacked the kitchen trying to figure out where it was coming from. None of us could really believe the microwave was singing! They never did find any other source. But that microwave played on and off until I sold the house and moved to Melbourne.

As weird as this sounds, I will not apologise for believing then (and now) that it was a message from Paul. Trouble is, you never know what this kind of message means. Did playing 'Danny Boy' mean Paul approved of selling the house? Did playing 'Jingle Bells' (another constant tune) mean he wanted me to stay put? That's the bugger about spooky events. How do you ever know how to decipher them?

Now weird stuff is happening again. Pia, as pragmatic a woman as ever lived, hears me banging around in the kitchen and comes downstairs. 'What in God's name is that awful music?' she asks. 'Turn it off, it's the middle of the bloody night.'

'I can't find where it's coming from.'

She pushes past me and rifles through the kitchen shelves. 'Must be one of those bloody musical kitchen contraptions,' she mutters, tipping baskets out on the counter. 'Ought to be banned.'

As suddenly as it started, the music stops.

'It's coming from in there somewhere,' she says, indicating a mess of kitchen gadgets, from garlic crushers to serving spoons. 'I'll sort it out in the morning.'

We both go back to bed. The music starts once more.

'I'm not bloody getting up again,' she calls.

And before long the music stops.

I lie awake, looking out at the night sky, clear and starry. A green satellite-shaped object appears and I wait for it to move on. A plane, I think, or a reflection of some kind. But it doesn't move. It hovers there. I think about waking Pia again but decide not to. I know what it is all about. I just have to wait to see what it brings.

Thank you, boys. They are looking after me. I know it. Bizarre? Delusional maybe? But not to me at this time.

Slowly, without quite understanding it, I begin searching for a house to buy.

It is late, about 10 pm. I wait at Church Point for a water taxi to take me home after a tedious, nitpicking day at the office. The nights are hardening as winter encroaches. Summer's lushness is being tossed off, like an irritating little brother. Tonight, there's no cloud around to soften the cold and it bites deep until the bones in my chest feel frigid. I pull my jacket tighter. Wipe my dripping nose.

The Point is almost deserted. Just me and a fisherman who is often here. He's harmless but he talks so quickly it's gibberish. He darts from bucket to bucket, slopping water. Moving on to the next chore before finishing the last. Always in a rush. A little mad.

I am too tired tonight to feel benign about his edginess. So I sit in the shelter at the ferry wharf, a little away from him, waiting for the water taxi. When there are no red and green water taxi lights in the distance and he starts to creep closer, seeking company, I move away.

'Just going to check the ads in the real estate window,' I tell him. He is too fragile to treat rudely.

Ads are lit up in a display window next to the ferry wharf office. There are faded pictures with price tags that make properties pipe dreams, not possibilities. I've seen them often. Unwilling, though, to return to the other end of the wharf and the feverish fisherman, I study the ads in detail for the first time.

In the top left hand corner, there's a rather bad photograph that I haven't noticed before, although it looks like it's been there a while, of a green tin house with an oddly shaped window. It is in

Lovett Bay. I assume it is on what I think of as the right side (north facing), because I know Lovett Bay quite well. The only house for sale (on the wrong side, south facing) is a rackety old fibro shack with a sinking pontoon and falling-down awnings.

The house in the photograph is all hard edges, corrugated iron, small windows and built like a fortress. Not my style at all. But the image niggles me on the trip home. It doesn't morph in with all the other buildings on display. Stands alone in my mind.

I will never be able to explain why but I call the real estate agent the next day and arrange to see it mid-week. When Wednesday rolls around the new real estate agent, in jeans and a bright white linen shirt, motors up to the Scotland Island house in a flaking tinny. The boat belongs to her assistant. This agent, all bouffant blonde and crisp creases, doesn't live offshore and sits in the boat with a frozen, tense expression. When I jump in she grips the sides fiercely, as though she expects me to sink it.

'Gidday. Great day,' says the assistant, a barefoot Scotland Islander. 'Let's go,' she adds, revving the motor.

'Couldn't get the water taxi for another twenty minutes,' explains the top agent, white-faced. 'Sorry about this.'

'Looking for a tinny just like this for myself,' I tell her.

She looks at me as though I need a lobotomy. I figure her career will soon move to solid ground where her car will be of more use.

We motor past *Trincomalee*, a lovely old white, weatherboard home that dominates the point between Elvina and Lovett. As usual, a big furry white dog, more suited to living in Alaska, lies on the jetty alongside the boatshed waiting for his mistress, a local doctor, to return from work. *Trincomalee* reeks of gentility and order, with regimented sandstone steps, scalloped stone handrails, a saltwater pool and boatshed. No tinny tied up, though. The good doctor gave up commuting long ago, except by water taxi.

When we begin to veer towards what I consider is the wrong side of Lovett Bay, I look at the agent aghast. 'We're not going to that awful old green shack, are we? I haven't got the slightest interest in that.'

The women nod. The assistant gets earnest. 'It's not awful. Just take a look. It has the most enormous potential.'

Potential. I hate that word. Especially when it's used by real estate agents.

'We're nearly there. Take a look at it anyway. Go on,' she insists.

I shrug. So what? I'm here now. 'Okay.'

The ferry wharf supports the usual wooden shack but this one is crammed with rank, overflowing wheelie bins. There's a box of empty wine bottles with good labels and a bin stuffed with a huge – even for Pittwater – number of empty Melbourne bitter cans and VB bottles. On the dock, there are fried food wrappers smelling of stale fat. It's a pigsty kind of welcome. We pick past the rubbish. Inside the shed every mariner businessman's calling card is pinned to the walls: 'Suzuki motors serviced', 'Tree lopping', Learn French at home', 'Tired of Housework?'

A red flag is tucked into the supporting beams.

'Hang the flag and the ferry stops,' the assistant explains.

'It's not on the regular route?'

She shakes her head. 'No.'

The raucous shrieks of cockatoos in the trees above are deafening. Their bright yellow combs furl and unfurl like squeeze-boxes.

'Jesus. What a racket.'

'What?' the assistant laughs. She adjusts a shoestring strap on her shoulder as we move towards the Lovett Bay boatshed. She's a sexy woman and she likes it.

An engraved sandstone sign declares 'Lovett Bay', '1895'. Huge sandstone boulders topple into a crescent-shaped beach where the sand is almost red. It would have been lovely except for the electricity pole bunged into the middle of it. I look up the hill where a ragged sandstone track climbs mysteriously through the bush.

'What's up there?'

'Another house.'

And no more is said.

We walk past dinghies racked in lines. An old wooden surfboard. There's mowed green lawn, smoke climbing lazily from a fireplace cradled at the base of two big boulders. Which is why it smells like a bushfire's just been through.

'That's called the Taj Mahal.' The head agent points at the mustard yellow house looming behind the boatshed.

'Why the Taj Mahal?'

It is blocky, with lots of glass and wood. Above the main building, a round room perches alone like a forgotten satellite. Not a bit like the Taj Mahal.

'Ken's palace for his bride.'

I visualise a handsome young man consumed with a grand passion for a demure young woman.

A tall, skinny bloke with dreadlocks, huge bare feet, tanned hands and ceramic blue eyes is scraping clean a yacht, bottom heavy with sea creatures. He stops scraping to let us past and smiles shyly.

Mussels, oysters, broken shell, grit and grime fester on the concrete, waiting for high tide to wash them back into the sea. I trip on the tram track that launches the boat. Quick tanned hands hold me up.

'Jesus. Thanks. Are you Ken?'

'No. No.'

There's a whiff of something foreign in his words. He points inside the shed, beyond iron, cable, wood and glue. Ken, grey-haired, wiry, around sixty years old, is hunched into a telephone, drumming up business.

'Ah.' So much for my notion of a young, lovestruck Adonis.

I decide I hate this part of Lovett Bay. It feels foreign and uninviting. Isolated and brooding. Then I see the house. Blinds hang brokenly. Dejection and depression enshroud it like an invisible cloud. Green summer mould clings to railings and shaded woodwork. Under the house there's a junk heap. Planks of wood, old windows, pots, pans, paint tins, chain, ropes, a clothesline, the water heater. It's a dump yard, I want to say. But I ask: 'Who owns this place?'

'Gordon Andrews.'

An expectant wait.

'Should that mean something?' I am a little arrogant because I don't want the house. There is power, isn't there, when you do not desire something?

We follow the path made from wooden sleepers hammered into the ground, supported by wooden pegs. Thick, plaited boat rope is looped on handrails. With the words *enormous potential* tolling painfully, I stomp up the final steps to the front door. Glass. No privacy.

'He designed the first decimal currency.'

'Huh?'

'Gordon Andrews.'

The head agent is impatient. I am not even playing the game.

The assistant fluffs with ambition. The house is rectangular, with two bedrooms at the far end. Sliding glass doors from the sitting room lead to a boxy deck that overlooks the bay. There is a kitchen, a bathroom which includes the laundry and a back deck where three stumps carved into gruesome faces surround an old-fashioned, wood burning brick barbecue.

'The bedroom walls could be easily removed,' enthuses the assistant. 'See, they're more like partitions than walls. If you built new rooms under the house, this could turn into a really big living room.'

I have fallen through a time warp and landed in the sixties. A built-in green sofa, bright red tractor seat stools, cubed shelving.

Masks leer and jeer from walls. Floor sanding ends raggedly at the entrance to the bedroom, revealed behind a calico curtain with wooden dowels weighting the hem.

'Why's he selling?'

'He's about eighty-five.'

'Right.'

Look at my watch. Time to go. I begin walking back to the boat, not even glancing behind me. 'Looks newly built,' I say.

'Yeah, in 1994. Gordon was the first to get going after the bushfires wrecked this side of Lovett Bay. Nothing left standing. Just his old bathtub in the middle of a smouldering, grey mess.'

'So he was about eighty years old when he started over?'

'Musta been.'

Shame floods my face in red splashes. 'Must be a courageous old bloke.'

'Cranky, more likely.'

But I understand now. Floor sanding that reaches as far as his energy. The homegrown masks replacing a lifetime's collection of art. The shoestring décor thumping with style. His own. Inimitable.

I make an offer and shock myself. I have no idea why I've done it. I don't want the house. But the offer is low, much lower than Gordon wants. So I assume it will be rejected. I put the house out of my mind on the ride back to Scotland Island. The nor'easterly has turned into a cold southerly. The big white dog is suddenly appropriate.

'Let's keep looking,' I say. 'A house with a deep waterfront. Winter sun. Lots of it.'

The assistant touch-parks the tinny at my dock with a crunch. The windows of the house are like fireballs, reflecting the western sun. I lose my balance for a moment and wonder if I'm being stupid, if the time for living with boat access is behind, not ahead of me.

I ring the lover and tell him I have made an offer on a house. I want his support and approval, perhaps because my father always told me not to worry about the big decisions: 'Your husband will make those,' he used to say as I grew up.

'What about my own cheque book?' I asked my father once.

'You don't need one. When you're married, your husband will manage the money.'

Ideas like that have a way of sticking to the walls of your mind. The concept is sown early that big details will be taken care of by *the man*. Even though women's roles had changed significantly since I was a teenager and I had waved the flag of liberation from the day I turned the first page of Kate Millett's *Sexual Politics*, I was still seeking approval.

But the lover flits around my questions, noncommittal. My hurt turns into anger.

'I'm about to spend a lot of money and you can't even give me an opinion!'

'Gotta go. The other phone is ringing.'

Yeah right! 'An opinion is not a commitment. Ultimately it's my decision. Right or wrong.'

'Gotta go.'

I wonder why I even mentioned the house. I don't intend to buy it. To get his attention? Probably. I can relax though. Gordon will never accept the price. I'll never hear another word about it. But as a group of us sail in the evening, my thoughts keep going back to the house. I start to see where I can make changes and mentally calculate what they will cost. If a couple of young self-sown saplings are removed, there will be a wonderful view of the waterfall on the other side of the bay. Maybe, just maybe, it has possibilities.

There isn't much wind at twilight, and it's a long slow sail. I've left a pot roast of beef braised in red wine in the oven in a huge, cast iron cassoulet dish that I carried back from Paris as hand

133

luggage on one of my travel assignments. Empty, it weighs a ton, and when it is full it is almost impossible to lift. But I love it and trust it. By the time we pack the boat away we are two hours later than planned and I joke about *boeuf brûlée*, but the smell as we walk up the jetty is delicious. Good old pot, I think. Worth every hassle at every airport x-ray.

Later, as talk drifts into the late hours and the tide drops, leaving boats stranded, I drift off to bed. I feel too tired to think. It's an aching tiredness and my bones feel too heavy for my muscles and my head is thick and muddled.

When the phone rings at seven thirty the next morning, I am shaky from too little sleep and too much red wine. For a moment, ludicrous hope blooms that it is the lover finally offering support. But it is too early for him to call.

I pick up the phone. I will be late for work. But what does that matter on a morning when I feel the stitching is unravelling anyway?

'He said yes.'

'Who?'

'Gordon! The house you looked at yesterday. It's yours!'

'Oh shit.'

'It's a great deal.'

'Oh shit.'

But I do not withdraw. I let the deal go ahead. I want a home base. Tiredness clamps like a vice on every part of my body. For more mornings than I care to think about, I have woken feeling as though I need to sleep for another six hours. It's a creeping exhaustion that builds through the day and often by lunchtime my eyes are gritty and I feel blurred, weaker in mind and spirit. Sometimes, I put it down to partying hard and a dysfunctional relationship. At other times I blame getting older. I tell myself I'll snap out of it once I have a house to call my own and my anxieties about where I belong are assuaged. Every day I find different reasons for this lessening of verve. But I avoid looking at myself *too* closely. I suspect I will not like the hard-drinking, duplicitous woman I have become.

This new move will mean more change. I wonder if it is time to learn to embrace it. I swallow a sudden fear of commitment and feel it going down like a hard-boiled egg.

'When does he want to settle?' I ask the agent.

'Will a month be ok?'

'Yeah. Sure.'

One more time, I think. I can pack one more time.

I crawl back into bed, the pillow cradles my head in a feathery bowl and I sleep for another six hours. This time when the phone wakes me, I am calm. Control has slipped neatly back into place. Exhaustion lingers, though, and I wonder why there is no excitement to rattle its grip. A new home. A new beginning. But I feel like a zombie. Is it age that muffles spontaneity? Or experience?

'Hello.'

I drill energy into my voice. Zip on the rubber suit of the happy mistress. Gay. *Toujours gai.*

'Hi.'

'Any news about the house?' the lover asks.

'Yeah. The deal's done. The price was too good to walk away from.'

'What d'ya pay?'

The phone crackles with easy intimacy. I have already hurled yesterday's lack of support into a chasm. I give him the figure.

'Let me check it out before you sign anything.'

And I slide easily into the illusion of being cared for.

He cuts off the call before I realise the conversation is dead. Always, always, he leaves only emptiness. A vast sliding track of words unformed, ideas unexpressed. There's never even the most ordinary, implicit kind of support couples take for granted. Ordinary. When had the state of *ordinary* become so damn desirable?

I call my solicitor and tell him what I've done. He is my husband's brother-in-law, conservative with a wild side he subverts into a love of bloodstock and thoroughbred racing. He is aghast.

'Boat access? Does that mean you can't get home on foot?'

'I could swim but it's a long way. Boats are better.'

'Have you got a boat?'

'No.'

'Do you want to take a few days to think about this?'

'No.'

I hear his breathing, his concern.

'I need a sanctuary right now. I think this is it.'

Silence. Then: 'Ok, love.'

And the deal is done.

'Why don't you come and have dinner with us soon?' he says.

How can I tell him that to hang around a solid marriage triggers a wave of yearning and a tide of self-loathing?

'Yeah. Soon. Thanks.'

Gordon Andrews invites me for coffee a couple of weeks after house sale contracts are exchanged. His voice on the phone is firm and youthful. 'Few things I need to explain,' he says.

'Great. Kind of you.'

We set a time for Saturday. I plan to take the ferry to get a grip on the transport system.

It's mid-April. Autumn and, to me, the most beautiful season on Pittwater. Nights are clean and cool, dawns break pink as a rosy breasted galah. The evenings close in and if the wind is from the south, it's pleasant to light the fire in the pot-belly stove and put a stew on top to cook slowly. It is dark now, when I leave to catch the morning ferry, so I carry a torch. The easy old goat track was mostly washed away during a big summer storm and I have to pick my way over submerged rocks. It is the day's first challenge and I have begun to think of the easy access to the Lovett Bay ferry wharf with relief.

On the Saturday morning I'm due to meet Gordon, the usual cheery faces peer through the bedroom window.

'Hi ya, Susan.'

The team from the house around the bend is off shopping. I lift a hand but not my head. Another hour in bed. Soaking tiredness. I vow to drink less, walk more, eat better, when I move house. Begin again. Again.

I look at the long, skinny stick of my arm. My skin hangs loosely and is aging into fine, gathered wrinkles. New, funny white spots, two or three, resist a tan. Are these age spots? The body slides along within its own time frame no matter how the mind instructs it. As I lie in bed, depression slips on like a second skin. There is no excitement about buying this house. I feel too tired even for that.

Gordon expects me at 11 am for coffee. I slouch around until I miss the ferry and have to call a water taxi. Rock scrambling is beyond me this morning.

I am not anxious to see the house. It is bereft of the cottage garden gentility I have always favoured, and I cannot visualise how I will fit in to its lean austerity. To give myself a boost, I search for omens. The day is sunny. Good. Water taxi prompt. Good. High tide. Good. Annette driving the water taxi. Good.

'Bought old Gordo's place, have you?' she asks.

Annette is soft-hearted, country straight, sunny-tempered with gentle eyes and a lovely smile. She wears cut-off jeans, a checked cotton shirt ironed to crispness, bright white sneakers and socks, and handles the boat like a racer using the wind as a second gear.

'Yep. Tell me about Gordon,' I ask. 'What's he like?'

'Wait and see.'

'I'll need you to get me home again,' I say when she drops me at the Lovett Bay ferry wharf. I feel suddenly stranded and unsure.

'Call me. Not much on so far. Shouldn't be a wait.'

She pulls away as I climb the yellow steps with the white safety stripes. The rubbish is gone, the wheelie bins are closed and clean. Another omen. They start to spin in my mind like a demented whirligig. 'Give up on the bloody omens,' I chastise myself. But my head has been in a foggy loop for so long, a single command will not change much.

It is quiet and still, this Saturday morning as I walk along the waterfront to see my new home. The boatshed is closed and deserted. An old yacht lies stranded in the cradle, her bottom scoured and holes patched with blobs of white filler. I realise I have no idea where I am. I do not know where on the vast Australian coastline Lovett Bay bites in. The water stretches ahead but I can't see how far. I have no idea if the sinister looking red escarpments that rise on both sides of the bay have names. I am clueless. Have I, I wonder as I climb the steps, made the most expensive mistake of my life?

Scotland Island is a large, ebullient community where the population is mostly full time and not made up of weekenders. There is always company if you want it. This little corner of Lovett Bay, as far as I can see, has four houses, one on either side of me and another hut, Japanese looking, behind Gordon's house. It's not exactly a bustling village. Who will I find for company? Who will go past my door and call in? This is not a thoroughfare. This is a dead end.

Gordon's front door is shut with a white curtain pulled across it. 'Closed!' it screams. 'Go back!'

I immediately assume I've come on the wrong day. But I knock. Then call. And call again: 'Hello? Helloo-oo?'

A grunt. Movement.

'Gordon? It's Susan.'

The curtain swishes back and Gordon peers suspiciously from behind metal framed glasses before he opens the door. I expect frailty. But he is sexy. He's tanned, and wears a bold silver necklace, black belt with a chunky silver buckle, a bright white, stretch T-shirt, blue jeans faded to perfection. His arms are heavily muscled and he looks strong.

'Come in.'

I hold out my hand and he grabs it in his bear paw which is callused and dry as snakeskin. So big it feels like my hand has been stuffed in a boxing glove. Under bushy white eyebrows, his eyes gleam with naughtiness – or is it challenge? He is irresistible. I have been told his new home is a retirement village in a nearby suburb and I wonder why. Leaving Lovett Bay after more than three decades could only be heartbreaking and you wouldn't do it unless there was no choice.

He stands aside and lets me in to the main room where his macabre masks dominate the walls, casting a manic pall.

Gordon notes my fascination. 'They're for sale.'

'Uh, they're great. Really. But I'm going to have to unload stuff to fit in here. Can't take on any more.'

He lets it lie and leads the way through the house to the front deck, furry with mould. I give myself a mental kick for noticing immediately that the windows need cleaning.

We step into an enclosed deck that's surrounded by a spiked picket fence so high it shuts out the water view if you're sitting down. Bronze caps shaped like fleurs-de-lis crown the corner poles of this corral and are oddly flamboyant touches amongst the masculine lines of the house. At the eastern end, where they catch the sun, there are green plastic boxes growing parsley, mint, coriander and Thai basil. Gordon is a cook as it turns out. Everyone, I think, is a cook on Pittwater.

At the front of the deck, the top rail has been carefully scooped in the exact centre and a little shelf added. The indentation in the wood, Gordon explains, is to rest your elbow. The shelf is to stand your wineglass. He points me to a lovely hand-hewn wooden bench and takes the canvas chair for himself. We settle at a slightly unstable, weathered grey table, handmade from a slice of a tree trunk.

'Did you build all this?'

He ignores me. The table is laid with plain white bowls and little white cups and saucers. There are broken pieces of very dark chocolate in one bowl. A mixture of dried fruit and nuts in another. Sunflower seeds or pumpkin seeds half-fill the remaining two bowls. There is raw sugar. No milk. It is all set out in a precise, beautiful, geometric design.

'I've got a couple of requests,' he begins formally.

'Sure.'

'My son likes the rug. Can I take it?'

I haven't even noticed it so I spin around and check out the floor. The rug seems to be a piece of manufactured carpet. Once it was called Berber, but I have no idea how it's currently marketed.

'Sure, take it. That's ok.'

'And the curtains. He can use those too.'

Made from flecked calico that Gordon has sewn himself.

'Fine.'

I loathe curtains anyway and wonder why he needs them here.

I look back at Gordon, wondering what's coming next, and I have a niggling sense of déjà vu. Then I remember. A bad-tempered old bastard disembarking from a water taxi in the weeks before Christmas. He'd staggered with his shopping bags and I'd reached to help him. Trying to take them to pass to him when he was solidly on the ferry wharf steps.

'Get away,' he ordered, his elbow pushing me aside.

I'd held my hands up in mock surrender and let him be. Shocked. Rudeness is not often encountered in an environment where everyone eventually has a turn at needing support.

It was Annette's shift driving the water taxi.

'What's his problem?'

She laughed. 'That's just Gordon.'

Today, though, he's polite. He is on a mission to sell me his furniture and as many works of art as possible. There isn't much space, it turns out, in his retirement home at Avalon.

'Coffee?'

'Yes. Lovely.'

'Good.'

He pushes himself up from the chair, moves into the kitchen unsteadily, his shoulders tipping a little off kilter. There is, after all, a frailty that cannot be disguised under the Jimmy Dean clothes.

Alone, I look at his stifled view of Lovett Bay. Gordon has created a textured, layered site. The shining green water is used as a backdrop for wispy conifers, spindly acacias, prostrate grevilleas and sapling gums, self-sown after the bushfires. Hue upon hue of peaceful green. The greenery is beautiful but I love to look at water and want to see more of it. A couple of saplings might have to go.

My mobile phone blurts, breaking the peace.

'How's it going?'

The lover. On a Saturday. Historic.

'Great! It's going to be fantastic.' I oversell, rushing for impact, waiting for the phone to go dead before I finish. But he hangs on the line.

'It's a lot of money . . . maybe too much?'

I hold back a surge of red anger. Advice after the event. The genius of hindsight. And what does he know about this area anyway? Not a bloody thing!

'Maybe. But who gives a rat's? Anyway, locals always think strangers are wood ducks.'

He laughs. 'What's a fucking wood duck?'

'Someone who pays too much.'

'Ok. I'll call ya.'

And he is gone.

Gordon returns with a pot of dense black coffee. We sip it. I wonder if he heard me, if he knows what a wood duck is. The acid hits my stomach and sets off waves of nausea. I reach for a seed.

'Just a couple of other things.'

'Uh-huh.'

He hesitates.

'Spit it out, Gordon. I'm unshockable.'

'It's the shelving in the sitting room. It's an original design. I'd like to take it.'

I wander inside, holding my demitasse. The shelving is a series of boxes, all different sizes, and crammed with sentimental treasures. A little cup. A postcard. A few bits of glassware. Some photographs. Stuff that only has meaning to him.

'Take it.'

I am tired again. I want to go home and lie down. But he hasn't finished.

'The table is for sale.' A stiff, knotted finger points at an exquisite blonde wood table.

'Gordon, I love the table. You built it, did you? But I have one.' My own battered table has a history, moments snagged in my mind by a burn, a stain, a mark. I will not trade it in for a part of Gordon's history.

'Perhaps, Gordon,' I say, thinking that it might be time for him to make an *offer* instead of a request, 'you could leave a very small piece of *you* here.'

'Such as . . .?'

'Nothing much. An old, signed postcard. A small piece of art.'

He looks at me silently for a moment and then nods.

'Then there's the fridge,' he continues.

'No, Gordon, the fridge stays. It fits the space in the kitchen. You can have mine, if you want it.'

He changes tack, aware of my rising discomfort. 'Are you frightened of snakes?' he asks.

'Snakes? Oh, snakes are ok.'

But it's a lie. Some stupid shred of pride that will not let me admit fear. In fact, snakes terrify me. Send me into hyperventilating panic. Turn my legs to lead, my head to the floury mush of an over-ripe rock melon. Growing up in Bonegilla migrant camp, I'd seen a lot. Red-bellied blacks, mostly. Some browns. As a child I'd quickly learned that screaming *snake!* would instantly snap a parent out of inattention. I overused the technique, of course. Once, baled up by a swaying black snake, eyes glittering, tongue flicking, I screamed and screamed and no-one came.

My father finally walked over. Tired of the racket. I stood rigid, too terrified to move, my screams more and more strangled. It was the first and only time I saw my father, a huge, towering, shuffling man, run. He grabbed a spade, flew in and whacked the snake's head off. The glossy black body wriggled frantically for a long time, going nowhere while its dismembered head lay immobile alongside.

We lived in Block 23, then, in a corrugated iron house amongst many others. Our home, with two bedrooms, a sitting room, dining room, kitchen and bathroom, was comparatively luxurious because my father was a ranking public servant, in charge of supplies for the thousands of post-war immigrants who tumbled out of box cars on dark nights. The migrants, from Latvia, Estonia, Lithuania – names that sounded thrilling and exotic to my young ears – were housed in long huts, single room by single room, wooden stairs at each front door. When I was given my first bicycle, just before my seventh birthday, I crashed that red, blue and white Malvern Star into every set of steps as I circled the huts, struggling to stay upright, reaching tippy toe for pedals my parents told me I would grow into in a flash.

'A big one, ja, that snake?' said Nicky, running to help my father. A woolly bear of a man from Yugoslavia, he gathered me up and stilled my tears and fear. Nicky looked after our garden and, in return, tilled some land to grow the kind of vegetables he was used to – capsicum, eggplant, broad beans. Not the kind of food my father ordered for the giant messes where everyone ate. Food so unappealingly stodgy and English that one day the Italians rioted in despair.

Often, Nicky earned extra income by babysitting my brother and me. We would laugh and dance and sing, bumping into old leather chairs strewn with gaily coloured tapestry cushions made by women in the camp. Long before my parents returned from their party, my father always beatifically drunk, I would collapse and sleep exhausted on Nicky's lap. My mother told me years later that his wife and children had been killed in the war. It explained the silent tears that sometimes ran down his cracked cheeks; tears of laughter, I'd thought, when they'd been pure grief.

I loved Nicky. All day, before the routine of school stole my freedom, he'd trundle me to and fro in his wheelbarrow. I tasted my first capsicum under his shiny-eyed coaxing, crisp and strange to a meat and potatoes kid. Juicy as an apple. To be with him, I'd jiggle my cot to the bedroom window when I was supposed to be down for an afternoon nap, strip off my clothes and climb out, falling the last couple of feet. I would run helter-skelter in search of Nicky, grazing shins, knees, elbows and chin. Scabs everywhere. Freckles bigger than sixpences on a face that burned to a crisp right through summer. I hated the hats my mother shoved on my head and chucked them away the moment I was out of sight.

'Mrs Duncan, here is your daughter. But we don't know where her clothes are,' was a common lament.

In that tight migrant community where people were bound together by the uncertainty of beginning again in a strange, new land, I was safe even if I didn't always find Nicky. We moved when I was nine years old, to a country town near Melbourne, where my parents bought the pub.

My fear of snakes stems from those early country days, but I don't want to tell Gordon I loathe them, so I lie.

'Glad you like 'em,' Gordon says.

'Why?'

He beckons and I follow, this time going out the back where he's a built a simple, raised brick barbecue. He lifts the tin lid. Coiled thickly, a diamond python sleeps.

'Lives here,' Gordon says. 'That's Siphon Python.'

'Right.'

'Wouldn't like to have him moved along.'

'Of course not.'

Gordon gazes fondly at the black snake with creamy dots that form diamonds along its sides. 'Quite beautiful, aren't they?' he says.

'Tell me about your work, Gordon.' I barely restrain myself from running back inside.

Gordon, who was labelled a dope at school, was actually brilliant. He just had a mind that went in a different direction to most other people's. During his career, which spanned more than sixty years, he became one of Australia's leading industrial designers. His most widely recognised achievement, though, was to design a new currency for Australia when we shifted from an imperial to a decimal system in 1966. His notes were bold and colourful, full of Australian imagery. Heroes, wildlife, the merino sheep that built Australia's early fortunes. Wonderful, wonderful designs. His banknotes were reproduced on tea towels and bath towels, money boxes, key rings, placemats and posters. And not a single royalty went into his bank account.

By the time we sit down and talk on his deck, he is riddled with bitterness. Bitter he never received the financial recognition he felt he deserved in Australia. Bitter about losing his original house in the 1994 fires. Bitter about not having enough insurance. But he is bitter most of all, I suspect, about going through the dastardly business of growing old and being forced to face it. His mind is a beehive of ideas his body can't follow through.

He uses salvaged wood, bits of rope and twine, wine bottle corks, broken glass – stuff gleaned from other people's rubbish – to create his designs. He sees beauty in practicality. Form follows function. But don't call it art. He is emphatic his role is designer, not artist. He makes swirling silver jewellery, heavy to hold, light to behold. I am told, much later, that people rarely bought jewellery twice from Gordon because he made them feel gypped. He would do the deal and, only on delivery, declare that a chain, a leather strap or some other integral part of the piece was not included in the price. The big commissions have long dried up, though. His attempt to fire up enthusiasm to reprint his biography, *A Designer's Life*, is unsuccessful. More or less wiped out by the bushfires in 1994, he has nowhere to turn for the cash he needs to ease the difficulty and expense of offshore living.

What saves him from being just another disappointed, twisted old man is his humour. No, not humour. His sense of the absurd. Around the barbecue, permanently fixed, the three sawn logs have been transformed into rude, larrikin faces with lolling tongues. They are Gordon's permanent guests. A perfect social solution. Over the next few weeks I learn that he feuded with almost everyone at some time. There's a bright red rooster painted on a mustard door leading to the bathroom. It's a little like Gordon, square-shouldered and strutty, and it brings life to a dead spot in the house. Chooks are great company. Was this his dinner guest each night?

What he struggles to show me that morning, are the hours of concentration, the hours of work, the intensity of purpose of every single detail in the house. But I failed to understand that until much later, when I thoughtlessly ripped out so much of his heart.

11

Two weeks after coffee with Gordon, the same boys, Andrew, Chris and Paul, the same barge of five months ago, arrive to help me move house. Again.

The boys know what to do so I don't have to be there. Don't want to be there. My mood is pessimistic. Every hazy plan I come up with to change the house is touched by a cold finger of uncertainty. If I look at my past form, there is no reason to expect life here will be any different. I want to change badly. I want to get fit and healthy, find my old energy. But I've tried so many times now, and I've fallen back into old patterns. Can I begin the slow, hard grind of change again? Can I do it alone? Can location help?

My last night on Scotland Island, I sleep less than I am awake covered by a blanket of wet sea mist that seeps under doors and through gaps in the wooden walls. In the morning, cardboard cartons are limp, as though they, too, lack the energy to begin again. This time, the move is timed for a 2 pm high tide. I plan to meet the boys at the new house in the late afternoon.

When I leave for work at 6.30 am, an early freezing westerly scoots down McCarrs Creek to bang at the doors, blowing hard. I put on an old grey tweed coat that I joke will outlive me. But the cold is on the inside as well. I feel ill. I don't know why. I blame it on apprehension. I hope the wind drops by the time the barge arrives.

Gordon has locked the house and the boys call me, stranded. Already on my way home, I divert to the retirement village to pick up the keys. I suspect it is a final gesture of defiance from Gordon but when I walk into the hotel-like reception area, past stooped old women glued to walking frames, my anger dissolves. 'This will be the end of him,' I think.

In fact, Gordon has reached the end. He is just waiting for it to find him. Less than two years later, he is dead, but not before I invite him back to see how I've changed his house. He is gracious enough to say: 'It's what I would have done if I'd had the money.' I think, in his shoes, I might have cried. Not long after his death, months only, I flick through a glossy magazine. Gordon's tractor stools, those with cowhide seats, are offered for sale. Three thousand dollars each. The resurrection of the sixties arrives too late to save him.

The water taxi drops me at the ferry wharf. Everything is unloaded and the garden looks like a refugee camp. Inside the house, there's a moss green wall with a huge, empty white space with pencil marks all over it. It's the unpainted gap left by Gordon's shelves. It makes the house feel like it's been abandoned and looted.

The boys bring in the furniture and stand holding it, wondering where it should go. Sofas are too big, the table too long. I ask them to rip out the bright green built-in sofa to make more space and it leaves a gaping hole in the plaster.

They see my growing distress and make suggestions. 'Angle the sofas like this. They'll fit,' Paul says.

They rush around, lifting, adjusting, until I have a room that functions. Table, chairs, sofas, coffee table. Anything that won't squeeze into this tiny space is stacked under the house in Gordon's old workshop, which I'd missed in my first, off-hand inspection.

'This is a bloody disaster,' I moan.

The boys console me.

'Look at this.' Paul leads me onto the front deck and points through to a cleft in the hills on the other side of the bay. 'What a view of the waterfall. Magical.'

I see the rocks but if there is water, it can only be a trickle.

'And what about this?' Pulling me to the back deck and into a little trellised space where Gordon has built a bench. 'You get winter sun here. What a place to lie and look at the bush.'

I lie on the bench. It is Gordon's length and a few inches too short for me. Paul shrugs his shoulders and gives up.

Another bloody brilliant mistake. The biggest yet.

I sit on a box labelled 'Mexican necessities' and wonder what on earth it means. I find the most pressing necessity – a bottle of red and a corkscrew. I hold it up to the boys enquiringly. They shake their heads, grab a beer instead.

'Gotta go before the tide's too low to get the barge out,' Andrew says.

'Ok, guys. Thanks a lot. For everything.'

They give me a hug and a kiss. 'It'll be right. You'll be right.'

I walk down to the barge with them, reluctant to be left alone. A black head in the water comes closer and closer.

'Bosun!'

A wet, happy Bosun emerges from the water, shaking a spray that lights up like a giant halo in the sunlight.

'Where have you come from?' I ask him, bending to rub his nose.

'Christ. We left him on the island!'

Andrew looks winded. He runs his hands over the dog, making sure he's intact after his marathon swim across the bays.

'Not even puffing, Bosun?' he says with relief, when he's sure the dog is fine.

This time, the dog is first on the barge, tail wagging.

'What's a barge without a dog?' I think, watching the tinny steer the barge into deeper green water. I think of Sweetie, her box of ashes. It's time to lay her to rest no matter what my future holds. She loved the water. Maybe, just maybe, a silent farewell and overboard.

Inside again, I reach for the wine. Drink myself into a crying jag, make up the bed, talk out loud to no-one. When the bottle is nearly empty, I shake the last drop into my glass and wander onto the front deck. The moon is high behind the house, lighting the bay, turning the mangroves along the shore into writhing bogeymen. It's low tide and there is a huge new beach where I'm used to seeing water. It's dry enough to cross to the southern shore without getting wet. I remember too late the real estate agent trick of only showing Pittwater properties at high tide.

Around midnight, I pick up my glass from Gordon's ledge and wander through the house and down the steps to the water. It's a still, cold night. The air is tangy, seagrass flops limply in dark patches. On the other side of the bay, a single light blazes. Another insomniac? There's a wooden pontoon, only slightly dewy, and I sit on it, looking around properly for the first time. My own slip, left by Gordon, has an upturned little fibreglass dinghy tied to it. Not much bigger than a bathtub. Finally got a boat. Can't see myself rowing it to the commuter dock, though.

My forty-ninth birthday is looming. Not much to show for it. Have I found my place finally? I look up at my house. I can always sell. This doesn't have to be forever. But the thought of another move is crushing and somewhere in that swell of self-pity I decide to give this everything I've got.

In the early hours of the morning, when it is still quite dark, I am woken by the sound of the back door sliding open. I cannot believe it is an intruder, not here, but then I hear breathing, heavy and regular, and a grunt. There's a clicking sound on the floor, a huge sigh and then silence.

My heart hammers as I get up quietly and move to turn on the light. I know I can scream. There are people next door to help. The switch moves silently and light floods the room from Gordon's funny little halogen spotlights strung together with industrial wire.

I look around. There is nothing here. Then I hear another heavy sigh, and the whoosh of breath rushing out of a mouth in what sounds more like contentment than threat. I tiptoe to the sofa and look over the back of it. A huge, fat golden labrador with impossibly big brown eyes looks up at me sweetly, then flops down to sleep.

'Get off, you bloody great brute! Get out!'

He opens one eye, shakes his head and goes back to sleep. I try to pull him off the sofa and he licks my face until I give in and climb into my bed again.

In the morning, before the sun is up, I wake with a thumping headache and vow, again, to go on a health kick. The dog stirs and this time doesn't seem to mind being asked to leave. I make tea and toast, and take it onto the deck to wait for the dawn. It arrives in a blood red rush, turning the escarpment a fiery orange and bringing the bay to life. As if on cue, birds begin racketing around and a school of tiny fish speeds past in a froth of water, followed by bigger, jumping fish that rise and plop loudly.

Five kookaburras join me, one by one, and eye my toast greedily. The littlest one is tousled, like he was late getting up and didn't have time to brush his hair.

'Scruff Bucket. That's your name.'

He tilts his head, his eyes never leaving the toast in my hand.

'You don't like toast. You only like meat. Give it a rest.'

He is the last to fly away. I go inside intending to shower and unpack but instead return to bed. There's no need to hurry. It's Saturday, and I'm going to be here a long time. When I wake it is nearly noon.

I squeeze in a lunch at Towlers Bay, drinking too much as usual. At some blurry point, Stewart leans across the table to me: 'You're turning into a drunk, you know.'

His words shock me into sobriety. 'Stewart, I have often seen you in the same state but I have never, would never, say anything like that to you.'

The entire table is silent. Watching. Waiting. Everyone's wine-glasses sit still, anchored.

'I apologise,' he says.

And chatter fires up as though someone's pulled the cord of an outboard motor.

But I *know* I'm drinking too much. And it scares me. As a kid, I hated alcohol. Watching my father negotiate life through a lurching haze put me off it for years. When I was nearly twenty years old, I'd go to parties and walk up to blokes with a beer in their hand and a sheen in their eyes and ask: 'Are you thirsty?'

'No,' they'd reply happily.

'Then you don't need this drink.'

I'd take their beer and tip it down the sink. I thought I was saving them from a future like my father's. But all I did was offend everyone and make them wary. I wonder now if I sensed early that alcohol might be dangerous for me.

Somewhere along the line I forgot all those fears and joined the drinking crowd. But a drunk? Me? All I'm doing is blurring the edges of a rather useless life, aren't I? I'm just having fun, aren't I? Filling in the holes when the lover leaves me and returns to his wife. Right?

On Sunday morning, I stay in my pyjamas and begin by cleaning the windows. At lunchtime, I sit on the back deck in the warm sun, a cup of tea in hand, the steam drifting lazily upwards. I have a ferocious hangover. Again. I vow to cut back on booze. Again. Not that it's a problem. It's a healthy move. Right?

A tall, grey-haired figure in navy blue trousers and a faded navy shirt, the kind you see tradesmen wear, picks his way down the hill from the Japanese inspired house that perches above the tall palm behind my house. He moves like a brolga, his legs impossibly long and skinny.

I wave my mug. 'Hi.'

'Hi. Love the two boys,' he responds.

'Oh. Yeah.' *What two boys?*

'I'm Jack. Welcome,' he says, coming across. He holds out a battered hand covered in scratches and grabs mine solidly but not painfully. Up close he looks as though he is part of the landscape. His fissured face matches the escarpment. His eyes reflect the blue of the bay. His skin is the reddish brown of the rocks. His roughly cut hair foams like white caps.

A horn sounds.

'Ferry's here. Gotta go. We'll get you up for a drink. Soon.'

He gallops down the goat track that leads from his house, trousers too short, bony ankles, lace-up shoes without socks.

By midnight the unpacking, as far as I can go within the space, is finished. The house sparkles except for the hole in the plaster and the big slab of white undercoat on the green wall. I have drunk gallons of tea. But no wine.

Monday evening, I get home early from work because I want to *be* at home as soon as I can.

Ken collars me in front of the boatshed: 'Listen, I'm quite happy to keep that fella on my land. Like him. What's he all about?'

'What fella?'

'The old Chinese bloke.'

Jesus. The bronzes. I suddenly realise my three Chinese statues, about a metre tall, Healthy, Wealthy and Wise, are missing.

'God, sorry, Ken, didn't know where the boys stashed them. Can you show me the spot?'

We walk around the edge of the shed. He points to a location below his deck. Wise, holding the pearl of wisdom, looks wistfully towards the bay through sprays of pink bougainvillea scrambling over a dead tree trunk.

'There are two others. Haven't seen them, have you?'

'You mean those blokes?'

I follow the line of his finger into my front yard. Healthy, holding a baby, and Wealthy, decked out in all his finery, stride across grass. Screened from the house by trees and in a gentle dip in the land.

'They're the ones. Thought I'd lost them.'

'Bit big to lose, aren't they?'

City dope, he's thinking.

'Leave him there as long as you want,' he adds. 'Swap him over for Wealthy, if you like. Could use a bit of that.'

'Couldn't we all?'

A week later, dusk rolls in from the east. It is mid-May and the air turns thin with cold as soon as the sun drops. The lover has finally found the time to come to Pittwater, his curiosity over-riding his loathing of boats and water. But he leaves after a quick house tour. Now, it's too early to sleep, too late to make something of the next few hours.

I vow to eat a proper dinner. My body, when I run my hands down it, is papery thin. Outside it begins to rain heavily, banging on the tin roof like a thousand drumsticks. There are no leaks anywhere. The house is solid.

I dream of dolphins with happy faces and wonderful smiles. They swim around me, chattering in the way dolphins do, and make me laugh in my dreams.

The next morning, the waterfall across the bay is frothing white and magnificent. It roars and I find myself busting with joy at the sight of it. I reach for the phone and dial a local builder to make an appointment. I am glad I am here. I just have to extend the house a bit and it will all be fine.

Two weeks later, I feel a lump in my right breast.

12

'Can't feel anything,' a local doctor tells me the next day when I stop by his office to get it checked out.

He is late middle-aged, dry skinned, smells faintly of tobacco. His eyes are kind and he is unhurried. I sit up from the cracked old leather examination bed as he pulls the screen so I can dress in private.

'Great.'

Yippee, is what I'm thinking. But he insists on a mammogram and I go confidently around the corner to the clinic. A South African woman, distant, methodical, resists my efforts at chat. She walks out with the plates and returns to do another set. Just the right side this time.

'Anything wrong?'

'They were a bit blurry.'

'Right.'

The mammograms go directly to the doctor and I forget to ring to make another appointment.

The receptionist calls me two days later. 'When would you like to come in?'

'How about next week? I've got a lot on right now.'

'Can you make it any sooner?'

'Why? I'm sure there's nothing to worry about.'

'How about tomorrow?' she suggests, and a worm of fear wriggles uncomfortably in my stomach.

'Is there anything wrong?'

'Doctor will explain.'

The next day I return to the same little cubicle of an office, sit on a tired old chair, while 'Doctor' reads the diagnosis. I have put my mind back into a field of golden pumpkins with Canadian geese flying overhead, as I always do when I feel I may not cope with what is happening. So I am detached. Tough. If I don't accept what he's saying, maybe it will go away.

He hands me a referral to a specialist, tells me to call him if I can't get a quick appointment.

'Do you understand what you have to do?'

'I know all about it,' I say. 'My husband died of a brain tumour, my brother died from thymoma.'

'Thymoma? Rare.'

'Doesn't matter how rare if it's attached itself to you.'

He is silent.

I pay the bill and walk to the car where I sit and cry. I cannot help believing I have done this to myself, that I am being punished for sins of the past and present. I think back to a moment, months earlier, when I returned from the assignment on the *Queen Elizabeth 2*, sick and nervous because I hadn't spoken to the lover for four days. Wondering who was filling his idle hours. 'This is the kind of behaviour that could give you cancer,' I told myself.

I still have a sliver of hope. Benign. Maybe it is benign, not malignant. I dial Fleury and ask her to find the best breast cancer specialist in Sydney.

'Who needs one?'

'Me.'

'Ah shit.'

I refuse her offer of comfort, refuse to go to town to stay with her. I want to be at home.

So much for happy dreams and good omens. I am a moron. Only a genuinely deranged person would put their faith in flimsy superstition. Guided by the boys? Idiot.

All the old feelings of anger and despair come surging in. The more I turn to the lover for support, the more he withdraws.

'Of course I'll support you,' he says. But he doesn't return my phone calls. He is called away suddenly during lunch. I believe the excuses. Cannot grasp that nearly three intense years can mean nothing to him. I ignore the flashing hazard lights.

'Most men would walk away,' I say, testing his resolve.

'I wouldn't like to think I'm that kind of man.'

But he is, of course. He dallies around my edges a little longer, waiting for the final prognosis, before he finally, formally, quits.

There is never a moment when I think: 'Why me?' Not even the morning three weeks later when I get out of my hospital bed to take a shower and look at my lopsided body for the first time.

Outside, through the hospital window, life scuttles on as usual, people hurrying to work, traffic clogging, the sun coming up and setting. And yet for me, life will never be the same.

Two weeks earlier, a soft-voiced technician, overflowing with kindness, stabbed me with a long, thick needle at the edge of my nipple. It hurt like hell and tears filled my eyes but I did not flinch.

'Sorry. It's terrible, isn't it?' she said.

I wondered if she'd ever been done to, instead of doing to. Pumpkins. Geese. Sunset. It was harder to pick up my mind and carry it to a beautiful place.

Then the wait in the specialist's office, high above the outside world, in a room where the windows do not open, the air is recycled. Ahead of me are two other women who look like hunted animals. They do not read the pile of aged magazines on the coffee table. The one with a half-inch halo of grey before her hair bursts into jet black is weeping silently. I study the grey roots intently. What's the point of getting your hair dyed if you're going to die?

Is that it? Or perhaps age has been transformed into a blessing instead of a curse.

A much younger woman is with her, dressed like a hippie. Her daughter, I guess. She talks like a tour leader. I want to tell her to shut up. There is no way to distract a woman who is waiting for a death sentence.

The other woman is with her husband. She looks old and beaten. He is short, his belly pushed into a too tight beige sweater, chins wobbling on his chest, patches of grey whiskers his razor has missed. He wears synthetic trousers and short socks that reveal milky blue legs. He does not look at his wife. I suspect he hasn't looked at her for years. Do I imagine his impatience and annoyance? Does he blame his wife for being selfish, having the affrontery to get cancer and interrupt his day?

I pull a novel out of my handbag and tune out. I jump when my name is called and follow the specialist into his office. Benign? Malignant? One word, life. One word, death.

On my first visit here, a week earlier, to schedule the biopsy, I'd set the rules:

'I watched my brother go through chemotherapy so I don't want chemo. If things are that bad, I'd rather buy a ticket to Tuscany and sit out death with great food, good wine and Dean Martin belting out "Volare" on a bad sound system. OK?'

'Deal,' said the specialist, an affable, grey-haired man used to women placing their lives in the bowl of his hands.

Today, I sit still and silent, my back ramrod straight. I am dressed up. A simple soft, grey woollen dress, my best pearls, even earrings. Shiny black Italian leather boots. No armour, though, is going to change the outcome.

'So do I buy a ticket to Tuscany?' I ask when the silence begins to feel like I'm being smothered by a wet blanket.

He opens the folder, pulls out some papers clipped together. Looks at them. Takes a breath. Does not look at me.

'Yep. It's Tuscany,' he says, finally.

Someone lets off a thousand tiny birds in my stomach, all beating wildly to escape.

'Thought it might be like that.'

'I won't be able to save the breast.'

Already it is an anonymous appendage. *The* breast. Not *my* breast. Or save *your* breast. *The* breast.

'Oh well. I've got two.'

A lifetime of my mother's corny jokes, mostly inappropriate, swizzle in my head. I am appalled at my own words. Am I becoming my mother? A woman who makes light of other people's catastrophes and creates her own? I am outwardly stoic. Not a drama queen. Not like my mother. Or so I tell myself. But the feeble joke still rankles. Takes my mind off my verdict. The rotten punchline is quintessential Esther. And then, instantly: 'So what? I will be dead long before I fully develop her most irritating traits.'

'The tumour is directly underneath the nipple.'

Tumour. I absorb the word. Miss bits of what he's saying. Hear only that my right breast is scheduled for the trash can. I wonder if that is where it actually goes, tossed out like a piece of steak that's gone bad. Then vanity kicks in. My thinness has reduced my breasts by four sizes. To lose one will not be so noticeable. I become silently fixated on trivial detail. Because I cannot utter the one question I want to ask. 'What are my chances?' It is a form of denial. And I am extremely good at that.

'Do you understand what I'm saying?' the specialist asks.

Worried my silence means I am about to faint or do something undignified like cry, he leans forward and adds a little more loudly: 'We also have to take out most of the lymph nodes under your right arm, to see whether any are affected.'

'Oh yes. Quite. Don't worry. I understand. I've been through all this before. First with my brother, then my husband. I know the routine.'

As I speak, I see doors stretching down an endless corridor like a long line of piano keys, slamming in my face.

House plans? Slam.

Holiday plans? Slam.

Work plans? Slam.

Get a dog? Slam.

Life? Slam.

In a wave of nausea, I confront my own mortality and wipe out, in an instant, the human instinct to look ahead. The waiting begins. Granules of hope are hesitantly pushed across the table. Then snatched back.

'We won't know how far it's gone until after the operation.'

Hope. 'Can you take a shot? Guess?'

'No. But I think you've had the tumor a long time.'

No hope. Long time equals time to travel through the body.

'What's the worst case scenario?'

'It's progressed to the bone marrow.'

'What happens then?'

'For most people, it's chemo.'

'What's the success rate?'

'Varied.'

'I told you. Chemo is not on.'

'Let's worry about that if the time comes. We won't know until after surgery, until we see if it's progressed to the lymph nodes.'

This is the moment, I believe, that I shut down. I do not ask any critical questions. My chances of survival? What kind of breast cancer? I do not want to know. Detail equals pessimism. No more questions, Susan. You are in control. You will take on the fight. You will win. Statistics don't apply to you.

A silent mantra begins: 'I am strong and my body is strong. I am strong and my body is strong.' With the first flicker of doubt, slip into the mantra, over and over again. Switch off the mad monkey spinning in my head. Laughing. Pointing. Sneering. *You brought it on yourself, Miss Fitz-Twiddle* – which was my husband Paul's name for me when he wanted to criticise.

I do not fear death, I understand in a flash. Cannot imagine the nothingness of it. I fear being ill and in pain far more. I know I will not go searching for miracle cures if the worst case scenario eventuates. I travelled that path with my brother. I saw, too, the ravages of successively more potent chemotherapy treatments and made the vow back then, naively, that if I were ever in the same situation, I would not go down that path. But that was then. This is now. My turn. Creeping around in a dark world of shifting sands where there are no straight answers. No matter what the outcome, there will never be another day that I will breeze through airily, another day lightly taken for granted.

I go through the process of scheduling surgery like a sleep-walker, feeling detached. The specialist's secretary avoids my eyes, and deals matter-of-factly with the details.

Seven to ten days in hospital.

Fine.

Is there anyone at home to look after me after surgery?

No.

Whom should they call in the event of an emergency?

My mother? No. A distantly located cousin? No. Work colleagues? No. The lover? NO!

Fleury, I finally decide. Good, strong, loyal, smart, the kind of woman who anticipates problems and solves them so successfully before they erupt that not many people understand how much she quietly does for them. And a friend, a wonderful, dear, funny, completely non-judgemental friend.

I walk out of the specialist's office, buy a bottle of French champagne and meet Pia at a hairdresser's in Darlinghurst. We laugh and joke our way through a cut, streaks and the wine. I am manic and a little crazy and Donald, the hairdresser, looks at us warily.

'What's going on, girls?' he asks.

'Nothing!'

'I'm missing something and you know how I hate that.'

'It's ok, Donald, nothing serious. Little trip to the hospital ahead. Nothing serious.'

If only.

It is late in the afternoon and Donald lets his little Jack Russell terrier, Lucy, come into the main part of the salon from her bed downstairs. Lucy is outrageous, cheeky, full of herself, a shocking flirt and she goes about getting her own way with the confidence of a beautiful woman. I watch her and I do not think about cancer.

'Where did you get Lucy?'

Donald gives me a card with the breeder's name, anxious that I, too, should have a little Lucy clone in my life. I put it in my handbag with the receipt for the hairdressing bill and forget about it.

Pia and I stumble out of the salon into the cold dark of a windy June night, streaked, smooth and shiny. Not a grey root in sight. Who would guess a little hard lump, no bigger than a pea, a slow growing, insidious little bastard, lurks under my nipple, threatening all?

'Will you be ok? Do you want to stay in town?' she asks.

'No. I want to get home.'

'What about dinner somewhere? You need company.'

'Don't be a dope. I'm fine.'

I laugh and smile, wave goodbye. As I slam the car door behind me, though, I cave in, suddenly limp. The effort of *toujours gai*, *toujours brave*, is exhausting. I want to wind back the clock. Return to innocence. Snatch back the security of believing death is a nebulous, distant issue (and never mine?).

I go home, not out to dinner as I once would have done. I do not want to be around friends. I want my home. I want the peace of Lovett Bay. I want the sound of the waterfall to put me to sleep. I want to wake up and watch the early morning sun turn the escarpment a burning orange. It is the physical world I crave, it is the physical world that I will most regret leaving. Already Lovett Bay has become my sanctuary. I will not give it up. Not for a long, long time. Not until I am too old, like Gordon, to get on a boat or carry the shopping up the steps. And even then, I think, I will find a way.

I sleep that night in fits and starts with the light burning constantly. It becomes a habit, to leave the light on. Waking from sleep, I want instant reality, not the mystery of darkness.

Insects ping against the lampshade, drawn irresistibly towards the fiery centre of the light bulb, and death. A pile of books lies untouched on the bedside table. Ruth Park. William Styron. Isabel Allende. Old favourites. But words that once inspired now seem to ring a different knell.

My mind flutters, screams, races. Is never calm. All the old cliches spin through my head: Regrets? Finest moments? Worst moments? And ultimately, the big one: What the hell is it all about?

I get up in the witching hour, around 3 am, when everything seems at its worst, and raid the bookshelves once more, seeking comfort this time, not escape. I pick up a slim volume that promises to help me find my guardian angel. I have no idea where it came from, have never seen it before. I take it as an omen and read for two hours before tossing it in the bin. If there is little time left, the banal is untenable.

Find the strength within, I tell myself. After almost a lifetime of 'take the risk but hook up the safety net', I am flying without a harness. This time, there is no fallback position. I switch off the lamp in the pewter light of dawn, reciting my mantra. *I am strong and my body is strong*. Again and again until it puts me to sleep.

Next morning, on the way to work, it is raining and I get wet racing from the water taxi to the car, but I don't care. The traffic is bad but it doesn't irk. At the office, someone is in my parking space and I do not even swear. I press the button for the elevator just once, even though it takes a long time to arrive. Already, my view of the world has changed. Don't sweat the small stuff.

I stride down the long corridors of the office, where the carpet is as grey as the air, past desks with empty screens and teetering piles of files. Here and there a head bends over a newspaper, the rich smell of coffee and fresh toast hovers fragrantly.

'Morning.'

The ritual greetings. Check out the eyes. Who has a hangover? Not me for once. The corner office is empty. The boss, a shimmering blonde with perfect lips, is late. Probably at the gym.

In Lego cubicles along the western wall, voices rise and fall on telephones. Stories bought and sold, pictures bargained for, souls for hire to the highest bidder. I once sat in a room where the father of a boy, only moments dead, called to sell his story. At the time, it didn't even shock me. It was a common enough scenario. Money, always money, the ultimate temptress, the final corrupter.

All day I sit in my cell and go through the motions, harbouring my little secret. *Toujours gai.*

As I pull on my coat to leave at the scheduled time of 5.30 pm instead of working late, I stick my head into the editor's office.

'I'll be needing a bit of personal time.'

'Why?' Not when.

'I'm having a breast lopped off.'

My voice wobbles. Which makes me furious. I turn to leave but she jumps up, a long, lean figure in tight black, gold jewellery, a huge, flashing diamond ring. She grabs my arm, leading me to a seat. Sits on the edge of her desk framed by a gigantic vase of powerfully perfumed oriental lilies. The smell is sickly.

'What's going on?'

The compassion in her tone nearly brings me undone.

'Breast cancer. Have to have a breast removed. Just take a few days. Shouldn't be away for long.'

'Are you sure of the diagnosis? Have you had a second opinion?'

'I'm sure.'

'What's the prognosis?'

'Don't know. Won't know until after surgery.'

'Are you frightened?'

'Oh no. Not a bit. It's much easier to deal with your own mortality than to face losing people you love.'

But it's a lie. They are both devastating.

Two weeks later, I check into hospital. Two weeks in which every twinge I feel becomes evidence of advanced cancer, every sleepless night a time to watch the flickering black and white rerun of my life and wonder how I should have done it differently.

A little thin, nervy man who looks vaguely familiar takes my details across a scratched reception counter and leads me to my hospital room. He chats away and I suddenly slot him into place.

'Did you have a plant nursery once, near the Blue Mountains?'

'Yeah.' But he is wary.

'I used to buy a lot of plants from you. How long have you worked here?' Idle chat, trivia. Anything to deflect attention from what will happen later in the day.

I think back. He landscaped a section of my garden a few houses ago, filling it with diseased plants. Every morning, waking with excitement, I'd race out to the herbaceous borders expecting a river of flowers only to find collapsed foliage, fungus-ridden roots. When I called to ask him the problem, he told me it was heat. The weather. High summer. Too much water. Not enough water. Now he tells me his marriage is over. He has sold his business. He seems broken.

He does not offer to carry my bag, which is filled with new pyjamas. Ones that don't need two breasts to look right.

'It's a wonderful room,' he says. 'Light, comfortable. Carpet on the floor. Curtains. Views. The best room in the hospital. But you have to share it until we can get you a private room. Probably in a couple of days.'

It is like being shown a hotel room but there's no mini bar, no fridge and check-out time isn't negotiable. The air is old and thick. The much-praised carpet has a large dark stain. The bed crackles with plastic underlay when I press it. The artwork is a metal panel with cords trailing from it – one to change the level of the bed, the other to call for help. The view directly across the road is of the hospice. I see it immediately and try never to look at it again. I am *not* going there. That is *not* my future. But sometimes at night, when I see the glow of a light burning until dawn, I think I understand that someone is trying to blaze away the spectre of death.

The day I arrive I stay in my street clothes for as long as possible, sitting and reading a book in the recliner chair by the bed. Nurses come and go, blood samples are taken, vital signs recorded. Allergies noted. I'm tagged like a steer for slaughter.

'Hi, I'm Maggie. You can get changed now.'

I look up from the pages of a novel I've read before. I want to know endings now, before I begin. Happily ever after or don't pick up the book. Suspense is no longer a thrill.

A nurse holds one of those white cotton robes with ties at the back. 'Put this on and get into bed. I'll be back in a minute.'

I want to shout that it's the middle of the day and nobody goes to bed at this time unless they're sick. And I don't feel sick. Tired, but not sick. That's the worst damned bit of it. Nothing tangible to fight. But I am silent. She is kind and happy. It's her fortieth birthday. A woman turning forty and she's excited.

So far the second bed has remained empty. 'Who's going into the other bed?' I ask the nurse when she returns.

'Woman with a brain tumour.'

'What stage?' Questions I do not dare to ask of my own condition.

'Not good.'

'How old?' Age. The new issue.

'Sixties. About.'

Maggie rolls up the rubber blood pressure bag, cool fingers lightly find the pulse in my wrist. She counts the seconds on her watch.

'Someone else did all this a while ago.'

'Yep. And it's going to happen on the hour, every hour, day and night for a while. Better get used to it, love.'

She pats my arm, tells me she'll be back with an injection shortly. Pethidine. The happy drug. Something to look forward to.

While I wait for nirvana, my room-mate is wheeled in, her hair caught up in a cotton cap, her face white and frail. She is slid from one bed to another, lightly, as though she has already shed most of her body. As soon as the nurses leave, her husband, daughter and son creep in, form a human chain around the bed, holding hands, heads bent. The daughter begins a prayer.

I don't want to be here. This grief and love is private. For what they are doing is saying farewell.

Surgery is scheduled for 2 pm. Unlike most schedules, this one is running on time. The pethidine shot calms me although it does not change reality, as I'd hoped. But by the time I am moved from stationary bed to mobile bed for the journey to the operating theatre, I feel everyone is my new best friend.

'Pethidine?' asks a nurse, pushing the bed from behind my head.

'Yup.' I am giggling.

'Great, isn't it?'

Above me, the ceiling spins wildly as I'm pushed around corners, into elevators. Bang. Bump. The nurses chat. Romance. Holidays. What's for dinner. I engage complete strangers in disjointed conversation. I remember many of them smiling down at me. Pity and humour in their eyes.

Then the countdown. A whack on my hand, find the vein, a jab. The sickening smell of anaesthetic, spotlights overhead.

'Count backwards from ten.' Voices are friendly, as though we've known each other for years.

I make it to seven and blackness descends.

I am angry when a woman's voice cuts through my world of peace, calling my name. I want her to go away. Shut up.

'Susan. Wake up. Can you hear me? Susan!'

Her voice gets closer and closer. Something big and heavy, suffocating, is shoved on my face. I try to push it away.

'You're hyperventilating, Susan. Can you hear me? Just breathe slowly. Slowly.'

I open my eyes and they are already filled with tears. I cannot remember a dream. Cannot understand my grief. The oxygen mask is heavy on my face.

'Good girl. That's it. Slow breath. Relax.'

I feel like a child, defenceless. I want to give someone my life, give away the whole responsibility and weight of it. A young face swims into focus. Bright and cheerful, young enough to be my own child.

'What's your name?'

'Susan.'

'Where do you live?'

'Lovett Bay.'

'Ok. We're just going to leave you here for a while, until the anaesthetic wears off. Then we'll take you to your room, ok? If you need anything just call.'

I wake up when I am being gently dragged onto the bed in my room. The ties on the hospital robe come undone and I feel exposed amongst strangers. Someone quickly covers me. I want to say thank you but I can't get the words to move further than my brain.

There are tubes in my hand, tubes in my chest, tubes filled with rainbow coloured fluids.

'Press this for pain.'

A little black cylinder is squeezed into my hand and my thumb placed on a red button. Press for escape.

'Don't worry, you can't overdose. It's self-regulating.'

There is hardly any pain but I press it all night, every time I wake. It is bliss to be able to gas the monkey at will. A small reprieve from the moment I will have to look down at my chest, note the new body formation.

Mid-morning the other bed has a new client. She is young and beautiful and her parents hover like hummingbirds. Her boyfriend slithers in and leaves as quickly as is decent. When she is alone, I say hello.

'What are you here for?'

'Breast reduction,' she says, eyes shining brightly.

'Oh.'

Then I recover enough to continue. 'But why?'

'People always look at my breasts, never my face.'

'Are you sure? You have a lovely face and a lovely body.'

Before we can continue, two nurses arrive to measure her vital signs. She goes off and returns hours later. She sleeps quietly through the early evening.

That night, very late, I hear panic in a nurse's voice as she stops by to do the hourly check. Buzzers are pressed, feet stampede down the corridor, there is a team around the young woman's bed in minutes. Equipment is hurtled through the door. Shock treatment. Then drugs.

'Come on, Genevieve, come on.' Urging, willing a response.

Her first words when she is revived are very clear: 'I'm so cold. I'm really, really cold.'

Is that what happens when you die? You feel colder and colder until there is only cold?

She'd overdosed. Someone forgot to record a second dose of painkiller administered before they brought her back to the ward from the operating theatre, and she nearly died. For smaller breasts.

Her boyfriend, if that's who she was really having the reduction for, does not visit her again. And then she goes home.

After a few days, hospital begins to feel like a safe haven. No need to think about being different yet. Everyone around me is branded in some way. Body parts are whisked out as quickly as a floating hair in a bowl of soup. Everyone wears pyjamas all day, most people wheel a steel pole with a plastic bag full of fluid attached. Daytime is bedtime, and so is night-time. It is a nether world.

There is no way of knowing how far cancer has progressed until after surgery and pathology on the lymph nodes removed from under the arm, so waiting for pathology results is terrible. More terrible to me than losing a breast. That was just a body part. Pathology will tell me if I have a chance of survival or if I should join the queue of the condemned.

After two days I ask the surgeon when he visits for the daily check-up if there are any results.

He is snappish. 'If I had news I'd tell you.'

It is the hope and fear mingled nakedly on my face, I think, that he finds difficult. But I ask again on the third day. Nervous now, that I will make him angry.

'I told you I'd tell you immediately. As soon as I know.'

I want to scream at him. Slap him. I have a right to ask! It is my future!

He checks the tubing running from under the skin where my breast once was, he feels the bones.

I ask him how his day has gone.

'Operated on a twenty-one year old this morning. Twenty-one!'

Slap. Perspective in a flash.

On the fourth day, I do not ask. But when he sits by the bed and sandwiches my hand in his, I can hardly breathe.

'One lymph node affected,' he says. 'And only the smallest trace measurable. Nothing really. A minute trace.'

'What does that mean?' At last I can ask.

'Not the best case scenario. But the second best case scenario.'

I had prepared myself for the worst in all the usual ways, the ways I had indulged in when the boys died, when grief had so overwhelmed me death seemed the only escape. 'Death is part of life,' I'd told myself. 'Remember the Buddhist who told Sophia – everything that is born must die. It might be my turn. Everyone has a turn. Face it. But don't give in to it.'

His words send me into a giddy spin of euphoria. Normal, I think, life can be normal again. Wind back the clock. A second chance. Thank you, God. I am dizzy with relief.

The surgeon snatches back control, steadies my euphoria. 'Of course there is no way of knowing what is ahead. All it takes is for one little cell to get through the lymph system to metastasise. There are no guarantees. Getting through the first two years without a recurrence is a start but we don't give you the all-clear until you've been cancer-free for five years.'

'All-clear?'

'Well, there's never a complete all-clear. We never know what's ahead, do we?'

He stands, takes my hand. 'So go home and enjoy life.'

The words sound ominous. I am on a slippery dip, hurtling towards hope only moments before plunging into despair. I look for hidden meanings in every word, study faces like I'll be examined on them. I am frantic and erratic. Which I disguise with a public mask of good cheer. *Toujours gai*.

The lover visits once. Quickly, in the early morning, on his way to the airport, which gives him an excuse to rush or he'll miss the plane. An international flight. He'll be gone for two weeks. His face, usually a featureless mask, registers shock when he sees me reach for a glass of water with the arm that no longer segues into a breast. My movement is slow and painful. Crippled. It is the moment, I think, when he finally understands everything has changed. It is the moment I understand the affair is over. It takes a while longer to accept it.

Eight days after surgery, I beg to be allowed out. The surgeon wants me to stay another two days. We compromise on one more day.

A lovely friend we all call the Witch, my brother-in-law's beautiful, voluptuous partner, takes me home, driving through a Saturday morning world. It is pristine, sharp, vibrant. All my senses are raging, picking up smells, colour, shape and shade. The great big black hat of doom has lifted at least a little. There is time, who knows how long, to begin again. Another chance. Don't blow it. Not this time. Because it's my last chance.

Kay, a friend and colleague, insists on coming to stay for my first week at home after surgery. I fight her but she is short, tough, opinionated, a genuine earth mother who never had children of her own. She bustles in anyway, loaded with fresh fish and vegetables, all sorts of herbs, crusty bread. A feast after brown paper hospital fare. We settle into a cosy daily routine of late breakfasts and early dinners. Each afternoon, we both take a book to our bedrooms. Kay sleeps though, long and deep, lulled by the tranquillity of Lovett Bay, the cessation of city sounds. I read.

I have long finished the hoard of Donna Leon, who writes exquisite whodunits set in Venice, and moved on to food and travel. I want only to touch the surface of life. Steer well away from the big issues. But in truth, I do not read much until darkness overlays the outside world and all I can see when I stare out the window is a reflection of my thin white face. Do I just imagine that I look ephemeral?

Even then, for a while, I tune in to the sound of evening. The fishwife screeching of white cockatoos reduces to a satisfied cluck. Noisy miners, nondescript brown and grey, do not slow down before bed but race from tree to tree, rowdy as a classroom full of teenagers. There's a final glissando from a full-throated magpie and, if I am lucky, a flash of emerald green and brilliant red as the king parrots wing home. It is the kookaburras, though, who ring the bell for lights out when they have their last laugh for the day. A lazy, deep-bellied laugh lacking the high-pitched, raucous joy of daybreak.

I read until Kay calls dinner is ready and we sit down to a beautifully set table, candles lit, as though we are celebrating. After what feels like a lifetime of drinking wine with food, I reach for a glass of water. It's time to change old habits but it is hard to be sociable without the crutch. And the evenings are full with time, when they used to slip away as fast as the wine.

Most days the phone rings regularly. Concerned friends, great friends. Their support means so much. They schlepped briskly through the hospital, arms full of flowers, hearts full of compassion, with lots of advice. Carrot juice. Apple juice. Vitamins. Chinese herbalists. Acupuncture. On and on. If it was that easy, I think, why do so many people die?

On her last day, Kay makes tortilla the detailed, traditional Spanish way she learned when she lived in Spain. By the time her husband arrives to take her home, it is golden and fragrant with garlic, rich with potatoes and eggs. It is the most delicious dish I have ever eaten. I devour an omelet that could satisfy four people.

Kay laughs happily. Her husband is wide-eyed. Kay feels the tortilla vindicates her visit. Her husband leaves a dish of lentils he has prepared, Chilean style. To build my strength, he tells me. And I want to cry.

It feels abso-bloody-lutely sensational to be out of the airless cocoon of the hospital, where illness and darkness are the norm. Away from the fetid stench of leaking bodies, a stench no amount of disinfectant can disguise. I wear a little woollen prosthesis that

I slip into the empty cup of my bra for the first three months after surgery. It's a pink satin covered lump and I hate it. I have already asked the surgeon if I might have the second breast removed.

He thinks I am frightened of a recurrence. But it is the thought of a fake body part that is repulsive. He tells me to wait a while. Think about it. But I am determined. I want no part of the little silicone blob that I am fitted for five months later, when the long, livid scar has healed. It comes in a pastel blue box, overprinted with sentimental twaddle about life, wonderful life. It is soft and pink and looks like a jellyfish. Every night I remove it from the pocket in my new, specialised bra and tuck it back into the box. So it will retain its perfect, perky shape.

When I lie down during the day, it shoots up defiantly while my other breast swells softly over the side of my rib cage. I give it a name. Tom Tit. Sometimes, I forget to wear it. Forget I need it. Because I have stopped looking in mirrors and do not notice the single lump where there used to be two.

Once you've had cancer it creeps around your mind like a whis-pery guilty conscience. Before every visit to the surgeon for a check-up, a niggling dread builds like a tropical thunderstorm. What is this lump? Why this ache? Minor physical discomforts, once so easily shrugged off, are filled with threat. Is it back? Am I already hurtling down the highway to death? I have rejected chemo but the pressure is on. I'm given case histories. One lived. One died. But statistics can be spun to mean what you want, can't they?

Memories of my brother lying in hospital, a drip drizzling a poisonous chemical cocktail through collapsing veins, surge into my mind every time I am pushed by one friend or another to have this drastic treatment. I spoke to John every day during treatments when I lived in Sydney and he in Melbourne. I listened to his voice weaken to nearly nothing. Once, he could barely speak.

'What's happened?' I asked.

'Had a bit of a bad night. Ripped the tubes out of my chest in my sleep.'

Nurses found him wandering the corridors, bleeding and hallucinating, trying to find his way home. The treatment, I suspect, had become harder to bear than the disease. But after they calmed him and put him back to bed he allowed the nurse to hook him to the drip once more because he was brave and his will to live was massive.

My case, though, is so different from his. Is the choice between chemo or no chemo really life and death? The surgeon has told me I am a borderline case. No lymph nodes contaminated means no chemo. Miniscule contamination? Up to me to make the decision. He also says he thinks a five year course of tamoxifen, two little pills a day to suppress my body's estrogen, will suffice.

'Hell,' I say, when he tells me about the pills, 'never thought I'd be so happy to be booked for the next five years!'

But a work colleague, high powered and persuasive, will not drop the case for chemo: 'Just go and talk to the oncologist.' She has done the research, like a good journalist, and she insists I write down a name and phone number. After two fraught days of weighing the odds, I make an appointment.

In the oncologist's waiting room wonderful paintings hang on the walls, fresh flowers grace coffee tables and lifestyle magazines – the succour of modern living – are piled high. I read directions on how to plant a *magnolia grandiflora* for future generations, learn the best thread count for bed linen, check out the newest trends in lighting. Anything to escape looking at the rows of filing cabinets behind the receptionist's counter. So many cabinets, so many files. Is there an epidemic? How many living, how many close to death, or dead?

I have not dressed up for this appointment. All I want is a healthy body. A healthy body turns rags into raiment.

When a door opens, a round-faced woman with dark brown hair and a cheery smile calls my name. She stands to one side and indicates a seat alongside her desk.

She wriggles around in her chair until she's comfortable and then pulls a file towards her, opening it to a letter from the surgeon. She gives the impression she's reading it for the first time, and perhaps she is.

'What would you do?' I ask her.

She sighs and leans back in her chair, swivelling in quarter-turns. She taps her bottom lip with a ballpoint pen then puts the pen down. Leans forward so her elbows are on the desk and her body is almost fully turned to me.

'I would have the treatment,' she says.

'Why? I'm told I'm a borderline case.'

'Because you have two types of cancer cells. One a greater risk than the other.'

I do not ask any more questions. I agree to the treatment and make an appointment for a couple of days after my forty-ninth birthday. I'm expecting to have lunch with the lover. He's never forgotten a birthday.

That night I call Sophia, seeking courage. No, seeking more than courage. I want her approval, I want her to tell me I am taking the best course. I want to believe that she has some magic power so that if she says *good girl* it will mean all will be well. Because I feel like I am spinning in a whirlpool of rage and confusion. There are no straightforward answers – or *clean* answers, as I come to call them. Will chemo guarantee I beat cancer? No, there are no guarantees. Is tamoxifen enough? There is no way of knowing. Can I be sure a little cluster of cells isn't already mutating somewhere else in my body? No.

At some point I begin to understand that my grip on life will always be tenuous. As it is in reality. Except that's not how we're taught to regard it. Life is blithely taken for granted by most of us – until it is threatened.

'My sense of security is gone,' I tell Sophia on the phone.

'Well, that's not a bad way to live,' she says.

'Next you're going to tell me it's another bloody gift!'

She laughs her big, fat, gorgeous belly laugh.

'Ah, darlin'. That's exactly what it is. Only fools think they're promised more than the moment they're in. And the only absolute cure for life is death.'

13

THE LOVER DUMPS ME formally at my birthday lunch. A lunch he does not confirm until the last minute.

When it seems like he will not call, I go to the juice shop at the organic grocery and order the drink with fresh garlic in the carrot and celery. It reeks all around me, all over me. But it makes me feel healthy. Then the phone rings and it's the lover and I regret the juice immediately. Lover before health, I ask myself? Surely not. That would be insanity.

'Are we having lunch or not?' he asks.

Why don't I just terminate the call, press a tiny button and zoom him into space forever? 'Yeah. Sure. Where?'

My phone drops out. Low battery. A chance to drive on, begin again as I promised myself I would. But I call back. 'Quick. Where?'

We make a time and place and the phone goes dead again.

I wear my uniform of jeans, loose shirt, Pia's discarded wind-cheater with its rusting steel buttons. I want to be interesting and sexual, revel in my last white napkin lunch before beginning chemo. But I feel I have passed my use-by date. I cannot even conjure up a smile. *Toujours gai* is gone forever. Soon I will be bald, without eyebrows and eyelashes, stamped as a person who now belongs to a different club.

The restaurant is beautiful, white tablecloths, perfectly tweaked table napkins, glittering glass. Lots of pale wood and slim waiters in black. The prettier the waiters, I think, the higher the price. We have dined here before. Often. The first time, I wore a mid-calf length flowing dress, my hair was freshly washed and styled, my shoes polished. I felt a million bucks as I walked down the staircase into the room. The lover introduced me to the owner, who ordered a bottle of wine and sat with us for a while, talking food, Italy, music. Life was always an event with the lover.

But it is winter now. Sunny and cold with clouds building over the silhouette of the CBD and we have a table on the deck. There are plastic blinds and gas heaters but it is still cold out here, and the view through the plastic is gluey. I keep my rusty jacket on to stay warm – or perhaps to hide a pink satin breast that often moves too high or low, giving the game away.

I read a menu that once tantalised but I have no appetite. The thought of swallowing makes me feel ill. I order fish because I think it is healthy but I have never enjoyed fish. I've always been a lamb or steak girl by choice.

I let the waiter fill my glass with wine and feel a sudden thrill at being careless of my physical well-being. I drink it recklessly and the cacophony in my head mutes instantly. Within a few minutes, I am quite drunk. It feels wonderful. Like days of old. Steady. Steady. But the second glass is gulped and it is enough to make me throw caution to the wind.

The lover reaches beside his chair and puts a shopping bag in front of me.

'Happy birthday.'

When I open it I find two books, one about the destruction of love, another about dogs.

'Trying to tell me something?' I ask. Another gulp, another empty glass. Because I know he is.

A conversation, years earlier, about the right way to end an affair: 'Never a phone call,' he told me. 'You go to lunch. At least.' And yet I cannot believe this is the official moment. It is my birthday, for God's sake. I have just lost a breast. I am about to begin chemo. How hard is it to give me one frivolous day to sustain me through the next few months?

He shifts in his chair, trying to make himself taller by straightening his back. The expression on his face is almost neutral but not quite. There is a hint of power. He drums the fingers of one hand – short fat fingers, I see with sudden clarity, when once I only noticed the buffed, clean shine of a recent manicure. He looks like an actor about to break into the defining soliloquy of the play.

'All my relationships eventually come to an end,' he says.

And I cannot remember anything else. I turn to reach for the wine and knock over the ice bucket. Ice slithers across the floor. Other diners stare. Waiters rush over to fix the mess, defuse whatever they sense is going on.

But I do not make a scene. I have never made scenes. I do not cry. I try for a line that is light (my mother again!) but come up with one that I am ashamed of to this day: 'I gave it everything I had. I guess it wasn't enough.' Jesus, where were the violins?

I see his jaw jut a little more. Power. Control. And I fall off the shaky edge of what I thought was love into hate and anger. Such a fine line. Passion of a different kind.

'We'll always be friends,' I say, but I'm lying. Because I'd rather see him dead.

When the waiter comes by with a fresh glass and bottle, I ask for the dessert menu. This time the lover is shocked and cannot fake neutrality. Was I supposed to get up and leave? Break down? What did all the other women before me do?

I slowly swallow every last mouthful of dessert. He can bloody well wait. But I am seriously drunk with an irresistible desire to get even drunker, to obliterate the event until I reach a stage where I cannot even remember where I am, who I am with. My wine goes down in gulps and I demand my glass be refilled.

The lover gets more and more aloof but never impatient. Even the stubby, drumming fingers are still. The performance of the damned has him riveted.

I look at him after what seems like only minutes and notice city lights with rain halos. Outside it is now dark and wet. I am deliciously, almost paralytically drunk, the stench of wine mingling unhappily with the raw garlic of my juice. At some point I hazily remember my mother, here for my birthday party, is waiting for me in a nearby restaurant where she is lunching with friends.

I stagger to my feet, thanking him for lunch, politely, like someone I don't know well, and leave. Just before I reach the door onto the street, I turn and ask him to call the restaurant where my mother waits. 'Tell them to get my mother to stand outside, that I'll be there in a moment.'

He nods. He is anxious to be away now. I suspect he has another date. Drinks with the new mistress. Poor cow. I hope she is stronger than me, that she gives him a run. But I doubt it.

I stagger the two blocks to my mother and then make her drive us to Church Point. Which is a pig of a thing to do. At home, she rarely drives further than her local shopping centre, which is three minutes away, and if she meets an oncoming car, it's a heavy traffic day. We're in Sydney city peak hour, Friday night traffic. It's a zoo.

She accelerates/brakes all the way home through rain and wind, never letting the speedo jump beyond forty kilometres while I fill the car with great big bellowing howls. She thinks I am going to tell her I have not long to live and she is silent.

Church Point appears around the final bend, familiar, friendly, like a safe haven. All the car spaces are taken, as usual, so I tell her to park illegally. By now, I have slid the afternoon into another part of my mind, to be taken out and dealt with later. I think I am being strong, but I am still just monumentally drunk.

A year later, I ask a shrink how I can go through a truly terrible situation and, not long after, behave as though nothing has happened.

He suggests I learned early to suppress unbearable truths, to compartmentalise.

'Men seem to be born with that facility,' I tell him, thinking of the lover.

The shrink looks at me sharply. '*Some* of them are experts,' he says.

I let the subject drop.

The Point shimmers in the wet. Tinnies joggle and clunk in the faint swell, tied side by side like Turkish slippers. The rain strobes through streetlights and textures the night, heavy enough to frost the water.

People in mustard, red, white and blue wet weather gear huddle under shelter, beers in their hands, unworried by the weather. This is Friday, the end of the working week, always a big night at The Point.

I scan the hooded faces. Who will help? Boxes to unload and an arm still tender where the lymph nodes have been removed, a chest where the scar is still a ruby slash. And my mother, nearly eighty. With swollen ankles and a bottom lip shaking from exhaustion and fear for her daughter.

'Matty,' I scream from the car, 'can you look after my mother?'

Matty is the man you call for any job too big to do yourself – rubbish removal, sandstone paving, bobcat work, new fireplace, even a sculpture installation. He is nowhere near forty but looks older, a once handsome face blurred by years of hell-raising. 'Matty's boys', as they are known, hover around him, a ragged collection. The core is Big Jack, the muscle, Scotty, the doer, and Bob, the fisherman. Others flitter on the periphery, slippery eyed, coming and going.

'Yeah, mate,' he says, his long thin legs blue with cold. A cigarette hanging from his purple fingers, a stubbie in his other hand. It would take a blizzard, I think, or a court case, to get Matty into long trousers.

He takes a last lung-busting drag on his smoke, sculls the dregs of beer from the bottle. With the style of the ritziest doorman, he ushers my mother into the Church Point world: 'C'mon on then, mate,' he says, holding out a work-stained hand.

My mother feathers up like a happy chook, smiles flirtatiously, flutters her eyelashes, slides her taloned hand across as though she's waiting for Matty to slip a ring on her finger. It's the kind of attention she loves. She whisks her fears into the bottom drawer of her mind and becomes, for a moment, a beautiful young woman again. The kind men fawned over and whose hearts she ruthlessly sliced to bits. Matty glides her down the jetty as though she's a fragile, ancient duchess.

Matty's boys, almost synchronised, finish their beers and come over to me like unsteady soldier crabs. Without a word, they take the boxes of wine and the shopping, two at a time, and in minutes the water taxi is ready for take-off. There will be a parking ticket, but does that matter? Money, once so carefully hoarded, has become a tool instead of a master. Might not have a future to save for.

'Will you be all right, mate, at the other end?' Matty asks.

He has seen my swollen face. No questions, though, that might intrude. The Pittwater way.

'Yeah. Thanks, Matty. Owe you a beer.'

'Yeah, mate.'

His long skinny legs pick their way back to the bottle shop. His boys close in around him halfway up the jetty, like a dark cloak.

The rain has stopped and the water is a black satin sheet. I watch the fantail of the water taxi's wake and think about swimming to the great big Pacific Ocean and sinking deeper and deeper until I disappear. And then a sliver of relief slips in. After the dozen or so half-hearted attempts to end the affair over the years, he has finally severed the cord. No more worrying about where he is, what he is doing, why he isn't returning calls. He loves me. He loves me not. It's a big fat not.

The wine and shopping are piled onto Ken's dock and I leave it all there. I'll deal with it in the morning. If it rains again, too bad. I'll get every guest at my birthday party – a quickly thrown together celebration – to carry a couple of bottles on their arrival.

That night, even my mother's snoring does not wake me. But the relief is turning back into anger. And, ever so cunningly, I slip away from the fear of cancer into the rage of the wronged.

The next morning there are questions in my mother's narrowed eyes as we sit over tea and toast at the kitchen table. I have the post-binge blues, a drilling headache. Red eyes, smeared mascara and, under the mascara, the old, dark shadows of self-abuse. Get through today. Tomorrow will be better. But tomorrow is the party. A final fling before treatment. I curse the stupid impulse. And the next day? Chemo. I feel shaky and out of control. Blame the alcohol. But there is no-one to call, no matter how unreliable, with news. No sharing. Even the illusion of a relation-ship is gone.

My mother tells me firmly that she prefers coffee to tea, so I reboil the kettle and make her a pot.

'Instant,' she says, 'will do in future.'

'I had an affair, you know.' As though saying it out loud will somehow give it substance.

'Had?'

'He ended it. Yesterday.'

'Oh, is that all it was,' she says lightly. 'I thought it was about something serious, you know, like dying or something.' She adds a casual aside: 'Anyway, men don't like mutilation.'

I scrabble for her meaning. Is she saying they are weak and can't cope with illness? Or that I am no longer desirable in any way?

She gets up and goes to her suitcase to get me my birthday present. It's a lace and satin teddy with matching knickers. Fragile. Feminine. Sexy. The style of top that will hang flatly and therefore emphasise where there is no longer any breast.

I say thank you and wrap it up again. A few months later I throw it in the St Vinnie's clothing bin. Now I know where I get my appalling ability to choose the wrong gifts.

Six days later, I wander around the rabbit warren corridors of Royal North Shore Hospital, searching for the right room for chemo treatment.

'It's an omen,' I tell Pia when I call her on the mobile, panicked, lost, afraid of what I am about to begin.

'What do you mean, an omen?'

'I'm not meant to have this treatment.'

'What do you mean, "meant"?'

'I just don't know what to do. What's right, what's wrong.'

'Well, why don't you ask someone for directions and make up your mind when you find the place?' Pragmatic as ever.

'Yeah, ok. I'll do that.'

'Do you want me to drive over and come with you?'

Of course I do. I'm looking for comfort. A gentle hand to hold on to mine and tell me all will be well. That there is life everlasting no matter what. But there are no fairy godmothers. No magic wands. None that work, anyway.

'Nah. I'll be ok.'

At the main desk I query a harassed receptionist. She directs me through grey, glossy painted labyrinths signed well enough for me to find the way.

At another desk, another receptionist hands me forms to complete. Once again, the actor in me has kicked in. I am bright, look controlled. But the staff here have seen every kind of behaviour, every frail defence. I don't think they are fooled.

There's an illusion of normality in the chemo ward. A tea room, with sandwiches and biscuits. Even cake. The more terrible the treatment, the better the goodies? I eat insatiably. Cheese and tomato on white bread, biscuits I haven't seen since childhood. Scotch Fingers. Milk Coffee. And then a chubby faced nurse calls my name.

I step from earth to a strange new planet where people sit around grey-faced and silent in large vinyl armchairs that hiss with every wriggle. Violently coloured drips hang from steel poles. Thin wires of life? Or delaying death a little longer?

No-one reads. Heads are dropped weakly on chests or turned to look out grey tinted windows over even greyer rooftops. Doing a silent stocktake of the past, perhaps? Not daring to dream of the future?

I do not talk to anyone. Look covertly at who has hair, who wears a scarf to disguise baldness, who looks well and is therefore just starting treatment. Who looks ill and frail and already half dead.

'Do I really need to do this?'

The nurse looks at me. Straight in the eyes. There is compassion and patience. How many times has she heard the same question? Unfair to ask. Impossible not to.

'No-one is forcing you to do this. Take a while. Think about it.'

'Would you have it, if you were me?'

She looks at my chart. 'Yes,' she says.

And I let go. 'Get through the hard stuff now,' I tell myself, 'so there will be no more in the future.'

I hold out my hand, palm facing the floor, and she slips the needle into the big vein just below my wrist. When the drip is flowing smoothly, the nurse walks away. I sit there, trapped, committed, flooded inside and out with tears.

I've chosen a chair at the back of the room, where the outside world is a distant smudge. To one side, almost behind me, there is a stretcher with an old, wispy haired man lying on it, with grey skin stretched tight across his cheekbones. Grey pants, checked shirt and an old, hand-knitted cable sweater. He is stick thin under his everyday clothes. Except for a tight, swollen tummy that points straight up.

The old man groans. Not loudly. More in anguish than pain. His wife, who reads a women's magazine by his bedside, pats the hand without the needle in it. But she does not look up from the pages of gossip where she is, no doubt, cavorting in a glamorous, healthy world.

I watch the clock through blurry eyes, willing the allotted two hours to fly past. Hurry up, drips, hurry up! Fluorescent red. Clear saline. Slip down the plastic tube and into my body and let me get out of here! But they don't hurry and I cannot move until the needle is pulled from my hand. I cannot even scream. In death's counting house, we are all polite.

When I walk out of that first session filled with my new, toxic blood I feel like a bug-eyed alien. In my pocket is a little bottle of pills. For post-treatment nausea.

'Drink lots of water. All day. Flush it out. Keep flushing it out.'

The nursing shift changed while the drip was flowing into my body. This new nurse is tall and dark and anxious.

'How much water?'

'As much as you can stand.'

'At night, too?'

'If you can.'

I walk to the car park, focus inwardly to assess any differences. Dizziness? Illness? Lightness? All I feel, though, is disconnected. Made up from a different recipe to the people around me. I check my hair in the rear-view mirror. Still firmly attached. I have been told I can expect it to start falling out before the second treatment. I dread losing eyelashes more than being bald.

For some reason I cannot explain, every time I stop at a red traffic light, I want to wind down the window and scream out to drivers sitting in their isolated bubbles. 'I started chemo today!' I want to yell. 'I'm not one of you guys any more.' But, of course, I do nothing.

My mind fizzes silently. If only I could turn back the clock. I do not want to be this person filled with stomach-churning fear and leaden despair. For a moment, I yearn for *toujours gai*. But it is *toujours gai*, I suspect, that's caused my problems.

I stay with Pia that first night, in her apartment in the city. We eat spaghetti for dinner at an el cheapo around the corner. I eat a mountain, and half of hers. That night, hookers and druggies scream abuse up and down the street. Cars slam on brakes, a truck grinds up the hill. City music.

When I finally sleep, it is to wake up drenched in sweat. The sheets are sodden. I feel like I'm on fire, or in a sauna. I have no idea what is happening. I shower, crawl back to bed. I don't need a sheet or blanket. And it is a cold, July night.

By morning, the night is a distant memory and I feel almost normal. I shower, dress and go to work. By the end of the day, though, I am mush. I want to go home. My home. I call Pia and tell her not to expect me.

'Call me if you need anything,' she says. 'Or do you want me to come with you?'

'Nah. I just want to be alone.'

And it's true. Because the kind of *alone* I'm talking about at Lovett Bay is the kind that feels like a haven.

At Mona Vale I pull in to the fruit market. Carrots. Apples. Celery. Garlic. Anything to restore what chemo has zapped. The woman working the cash register watches as I reach into my bag for cash. The little needle spot on my hand purple now, with bruising.

'Chemo?' she asks.

She has pale skin and faded dyed blonde hair. Looks worn out.

'Yes?' I turn the word into a question.

'I had it ten years ago. You'll be right.'

I want to grab her and kiss her. For a moment, I am not flying alone in an unknown vortex. She's had it and survived. I will too.

At home, I reach for the phone, planning to join a cancer support group, the kind I rejected when I received a follow-up call after surgery. But I stop before I dial. The idea of sitting around talking about cancer is abhorrent. I want only to think about living.

That night, I look at the anti-nausea pills and reject them again. I do not feel ill. On the bedside table I line up a jug of water, a glass, a stack of books. The arsenal, as I come to call it.

For dinner, I eat tuna out of a can. Standing up. In the kitchen. Then I walk onto the deck, just to sniff the air, like an animal searching for the familiar scents of home territory. It is damp and cold and clean. When the metallic thread of chemo rises up in my mouth, I breathe deeply. Briny. Sweet smell of composting leaves. Of earth. Unbidden, an image of death, of lying under the earth, rushes in. Bury the thought. Bury? Anyway, I think, it's Lovett Bay for my ashes. Here, and only here.

At 3 am with a full moon blasting through the bedroom window, I sit bolt upright. Before I can get up, I have vomited all over the floor. I should have taken the pills. I am too exhausted to move and leave the vomit there. I am absurdly thrilled that I don't have carpet or even a rug in the bedroom. Less to clean up. Drink some water and go back to sleep.

At work the next day, I cannot get warm, cannot think straight. The screen blurs, the phone jangles. Mental or physical? Does it matter? I am still debilitated, pushing to go on when all I want to do is lie down and close my eyes. I thought I understood the meaning of 'bone tired', but I didn't. Not until now. But I refuse to give in. I keep going to work. Day after day. Perhaps because it seems so ordinary. It's the contact with other people that allows me to check whether my mind is spiralling into a kind of madness or whether I'm still seeing the world rationally. Long, silent conversations with yourself have a way of sending you nutty.

A week after my first treatment, I'm back in the waiting room with the beautiful paintings. I hear the oncologist behind her closed door talking to a crying patient. A low murmur, nothing defined except the sobs.

Then it's my turn. We trade standard lines.

'I'm fine. How are you?' she asks.

'Fine.'

I have told myself to think of the treatments as a four-part series. I have had one, so I am one-quarter of the way through. After the next dose, I will be halfway through. When you're halfway through, it's nearly over. Once it's over, everything is level again.

'Feel all right after treatment?'

'Yep.' I forget to tell her about the sauna sweat on the first night.

'Any nausea?'

'Oh, yeah. Threw up on the second night.'

She looks shocked. 'That shouldn't have happened.'

Why did I feel like I'd blundered? 'Well, it did.'

'Did you take the pills?'

'No.'

'Why not?'

'Because I didn't feel sick until I suddenly threw up.'

'You're supposed to take the pills for the first three nights after treatment.'

'I thought you only took them if you felt sick.' I've never been good at understanding instructions.

She sighs. 'No. Take them next time, ok?'

'Ok.'

She gives me a referral to a nearby blood testing clinic. Tells me to arrange a test one week before my next treatment, which is scheduled in three weeks, to make sure I've remade enough white blood cells to replace the ones that have been nuked.

The vein in my left arm is in for a pounding. My right arm is off limits for even a blood pressure test. Lymphoedema is the big bogeyman. Swelling that will not retreat, leaving one limb much bigger than its partner. Without the full quota of lymph nodes, my arm is no longer as efficient at cleaning out bacteria. An infection of any kind is a danger – from a knife-cut while peeling the potatoes, to a mosquito bite. Do not even take a long flight without wearing a pressure bandage, I'm told.

It takes a few scares until I accept that a small tube of antiseptic is my new constant companion. But I instantly reject babying my right arm. Not practical in an environment where everything is carried in and out. I understood, from the moment I met Gordon, that to lose your strength signals the end of life on the boat-access-only shores of Pittwater. That is not an option for me. I tell my arm, like a separate sentient being, that it has to perform.

During the second treatment, I endure but do not cry, although I want to flee and be gone from that room of last resorts as quickly as I can. I hate the thin, dead smell of chemo. Hate that falsely cheery cocoon where we sit around in those *hissing* chairs. Strung up to chemicals so deadly, when the old boy's pee bottle spills, men arrive in white boiler suits and contamination masks to clean up. I did it, I think now, because to walk away would have been the easy option. Another possibly life-threatening stab at denial. No more easy options.

After that second treatment, I behave quite bizarrely when I leave the clinic. I sing out loud in the car and arrive back at Church Point almost euphoric, adrenaline running hard, my heart racing towards some invisible finishing line. I wait for the water taxi, toe tapping, humming a silly tune about *a song and a señorita*. Glance every now and then at the little speck of pure white cotton wool taped over the puncture in my hand. As I wait, I invite almost total strangers (no-one who lives in this part of the Pittwater community is a *total* stranger) home to dinner. All they have to do to get an invite is catch my eye. I am manic and a little mad. Am I trying to fill the long empty hours of the evening before crashing into uneasy sleep?

I know I am worn out but invitations to one and all come tumbling out of my mouth before I even think about them. Perhaps it's desperation, wanting to be centred in normality. To be around people who have dreams, who talk about kids and cooking and boats and fishing . . . and holiday plans. Who plant gardens to enjoy in twenty years' time because they have no idea, yet, what it's like to have the curtains drawn on dreams. As I am dropped off at Ken's dock at the Lovett Bay boatshed, I add up the number of people who have said yes to dinner. About eight, I think. Easy.

There is a man on the pontoon. Middle-aged, with dark, wavy hair and eyes so brown they seem black. He's helping one of the boatshed boys carry a mast.

'Do you need another pair of hands?' I ask. 'I'm *really* strong.'

'We'll be right,' says the stranger.

When the mast is laid on the jetty, the stranger stands and looks across the bay. Shoulders hunched. Bright white T-shirt ringing his neck under a navy windcheater. Worn working boots below his jeans.

'Hello,' I add.

'Uh-huh.' His face is weary but deeply tanned, though summer is well over.

'I'm Susan. I bought Gordon's place.'

'I know.'

'Oh.'

Silence. Then he remembers the normal protocol. 'Oh, I'm Bob.'

'Do you live around here?'

'Yeah.'

He spins and points up the winding sandstone path to the pale yellow house with the graceful columns. Says nothing.

'Oh, so that's your house. I've wondered who lives there,' I say.

And then it registers. His wife is ill. Cancer. I'd heard about it sometime. But wallowing in my own fog, I'd pushed the information to one side.

'Come and have dinner tonight,' I babble, trying to fill the ballooning silence.

'I don't know,' he says. 'My wife . . .'

'Yeah, I know. Cancer. Me too.'

I hold out my hand for him to see the little patch of cotton wool.

'Then you understand,' he replies. 'But I'll ask her. Let you know.'

He moves off along the jetty, one shoulder lower than the other, walking crookedly. Head bent low.

'Seven o'clock, if you can make it,' I call out.

He stops and turns, head hunkered deep into his shoulders like a turtle. 'Might be too late for her, she gets tired. Thanks anyway,' he says.

'How about six?'

'I'll ask her.'

'Ok.'

I watch him walk towards the pathway that climbs to his house. At the dock next to the ferry wharf, his dock, I now realise, he bends and picks up a coil of shiny green hose and a bag full of groceries.

About half an hour later, the phone rings.

'Thanks but we won't come to dinner,' Bob says.

'Oh. Everything ok?'

'Barbara's a bit tired, that's all.'

'Ok.'

Intrusive. I've been intrusive and pushy. Feel I've overstepped some fragile line. I back off.

'She says lunch would be good sometime,' he adds.

'Oh! That's terrific. When would you like to come? This Saturday?'

'I'll talk to Barbara and let you know.'

I put the phone down, vaguely exasperated. I'm used to instant results and Bob, I think, is hard to get a lot of words out of.

Some nights, the moon is so bright through the bedroom window I have no need of a light. Not even to read a book. I plunge into master food writer Stephanie Alexander's odyssey into south west France. Reading about food is endlessly reassuring. There's a predictable outcome, a vicarious pleasure and no-one is ever threatened. Her mouth-watering account of making a traditional peasant dish called *Poule avec sa mique* (chicken with a dumpling) is inspiring. First, you bone a chicken and make a rich stock from the bones, and then the flesh is stuffed with a blend of tarragon, chopped ham, pork mince and breadcrumbs. The boned, stuffed bird is then wrapped in muslin and poached – along with a large, tasty, juicy dumpling – in the stock heavily laden with vegetables.

Its difficulty fascinated me. First the boning, then the stock, then the stuffing, then the dumpling, then the grand finale, when it all comes together in a slow simmer until it is ready to be sliced and served in bowls with plenty of broth and slices of the dumpling. I read it over and over for a while, tempted by its complexities. I vow to make it one day. Which becomes a tiny rub on a steamy window to take a tentative glimpse at a future.

In the cool hours before dawn, as I sip endless glasses of water, the idea of spending a whole day cooking a 'simple' meal is incredibly tempting. So much easier than the racking business of sitting at an office desk. My concentration at work, after the second treatment, is scatty. I scramble around my head trying to link thoughts and words. When I read them back, they are disjointed, jumbled, frighteningly inept. Frightening because this has been my livelihood and I am losing the skills. It's not just that I *can't* concentrate, it's that I cannot stop my mind from shooting off in a thousand different directions.

My childhood. Was my path, even then, mapped out? My relationship with my mother. Is it my fault? What has made me what I am, and what has brought me to where I am? Would a turn left or right instead of ripping up the middle have changed the outcome of my life? How can I recognise the defining moments? Would I have done it differently if I knew then what I know now? And the biggest question of all. When weighing up the balance, have I managed to live my life with more honesty than prevarication, more compassion than cold-hearted judgement?

It is a chilling mental game because a million failures, some bigger than others, rear up and the memory of a few leave me reeling. Is everyone's life like that? Or just mine? Am I more flawed than most? Or am I again falling into that viper pit the shrink warned me about so long ago, the one in which I think only of what I *didn't* do (for the boys, when I had the chance) instead of what I *did* do? Is dwelling on the negative a strong personal characteristic – and if it is, should I reprogram my mind?

Easier by far, I decide, to follow the directions in a recipe than to try to fill a glaring white page with words. Best of all, there are results in a short time. And there's no-one to tell you to do it again because they'd like it presented a different way. So it isn't that hard when I step into one of the grey carpeted cubicles one morning soon after the second treatment and withdraw (again) from my career. I have heard, anyway, that they're looking for a replacement for me.

I wear a mid-calf, beige, knitted skirt. A matching polo-necked sweater. Tan boots of the softest leather. Underneath all this, knitted leggings, a white skivvy. And I am still cold. Even in the fan-forced oven of the office.

I sit in the straight-backed chair opposite the business manager (the blonde is on holidays) and take control. It is wonderful, the freedom of having nothing to lose.

'I've heard you're looking for a replacement for me,' I tell her flatly.

She swallows and looks at the file – my file – on her desk. She is not a bad woman but trapped in the age-old dilemma of doing what's been asked of her or doing what she feels is morally right.

'Where did you hear that?' she asks.

'All over town. I even know who's been offered my job. I can't work out, though, whether you're lining someone up to replace me now – or because you think I'm going to drop off the twig shortly?'

'Oh,' is all she can manage. My bluntness has shocked her.

'It's ok,' I relent. 'Let's just be adults, admit what's going on and come to some kind of arrangement.'

Her face stains with red but she smiles. I've taken away the need for lies and deception and she is, at heart, a kind and honest woman.

'That'd be wonderful,' she says.

'What I'd like to do is to walk out of here today and not come back.'

'I'll see what I can do for you. I'll do my best.'

And I know she will.

By lunchtime, I finish my goodbyes, climb into my car and vacate my parking space for the last time. If I didn't feel so absolutely wrecked with tiredness, I would have sung out loud. What matters now is living. Not existing.

As I round the bend where the dinghies play their concert in time with the waves, I wind down the window and let the cold air rush through the car, just so I can breathe in the salty air. No more office deadlines. My only goal now is to get well and survive. And to make *Poule avec sa mique*. It's the kind of dish you have to make at least once in your life.

≈

A few days after quitting my job, the phone rings in the middle of a silent morning and I jump with fright.

'Hello?'

'It's Bob.'

'Hello. How are you? How's Barbara?'

'She's . . . ah . . . lunch. We can make lunch on Friday. She'd love it.'

'Great. It will just be us. No-one else.'

'That's good.'

'Is there anything she can't eat?'

Since chemo, all fish, except canned tuna, tastes like wet cement to me. Lamb is fine. The thick, sweet smell of beef sends me fleeing from the kitchen.

'No. Anything is fine,' he says.

The phone goes down abruptly. Not a great talker, this Bob. After growing up in a family that equated charm with glibness, his reticence is disorienting. A whole bunch of polite little asides go unuttered, like I've been cut off midstream. But it feels clean. There's no bullshit.

I've spent a lifetime listening to people use other people's needs as an excuse to get what they want (and doing it myself). Don't want to go to a dinner party? Use the kids as an excuse. Don't want to tell someone his work is bad? Use the editor as an excuse. Don't want to face the truth about yourself? Blame other people. Want something badly? Manipulate until you get it. In the end, it's all dishonesty of one kind or another, born out of a lack of personal courage. How often I've said something untrue because I convinced myself it was kinder. Only it wasn't really. It was just easier for me. Cancer, it seems, has already given greater clarity to my view of the world.

I put the phone back in the cradle after talking to Bob and rub my prickling head. Hair drifts down in a sunbeam of light and lands on the floor like snipped threads. *My* hair. This morning, the pillow looked like a moulting dog's bed. Soon I'll be bald. *Hat* gets added to the shopping list. Make an appointment to get my hair trimmed – that's the hair that's holding on defiantly, mostly on the top of my head. But it is thinner. Noticeably thinner when, forever, I've had a thatch thicker than a bear's winter coat.

I plan Bob and Barbara's lunch with the care of a christening. Food, which I've shovelled down with abandon for so long, is newly holy, the stuff of life. Each meal is one less to experience, ticked off, like days on a calendar.

At the hairdresser's, Simon, who would rather be an actor, takes a close look.

'See this' he says. The hair around each temple is rubbed to almost nothing. I look, but not too hard. No time for mirrors.

'It's a sign of what's to come,' he says.

He is kind. But I know what is to come. 'Just do what you have to,' I tell him.

He reaches for clippers in his industrial grey salon next to the chicken shop in Mona Vale and starts at the back, perhaps to ease the shock. I bury my head in a book until he tells me I have to look up so he can level the sides. It's a close-cropped shave that reveals the shape of my head in detail. I expect to be horrified but I like it. Which is great. When you don't have a choice you might as well accept the status quo.

'I reckon you've got a couple of weeks before it all falls out,' he says.

'Ok.'

'Sorry.'

I feel a swell of loyalty to him. So many are appalled by the merest whiff of illness.

He holds up the clippers. 'I've given you a number one. When it starts to grow back, we'll increase the numbers. When we're shaving at number six, you'll be able to let it grow.'

'Right.'

I cruise Mona Vale searching for a hat but it's winter and stocks of summer hats are nonexistent. On one side of the main street there's a serendipitous collection of shops aimed at middle-class women who like natural fibres in their casual wear and a touch of glitter in dress-up clothes. On the other side, the takeaway food shops layer the smell of deep fried chicken heavily in the air. Along with the exhaust of idling cars waiting for someone to pull out of too few parking spaces, the atmosphere is rank.

My stomach flip flops. A burning taste of chemicals rises up and my legs suddenly feel like balloons filled with concrete. I drag myself into a coffee shop to sit for a while. To stop the Persian carpet patterns behind my eyes. To adjust to the unfamiliar sensation of weakness. It's not just unpleasant, it's downright scary. The desire to lie down immediately in the café and sleep like a hobo on a park bench, oblivious to the world, is overwhelming. I close my eyes for a moment.

'Would you like to see a menu?'

The waitress wears a T-shirt that fails to stretch low enough to meet the top of her jeans. Her tanned stomach is flat. A silver ring winks from her navel. It is impossible to look anywhere else.

'Coffee. Flat white. That will do.'

She flicks the menu away cheerfully. My eyes clang shut again. Just a few moments. That's all it will take. It is the kind of drowsiness that kills long distance drivers.

Coffee arrives with a deliberately loud clunk. They are not used to seeing people doze at café tables in Mona Vale and they find it disturbing. I drink up quickly and leave. The caffeine acts like a hit of adrenaline.

Outside, the hat search begins again but I hesitate to try on the few I find. When a saleswoman insists I try on a hat that costs more than a week's grocery budget and is better suited to the Melbourne Cup than tinny travelling, I turn on her. Angry.

'My hair,' I explain forcefully, 'is falling out. I will leave a great handful of it in your tizzy, clean hat if I try it on.'

She backs off. Silent. But I have noticed the recoil in her heavily made-up eyes, recoil not at my anger but at what she suddenly realises is not a punk haircut but a sign of illness.

Two shops further along, I pick up a white cotton summer hat with a small brim that I can pull low. It costs twenty dollars, wraps into a small ball, washes easily and will keep off the sun. I pull it on, pay and leave.

Over the next few weeks, when I am finally completely bald, I encounter great swathes of compassion from most people. Men stand to give me a seat on the bus, old women pat me on the arm in silent sympathy as they pass, salesgirls lift heavy items into my supermarket trolley. It is a deep, enveloping kindness that is completely new to me. In turn, it makes me able to be kinder than I have ever been before. Occasionally, though, I see retreat and fear in the eyes of strangers, as though to come near might risk infection. Their reaction is not offensive. It is fear of their own mortality that they cannot face, not my bald head, grey face and dark-circled eyes.

Back at Church Point, the water taxi nudges into the ferry wharf and I pass over the shopping, bag after bag. Plastic. Must do something about that. Save the world then save myself. Or should it be the other way around? It's low tide. Extremely low. The step into the taxi with its chipped pink paint is a long way down. A month ago I could have jumped in, holding bags in both hands, balancing easily. Now I hesitate. Weakness. Feeling leaden legged and lightheaded at the same time. Bob is driving (is everyone called Bob?) and without a word he puts out a hand. I grab it and step down safely.

'How you doing?'

'Great.'

'Yeah. I can see. Got someone at the other end?'

'Just drop me at Ken's dock. It'll work out.'

He cruises slowly from The Point towards Lovett Bay, staying within the eight knot speed limit until we pass the marker. Then he revs *Pink Lady*. The bow lifts high until only the sky is visible, then the taxi slowly settles on the water like a broody hen. The landscape rushes back into position. Spotted gums like sentries, blue water sliding into deep green in the bay. Coastlines like broken honeycomb. White cockatoos. Always white cockatoos. Sulphur-crested, big, loud, incredibly clumsy. Wonderful.

Fine salt spray dusts my face, soothing and cool. My heart lifts as urban life gets further away. *I am strong and my body is strong.*

We speak no words over the growl of one hundred and fifty horses. Too beautiful to speak. Too tired to speak.

When we reach Ken's dock, Water taxi Bob passes out the grocery bags and asks again if I'll be ok.

'I'll help you get them to the house,' he offers.

'It's good exercise. Keeps me fit,' I reply.

He shakes his head, eases *Pink Lady* away from the dock, does a U-turn and takes off with a wave. It will take about four trips to get everything into the house. I grab a handful and head off. *I am strong and my body is strong.*

Ken is in the boatshed, sanding a wooden mast to satin smoothness with a buzzing machine when I walk past with my new haircut. He pulls off his breathing mask.

'Gunna join a rock band, are you?'

'I'll be bald soon anyway.'

Ken looks stricken. I have not mentioned my illness to many people.

'Jeez, mate. What's going on?'

'Bit of treatment, Ken. Nothing to worry about.'

And because he has always been a private, self-sufficient man, he asks no more questions.

'Boys! Help Susan with the shopping!'

The boys, spiky haired, ragged and billowing with health, leap to grab bags. In minutes, everything is piled at the front door and they have scampered back to the boatshed, barefoot even in the winter cold.

Cinnamon, the German pointer owned by Ken and his wife, Jan, lifts an affectionate muzzle when I walk by, ready for a pat. She is sweet and docile – until Ken pushes the button to send a cradled yacht sliding down the tram lines into the water. Then she goes berserk, barking hysterically and chasing the boat. Nothing stops her, not even Ken's loud, threatening yells. She is also extremely territorial. When any passing dogs venture onto boatshed land, she rounds them up like sheep and sees them off.

'She thinks she's a queen,' Jan tells me one day. She tells me, too, that when Cinny was a puppy, she refused to come in at night. To lure her, Ken would have to start the engine on the tinny. 'She loved a boat ride,' Jan says indulgently. 'And she came every time. But Ken had to take her for a spin when all he really wanted to do after a hard day's work was have a cleansing ale!'

By four thirty, the groceries are packed away and the sun is a sinking orb. The bay shimmers like a copper tray. From the deck I can see the boys, showered, wet-haired, squeaky clean in only slightly less ragged clothes, hovering in the frail warmth of the last rays. They are still barefoot.

When the sun drops behind the hill that rises from the cleavage of Lovett and Elvina bays and a sudden chill unfurls, sinking the temperature three or four degrees, the bay slides from copper into a still, silver slate. The boys leap into their tinnies and, with a roar, head off to wherever home is.

For Veit, the tall young man with the shy smile and ceramic blue eyes who stopped me from falling the very first day I came to look at Gordon's house, home is his sixty foot, steel-hulled, half-finished boat moored in the middle of the bay. Summer or winter, he lives on her. She has no name yet. Veit is waiting until he meets a woman who will share his itinerant life. He will name it for her.

One day when he's giving the boat a clean at Ken's wharf, he calls me on board for a tour. The space is huge. But it is mostly empty. A carcase. There is not even a loo. In winter, the stove, where he cooks stir fry and mountainous quantities of rice, provides the heating. In summer, he sleeps on the deck. He dreams of turning her into a glorious new beauty with sofas and bathrooms and curtains framing the portholes.

'Can you see it?' he enthuses.

'It will be wonderful.'

'I've got the space, that's a big start. Could be a beauty. Lotta work, but that's boats. Pretty comfy now.'

He flits from space to space. Incredibly graceful for someone well over six feet tall. No shoes. Never any shoes. His intricately patterned sweater, knitted long ago by a doting German mother, is worn through at the elbows. The faint smell of diesel clings to him.

'The main cabin,' he announces as though he's revealing a box on a television quiz show. But there's no drum roll. Only a king size mattress on the floor, doonas, pillows, rumpled bedding. It looks incredibly decadent but I can't think why. Perhaps it's the size, which gives an unspoken signal that he is looking for someone to share it.

'A bench here. Table here. This is where I'll put a shower.' He ends the grand tour with a wave of his arm.

'Veit, it's fabulous.'

He goes flat suddenly. 'It's a dump, isn't it?'

'No. It has huge potential.'

'It's a dump now, though. A mess.'

'You're a shipwright. You bring boats to life. That's what you'll do with this one.'

'Yeah.' But he doesn't sound as though he believes it.

Everyone has a dream on Pittwater. To catch the biggest fish. Sail the fastest race. Return a wrecked old boat to former glory. Maybe just to kayak under a moon so big and bright it turns night into day. Dreams that cost almost nothing except effort and are therefore possible.

There is a classlessness amongst the permanent population here, one that the weekenders do not entirely understand. Weekenders roar in to eat and drink and barely wet a toe even in the heat of a summer day. They are not persuaded, most of them, to join in the abandoned joy of skinny-limbed kids leaping from docks and begging, as a tinny passes, for the driver to rev the engine so they can get an extra thrill from diving through the fizzing wake. For them, and I do not mean to sound smug, the only social infrastructure of note is trade. Plumbers, electricians, floor sanders, path builders, retaining wall specialists. The human core that revives houses left empty for too long. Or marine specialists that keep boat engines humming, yacht bottoms scraped clean, moorings serviced. The essentials of *boat-access-only* living.

The rushing weekenders who successfully manage to straddle both Pittwater and urban life tend to be the people who love boats. Not in a way that makes sense to most of us – that is, to climb on board, go for a gentle row, paddle, sail or chug, have a picnic and return to the mooring – but deeply and passionately. Anything that floats will do. A little putt-putt, a launch, a sailing dinghy. And if it is a wooden boat, ah well, that is truly the stuff of dreams. Prized and cherished, handled gently as a newborn babe, these boats are scraped and polished, painted and shined, and glisten on their moorings or sailing on the water. They are treated like priceless works of art.

Ken has a wooden sailing boat called *Sylphine* with a

voluptuous, spreading hull. He's begun a two year project to fibre-glass over the wood. 'Lower maintenance, mate,' he explains when he raises her out of the water and nestles her in the cradle where she'll be worked on. He builds a temporary roof to protect her from the weather and treats her like a Fabergé egg.

'Aren't all boats high maintenance?'

'Yeah. But this will be less high,' Ken says, grinning.

Perce, a gorgeous, beautifully mannered shipwright who once owned and skippered a restored and glamorised old navy (wooden) boat around the coastline of Australia, has the perfect Pittwater wooden launch. Called *Perceverance*, it is the most coveted boat hereabouts for its practical beauty. To sit at a dinner table with Perce is like taking an ocean voyage with an ancient mariner. He knows the history and specifications of nearly every boat on Pittwater and far beyond. He can tell you the name of the man who designed it, who did the woodwork and whether it will travel easily in choppy seas, or toss you mercilessly.

All boats are known by their names or their class, unless for some reason they are nameless and then they are known either as no-name or by the letters and numbers on the mainsail (*KA2*, for example). When you wait for the ferry, you wait for the *Curlew* or the *Amelia K*. Or when a working barge goes past, it is the *Trump* or the *Laurel Mae*. Rarely 'Bomber's' or 'Toby's and Dave's barge'.

I knew Toby years before coming to Pittwater, when he sold advertising for magazines and newspapers and dined in five star restaurants at his employer's expense. His shirts were always eye piercingly white, his trouser creases sharp enough to cut cakes, his hair regularly trimmed. He still worked in the media when I found him, one day, at Church Point, having a Friday evening beer before catching the ferry home. It was a winter's night, I recall, and he wore a heavy, navy overcoat, shiny black brogues. He had not yet loosened his striped silk tie. His girth reflected a life spent in exotic restaurants.

'Toby?' I asked, hesitant and unsure. He was out of context.

'Gidday.'

He hugged me, engulfing me in the smell of beer and tobacco. The same Toby. He reached for a roll-your-own. Lit it. Offered me a beer.

'What on earth are you doing here?' I could not believe for one moment that Mr Urbane might have an offshore bolthole.

'Bought a little place on Scotland Island. Live here.'

'Really?' I thought, how little we really know about what goes on in people's minds.

After that, we met from time to time, passing through The Point. We exchanged industry gossip, caught up on news of old colleagues. Soon, I noticed more cynicism than humour edged into his accounts of life in the advertising world.

One day I heard he'd bought a partnership in a boat. A barge, the *Laurel Mae*. And he intended to run it as a business.

'Do you know what you're doing, Toby?' I ask him one evening when I'm passing through The Point and he's amongst the crowd having a beer before climbing on the last ferry for the day.

'Oh yeah. As much as you ever know what you're doing.'

It is a fine day, about a month later, when I find Toby in his grand wheelhouse on the *Laurel Mae* at Cargo Wharf, at lunch-time. He looks up and waves and I wander over. He emerges on deck in a faded grey singlet. Faded navy shorts accordioned at the crotch and socks the same colour as the clay at Cargo Wharf. His boots are a kaleidoscope of Pittwater soils.

He has a sandwich in his hand, a high pile remaining inside a brown paper bag, waiting to be eaten.

'What's for lunch?'

'Devon sandwiches. With tomato sauce.'

'That's a big call after dining five star for most of your career.'

'Wanna know something?'

'Yeah.'

'I've never tasted anything better in my life.'

He beams. Stomach newly flat. Arms muscled and tanned. A new man. His own man.

The *Laurel Mae* is a great big, broad beamed barge with a hull made from spotted gum. Thirty people could waltz on her pitted deck and not come close to the edges. They'd have to dodge the crane in the centre of the deck, though, with its giant rusted hook and ropes as thick as wrists.

'Wanna see inside?'

I follow him on board to the cabin, which is clean and braced in the corners with quite beautiful, pale blonde huon pine wood.

'Grown knees,' says Toby, patting the bracing knowledgeably. 'That's what they're called.'

'What's a groan knee?' I ask.

'Grow-*en*,' he replies. 'It's wood taken from the natural knee bend in a tree, which makes the brace stronger than using two pieces of wood.'

The cabin is big and meticulous. Tools are neatly in boxes, phone books lined up on a ledge alongside business envelopes and receipt books. The floor is painted green in here, but where the captain stands at the helm, it is worn to bare wood.

'Don't miss your office desk, then?'

Toby grins. 'Not a lot, mate.'

'How's business?'

'Yeah. Not bad. Not bad.'

'Toby?'

'Yeah?'

'Do you actually know anything about the barge business?'

'Not much, mate, not much. But I'm learning quick.'

Cargo Wharf, where the *Laurel Mae* is tied up, is the industrial estate of Pittwater. Huge bags of sand, with giant handles like a woman's shoulder bag, are lined up to be lifted by crane from land to water, along with bundles of wood, pipe, tin, and other landscaping and building supplies.

Twice a week the reeking garbage truck is driven onto a long flat barge from Cargo Wharf and ferried around the bays and Scotland Island. Garbage, which is piled in bins at public ferry wharves, is tossed into the truck's gawping black hole, where it is crunched and munched and swallowed whole. Bagged garbage is picked up from private docks by a couple of lean young blokes who splash around, mobile phones to their ears, on a long, flat barge. They pick up bags and chuck them like pillows into bins on the barge, missing only occasionally. When that happens, the bag sinks slowly to the watery bottom and in Lovett Bay, and probably everywhere else, locals wait for low tide and try to tidy up.

One Sunday when I'm on the way to Church Point in the water taxi, I see the two boys who are usually on the garbage barge quietly sailing around in an exquisite little wooden boat. It looks antique and quite delicate and it's been sanded and painted to perfection. When I catch the boys clearing the garbage at Lovett Bay a few weeks later, I ask them about the boat.

'Bit of a passion, mate,' they say. 'Old wooden boats. Yeah. Bit of a passion. Found her rotting and did her up. Saved her. She's pretty bloody beautiful, isn't she?'

I do not fully understand the grip of boat passion until Steve, who lives aboard his boat in McCarrs Creek, his dreadlocks newly shorn, his little black and white mutt, Minnie, prancing busily alongside, explains that for him, the only romance in life comes from boats. 'They are,' he says, uncharacteristically serious, 'the love of my life. I live . . . for boats.'

And then as we walk along the roadside at Church Point, Minnie following at a trot, we plunge into a heated debate about whether browning meat is a good idea or not, as a prelude to creating a thick winter stew. The kind that transforms into a heavenly soup when the meat is gone.

'It's essential,' Steve says.

'Yeah, but most people chuck all the meat in a pan at once and the pan loses heat so the meat goes grey instead of brown.'

'Mate, that's the cook's problem. If you're any good, you do it handful by handful and sear it quickly so the juice stays in the meat.'

'Yeah. Which means it shouldn't dry out when you stew it.'

'You've got it! That's the whole point. But do you reckon you need both parsley and celery for flavour?'

'Individual taste, mate,' I say. 'Personally? I'd use both. With carrots, onions and a bay leaf or two.'

'Yeah. Me too.'

One day I ask Steve to explain *why* he is so passionate about boats.

He squirms for a minute or two, uncomfortable with the thought that he might reveal something essential about himself. 'Dunno, mate.'

'But you must know. You're obsessed with them.'

'Yeah. Well maybe it's because they're there.'

I lean in the groove Gordon so cleverly fashioned to comfortably cup an elbow with a glass of wine in hand. It is cold on the deck, and the damp is heavier than a spring dew. The chill seeps through my sweater and my jeans feel frigid enough to ice a martini. It is that time of day when the sky is pale grey and the trees silhouetted on the ridge tops look like pins on a cushion.

To pass the time, I think about ideas to transform the fortress mentality of my house. Maybe wide, sliding doors from the bedroom onto a new, vast deck, so in summer I can push my bed outside. Live in the physical world, if by then that is the only way. If I am bedridden.

It's a dreadful word, and I rear back from it. My Uncle Frank is right. You've got to watch your noodle all the time. Turns on you in a flash, fills your mind with crabby, unhelpful little ideas if you're not constantly vigilant. I will not be spending days in bed, inside or out. *I am strong and my body is strong.*

I stride inside and grab a pencil and a piece of paper. Draw, erase, draw again. But then the fear of illness trickles in once more. I throw the pencil down. Stop it, I shout silently. You cannot afford the luxury of ambivalence. To let your guard down is reckless!

And life is like that now. An emotional seesaw. Live? Die? Which force is winning today? Which will win tomorrow?

I put aside the pen and paper, too tired to continue. I peel off my clothes, put my fake tit in the underwear drawer, pull the quilt around me and reach for cookbooks piled high on the bedside table. I flick through pages searching for ways to make the baby leg of lamb for Bob and Barbara's lunch irresistible to a woman whose tastebuds must be fickle and dulled.

Hazy ideas float through my mind as I skim recipes. Where *would* a fireplace go? What about the kitchen? The walls between bedrooms and living room do not reach the ceiling. Should I raise them to be a proper noise barrier, or leave them as they are because it makes the house feel wonderfully casual and shacky?

I settle on a recipe for the lamb at the same time as I vow to call the builder. Bugger it. If I'm going to die in the foreseeable future, I am going to die in comfort!

On a glorious Pittwater night my friend Michael, who took over the lease on the Scotland Island house, paddles over by the light of a fabulous moon. He knocks on my door and walks in, leaving wet footprints in his wake. I am in bed but not asleep when he sticks his head around the curtain, which passes for a door in my shack, and tells me to get up.

'Come on, come on. This is too good to miss,' he says.

He is new to Pittwater, I think a little crankily, as I get up and follow him outside in my pyjamas. But he is right. The night is spectacular. The escarpments shimmering with silver, the night sky undercoated with the softest pink. The whole bay shining and, right through the middle like a silver stairway, light accordions out to sea.

We manoeuvre the kayak past the mangroves to the point where Salvation Creek, which runs down from the national park, joins Lovett Bay. It is a beautiful creek in a damp gully where life and growth is rampant. In the first days of moving to Lovett Bay, I wandered at low tide to find out for myself what lurked at the end of the shoreline. As I stepped from the open bay into the gloom of a rainforest, thousands of insects hurtled in the light and shadow. Palms as tiny as cocktail umbrellas sprouted wildly, delicate maiden hair cascaded and forests of fungi filled the air with a stewy smell. Moss, thicker than carpet, softened sharp-edged rocks, and after scrambling over huge, slippery boulders for a while, I found a waterfall. Later I was told that this is the creek that never dries up, even in the most severe drought. The name, Salvation, is fitting.

At low tide, the creek trickles onto the sandflats, at high tide, it is still too shallow for any boat bigger than a tinny. So there is never any boat traffic here. As we paddle along, the silence is lyrical and we do not speak as we turn and glide smoothly back to the house.

'Thanks,' I say.

My friend nods and keeps paddling his way home.

Friday morning is quite beautiful. Sunny, crisp, vibrant. I stroll to the fringe of the night's high tide. A big one, spilling a foot or so over the sea wall. It is not long past the time when the sun swathes the bay in an orange glow, when the tree tops look like they are burning. About four or five early morning kayakers glide past as usual, their paddles dipping into the dark satin water. First one side – whoosh – then the other. Occasionally they nod in my direction and I wave in a small gesture to create only a small disturbance.

The boats on their moorings hover over their reflections like conjoined twins, bright white most of them, with blue sail covers, blue as the sky. Sea eagles who nest on the Elvina side of Lovett Bay, high in the rocky escarpment where no human can disturb them, swoop and soar. Is it a mating ritual? Or is the day, for them also, too exquisite not to feel a surge of joyful energy? Perhaps they are simply letting off steam.

Mid-morning, I call the builder on his mobile. 'Think I'll go ahead after all,' I tell him.

'Right,' he replies.

'When can you come over for a chat?'

'I'll call you Monday with a time. Does that suit you?'

'Yeah, great.'

There's a long pause.

'How are you doing?' he asks tentatively.

'Who knows?'

'Right,' he says quickly.

After I put down the phone, I wander into the kitchen to get lunch going.

The lamb goes into a chipped, heavy, cast iron pot with a broken knob on the lid. Dropped it once on a tile floor. Chipped the tile, too. I squeeze a bulb of garlic until it breaks up and chuck all the pieces in with the lamb. Unpeeled. Peeling garlic can sap your creative spirit and anyway, it burns too quickly. I drizzle balsamic vinegar over the top so it collects in a glossy brown pond in the base, chuck around plenty of salt and pepper. The lid goes on and the whole lot is shoved into the oven to cook on a low heat for about three hours. At the end of that time, the lamb will emerge with a caramelised skin and flaking, moist meat infused with the nutty flavor of roasted garlic and the sharp sweetness of vinegar.

There are little new potatoes, green beans, baby carrots and a salad of bitter leaves – bitter greens are good for the liver. Barbara's liver is under assault from chemotherapy and so is mine. Every little bit helps. There is no dessert. Just crisp fresh apples, pink skinned and voluptuous, and a hunk of pale yellow cheddar cheese. Ok, so cheese is not good for the liver. But it's wonderful for the spirit. Balance is what life is all about, right? Yeah, right.

I do not know what to expect of Barbara. Have never caught even a fleeting glimpse of her. She and Bob live high above the ramshackle waterfront neighbourhood and the path from their house to their dock does not pass my home.

When the lunch is organised, I wander onto the deck where the table is set. The day is warm enough for a T-shirt. Soon, the sun will swing around and make it feel like summer. But the light arrives late in the morning and fades early. Thin. Brittle. Watery. It's undeniably still winter.

Bob and Barbara appear from the front of the boatshed about fifteen minutes early, walking slowly. Bob's arm around Barbara's waist. She is talking and her words float through the day. I cannot make them out and do not want to. There is an intense intimacy about the two of them. A grimy little grub of envy is born and quickly slain. I turn into the house and pull the sliding door behind me gently, so the noise won't intrude on them. But I have seen that Barbara walks slowly, stopping often as though to catch her breath. Using conversation to camouflage her little rests. By the time they reach the front door, they are perfectly punctual.

'I'm Barbara.'

She holds out a long, slim hand and smiles, looking directly at me. Her face is long and thin, her eyes are the kind that can be said to sparkle.

'Come on in. It's really lovely to meet you,' I say, standing aside for her to pass.

She comes in a few feet and looks around the room, and then she walks slowly to the sofa, easing herself carefully onto it. As though a jerky movement might hurt too much. She sniffs the meaty, garlicky air.

'Lamb?'

'Yeah, is that ok for you?'

'Yes. Thank you.'

Bob is dressed up. A T-shirt *with* a collar. He plonks a couple of bottles of wine on the counter, a red and white, both very good, and sinks shyly into silence.

I rush around, filling in the empty spaces with action. Opening the white wine, peering into the oven although the covered pot can tell me nothing, hauling down wineglasses from the shelf.

'Can you pour the wine please, Bob?'

I lift the lid on saucepans, check under the damp tea towel to make sure the salad hasn't suddenly gone limp and curse the impulse that made me hold back from inviting a couple of extra people over to relieve the pressure of discovering a comfort zone with strangers.

Then I fall back on the old journo's technique of asking questions to settle my nerves and their shyness: 'So! How long have you two lived here?'

Bob begins to answer. A pair of king parrots, red and emerald green, male and female, take up positions on the rail outside, like an audience in fancy dress. He struggles for the right words, his face rubbery with a quick succession of expressions.

Barbara slides smoothly in. Bob watches the parrots as Barbara weaves her tale. 'First glimpses are often last glimpses,' she says.

I do not understand her and must look confused.

'How often in life do we see something that catches our attention for a moment but is never seen nor thought about again?'

'Yes,' I say. Because it seems expected. But I have no idea where it is all leading. I move to sit on the sofa opposite her, to concentrate better.

She is quiet for a little while, as though gathering thoughts and energy for the story she is about to begin. Her face is pale and her hair golden with coppery highlights. Her hands rest in her lap. Elegantly crossed. Looking back, I cannot remember what she was wearing that day. Perhaps because her eyes, the colour of curaçao, make the rest of her seem drab. She could hide nothing behind those eyes. Had nothing to hide. Until later, when she tried to hide the pain.

Bob leaves his position watching the parrots and sits beside her. He takes tiny, regular sips of his wine.

'How long ago did you come here?' I ask.

'That first glimpse? January 28, 1993. We didn't move here until later, though.'

'You remember the exact day!'

'Oh yes. I'll tell you why in a moment.

'We were bushwalking, Bob and I, along a section of the North Lovett Bay fire trail. Trying to find the public wharf,' Barbara begins.

'The trail had become indistinct and eroded, with archways of evil lantana ready to spike unwary bushwalkers so we never found the ferry wharf and decided to retrace our steps.'

Bob's eyebrows soar, dip and weave with his wife's words. Then his chin sinks lower into his chest. He has heard this story before, probably quite often. But he lets it run. He likes hearing his wife's voice. Perhaps he knows she has very little time left to get everything said.

As they turned, she explains, they looked down to the water, velvety and green. Barely visible through swathes of pink flowering lantana and dense bush, Barbara saw the rear of a large old home.

'It was the roof I saw at first. Old terracotta tiles covered with lichen. And three chimneys. There was a rigid symmetry to the lines of the house and the cream coloured bagged walls were unusual. I felt, I confess, a hint of mystery.'

'Go on,' I interrupt, getting up. 'I've just got to get lunch ready or it will spoil.'

'Don't worry. The story can wait until we're all sitting down. Bob? Could I have some water, please?'

In the kitchen, I hand Bob a water glass and begin piling vegetables on a platter.

'Will you carve?' I ask, after Barbara has her water.

'Love to,' Bob replies.

I pass him a knife and fork, and put the lamb on a large carving dish. Then I tip the clear jus from the pot into a warm gravy boat, grab plates from the warmer drawer of the oven and start loading the table with everything we need.

'Lunch is ready,' I tell Barbara. 'Do you want to come to the table now?'

Bob leaves the lamb and goes to Barbara, helping her get up from the sofa with subtlety. As though it is more about gallantry than giving physical support. When she is seated, he comes back to the kitchen to help.

'Watch out for Scruff Bucket, the kookaburra,' I call to Barbara. 'He's partial to lamb and the bloody magpies will eat the nose off your face if it looks tempting enough.'

Bob thoughtlessly pulls off a sliver of caramelised meat from the top of the leg of lamb and chews it happily. Then he realises what he's done and looks at me apologetically.

'Sorry. Hope you don't mind. Forgot I wasn't at home.'

I reach for a knife, slice off the textured and richly flavoured bit of meat around the knuckle. Pass it to him. His face lights up. He pops the meat into his mouth, and licks his fingers loudly. Then looks horrified again.

'Sorry. Done it again. Keep forgetting where I am.'

I laugh. 'I don't care if you pick up the whole leg and eat it with your fingers.'

He moves off with the lamb. It seems mad, but I could swear he gives a little skip.

I pick up the salad bowl. The salad, purplish radicchio and thinly sliced red onion vibrant against the white bowl, resting on the yellow-green leaves from the heart of a cos lettuce. I'd thought about throwing in the jarring red of a ripe tomato. Held back at the last minute. A lifetime of overdoing. Time to learn a little restraint. Maybe. Hopefully.

'So you've seen the back of the house. What then?' I ask Barbara when we're all sitting down.

Bob lays slices of lamb out on a plate as carefully as if he was arranging flowers. Adds vegetables, passes it to Barbara. All small portions. Like a child's. He does the same for me, but the portions are larger. When his own plate is ready, he sits down, raises his glass.

'To new neighbours,' I toast.

'I can drink to that,' Bob says.

We all clink glasses and it feels oddly festive.

Barbara moves the food around her plate. Not eating much. When there's half an inch of wine left in her glass Bob tries to pour more but she waves him away.

'So go on with your story,' I say. 'You've just seen the roof and the bagged walls.'

'Oh yes, that's right. Well. I looked at the building and said to Bob, what a lovely looking old house.'

She spears a little meat. Chews it slowly.

'What did Bob say?' I butt in.

Bob looks up from his food. 'Damp in winter. Faces south. Escarpment to the rear. Cold. No way.'

'So you were looking for a place to buy as you walked the tracks around here?' I ask.

'Uh-huh,' Barbara says. 'We'd lived in Mt Eliza in Victoria for most of our lives. Bob wanted a change. I did too. But we weren't looking for anything offshore.'

'What we wanted to do was escape the kids,' Bob says, interrupting with a grin.

Barbara looks at him. They smile at each other.

'Our family had grown up and they were all doing well,' Barbara says, softening his jokey explanation. 'They didn't need us any more and we felt it was time to lead our own lives. But Bob was right about the house that day. With the escarpment hard up against the back of the building it had to be cold and damp.'

So they retraced their steps, she says, without even a backward glance and never thought about the house again.

'But that doesn't explain –'

'Just give me a little time,' Barbara says, laughing at my impatience.

'Sorry, ok. I'm always in a rush to get to the ending.'

'In September 1993, we rented a house at Newport on the northern beaches and started searching for a home around Pittwater in earnest,' she continues. 'Our criteria was low maintenance, two bedrooms, no swimming pool, plenty of parking. We wanted a home to use essentially as a base for travelling. Which we'd been promising ourselves we'd do for years.

'But you know how it is, first there's babies, then Bob was establishing his business, then the babies grow into teenagers and you become the taxi driver. You seem to run around frantically and it feels like it's never going to end and then one day, you look up from washing the dishes and think I've done my job as a mother, now it's time for us.

'After a couple of months of looking at houses from one end of Pittwater to the other, we'd found nothing in our price range and we were getting desperate. So Bob and I decided to contact a local offshore real estate agent to see what was available in boat-access-only homes.'

On a balmy afternoon in November 1993, Barbara looked at eight boat-access-only properties on Scotland Island and the western foreshores of Pittwater.

'There were a couple of possibles on the south side of Lovett Bay,' she says. 'But it was a disappointing day. Nothing came close to the house of our dreams.'

Late in the afternoon, Barbara climbed wearily into the real estate agent's boat to go home. There were a whole lot of brochures on the floor of the boat and she picked them up, glancing at one picture of a rather beautiful house with a long, columned verandah. The house was called *Tarrangaua*. Built, according to the leaflet, for Dorothea Mackellar, an icon of Australian poetry who wrote 'My Country', a poem that sums up every Australian's nostalgia for a wild, untamed landscape.

'The real estate agent was just as tired as I was,' Barbara says. 'But I wanted to see the house. Just out of curiosity. It was way beyond our price range. But it would be an interesting end to the day and I'd tell Bob all about it.'

Barbara walked slowly up the sandstone steps, about eighty or so, she estimated. Out of breath, she climbed the last few steps up to the verandah and then paused. The beauty of the house and the environment was almost shocking. She put her hand on the wide, smooth balustrade at the top of the steps and looked and looked. The view across Lovett Bay and east along Pittwater towards Clareville was simply spectacular. Then she turned and faced the house.

'Time seemed to stand still,' she says.

We have stopped eating, Bob and I. Barbara's food, too, lies barely touched.

'Then I stepped forward and opened the front doors, eight panes of glass in each door. They swung into a long sitting room with polished wooden floors and beams in the ceiling. I felt that glow of reaching one's place. Do you know what I mean? That warmth that runs through you when you walk into a space and feel serenity?'

'As though you've found where you belong?' I suggest.

'Exactly!' she says, smiling. 'Perhaps that's how you felt when you bought this house?'

'That's another story,' I say. 'Let's finish this one first.'

She laughs a little and sips her water.

'When Bob returned from a business trip the following evening, I told him I had found three houses. Two were within our price range. One was a dream. I thought he would dismiss the dream immediately. It was the early nineties, not long after the stock market crash, and we were in the middle of the worst recession since the Depression in the thirties. But he was curious, I think, perhaps because he could see how I'd been entranced. So he came with me to see them all, including the dream.'

The property on Scotland Island was basically a pull down and rebuild option, but it was a lovely piece of land with wonderful views of Pittwater. The other house was on the north facing side of Lovett Bay.

'But Bob looked at it closely and felt it had been built too poorly. It was one of those houses that was just a bit too good to demolish but not good enough to live with.'

And then there was *Tarrangaua*, with its graceful verandah and echo of a more innocent era.

'Exactly, to the dollar, double our budget,' Barbara says.

Bob climbed the stairway behind his wife, pausing every now and then to look across Lovett Bay. Neither of them said much, not even when they reached the house. Barbara let Bob enter the house first to wander alone for a while, through the rooms and into the back courtyard where an old rock retaining wall sprouted rock orchids and ferns. After a while, she followed her husband inside and found him standing in a small room at the eastern end of the house.

'I could see that, like me, he felt comfortable. As though he was home,' Barbara says.

He looked through the armies of spotted gums, some of them shedding their salmon pink bark to reveal smooth, lime green trunks. Then he turned to his wife and slipped an arm around her shoulders.

'I always thought Shangri-La would be to be able to sit in your office and look out your window at your boat,' he said to her.

'There was a smile on his lips. A faraway look in his eyes,' Barbara says. 'I knew then that he loved the house – not just because it was set well beyond the neighbours and surrounded by ragged bushland, but because of the atmosphere it created. There was order – but also wildness. Simplicity – but with an overriding formality.'

Bob says: 'I found out later that the house is always referred to as Pittwater's *jewel in the crown*. And in a strange way, it is. Not because it's the biggest or grandest house, but because it has such . . . such presence. Yes, that's the word. Presence.'

'But it was twice our budget and I didn't know how we could find a way to buy it,' Barbara adds.

When she voiced her misgivings, Bob just smiled. 'Let me worry about that,' he told her. And the business of buying the *house on the high, rough hill* began.

The story seems finished. The sun, by now, is hard on my back, like a warm blanket, but it shines in Barbara's eyes. I'm about to go inside to get her a hat but she continues talking and I sink back into my seat. Bob refills my wineglass and his own. Barbara waves him away from her glass.

'There were two quite strange coincidences before we took possession of the house,' she says. 'First, we realised the house was the lovely old home that we had seen from the rear on our bush-walk the previous January.

'Second, the contract of sale was to have been exchanged in

late December but we had business commitments and a daughter's wedding in Melbourne, so we asked if the date of exchange could take place on January 26. *Tarrangaua* was of national importance and Australia Day seemed appropriate. But it was a public holiday so the date was moved to January 28, 1994.

'I didn't realise the significance of the date until a couple of years later when I was throwing out some old work diaries. I was amazed to discover I'd noted the bushwalk on January 28, 1993. So we took possession of this wonderful old house a year to the day from that first glimpse.'

Barbara looks around the table at us. The story, it seems, is ended. But we are all silent for a little longer.

'Are you happy, living there? Was it the right move?' I ask her after a while.

'These have been the best years of my life,' she says.

And because her life is visibly running out, there is nothing more to say. Bob reaches for her hand across the table and holds it tightly. Barbara smiles at him in a way that closes other people out, then gently withdraws her hand.

Lunch drifts along again and we exchange information about ourselves. Bob is fifty-six years old, they have four children, love sailing, and Barbara is passionate about bush regeneration, which is why she hates that *evil* lantana. Bush regeneration is big on Pittwater, she tells me. It means clearing out introduced and often invasive species and giving the original Australian bush a chance to regrow.

'It's a skill even enthusiastic bush regenerators don't always understand,' she says. 'The Australian bush is so fragile, so easily trashed. People rush in and get it all wrong and do more damage than good.'

'Actually, Barbara, I don't know much about the bush and native plants.'

'Not many Australians do.'

She smiles wryly, and then looks me straight in the eye. 'Why don't you learn about it? This is the best place in the world to start.'

I shrug, non-committal. I grew up with gardens proudly filled with plants from around the world, the kind that give you lots of cut flowers for vases and a big, colourful, perfumed spring show. To me, the Australian bush can be lacklustre, even downright unfriendly. It's full of scratchy plants that spike and lacerate and it's always dry and crackly with dead branches and spindly, struggling plants. There's usually an ants' nest right where you decide to sit down, and spiders, snakes and leeches. Magnificent in a wild way but there's not much that's lush and inviting about it at all. It's not the kind of place you'd want to wander into with a book and a blanket for a lazy afternoon. Ok in its place, in other words, but not in your backyard.

'I like walking in the bush, Barbara, as long as I'm on a track, and I love the smell after it's rained. Sort of new and lung cleansing. But I like a garden to have flowers, and ordered beds with spaded edges. And trees that change colour with the seasons and foliage that's a dense or vibrant green, not grey and washed out. I like the bush to stay in the bush.'

I break off because I see her smiling and there's a dreamy look in her eyes. 'That will change, you know.'

'Maybe.'

'Places can change people, weave a kind of magic.'

'Perhaps,' I reply.

At the end of lunch, when it's too cold to sit on the deck any longer, Bob and Barbara get up to go home. At the front door, Bob holds Barbara's bright purple jacket so she can slip her arms into the sleeves. But she ignores him and turns to ask: 'Are you enjoying living here?'

'Oh yes, I love it.'

'We knew Gordon, you know. Not well, but enough.'

'Gordon was the first to build after the fire,' Bob says.

'Yes. Tough old bloke. He's going to hate me soon, though. I'm going to extend the house.'

'Are you?' Barbara asks, surprised.

'If I'm going to die, I'm going to die in comfort.'

Barbara laughs. 'Oh, you'll be all right.'

And she says it with what seems like prescience, so it gives me comfort. I remember then, living with the boys when they were dying. Remember the importance of setting manageable goals, talking to them about the future. Buying them clothes that, in my heart, I knew they would never wear. Seeing hope and optimism flood their faces. Taking away, even for a few minutes, the heavy tread of death.

Still standing at the front door, we launch into a discussion about the best builders, plumbers, electricians and architects on Pittwater.

'It's a minefield,' Barbara says, 'unless you know what you are doing.'

'I figure I'll get the most experienced offshore builder in the area and leave it all to him.'

'Oh no,' Barbara says, quite shocked, 'that won't work. You'll have to monitor it every step of the way.'

'Good God, no. I don't even know which end of a hammer is the right one. Pointless. Have to trust them. It'll be fine.'

'Bob will help you,' she says, as though she is used to guiding him and he doesn't mind.

'No way! You guys have enough to do.'

'If you have any questions, if there is anything you don't understand, then please ask me,' Bob says. It's his longest sentence so far.

Barbara insists again that Bob help to oversee the project and I decline again. But I cannot tell her it is because I know what is ahead of Bob, as her carer. There will be no time and even less energy for anything outside Barbara. They are the ones, I think, who will need support.

'Tell me, do you know anything about Dorothea Mackellar?' I ask, trying to change the subject.

Barbara smiles. 'A little,' she replies.

'I'd like to find out more about her.'

'Come for a cup of tea tomorrow.'

To be honest, I don't *really* care much about a poet who's been dead for thirty years. But I agree because I like Barbara's company and I really have nothing else to do and it takes my mind off cancer.

During that first lunch, the first of many, Barbara and I never talk about the illness that threatens both our lives. I wonder later if we were simply in denial. Lunch was so blessedly mundane. A gentle exchange of information between new neighbours – just enough to keep escape routes intact for a quick exit if one of us turned out to be mad or, worse, a crashing bore.

14

THE MORNING AFTER LUNCH with Bob and Barbara, I feel too tired to vacuum, and gardening is out because every time I bend over and then straighten, the world swims dizzily for about three minutes and I'm overwhelmed by a desire to throw up.

I wander around aimlessly, trying not to think about the big issues but they sidle in easily when your mind is unfocused and your hands lying idle. I decide to clean out a couple of handbags – seldom used now that I don't go to work every day. In one, I find the card with the name and phone number of the Jack Russell breeder that Donald the hairdresser gave me. On a whim, I call her.

'I've got a real little darling pup,' she enthuses, 'gorgeous, so gorgeous a friend wanted her immediately.'

'Oh, so your friend wants her?'

'Oh no! She already has three dogs. She'd take her, though, if she didn't already have three dogs. And her sister. She's gorgeous too.'

'Your friend has a sister?'

'No, the puppy has a sister. There's two of them. The last of the litter. Don't know what I'll do if I can't find homes for both of them.'

There's a big sigh from the other end of the phone. Visions of lethal injections, glue factories, everything horrendous, flash through my mind.

'I suppose I could take both of them.'

'Oh, luv, I'd give you a discount if you did that. Fifty dollars off each of them.'

Great. Only half the national debt. But I am in *live for the moment* mode. Forget about the future. There may not be one. Who should I leave the dogs to if I die soon? Pia, of course. She used to have two King Charles spaniels years ago. Two dogs are, for her, normal. There go the death thoughts again. Crush 'em instantly. *I am strong and my body is strong.*

The breeder talks incessantly. I don't hear most of it. A few words sink in. *Worms, raw eggs, house-training.* But I am not concentrating. I am trying to understand why I think taking on two little puppies seems like a good idea when I hardly have the energy to walk to the water taxi.

'Are you there, luv? Are you there? Did you get the address then?' she asks nervously.

'Oh yeah. Right. For the cheque. Run that past me again?'

'I'll let you know the flight details. The puppies will be on the plane from Canberra next Monday. They have names. Ibis and Iris. Lovely, aren't they?'

'Oh.'

''Course you can change them if you want.'

'Right. Great. Thanks. Call me when you know the arrival time.'

'They're house-trained, too.'

'Fantastic.'

'Well nearly. And they come to the call of PUPPPPIEEEES!'

An ear splitting squawk reverberates down the line and, muttering a quick goodbye, I hang up. Sisters, I think. Sisters. Well, they'll keep each other company.

There is a quirk in my personality that makes me take on double what is feasible. I always push the limits. I am not sure, even now, whether it is ignorance, innocence or bull-headed stupidity. The trait filters through every aspect of living. When I cook, my husband always said I made enough to feed the Russian army. At his funeral, for God's sake, the priest recounted the details of a lunch I'd prepared for the christening of one of Paul's grandchildren. I made enough, he told the congregation, for him to take the leftovers back to the seminary where they fed the brothers for a week.

I'm not sure where the impulse comes from. Was it growing up in the country where one minute there was bounty, the next nothing? Was it a lifetime of my mother telling me at parties to 'FHB' (Family Hold Back), in case there wasn't enough for all? Did I suspect a thin line of meanness in my spirit and therefore made sure to overcompensate?

My long-legged neighbour from up the hill, Jack, came closest, I think, to fingering the source of the problem. 'You have,' he teased at a lunch a few months after I bought Gordon's house, 'an almost morbid fear of running out of food.'

But why? Why still, after all these years? I haven't gone hungry since I lived in London when I was barely twenty-one and the best I could manage after paying rent and transport to work (as a receptionist for United Press International) was muesli for breakfast and baked beans for dinner. Forget lunch. Even then, life wasn't lean for long. I eventually got an evening job three days a week as a barmaid in a pub around the corner and the chef took a liking to me. Fed me every night and sent me home with enough to see me through to my next shift. Truth is, I have no idea why I always over-cater. Perhaps I'm just no good at working out quantities.

The idea of the puppies is hugely cheering and I do what every new dog owner does – avoid thinking about house-training, dog hair and exercise routines and think, instead, about warm, furry little bodies and unconditional love.

My diary is littered with gruesome appointments. Blood tests. Chemo dates. Naturopath consultations. GP appointment. Lymphatic massage. But the day is free on Monday. Why all the medical appointments? Because when your life is on the line, you grab every remotely rational sliver of help – or do I mean *hope*? For the first time in my life, instead of taking my body blithely for granted, I am aware of every tiny function, from a wriggling toe to cracked lips. The body's toughness and fragility is astounding when you think about it. A deep cut in the wrong spot and you can bleed to death. And yet you can be injected with poison and you will recover.

Watching my own body so closely makes me, in turn, study everything that grows. Trees, flowers, animals. And by studying what makes them thrive, a subtle logic begins to prevail in the way I look after myself. Drink alcohol? Pay the price. Eat rubbish? Pay the price. Do everything right? Enjoy the well-being.

It's about three hours until I'm due to have tea with Barbara so I check out the fridge to see what's there to make a cake. Eggs? Yes. Butter? Yes. Lemons? Yes. Ok, so it's a lemon cake. One of those quick ones you whiz up in the food processor with lots of butter and eggs and that turn out as light and luscious as a hand-beaten sponge and takes only a few minutes to make. It fills the house with a buttery/eggy fragrance that sets the mouth salivating. Is it possible to smell the lightness of a cake? I think so. When it's cooked, I turn it out on a plate immediately and coat it with a sugar and lemon juice syrup with a big slug of gin added. Bugger our livers, I think, and with that thought comes the understanding that it will always be a struggle to do only what it is good for the body. And it is better, perhaps, to aim for balance.

That late winter afternoon, I climb the sandstone steps to *Tarrangaua* for the first time. Carrying a bloody huge cake after doubling the recipe. Overdone it again. Twenty-two generous slices. Easily. There will be three of us. Oh well, Barbara can freeze it. Pull it out when people call in. As they do, when you are ill.

The steps are steep and uneven. Dizziness swoops in. I have to stop and put the plate down and then sit. From out of nowhere, my skin prickles with a mass of burning pins and needles. I whip off my hat to cool my body and wonder what is happening to me. When the world stops spinning, I look across the bay, the cold from the stone steps seeping through my trousers and cooling me down. Chemical poisoning, I decide. That's all it is.

Yachts are etched with the fine gold line of a late sun. The waterfall runs in a muffled rush. Green on green. A thousand hues. There is an old work boat moored in the bay. I can see her clearly from my perch on the steps. Although she still floats, her buoyancy is the fittest part of her. The wood is tired, the paint peeling. The small cabin where the wheelhouse once stood is half missing, rotted, damaged, whatever. And yet, from a distance, there is nothing sad about this tired old vessel. Because she is beautiful. Her bow rises fluidly and elegantly. Her stern lifts almost flirtatiously and she is long and slim, like a satin-gowned film queen of the thirties. 'That might be a little project one day,' I think, getting up and tackling the stairs once more. 'Bring her back to glory.'

Barbara waits on the verandah, on the western side of the house where she is in the sun and protected from the breeze, sitting in a cane armchair. From the top of the steps, a little way from the house, she looks like a photograph of a woman from a long-gone era, fragile, delicate, with the ghostly pallor of early black and white pictures. The moment feels surreal. The house, settled high above old holiday shacks and nouveau glass palaces of nearby Frog Hollow and the south side of Lovett Bay, is quietly authoritative. Not casual. No holiday spirit about it. Just solid and graceful.

'How are you?' I shout from the lawn.

Barbara waves, indicating I should use the front door steps to reach the verandah, which gleams dark brown, as though polished, and stretches the length of the house. About eighty feet. It makes the current era of decks and platforms seem abandoned before completion.

I plonk the cake on the table and sink into another cane chair. Rearrange cushions for comfort.

'Bit of a hike up here. How do you do it?' I ask.

'Keeps you fit,' she replies, looking at the cake.

'What about after a few drinks?'

'Did you notice the turn? The corner? Near the top?'

'Yeah. Where you move towards the back of the house instead of parallel to the coastline?'

'Yes. That's known as Barb's Rest. Bob and I were at The Point one Friday evening. It was summer and hot and thirsty weather. We had a few drinks to cool down, and then a few more. I made it home as far as the turn when I quietly sat down and decided it was the perfect spot for a bit of a nap.'

We laugh.

'This is a place where, if you are not careful, drinking becomes a way of life,' she adds.

'My dear, I am – or was – a journalist. Drinking *is* a way of life.'

She looks at me without smiling. Her blue eyes flat. 'Not much gets done if you drink a lot.' Don't waste time, she is saying. Not when we both know it is finite.

On the round wooden table in front of her there is a stack of books and old magazines.

'There's a bit of a mystery about Dorothea,' she says, leaning forward, businesslike, moving folders around. She pushes the cake aside as though she doesn't quite know what to do with it.

'Lemon cake,' I say to help her out. 'Thought you could freeze leftovers. Pull it out when you need it.'

'Thank you. Looks delicious. I must say, it's the biggest cake I've ever seen.'

She gets up from her chair and goes into the kitchen, calling to Bob. There's the sound of shuffling feet coming down the hallway.

'Susan's brought a cake.' She pauses, looks down at the cake. 'All of it is here to stay.'

Bob comes to the kitchen door that leads to where we're sitting, nods to me and looks at the cake. 'Big cake. Cup of tea?'

'Oh yes. Lovely. Thank you. With milk. No sugar.'

He disappears.

I turn to Barbara: 'Mystery?'

'Mmm.'

Bob materialises from the kitchen. Two plates each bearing a slice of cake. Half the size I would cut.

Barbara takes a bite. Says nothing for a minute or two. I reach across and sift through the material on the table. A document, bound in plastic with a clear cover and a cheery yellow back, catches my eye and I pull it out. It is titled 'Search for Solitude', subtitled 'Dorothea Mackellar and her Lovett Bay retreat'.

'What's this?' I ask.

Bob returns carrying flowery bone china mugs filled with steaming tea. It smells like it's made from tea leaves, not tea bags. He puts a cup in front of each of us without a word and then goes.

'Bob's working.'

'Oh.'

'On a design for a new kiln.'

Barbara sips her tea, breaks tiny pieces of the cake and eats delicately.

I flick through the document, shovel the cake down my throat in large lumps.

'It's a project I have begun,' Barbara explains about the yellow folder. 'And one I hope you might finish.'

I look at her sharply. She avoids eye contact. Continues to break tiny pieces of cake.

I want to ask her what she means. But I know what she means. And to ask would be rude. Somehow reduce the moment. She does not want me to pretend I do not understand what she is saying. So I do not waffle on with *you'll be fine* said in a dozen different forms. I am not grinning and *positive* when Barbara is clearly confronting the most difficult reality any of us ever faces.

My friend Sophia, the Buddhist, taught me truth is easier to handle than lies.

'I may die soon,' I said to her one day. I expected her to tell me it was rubbish, to pull myself together.

'Yes,' she said simply. 'You could die soon.'

For a moment, I was furious with her. She was supposed to prop me up emotionally, wasn't she? Then I loved her for her answer. She was the first, in a long line of doctors, friends, family and colleagues, who actually articulated the word *die*. It was a relief and, with her, I didn't ever have to pretend everything was fine and, that there'd be some kind of Pollyanna-ish end to it all when it was just plain hideous.

So I wait silently for Barbara to go on, to unveil the mystery, whatever it might be.

'That's the research I've done so far,' she says finally, pointing at the document in my hands. 'Read it, and tell me what you think.'

'What's the mystery?' I ask again.

'Come back to me when you've read that. Then we'll talk.'

'Ok. By the way, I'm getting a new puppy – well, two new puppies. They arrive on Monday.'

'Now there's trouble,' she says.

I walk down the sandstone steps clutching her research, not convinced, I must admit, that there could be anything too interesting in the life of a long-dead, spinster poet. 'And how much trouble,' I ask myself crossly, 'can two little puppies be?'

That night I put Barbara's work aside and check out the bookshelves again – this time for anything to do with raising and training puppies. There's nothing. When Sweetie was a pup I went to boot camp training sessions at some doggie training school about an hour's drive from the Nepean home. It rained every Saturday and I slushed through a boggy paddock with niggling sensations of having drunk too much the night before. Saturdays were often delicate. The result of winding down after a big week.

I realise with surprise that I do not miss journalism, haven't thought about it since the day I closed the door on my last job – almost a month ago, now. I know instinctively that the gut-churning thrill of looming deadlines, the chase for the big exclusive and the rat-gnawing fear that you'll fail to fall over the line no longer appeal to me. The part of my nervous system that thrived on adrenaline has worn out. What I once found thrilling now makes me feel weak and threatened. It isn't until a few years later that I work out the only reason to feel fear is when you haven't covered all the bases. Haven't put in every ounce of possible grunt. If you could have done no more, then there can be no sense of failure. Not just in journalism, but in everything. From making a cake to cleaning a loo.

It is that same fear of being called on to give more than I'm now capable of that makes me wonder if I should cancel the puppies. Can't look after myself properly at the moment. How can I cope with energetic young pups? Then the image, quick as a flash, of soft, warm bodies. Cold, wet noses. Unfettered exuberance. Companions. Love. Two little beings that are honestly my own. So I don't reach for the phone to cancel. Let it happen. For better. Only for better.

I go to bed early feeling exhausted. Dinner (two lamb chops) sets off waves of nausea. Chemo makes me feel like I'm constantly seasick. Only lying down stops the rolling disorientation. Even reading gets hard.

The phone rings when it is cold and dark. It's the breeder with the arrival time for the puppies. Ready for pick-up at two thirty the following day. I cut the conversation short. Too tired to be polite.

Then suddenly a toe-tingling heat, pins and needles again, rises like a surging surf and swamps me. Sweat explodes all over my body. I throw off doonas. Unbutton my pyjamas. Sweat rolls down my back. I fight the urge to vomit. Then, in moments, I'm back to a teeth-chattering cold. I haul the bedclothes back on then, just as the cold seeps out of my body, another flush explodes. Fast and furious. Is this a new kind of hell?

I sleep on and off, my mind in a drowsy half-reality, buzzing with people I've never seen, places I've never been. I have no idea where these blank faced beings in my subconscious come from, and I do not care. I let them chatter away in conversations that mean nothing until I fall into an uneasy sleep a couple of hours before dawn.

I phone the oncologist in the morning. 'What's going on? I keep feeling like I'm going to explode with heat and the next minute, I'm freezing.'

'Hot flushes. You're in menopause.'

She is happy. Chemo has done its job. The estrogen has leached out of my body.

'How long does it last?'

'Couple of years. Often five. Sometimes a lifetime.'

'I'd better be in the couple of years scenario.'

'No way to tell.'

'Is there anything I can do?'

'Nope. Hormone replacement is not for you. So hang in with the flushes, ok? Just hang in,' she says.

'Yeah. But this feels like the last straw.'

'I know you don't think so now, but you'll get used to them and they'll start to lose their intensity in a couple of years. Roll with them, if you can.'

I hang up in despair.

Within a week, the last shreds of my ability to concentrate evaporate. Any close-fitting clothing makes me feel like someone is pulling a noose tight around my neck, choking off the air, suffocating me. I stand at bank tellers' windows and see wariness in their faces when I suddenly break into a drowning sweat. I know I look desperate because that's how I feel. Chemo has left me with very little control over my body. Now I have even less and I feel semi-hysterical most of the time. Panic attacks, which engulf me for no reason at all, hit me anywhere, but for some reason, mostly in supermarket parking lots. If I'm shocked by a loud noise – a car backfiring, a door slamming – I burst into tears.

The flushes surge in at around twenty minute intervals, although there may only be a five minute respite. I spend a lot of time putting clothes on and then taking them off. Sometimes the desire to strip everything off is almost overwhelming, even in the middle of a busy street. Anything to cool down before I explode. It's a new hell. And I hate it. I hate the absolute bloody weakness of it all. But I will not – I abso-bloody-lutely will not – give in. I know forever more now that one gift cancer has given me is the knowledge that life, in just about any form, is utterly precious. I doubt I will ever be careless of it again. The new measure for everything from irritation to disappointment is simple. Is it life-threatening? If not, don't worry about it.

I call the water taxi when it's time to pick up the puppies. Outside, the cool air feels like stepping into a refrigerator in the middle of my own personal heatwave. I whack on my hat and say hi to the boys as I pass the boatshed. It is lunchtime. They sit on the cold concrete on a cold day, eating two-inch thick sandwiches, surrounded by the synthetic smell of instant coffee.

Alongside the ferry wharf, on their own pontoon, Bob and Barbara's two tinnies rock with the swell in what looks like mute conversation. They are not the conventional open tin dinghies ordinarily found around the bays. The big one is squarish, with an aluminium cabin and three V-shaped hulls, The smaller one has a conventional dinghy body with a pointy nose and a rounded middle, but the same hard metal cabin as the bigger boat. They look a bit like Thomas the Tank Engine and as stable as tennis courts. I can't help thinking one of them might be a perfect commuter boat for a beginner driver like me. I could slap, bang and bash them up against docks and barely feel the bumps.

Water taxi Bob is on duty today. When I first arrived at Towlers Bay in what already seems a time as distant as The Dreaming, I'd tried to get a herb and vegetable garden going at Stewart's house. The soil there is sandy and poor, and I hauled bags of fresh chicken and cow manure and bales of lucerne in an effort to build it up. Water taxi Bob didn't even hesitate to take on the cargo, which ponged like a poultry farm. He just reached for the bags and bales and loaded them onto his immaculate boat. Years later, he tells me he ripped the carpet from the floor of the boat and dragged it behind in the water for about three hours to kill the dung smell. I love water taxi Bob. He's a gentleman.

'Off to another treatment?' he asks.

'Nope.'

I don't want to tell him about the puppies, want them to be a surprise.

'What time does your shift end?' I ask.

'Today? Three.'

He'll be gone before I return, so I tell him: 'Picking up two little puppies. Jack Russells. Sisters. From the airport.'

'Yours?'

'Yep.'

'Now there's trouble,' he says, laughing deep and so wide a shard of sun hits one of his silver fillings and creates lightning flashes.

I wonder briefly why everyone keeps mentioning the word 'trouble'. Puppies can't be too hard to handle, can they?

The traffic feels like playing dodge 'em cars. It's nearly two months since I drove through crowded city streets. Downturned mouths, tapping fingers on steering wheels, people who honk and hoot and then shake their hands in mock despair when I fail to accelerate fast enough for them. Everyone around me seems to be going at a ball-breaking, frantic speed. I recall a hundred cranky moments when I, too, ranted and raged at all those grey-haired drivers with fading eyesight and wavering concentration who moved too slowly. Now I am like them. Lovett Bay has changed my pace and I get a sudden glimpse of what it will be like to be old and left behind by youth and technology. But with Lovett Bay as the backdrop for aging, the prospect doesn't seem too awful. Neither does aging, now that there's a chance I may not get to experience it.

I hear yapping from the moment I step out of the car at the cargo terminal of Sydney airport. Two sets of high pitched yelps, constant, ear-piercing, semi-hysterical. Completely furious. The clerk is pathetically grateful to hand them over in their doggy carrying case and wishes me a fervent 'Good luck'.

I load them into the back of the car and open the cage door. The first puppy to poke out a velvety little nose I call, Vita. The second, shyer but bigger, with the gentlest face and roundest brown eyes, I call Dolce. I know it is corny but I don't care. Sweet life, gentle life. That's my goal. They will be constant reminders of all that is good.

I lift them out of the cage, each small enough to fit in one hand, two warm, frightened little puppies that lean against my chest as hard as they can. Their hearts race and they smell like fresh bread. I inhale deeply and it drowns out the smell of chemo that comes up from my lungs with every breath.

Vita's face is tan. Matching hindquarters lead into a tan tail. The rest of her starry white coat is short-haired, not curly like some terriers, and her legs are longer than conventional, which means she doesn't have the tummy dragging look of some Jack Russells. She is pure female. Sexy. Knows her own beauty. She reminds me, don't ask me why, of Lana Turner.

Dolce's face is also tan but with a little black through it. She has a white blaze, and fluffy mutton-chop whiskers. She has the same white through the body, but stained here and there with shadowy brown patches under her thin white fur. Her tail is tan but the tip looks like it's been dipped in white paint. When it wags, it's like a frantic flag of surrender. Her head is too small for the rest of her body and she gives the impression of being messy, lacking the aura Vita exudes. Her confidence is shaky. I hold her harder. Soothe her with more focus. Vita is already looking around, scoping the landscape.

I put them in the doggy cage for the drive home. They are quiet in the back. *Good puppies.* They may not be perfect specimens of the breed but I like that. I feel we all match each other.

I pull into the supermarket car park and lock them in the car. After a quick scoot around the aisles, stuffing the trolley with dog food, dog collars and leads, and doggy treats, I tiptoe back to the car. Listening for a racket caused by two frightened puppies.

All quiet. *Good puppies.* Open the rear, throw in the grocery bags. They spring up and down, their little round pink tummies freckled with brown spots, pressed against the sides of their cage. Already so pleased to see me but I resist the desire to pick them up. They will settle in at home in a minute. Of course they will.

Annette swings the pink water taxi in to dock, churning the water like a flamenco dancer's frilly skirt.

I load the puppies on first.

'Who are these?'

'My new family.'

'Oh . . .' She goes quiet. A cold wet nose pushes through the bars to get closer to her fingers.

'They are . . .' she says. 'They are . . .'

'Heaven!'

'Yep. That's the word.'

But she leaves me with the feeling she was going to say something else. A word that didn't have quite the same meaning as 'heaven'.

Annette climbs back into her driver's seat, puts her feet on a raised, homemade step for comfort and balance, slowly guns the motor and swings away from the ferry wharf. Her hair is always perfect. Wonder how she does it in the wind and rain? Never seen her bad-tempered either. She always wears pink or navy or both with lots of white. She does a hard, often dirty job but she always looks clean, and serenely, effortlessly female.

The puppies are frantic when the throttle moves forward and the boat, *Little Bits*, rises high before levelling. I try to soothe them but Dolce throws up. I feel for her. I get seasick too.

At the Lovett Bay ferry wharf, Annette hands up the smelly cage. 'Happy families,' she says, screwing up her nose.

Later in the afternoon, I put collars and leads on the puppies and take them up the hill to visit Barbara. Her wide smile erases the tiredness from her face, and she scoops them onto her lap, inhaling their wheaty puppy smell.

'I haven't had time to read your document yet,' I explain, settling in for what is to become a ritual cup of tea.

We sit on the verandah in the late afternoon light. The escarpment broods in shadow. Great swathes of towering eucalypts, backlit by the setting sun, roll like moss down the hillside. Near the house, the feathery foliage of wattle trees bleaches to gold and a border of agapanthus defines the edge of the lawn. The colours just before evening closes in are denser, richer, lusher, and the bay gleams like polished brass.

'Read it when you're ready,' Barbara replies.

Bob, again, brings slightly underfilled mugs of hot tea and slightly undersized slices of lemon cake. Then disappears back into his study. The tea has the same earthy smell that came from my grandmother's kitchen when tea was routinely brewed strong and black on a wood burning stove or in a sooty billy hanging from a hook over the gigantic, fifteen foot fireplace in the sitting room.

Bob's tea always makes me think of my granny, whose name was Henrietta and who always wore a 'pinny' (apron) over her clothes, tied tight around a tiny waist. She used to buy Bex, a powdered painkiller, by the carton load, and every afternoon she'd disappear into her bedroom with a cup of tea and a Bex, to have a lie-down. My Uncle Frank says she used to take a Bex if she thought she *might* get a headache. She died at sixty-three. Probably from kidney failure, although no-one quite knows.

She was a superstitious old girl, my granny, who believed she had second sight. She passed on her *I told you so* kind of magic to my mother, who wielded it indiscriminately. For years I believed that my mother had some kind of ability to see beyond the natural. As a result, my childhood was hostage to superstition.

'Old Etty died,' my mother would tell me. 'Saw it coming. Picture fell off the wall last week.'

I would wonder briefly why – if she saw it coming – she did nothing to warn the old girl. But my doubt always felt disloyal so I kept silent even though it seemed to me that she was usually wise *after* the event and never *before* it.

My mother has her own long list of rules to obey to keep the spirits satisfied. Never put new shoes on the table (bad luck). No carnations or lilies in the house (death in the family). Never cut your fingernails on a Sunday or Friday (more bad luck). Never turn a mirror or painting to the wall (more death). Never give away a knife without getting a coin for it (cuts a friendship). Seeing crows (watch yourself, you could be in mortal danger). Picture falling from the wall (death). And on and on.

As a child, though, I wondered if my mother also knew the thoughts that ran through my mind. She certainly let me believe she did. Which gave her a lot of power until I was old enough to toss off the hocus-pocus. She was a good guesser, though, I'll give her that. Although my brother told me my face was as easily read as a book. Still is, apparently.

One day I plucked up enough courage to actually ask Mum why, if she'd foreseen a calamitous event, she hadn't done something to stop it.

'You can't intervene in the natural course of life,' she replied.

'Then what's the point of having second sight?'

I got a pat on the hand and a sad little shake of the head, as if to say that one day, when I grew up, I would understand all. Maybe she had a point. Musical microwaves, little green satellites, my obsessive search for omens when I didn't want to make a decision . . . I wonder, though, whether omens were my scapegoat, a device that I conjured up to allow me to take actions I knew were intrinsically wrong. Cross two creeks in one day bearing the lover's name? It must mean the gods are smiling on the relationship, right? Of course not. But for me, in those cyclonic times, it was enough to make me feel the gods had pressed a waxed seal of approval on the liaison.

I have not seen the lover since my dreadful birthday lunch, nearly two months ago, nor had a phone call from him to see how I'm doing. Have I been amputated from his mind or just quickly and cleanly filed away. I wonder if he ever gets a tingling, as I do from the empty space where I once had a breast, when he sees a tall woman in the street that could be me. Sometimes, I try to conjure his face. The deep brown eyes, so hard to read, and the long thin line of his mouth. Easy to read. I am surprised to find that his image is already blurred in my memory. Would I pass close by him in the street and not notice? All that anguish and pain and I cannot even recall the way the pieces of his face fit together.

I sip my tea and wonder whether Barbara would like to hear about my granny and *her* tea, but before I can say anything she passes me a pamphlet covered in crude, ugly drawings of a fat little creature with a pointy head and eight legs.

'What's this?'

'Now you've got a couple of dogs, you'd better find out about ticks.'

My face must have gone even whiter than usual. 'Ticks?'

She points at the drawings. 'That's the life cycle of ticks. The ones that can kill a dog are the fully grown ones, the paralysis ticks.'

'What do you mean, kill? They don't really kill a dog, do they?'

'Oh yes they do.'

'But there are dogs everywhere on Pittwater. How come they're not all dead?'

Barbara smiles. 'I guess you haven't been here for the tick season so you don't know much about them.'

Barbara begins to shake with laughter and she looks at me and apologises. 'Sorry,' she says, almost hiccuping. 'The thing about ticks is that they attach themselves to you in very awkward spots. The first tick Bob ever got . . .'

The story emerges slowly, through more laughter. They'd spent a morning walking a scrubby, bushy block of vacant land during their search for a place to set down new roots.

'When we got home, Bob went to the toilet and felt an itch in his groin,' Barbara explains. 'He scratched for a couple of minutes but the itch didn't go away. So he sat on the toilet and took a closer look.'

'Saw a whole lot of little black legs waving at me,' Bob says, walking in on the conversation. 'From the end of my dick!'

Now they're both laughing.

'Neither of us knew what to do because we'd never seen a tick before so we climbed in the car and went to the local medical centre,' Bob continues. 'There was an old bloke with shaky hands on duty. He came towards me with tweezers and this shockin' shake and I thought, hell, I hope his eyesight's better than his hand control or I could be damaged for life!' He drops down beside his wife, winds an arm around her waist. 'Barbara was laughing so hard I had to drive home. And I was the wounded one!'

For a moment she tilts her head onto his shoulder and there are tears in her eyes that I mistake for sadness. But she's still laughing. Bob plants a loud, squishy kiss on her cheek.

'Got work to do,' he says, getting up.

The puppies are dozing peacefully on Barbara's lap. They're tiny and vulnerable and I can't bear the thought of anything happening to them. I take Dolce from Barbara and tuck her under my chin, snuggling into her fur.

'So much for paradise, huh, little puppy? We're going to have to learn about these ticks then, aren't we?' I have quickly fallen into the habit of talking to the puppies in a way that non-animal lovers find borderline mad.

'Take the pamphlet with you. I've got another one,' Barbara says.

We sit silently then, until the sun drops below the hillside and the chill slams in, which is my signal to go home.

'Stay and have dinner,' Barbara suggests, breaking our pattern.

I don't need any persuading. The idea of going home to a cold, empty house isn't half as tempting as staying in the warmth of *Tarrangaua*.

'How are you getting on with the neighbours?' she asks, going into the kitchen to tell Bob I'll be joining them for dinner.

'Great,' I say, following her in. 'Well, I've seen more of Ken than anyone else because I walk past the boatshed all the time. But I've met Jack and his partner, Brigitte, and their two gorgeous boys. No-one seems to live in the house at the end. I've never seen anyone there.'

'They're weekenders, but they don't get here very often. Good people, though.'

'I haven't met anyone who isn't.'

Barbara smiles with a glint in her eye. 'You will!'

Bob is pulling vegetables out of the fridge.

'Susan's going to stay for a meal. Can you manage?'

'That's great,' he says.

I follow Barbara into the sitting room and scoop the puppies onto my lap. They fall asleep immediately, curled into each other, their little black noses touching lightly, eight paws linked as though they're holding hands.

'I'd like to build a garden,' I tell Barbara. 'Gordon's made a great start but I want to enlarge it.'

'What kind of garden?'

'Well, a few flowers for a vase. Some herbs and vegetables. Maybe some low growing shrubs along the boundary of the property so everyone who passes can't look directly inside the house.'

'Native or non-native plants?'

'Haven't given it much thought.'

'Well, I'm probably biased in favour of natives. I reckon the bush should be allowed to be bush. Most people around here think like that and we'll pressure you a bit to follow that line.'

I feel hackles rising as she speaks. I figure it's my land and I can do what I want. 'I'm the kind of person who doesn't much enjoy pressure,' I say slowly. 'The kind of person who'll plant a rose hedge if people get too bossy.'

She looks at me for a moment and says nothing. Torn between her passion for all things Australian and keeping the balance in a new friendship. Then she shrugs. 'The bush has a way of sorting itself out anyway. A word of advice, though, if you don't mind. The wallabies will eat just about everything you plant and the cockatoos are merciless when it comes to breaking the buds off flower stems. A formal sort of garden could involve a lot of expense and heartbreak.'

Bob comes in with a bottle of red wine and some glasses and looks at us enquiringly.

Barbara shakes her head. 'Not for me. I'll have a little bit of brandy and a lot of dry.'

'Susan? Wine?'

I think about saying no thanks for half a second and then nod.
'Red would be great. Thanks.'

Bob pours my wine and returns to the kitchen to fix Barbara's
drink. There's a constant ping coming from the kitchen and Bob's
tuneless humming. When he returns with Barbara's drink, he
tells us dinner is ready. We sit down to carrots, beans, zucchini,
pumpkin, potato and cauliflower and a piece of golden, crumbed
chicken. When I cut into the meat, it oozes thick rivers of butter
and garlic.

'This is yummy. Thank you.'

Bob grins and raises his glass as though he's going to make a
toast but he doesn't say anything.

'So, tell me what summer is like. Do you see many snakes?'

'Yeah,' Bob says, 'but they're usually more afraid of you than
you are of them. And the pythons, you know they're harmless,
don't you?'

'Saw one when I was staying at Towlers. On my walk to the
ferry. Huge thing, it was, just sliding across the track in front of me
ever so slowly.'

'You're better off letting them hang around,' Barbara says. 'They
eat the rats and mice and they don't let other snakes – poisonous
ones, like red-bellied blacks and brown snakes, move into their
territory. At least that's the theory.'

'Gordon showed me his python. Sleeps in the barbecue.'

'Siphon?'

'Yeah, that's his name. I steer clear of him.'

'He won't hurt you.'

'Yeah, well . . . I let him have his space. Anyone ever been
bitten?'

'Never heard of it.'

When I look up from eating, I see the puppies have climbed
onto the sofa where they're asleep.

'God, sorry. Look at the puppies.'

I jump up to move them to the floor, but in unison Bob and Barbara tell me not to worry. 'They're fine. Let them be.'

They're rock bottom exhausted. And Barbara looks worn out. So as soon as we've finished eating, I get up to go. As I push back my chair, Barbara claps her hands quickly and loudly, and a giant, hairy black spider falls from the ceiling.

I scream. Feel like I'll faint.

Barbara laughs, unaware I'm dizzy with fright. 'It's a toy,' she says. 'Don't worry. It's a toy.'

But my heart beats wildly. I don't feel strong enough for this kind of joke. Bob must see it written on my face. He takes Barbara's arm and says once is enough with the spider joke for me. The shock has sent me into a huge flush. Sweat erupts from every pore.

I hook up bleary-eyed puppies to their leashes and borrow a torch. On the way down the steps I imagine boojums lurking in every dark corner, giant ticks on every illuminated blade of grass. I duck and weave to avoid touching overhanging boughs and jump into the shower immediately I get home, pulling the puppies in with me. If they have a tick it is going to be either scrubbed off or drowned.

The puppies stand wet and shivering, shattered and hurt. For them, the day has turned sour. I dry them off and make up their bed in the corner of the bathroom where I've put a ticking clock that is supposed to sound like a mother's heartbeat. Then I add a hot water bottle. Next, I spread newspaper all over the floor. A precaution only. The walk home was a final piddle stop before settling in for the night and they're partially house-trained. Right?

It never occurred to me to ask how 'partially' fits with 'house-trained' until the next morning when I walk into a bathroom that looks like a shit storm. With a stomach already nervous and tender, I quickly close the door and retreat to the kitchen. Put on the kettle. Not ready to cope yet. But the puppies are awake and alert.

The yapping begins. To quieten them, I open the bathroom door and let them into the sitting room where they both piddle instantly. Does house-trained mean they make a mess *inside* instead of *out*? It is the beginning of chaos, a chaos that escalates daily. About the best that can be said for it is that it takes my mind off cancer and the ex-lover.

Over the next few weeks I test the breeder's notion that the dogs are trained to come to the call of 'puppies!'. They do. But only when they want to. They quickly become known around the bays as the 'terrierists', two tiny, shiny white streakers who think they've landed in the best backyard in the world. Every day an adventure filled with lip-smacking opportunities.

At first, people are patient. And I have no idea when the puppies take off at dawn (when the first yapping begins and I let them out so I can return to bed) that they are wreaking havoc over kilometres of land – private and national park. All I know is that they run off and return a couple of hours later, happy and tired and ready for a snooze. I assume, as little puppies, they will hang around the neighbourhood, too timid to test the unknown boundaries where spiders and snakes, goannas and wallabies, and every kind of scary critter, including *ticks*, lurk. They are on the rampage, though. And the mad, yapping hunt begins from the moment I let them out. But no-one says a word to me. Although I hear later it is a nonstop topic at every dinner party around the bays. Everyone knows I am being treated for breast cancer. No-one wants to add to the burden. And no-one knows what to do.

As if the rampaging isn't bad enough, things are even worse on the nights I go out. Leaving them locked inside. With the unabated fury of the righteous done wrong, Dolce and Vita begin an incessant, high-pitched yap that carries up the hill and over the bay. When one takes a rest, the other starts up. They're relentless. Mostly, though, they yap together at a pitch that has the same effect as fingernails scratching a blackboard. My neighbourhood is fracturing. Across the water, over which the sound carries with an exquisite, ear-piercing purity, windows are being slammed shut, televisions turned up, and partners start to argue about how to handle the problem. Even the boat dwellers, the most laidback and tolerant of all because they live aboard illegally, are pacing their capsules, grinding their teeth, patience worn out.

I, of course, know nothing of this. The yapping starts only after I leave home. And it stops when the puppies hear the water taxi return. To me, it feels like I leave in silence and come home in silence to two warm little bodies springing excitedly at the front door as though I've been gone for years.

One morning, Bob calls. 'Ah, well, it's um, it's, well, the puppies,' he begins. 'Debbie's rung me.'

Debbie's from Frog Hollow, the dark, misty bay east of Lovett where there are also only five houses.

'What's Debbie's problem?' I ask Bob.

'Ah, well, they're chasing . . . um . . . the dogs, well, they're chasing wallabies,' he finally blurts out.

'Why didn't Debbie call me?' And yet, as I ask the question, I realise I barely know her. Each bay is its own tight community with informal hierarchies.

'She called Barbara and Barbara thought I should tell you,' he says, his words suddenly coming out in a rush. 'Because we've thought of a way to help.'

'Is it serious, then? Are people angry, or just Debbie?' I ask.

Bob's reply is slow, the words carefully chosen. I do not know enough about him to understand that he never says anything he doesn't mean, never offers anything he can't deliver, never makes promises he has no intention of keeping.

'Nobody is angry, they are concerned,' he says. 'People live here because they love the wildlife and the bush. They don't want to see it harmed.'

'What harm?' I ask with iron in both syllables.

'The puppies are causing a lot of trouble, chasing wallabies and brush turkeys . . . and it's better to face the problem now before it gets too big.'

'But they're puppies, they're not big enough to hurt wallabies. And birds can fly away. This is just hysterical stuff, isn't it? I bet Debbie doesn't like dogs!' I fume.

'It's not only Debbie,' Bob says. 'Brigitte's unhappy. Maureen around in Towlers has seen them running wild. She worries about the puppies *and* the wildlife.'

I look across the room. The puppies sleep silently on their fluffy sheepskin bed just inside the back door, curled into each other like the underside of a cowrie seashell. They look peaceful and inno-cent. And too tiny to do any damage.

'But they're so little. They can't be causing much trouble,' I insist.

'There's two of them. Which means they're a pack. And packs, eventually, do damage.'

Bob says he'll come down in the late morning to work out a plan and suggests I take them out on their leashes for the next few days instead of just opening the back door and letting them run free.

'What you need,' Bob says when he arrives later, scruffy in dusty work clothes, one trouser leg hooked into the top of a boot, 'is a dog run.'

'No way! I am not going to cage these puppies. I cannot, I just cannot do it to them. I'd rather take them with me wherever I go.'

I hand Bob a cup of tea and he drains it quickly, as though it's lukewarm when in fact it's scalding hot. He focuses on the tea leaves, staring any place but at me.

'I'll put in the dog run anyway. We'll see what happens,' he says quietly but firmly.

We are silent for a while. I am inwardly raging, convinced it is more a political exercise to keep dogs out of the area than any real threat. I do not even think to say thank you, to appreciate he is trying to help.

'Er, there's been another problem,' Bob says, still not looking at me.

'What!'

'When you go out, they yap. They never let up. Doesn't matter if it's day or night. Apparently you can hear them in Elvina Bay.'

'Do you hear them? Up at *Tarrangaua*?' I ask.

'No, but I have heard them. It's pretty terrible. Sorry to be the one with all the bad news. But their yapping is the kind that drives you nuts.'

'Like I said, I'll take them with me when I leave the house. That will fix both problems.'

Bob builds the dog run in the backyard that afternoon. But I won't use it. Every morning, still in my pyjamas, with a dressing gown over the top and a black woollen hat that my husband wore when radiotherapy made the hair on one side of his head fall out, I put the puppies on their leashes and take them for a walk. They are anxious and resentful at having their freedom curtailed and pull hard on their leads, coughing and choking and glaring at me. They are miserable and so am I. But the word goes around. I am trying to train them. The unspoken, unspecified pressure eases.

Jan, next door, is encouraging. 'You're doing a good job. Keep it up,' she says.

But in my vulnerable state, I feel as though I am at war with Lovett Bay and most of the Pittwater community.

Hot on the heels of the puppy problems, I have a routine blood test and my white blood cell count is so low my third treatment has to be postponed. The result makes me feel like I am fading away, being slowly poisoned to death. Since chemo started, I've tried to deny the weakness and dizziness, the feeling of being constantly cold in between flushes. But this latest blow shakes my belief in the power of positive thinking and makes me wonder if I'm being a damn stupid fool to think I can use my mind to help me get well. How much of our physical well-being is tied into our emotional health? No-one's ever been able to figure it out. Not scientifically anyway, only anecdotally, which doesn't cut it in science.

The reality is that most days, I am crying tired. I am stick thin and I have no energy. The dreaded hot flushes wake me at twenty to thirty minute intervals nearly all night, so I never seem to sleep long enough in one go to make it count. I feel as though my body is made up of bleached paper. But I tell myself every day, over and over, that *I am strong and my body is strong* until I believe it, despite the evidence to the contrary.

The blood test news knocks me flat, though. My own, western doctor tells me chemo is chemo and you just have to handle it. The naturopath has told me to buy a whole lot of food supplements to help me put on weight. I'm also taking a mountain of vitamin pills. And I still can't stumble over the line for the third treatment without an extra week or two to build up my white blood cell count. It's firm, scientific evidence of a frailty I refuse to acknowledge.

To boost my body I make an appointment to see a Chinese herbalist recommended by one of the naturopaths I am seeing. Chinese herbalism is just about the only avenue I haven't investigated. Maybe it's going to work brilliantly but, like everything else in this ferocious business of treating cancer, there's no way of proving its effectiveness.

In his North Sydney office he tells me my pulse is very weak, not the pulse checked in western medicine, another, deeper pulse, which explains why I feel quite shockingly frail. His words scare the shit out of me. He writes out a prescription in Chinese and leads me into the reception area to a wall of jars filled with ingredients that look like the stuff of black magic – dried old bones, ground seashells, old bark, animals' intestines. I try to ask him what is actually *in* the jars but his English is erratic. 'Good Chinese medicine. Good Chinese medicine,' he answers to every question.

He hands me seven brown paper bags each containing his mixture of dried brown bits and shell grit – well, that's what it looks like – with instructions to boil up one bag's worth every morning. I must drink one cup of fluid at the beginning and end of every day. It's a five year plan and I must not miss a day. I know that's impossible before I leave the waiting room. And I hate the pressure it applies. If I miss a day, does that mean all is for nothing?

The bill is around one hundred and eighty dollars, and I need a follow-up appointment in seven days. The costs are not reclaimable from medical insurance, like so many naturopathic remedies, and my medical bills are soaring. Memories of the boys and the search for miracle cures come surging back. Am I being a mug to try anything? No, just desperate, and desperate people do desperate things. My life is becoming increasingly bizarre. As each new hurdle comes along, I create a structure to deal with it.

To help me cope with hot flushes during the night, I've set up a little fan on the bedside table, which I keep on all night. Of course it's still winter, which means it sends an arctic gale across the bed, but that's ok, because I sleep under the doona until a hot flush hits, at which point I poke my head out, like a turtle, until the fan cools me down, and then I hunker under the doona again.

Every morning, I tip the contents of a brown paper bag into a saucepan and simmer it for half an hour, filling the house with a smell like decaying mushrooms. Then I strain half the concoction into a cup and drink it down as quickly as possible. It tastes absolutely foul. The other half of the brew is to have with dinner. Breakfast consists of lecithin, Missing Link, ascorbic acid, fish oil, flax seed oil, calcium, and on and on, all tipped into a blender with soy milk, a banana and maple syrup. That's followed by a handful or two of vitamins from what looks like a personal apothecary lined up on the kitchen bench. My entire life is focused on taking care of my body.

Meanwhile the puppies haven't spent long sleeping by the back door. In a weak moment I lifted them onto the bed for a quick cuddle and they immediately assumed instant ownership of the entire area. Now, the bed is a mishmash of muddy paw prints and dog hair, and I don't give a damn. Dolce sleeps pressed hard up against me. Vita is more distant, curling tightly at the far bottom corner, as though she's the gatekeeper. They are comforting.

Obi, the gorgeous golden labrador, calls in regularly and the puppies have fallen in love with him. Vita jumps all over him, licking his face, teasing him to play with her. Dolce lies alongside him on the floor and puts her head in his huge mouth. The first time it happens, I nearly faint. But sweet, gentle Obi spits her out like a cherry pip. He is truly the Rhett Butler of dogs.

One night I dream of golden sunlight and of my brother as fit and handsome and blonde-haired as he'd once been. In this dream I feel rested, unafraid and strong, and I want to follow his joyful face. His world seems carefree. Although he beckons with a radiant smile, I refuse to follow, begging instead that he stay with me. To this day, I feel I could have chosen to die at that moment. It was simply a matter of letting go. I could have silently let go of the will to live and faded with him. I wondered if that was what dying felt like. A slow, slow fading until the last little speck of you disappears. But I chose not to let go.

There is no doubt, though, that my body is highly toxic. One night when the puppies still slept in the bathroom, in their early days of proper house-training, I got up to go to the loo. I didn't want to wake them so I went outside to pee on the grass at the back of the house. About two days later I noticed a dead patch in the midst of the green. For a few moments I couldn't figure it out. And then I remembered. My pee was so toxic I killed the grass. That patch stayed dead for nearly a year.

15

WHEN FLEURY CALLS A COUPLE of days after the blood test results, I burst into tears on the phone. 'I feel as though it's one thing after another. I never seem to be able to recoup before the next onslaught.'

Before I can even put up a protest, she arranges for Sophia to come and spend time with me. The pretence they devise is that Sophia needs quiet time to work on her book about the Lama Yeshe. Lovett Bay is ideal, they insist. I let them think I believe them.

Within a day, Sophia is running the household like she's been here forever. She walks the puppies. I sleep as long as I wish. We eat lunch and I go back to sleep.

When I shop for supplies, I come home and there is Sophia, waiting at the old wooden ferry wharf, Walkman to her ear, gyrating in a dance all her own in amongst the wheelie bins and overflowing garbage. Orange trousers, orange skivvy, her old navy cashmere sweater darned over and over at the elbows, heavy walking shoes. When the water taxi gets close enough to drown out her music, she turns, this white-haired woman whose face is jammed with smiles, and waves.

"Lo. How are ya?'

'Good.'

'Yeah.'

She reaches for the shopping, which means I walk up the steps to the house empty-handed and light, and pause only once or twice to stop the dizziness.

While I am out, the laundry mysteriously appears clean and folded in my cupboard. The floors gleam, appliances on the kitchen benchtop suddenly sparkle. But I never see her hold a broom or a sponge. Which gives me the illusion that it all happens as if by magic and means I don't feel I must get up and help. When I try to thank her, she asks, 'What for?' She tells me I am teaching her so much in this funny little corrugated iron shack with its half-walls and condensed spaces.

'Yeah? Like what?'

'Silence. I am learning about silence.'

We are sitting on a sofa each, sipping tea, mid-morning. Feet up, heads cushioned comfortably. It's a blaster of a day. Looks pure, but the southerly has set in and the glass, when we touch it, feels iced. We are tightly wrapped in clothes, the heating is at the max. Our hot tea, laced with honey, steams fragrantly.

'This is not a quiet place,' I say. 'Those bloody cockatoos –'

'A different kind of silence,' she cuts in. 'How many houses do you walk into where there is the background babble of a television or a radio? The silence in this house lets you hear life.'

'Oh, get over it.'

'No I mean it. And there are huge swags of time. Empty. Waiting for you to fill them. No distractions. That's a gift.'

There is the silence, too, between us. Long periods. Never gloomy. Cleansing, in a way. Enough quiet to sort through a jumbled mind. A whole day might pass when the only words spoken are 'Feel like a cuppa?' On other days, we sit in pools of sun on the back deck, stripped to T-shirts, basting in the heat, and we talk. Or I do. And it begins to feel as though someone is loosening shackles.

One day I ask her if she ever dreams of another relationship.

She hoots with laughter. Her blue eyes dance. 'Sex, you mean?' she says.

Stung, I retreat a little. 'Ok, well what about the comfort of a partner, the sense of not being alone?'

'In my experience, having a partner can make you feel *more* alone.'

'Well, it's gotta be the *right* partner,' I say, refusing to give in.

'Sometimes you don't know who's right or wrong before it's too late.'

She has a point. I dump the conversation.

Sophia gives me peace. And has the grace to tell me it is a gift I've given her. And she listens and listens and listens. Where have I gone wrong, I want to know, so that my lover left me? What did I do? What was missing in me? Much later, I understand it was easier to focus on my dead affair and the past than to look at the future.

'It's over, Susan,' Sophia tells me one cold night. 'Let it go.'

And then we talk again and she asks questions.

'Do you hate him?'

'No.'

'What do you wish for him?'

'Happiness.'

'That's good. It takes great love to be able to wish happiness for the one you love but cannot have.'

But there is anger, too, and one day I hint at how much of it there is inside me. Anger at the cruelly timed dismissal. Anger that what I thought had meant so much to both of us was simply an illusion of my own. A mad fantasy I mistook for care even though I knew it could never be any kind of commitment.

Under her careful questioning and prompting, though, I find a way to close down the bitterness and let go of the anger. I learn to loosen the iron grip of self-pity. On days when I succumb, Sophia always finds a story to tell me of a friend whose child is ill, whose son is dying, whose husband has dementia – so many others, with no upside in their lives. It is never a lecture, nor even a way to inflict guilt at indulging in long bouts of self-pity. It is a way of building a set of balances in my head. Feel bad? Fine. But remember, it could be worse.

Halfway through Sophia's visit, I ring a friend and ask if I can borrow her boat to learn to drive. She is a weekender, one of the people who come to Pittwater to 'lunch'. Her boat is fibreglass and has comfy little padded seats and a canvas awning to keep off the rain or the sea spray if the wind is blowing the wrong way. Her instinct is to say no. I can almost hear the word. But she can't bring herself to be mean spirited when she knows I am ill, so she says yes.

I worry Sophia misses her morning papers. As a newspaper columnist, part of her job is to keep up with the news. So if I learn to drive a boat, we can motor over each morning, the two of us, to get the papers and perhaps a cup of coffee and rejoin, for a short time, *the crowd*.

The boat key is under the pot plant alongside the house keys. Weekenders lock their homes. Full-timers wouldn't even know where to find their keys. I put the key in the ignition and the boat starts. We untie and set off. Easy.

'Nothing to it,' I yell over the engine.

After months of waiting for ferries or calling water taxis – which are expensive, making you think twice about using them – the instant freedom of a boat is fantastic. It's like owning your first car. The whole world suddenly becomes accessible.

As we slice through the water, there's not even the whisper of a breeze to blow us off course. Brimming with confidence, I push the throttle forward, as I have seen Annette do on the water taxi, and the boat points heavenwards before settling back down on the water.

'Jesus!' Sophia shrieks. Her hands grip her seat. Then her hair. Then the dash in front of her. I laugh. Terrified and jubilant. Why did I think this was going to be so hard? We roar along, slippery dip smooth.

'How about fish and chips at Palm Beach?' I yell.

Sophia can't hear so I throttle back. Suddenly. And we both

almost crack our chins on the dash as the boat comes to a sudden stop.

'What did you say?' she asks. Sophia tries not to show her nervousness.

'I was thinking about fish and chips at Palm Beach but maybe we should skip it. Do it another day.'

The heady freedom is suddenly dulled by the realisation that I am dangerously ignorant about boats. There might not be roads but there are rules, and I haven't a clue what they are.

When we see the *Curlew*, all blue and white and matronly, cutting through the water towards us, I panic. Sophia's laugh has an edge of hysteria. I stall the boat trying to rev it to get out of the way. The ferry pulls around us. Horst, who's driving, scowls. How many dumb, reckless boat people does he have to avoid on a single shift? I wave in apology but he ignores me. The handful of passengers, seated like memsahibs on the stern seats in the open air, look mildly amused. One even waves. But I am humbled. No longer invincible.

'Shall we still try for the papers?' I ask weakly.

Sophia looks at me sternly. 'Are you mad? We barely missed a ferry! Forget it!'

'Right.'

The engine comes to life again with the first turn of the key and we motor home sedately. I swivel, doing 360 degree scans of the area, watching for oncoming traffic. By the time we reach the dock, we've both had it. Nerve weary.

I look at the ropes. Look at the cleats on the pontoon. Look at Sophia. She is still seated and seems to be breathing deeply. Her eyes are closed.

'How do you tie up a boat?' I ask. I've untied one heaps of times. But never tied one up. Boat owners do that.

Sophia's eyes open slowly, refocusing on the familiar, solid world of earth and trees. 'Dunno,' she says, rising slowly from her seat.

She steps off the boat carefully and walks, duck-like, up the ramp. When she is reunited with solid ground, she turns. 'Boats,' she says, taking a deep breath and tucking her chin into her ample bosom, 'are unnatural. I am going to the house to put on the kettle and have a whisky.'

Sophia grew up in the Victorian high country where water comes in rivers or dams. You might have an occasional swim on a blistering day during a heatwave, when the house is hot enough to cook you. Or go trout fishing from the bank. But no-one has a boat. She rode horses, though, almost before she walked. Stick her in the middle of a sheep or cattle muster and she'll wheel a horse on a tuppeny bit and eat dust with the toughest stockmen during ten to twelve hours in the saddle. She doesn't lack courage. She just doesn't understand boats. Neither do I. Not yet.

Her orange legs carry her up the slope to the house. Each foot hits the ground and seems to dig in a little.

I secure the boat using shoelace knots with big bows. It looks weird but it should hold even if a sudden, tricky winds erupts from nowhere.

The next day when I wander out onto the deck to make sure the boat is still there, the tide is out. The boat is aground, heeling awkwardly to one side.

'Ask Ken if it's ok, or whether we've done some awful damage,' I say to Sophia when she joins me.

She puts down her cup of tea. 'Right!'

She disappears inside the boatshed, emerging moments later with Ken. He's unshaven and wearing layers of winter woollies. Only the boatshed boys seem immune to the cold. She points and waves her arms around. Crouches and then falls forward. Without hearing, I can tell she's giving him an account of our first solo voyage. His body shakes with laughter and it's not easy to get a belly laugh out of Ken. I assume the event is growing in the retelling. Finally, Ken shakes his head and they split.

'He says not to worry,' Sophia reports on her return. 'There's no damage. But we shouldn't leave it there too long.'

'How long is too long?'

'Oh, you know.'

'No.'

'Ah shit.'

She returns to the boatshed.

'Too long is when it starts to do a bit of damage,' she explains a few minutes later.

'Oh. Right.'

There's just nowhere to go with that.

Over the next couple of days, the weather starts to pick up and the wind whistles into the bay. Sophia decides to weed the rear garden and I take a book to read in the shelter of the back porch while she works.

'Remember those shasta daisies I took from your garden in Melbourne?' she asks.

'Yep.'

'I'll send up a few cuttings for you. Go great out here.'

'They came from Paul's father originally,' I tell her. 'He gave us a couple of slips when we moved to the white elephant on the Nepean River. Then I took a couple of bits to Melbourne for the garden there, then you took a couple of cuttings for your garden when I left Melbourne. Now you're going to send cuttings back to me here! That's just about full circle, don't you think?'

'Seems appropriate, huh?'

Sophia quits weeding at four in the afternoon and goes inside for a shower. A couple of minutes after the water is turned on, a loud scream comes from the bathroom.

'What's the matter?' I call, panicked.

'Ticks. Ticks. Bloody ticks all over me. Ah!'

'Get in the shower and wash them off.'

'They're under my skin. There's bloody hundreds of them.'

'Can I come in? Can I have a look?'

The bathroom door, with Gordon's wine bottle weight balance which closes it automatically, is slid back roughly. Sophia stands there in her underwear.

'Look!' she says, pointing at both legs.

They are covered in tiny red welts with a black spot in each of them.

'Hang on.' I rush for Barbara's tick pamphlet and flick through the information.

'They're seed ticks,' I announce, proud of my local knowledge.

'A tick is a bloody tick,' she replies, unimpressed. 'I don't care whether it's a seed tick or a cattle tick. What do we do?'

'Well, I don't know. Pull them out, I suppose. Hang on, I'll ring Barbara.'

The bathroom door closes, the shower is turned on again. When I get off the phone, Sophia is still muttering under the shower.

'Barbara says get a razor and shave them off,' I yell out to her. 'Then slap on some antiseptic. There's a razor in the cupboard. Antiseptic, too.'

There's no sound from Sophia. Then I hear the cupboard being opened.

'You ok?' I call.

'Ask me in a day or two.'

A couple of days later, when the welts have subsided a little and the sting has gone out of the bites, we've just about forgotten the fear and idiocy of our maiden voyage.

'Feel up to another go in the boat?' I ask.

Sophia looks at me with a frown.

'Just a little excursion,' I plead. 'To the Church Point store. For a newspaper and coffee and perhaps, if the pastries look scrumptious, we could split one?'

She sighs and grabs her jacket. 'Let's go then,' she says, a suggestion of martyred resignation in her voice.

It takes about ten minutes to untangle the knots. Sophia waits inside the boat, eyebrows raised. When we are finally untied, I jump on board. The breeze is quite brisk, the water a little choppy. But it's a fine day.

I turn the key in the ignition. Three times. The engine screeches but fails to catch. I look up at Sophia to see if she can figure out the problem and notice that land is a good swim away.

'Who would have thought wind could move us so fast?' I say, nervously.

'That's what boats are about, isn't it?' Sophia says dryly. 'I thought you knew about stuff like that.'

We both realise there is absolutely nothing we can do. Just drift. Until someone sees us and helps. We begin to giggle uncontrollably.

'It might be an idea, next time, to start the engine *before* we cast off,' Sophia adds.

'Yeah.'

And the giggles erupt again. It takes a minute or two before we hear Ken's voice.

'Give it some choke,' he shouts from his jetty.

'Where's the choke?' I shout back.

'It's the lever above the throttle. Lift it up.'

Looking down, I see a little flap of plastic that could be it. I lift it. Turn the key. Once. Twice. The engine gargles into a full-bellied roar. We wave to Ken to say thanks but he's already turned back into the boatshed.

'We're off!' I announce happily.

But this time I ease the throttle forward slowly. I look around, get the feel of the steering, which is like a car. Turn the wheel to the right and the boat goes to the right. Left is left. I have a dim memory of tillers doing the opposite, but maybe that's the old-fashioned way of boating.

We cruise sedately and the water becomes a highway to

anywhere. A thrilling sense of absolute freedom rises up and, for a moment, immortality seems easily achievable. Panic doesn't set in until Church Point looms. The two ferries, one docked and one sounding the final bell for passengers, are tied on either side of the wharf. In between them, people are coming and going in tinnies at what seems to me to be reckless speeds.

Sophia is rigid, her face stony.

I decide to aim for the pontoon at the rear of the Church Point store. There's a large deck where daytrippers and some locals read newspapers over a cup of coffee. As we chug in, I can't help feeling everyone is watching, pointing and shaking his or her head. I line up the boat to come neatly (I hope) alongside the pontoon. It's low tide and there are sharp-edged pylons and the rank and gloomy underside of the deck ahead.

Until you've been steering a boat for a while, it's impossible to judge speed and distance. It's not like a car when you hit the brakes and it stops. There are no brakes in a boat. You need to judge coming in slowly enough to grab the cleats without ripping your arm off, fast enough so you still have control if there's a wind, slow enough so you don't crash. But I've misjudged badly and we're going much too fast about ten feet from the pontoon.

'I'm gunna jump off and tie up,' I tell Sophia, who looks stricken at being left on board alone.

I pull the throttle into neutral, kill the engine and leap.

'Ah shit!' I say in frustration.

Sophia is hopping quickly from one foot to another. Spinning. Making a low gurgling sound.

'What? What?' she asks.

'Forgot the rope!'

The boat quietly churns forward under the deck, coming exquisitely to rest between two leaning pylons.

'Chuck me the rope,' I tell her.

She spins blindly. 'Where's the bloody rope?'

'It's on the bow. You'll have to reach through the front to get it.'

I leap up the steps to kneel on the restaurant's deck. Sophia passes me the rope and I pull the boat around, sliding it into deeper water. When we are lying alongside the pontoon, tied quite neatly with more shoelace bows, there is scattered applause from the coffee drinkers.

'Second go in the boat,' I explain to anyone who cares to listen.

No-one responds. Sophia steps off with as much dignity as she can muster and we go inside to order enough food to keep us busy for an hour. Neither of us wants to climb back into the boat too quickly. We need recovery time.

When our coffee arrives, Sophia takes a sip and finds her voice. 'It might be an idea, next time, to grab the rope *before* you leap off the boat,' she says tightly.

'Yeah. I'll remember that when we get home.'

'Terrific.'

We settle into our normal silence, flicking pages. There is nothing in the papers that has any relevance. Not to Pittwater life. And anything beyond Pittwater life seems just too big to embrace. I can't change the course of the war over the Gaza strip by reading about it, can I? I turn away from the papers and look around. It's a constantly changing view. Dogs. People. Boats. Kids. Ferries. Water life. Busy but low-key. No harassed faces. No rushing.

When both ferries move off, the fishermen return to their spots and drop lines off the end of the ferry wharf. Kids squat and watch the day's catch in the buckets intently, as though any minute the fish might come alive.

We sit there long enough for the tide to turn. Warmed by the sun. Filled with food.

'Ready to hit the track?'

Sophia looks up over the rim of her glasses. She has read every story on every page of the newspaper. She checks her watch. Looks around. There is no other way home that doesn't involve a long swim or the expense of a water taxi. She sighs long and loud. Tidies her newspaper and tucks it under her arm.

'Let's go,' she says.

We both get on the boat and I start the engine. It ticks over first go. Then I untie. Coiling the ropes neatly. Then I reverse slowly out of the space.

'Think I'm getting the hang of this,' I say.

Sophia does not respond, does not even look in my direction. Her eyes seem to be closed and I'm not sure she's breathing.

When we're clear of the wharf, the deck and any traffic, I slowly ease the boat forward, pointing home. Sophia's chest seems to lower slightly. Her eyes open. A good sign.

The wind has dropped. We make it to the entrance of Lovett Bay, slide in alongside the northern shoreline and slowly motor the final leg. At the pontoon, I grab a rope and jump off, tying up neatly. Then I look up and see the boat drifting away.

'Jesus.'

The rope is tied firmly to the dock. It's just not tied to the boat. Sophia looks ready to explode but she is still close enough to throw the rope to. She catches it and holds tightly while I pull the boat in.

'Had enough of this for a while,' I say.

'I'll say.'

At the weekend, my friend comes and collects her boat.

'How did it go?'

'Great. Yeah. Really great.'

Sophia, good Buddhist that she is, turns into the kitchen to make tea. Says not a word.

'Gotta get one of my own,' I add.

'Only way to really learn. Lots of practice. That's the go.'

≈

A few days later, as night spills in, I sit at the old wooden kitchen table already dressed in my pyjamas with my woollen beanie pulled tightly over my ears. A new blood test has revealed my cells have built up and tomorrow is third chemo treatment day, two weeks overdue. Sophia is coming with me to sit in that awful grey room full of grey faces. I'm so grateful. It is a terrible place to be alone.

Outside, heavy rain hits the tin roof like a crazed drummer. At the kitchen sink, Sophia washes lettuce for a salad to have with soup made from lamb shanks and root vegetables. It's a soup from my childhood and the merest meaty whiff triggers waves of nostalgia.

'You wash each leaf so tenderly,' I observe. 'I just chuck 'em all into the salad spinner, swizzle them around, spin, and there you go.'

Her way of answering is to tell a story about Lama Yeshe. One day, a woman whose turn it was to cook, Sophia says, was washing a big bunch of spinach roughly and hastily. Lama Yeshe saw her carelessness as he walked past the kitchen and came inside to take over her work. He washed each leaf with infinite care. The young woman got the message.

'I learned that if you do a job, do it as though it is the most important job in the world,' Sophia explains. The satisfaction, she adds, is immense. And there is no boredom because you are thinking about the task, giving it your best.

'If you demean your work, you demean yourself?' I ask, needing, as usual, to have the concept hammered into a few words.

'Like that. But broader,' she replies.

Much later into the treatment, when even sweeping the floor is unthinkable, I long to be able to do all the old physical chores I'd once resented. Cleaning. Weeding. Ironing. I suddenly see them as a privilege of the fit and healthy.

≈

A few days before Sophia sets off home, I ask her what she wants for herself.

'Enlightenment,' she tells me. 'But I'll settle for just being able to dump my pride and ego.'

When she finally leaves, it is like losing a sister. The house feels as though the vibrancy has gone out of it. But she's already stayed longer than she should have. At home, as well as writing her weekly column, she visits people in nursing homes and also works for the Jewish Library where she helps Holocaust survivors write their memoirs. She is useful.

Sophia tells the neighbours what I might need, arranges for Veit, from the boatshed, to call in regularly. She tells him to use the washing machine, which gives him his excuse to knock on the door. To me, she says he needs somewhere to do his laundry and how perfect it would be if he could use my washing machine. No debts. No-one a martyr. We become friends, Veit and I. I cook for him often, which means I bother to eat. I'm sure Sophia knew that would happen too.

After she leaves, I have no-one to babysit the puppies so I ask my friend Michael, who took over my lease on the Scotland Island house, if I can drop them at his jetty when I go out. They'll be safely confined to the island where most of the dogs roam happily.

'Fine. As long as they don't cause any problems,' he says.

I load them onto the water taxi and drop them off on the way to Church Point and swing past on the way home in the water taxi to collect them. I call loudly and clap my hands. Two little white and tan streaks flash down the jetty, faces happy, tails frantic with joy. They jump on board like sure-footed sailors and off we go home. It seems a perfect solution. And they love it! They wait expectantly every morning for the big trip to the fun park. If we don't go, they curl on their bed, nose to nose, paws to paws, in silent disgust.

One mid-week evening I pick them up just before dark and the phone is ringing as I walk up the steps to the house.

'Hello?' I say, short of breath.

'Uh, Susan, it's Lewis. From the Island.'

'Hey, Lewis, how are you?'

Lewis is an electrician who has a wonderful spaniel called Billy. When I lived on the Island and the hot water service broke down, Lewis fixed it.

'Ah, good, mate, yeah, good. Um, it's about the puppies,' he mumbles.

My heart sinks. No call about the puppies is ever a good call. 'Yes?'

'They got into the house, into the cupboard with the dog food. Finished it off. Don't mind 'em eating the food, but don't want 'em tracking through the house when we're not there.'

'Sure. Quite understand. I'll keep them home in future.'

On the weekend Michael rings to tell me there're complaints coming in from all over the Island. The puppies have been on the rampage. Chasing cats, chooks, other dogs, anything that moves. Uncatchable, always running just out of reach.

'Sorry, love, but you can't drop them here any more,' Michael says. 'I want to relax when I get here, not be bombarded by upset neighbours.'

'Absolutely. Quite understand.'

He softens the words with an invitation to dinner. 'Bring the puppies. We'll nurse them until you go home.'

Over the next few weeks I realise my only remaining recourse is to take the puppies everywhere with me. Into the city. Into Mona Vale. Make the car a second home. But they are not good travellers and throw up as soon as we start winding along McCarrs Creek road. Then they trek vomit from one end of the car to the other. I load up paper towels and disinfectant, I try driving slowly around bends. But the vomiting keeps up. As a last resort, I fence off the car seats and put a disposable covering on the carpet in the back of the station wagon I bought after I sold Fearless Fred when

Sweetie died. Didn't seem much point having a ute in the city unless she was there to use it.

As soon as I leave the car, the puppies rip through the barrier easily and plunge into the groceries stacked on the seats. I arrive home with half-eaten mince, chops and chicken. So I try packing groceries into storage boxes. It works, but without the groceries to keep them busy, the puppies yap incessantly. It gets so bad that the parking attendant beneath the surgery of my naturopath asks me to find somewhere else to park. Their yapping penetrates the walls of the shopping centre and drives shoppers to despair.

I am close to despair myself. The physical effort of taking them everywhere, pee stops, cleaning up poo from sidewalks, worrying about them locked in the car on sunny days, worrying if they are locked in the car for too long when appointments drag overtime, is too much. It feels like a sea is closing in over my head. The dreaded dog run begins to look more and more attractive.

One morning I shower and wander out onto the deck in my dressing gown. The lawn is covered in fluffy white balls. It looks like it's been snowing. I wonder where it's all come from.

Back inside, I reach for my clothes. Jeans, knickers, bra, T-shirt, little satin covered fake tit . . . no little satin covered fake tit anywhere. I finally sit on the bed and think. It's not the kind of appendage you pull out somewhere and leave behind by mistake. Slowly, the image of pure white balls of fluff scattered on the lawn begins to make sense. It's all that's left of my prosthesis.

'Puppiiiiiies!' I scream.

They roar up to me, tails wagging, happily anticipating wonderful treats.

'You little bastards,' I yell.

They look at me, hurt written all over their faces. They look at each other, confused. Then back at me. Then on some silent signal they turn together and walk away, tails curled under their tummies.

I grab a pair of socks and try to beat them into a tit-like shape.

I look like a teenager aiming to increase her bra size but only on one side of her body. I toss the socks back in their basket and opt for a large, loose sweater.

The puppies' escapade has forced me to face going in to the city to buy a proper, silicon prosthesis. An excursion I've been avoiding for a couple of months. Denial, again.

During one of my regular teas with Barbara, I tell her about the problems with the puppies in the car parks. I try to make it sound funny but she sees through the humour to the frazzled woman underneath.

The next day Bob calls: 'We've got a courtyard at the back of the house where the puppies can stay while you're out.'

It feels like someone has just lifted a concrete hat off my head. 'Thank you, Bob. Thank you.'

'Barbara said things have been a bit chaotic.'

'Just a little bit. Bob?'

'Yes?'

'Please tell Barbara I'm about to read her document. I'm sorry it's taken so long. Embarrassed it's taken so long.'

'Don't worry about it. You've had your hands full.'

Bob and Barbara become surrogate parents to the puppies, and fall in love with them, giving them free run of the house and verandah. They do not tell me until a couple of months later that one of the puppies chewed a large lump out of the doormat, a huge, irreplaceable hand-woven mat that had been custom made for Dorothea Mackellar in the 1920s. And they only mention it then because I ask how the mat was damaged.

One evening when I'm struggling with the shopping, Jack from up the hill grabs the bags from me. 'Leave your shopping at the ferry wharf in future,' he tells me. 'I'll carry it up to the house for you.' Help seems to come from every direction and the weight of coping alone lifts immeasurably.

Mostly, I manage my own shopping but if I can't, I leave it at the ferry wharf and it silently turns up at the front door. No-one ever looks for any thanks.

When I have my final chemo treatment, a week after the scheduled time because my white blood cells are slow off the mark again, it is nearly four months since it began. I celebrate with Bob and Barbara at *Tarrangaua* with a cup of tea and a slice of cake. The partying has slowed down to almost nothing and it feels good.

Around the same time as chemo finishes, the builders call to say they're ready to come and discuss plans for the extension on the house. I know exactly what I want. A simple house where the outside is allowed to be part of the inside.

'That's where all the beauty is,' I tell them, over more tea and lemon cake. 'The house shouldn't distract but, instead, frame the outside.'

I feel a stirring of precious energy, so precious I can't afford to waste it, so when the ex-lover eventually calls – who knows why? – I let the answering machine pick up his message. I do not return the call. But I am beginning to see what he's done *for* me instead of *to* me and it frees my mind.

One night, with the doggies tucked in bed beside me, a hot water bottle at my feet, my silly woollen cap stuck on my head, I start to read Barbara's document. It is her research into Dorothea Mackellar's life and the history of *Tarrangaua*. It is enormously detailed, right down to the amount of backfill needed for the dry stone retaining wall (1.2 metres). Interesting only to locals, I suspect, or people who wander past and are curious about the pale yellow house on the side of the hill. Towards the end, on a page of its own, she writes this extraordinary tale:

About a year and a half after we moved in, I looked out the window from my study, which had once been Dorothea's small and simple bedroom, and saw the strangest sight.

There was a woman, wearing a longish dark dress and a huge sun hat, walking quite sadly, it seemed to me, with her head down. Her steps were slow and a little tentative, as she headed towards the steep slope leading to the water's edge.

She disappeared for a moment, and then came back into view but I still could not see her face. And then she followed an old sandstone pathway, narrow and rarely used, to the waters of Frog Hollow. The little bay to the east.

I felt she had stepped out of another era, but that seemed fanciful, so I tried to think who she might be. I thought briefly of the neighbours but dismissed the idea. Her shape was all wrong to be contemporary. Her ankle length dress, in a fabric that also seemed from another time, fell in thick, heavy drapes in that old-fashioned russet brown that was so popular after the first world war. And her hat was large, straw and similar to the style seen in photographs of people in the 30s.

It was a mystery to me.

I didn't mention this 'sighting' to Bob. I felt silly and melodramatic. Because I knew from the first moment the figure appeared that she was a ghost. The ghost of Dorothea.

I am a pragmatist by inclination. But I know what I saw. I remember the day quite clearly because it was Melbourne Cup day. As every Australian knows, it is the one day of the year when we all seem to be gripped by a mad, gambling frenzy. The nation comes to a stop for the three minutes or so it takes for the best horses in the country — and from around the world — to race for a prize of millions of dollars. Not a day any Australian would easily forget.

I was catching up with office work, sending out a few accounts and invoices, wondering whether Bob and I should go over to the Scotland Island Fire Shed to watch the race. A lunch and a few drinks are an annual Cup Day event there.

Bob was in his work shed designing a new piece of equipment to make poisoning that dreaded weed, lantana, a simple business. But as I said, I felt a bit silly. What was I going to say? I think I saw a ghost? Bob would have told me to have a cup of tea and a rest.

So I said nothing. But I sat and waited, and skipped lunch on Scotland Island, hoping she would return, my sad figure in dark clothing, and that I would be able to see her face this time, without the concealing shadow of her hat.

She didn't return that day and I have never seen her since.

But this much-lauded and loved Australian poet intrigued me. How little I knew about the woman who had built this house where I now lived so happily, content and at peace. Did she, too, find peace and solitude here? Is that why she came here?

And the house? What about the house? I knew it had been designed by Hardy Wilson, a famous man in his day. But I knew nothing about him. So I began my research.

I put the document down, finding it hard to believe Barbara, cool, practical Barbara, thought she might have seen a ghost. No, not might. Thought she *had* seen a ghost, the ghost of Dorothea Mackellar.

'You're the first person I've told about that ghost,' Barbara says when I call in to see her the next afternoon. She is in her night-wear. As she mostly is, these days. 'I've always wanted to follow up seeing that ghostly woman with someone who knew Dorothea,' she adds. 'I need to know if this apparition had any resemblance to her, if Dorothea wore dark clothes, and liked sun hats. Could it have been her ghost or was it someone passing in fancy dress? That, you see, is the mystery I would like to solve.'

I've baked scones and we tuck into them, piling on strawberry jam and cream. Rolling the scones around in our mouths, the crust, the inner softness, the sweetness and then the pure fat. Following each bite with a sip of bitter, hot tea.

'There must be someone around who remembers her,' I say, talking with a mouth full.

We are in the big, beamed room that so thoroughly seduced Barbara on her first visit with the real estate agent. Outside, an angry, icy westerly wind recklessly hurls small branches through the air and dead fronds from tall cabbage palms spin earthwards like lethal spears. The sky is black. As the wind builds, our ears tune in to the sounds outside. The rushing whoosh and, suddenly, the rain. I wander over to the window, my steaming mug of tea held tightly. Outside, the spotted gums, so tall they block the sun at noon on a winter's day, twist and bend. They could easily crash down on the house.

Barbara reads my mind. 'They've stood for years. In much bigger winds than this,' she says calmly.

But I have heard, usually on a still day not long after big winds, the sudden gunshot crack and then smash of a tree as it lets go of the earth somewhere in the national park. There are no tall trees near my house so I never feel threatened, but at *Tarrangaua*, the trees loom over the house, not one or two but dozens. Where is the rule, I wonder, that says trees may only topple where they will do no harm?

'What about the old-timers around here? They must remember Dorothea?' I ask, deciding to worry only about situations I can control.

The wind picks up the rain and hurls it onto the verandah. The table and chairs where we usually sit turn black with the wet. Water pools in the western corner. One chair scoots along the entire length of the verandah as though it has a life of its own.

'Water's building up in the corner,' I add. 'Might do damage if it sits there too long.'

'Bob will see to it,' she says.

I move back to the sofa. Reach for another scone.

'Why don't we try to find a couple of them? Old-timers. Take a cattle prod to their memories,' I suggest.

'Not that simple,' Barbara says. 'Pittwater is a funny place. People come here full of enthusiasm. Love the summers, the boats, and the life. But many don't stay. After a while, it gets too hard. Loading the shopping. Docking the tinny in strong winds. Running out of petrol in the middle of the bay. Two years sorts most people out.'

'Yeah, the removalists told me two years is the deciding point. But there must be someone.' There always is, I think.

Bob walks in from his workshed, smelling of wood shavings. Cold air hangs off him.

'Figured it all out?' he asks.

He reaches for a scone. His hand not quite thoroughly scrubbed. Slaps on too much jam. His tongue quickly tidies the sticky red dribble. The puppies look up. Beseeching. A crumb? Bob ignores them and in a minute or two they settle. Tiny puffs of disgruntlement and disbelief. They know they are irresistible.

'We're trying to figure out who's lived here the longest. Who would have known Dorothea Mackellar,' Barbara explains.

Bob moves in front of the fire. As though he needs to thaw. The front of his faded grey trackie top is streaked with dirt, his pants are pouched at the knees.

'Won't be easy. The locals who lived here all year round, not the weekenders, are probably dead,' he says.

Bob licks his fingers, one by one.

'Dorothea died in 1968,' Barbara says. 'And she didn't come here for the last eleven years of her life. So that means we're looking for people who were adults, or at least old enough to have accurate memories, about forty-five years ago.'

'That can't be too hard. I'll start asking around.'

Bob and Barbara exchange a smile, making me feel like the village idiot. Barbara has searched for six years without success. But a gritty little kernel of determination settles inside me. I have never enjoyed being beaten.

'Bit of a challenge for me. Fill in some time,' I say flippantly.

Bob moves from the fire. Throws on a log. 'Got a bit more to do. Then I'll come in.'

Barbara asks: 'Have we got enough for three for tea? This weather won't ease for a while.'

I get up. 'Thanks, but no. I want to get home before dark. Get the puppies settled.'

No-one tries to pressure me.

'Come on, puppies,' I say, 'let's attack all those steps and go home.'

'There's an old pathway,' Barbara says, 'that runs from Bob's shed to the back of your house. It's overgrown but Bob will clear it. Easier than going up and down the steps.'

'I've never noticed it. How long's it been there?'

'Years. Once, a doctor owned the house directly behind you. Where the old chimney still stands. According to local legend, he was in love with Dorothea and used the path to visit her. Locals call it Lover's Lane.'

'Did Dorothea return the affection?'

'Not according to legend.'

'Then we should rename it. How about Barb's Lane?'

Barbara smiles and, for a moment, weariness falls from her eyes.

'Oh, Lover's Lane will do. I think it will have its day again, that lane,' she says.

It seems an odd response but I let it go.

Bob and I walk out together. In the laundry, I pile on clothes – scarf, sweater, jacket.

'Put this on.'

Bob hands me a bright yellow, slightly ripped slicker.

'Sure you don't want to stay until the weather drops off?' he asks.

'Nah.'

I bend down, grab the puppies, one under each arm. Just in case the thrill of discovery overwhelms them and they decide to rush off. I open the back door and peer out. It's dark enough to be late evening. Light from Bob's shed shines like a beacon.

'So what goes on in that mysterious shed of yours?'

'Bit of this. Bit of that.' He pulls his collar up. 'Come and have a look.'

He grabs a puppy. Stuffs her down his shirt. It's Vita and she squirms with delight, licks his face. I do the same with Dolce, who is less entranced.

We run for the shed, a dark brown weatherboard building about ten metres from the house. I have passed it many times now, heard a radio and mistaken the chatter for a group of people gathered in the shed. Called out hello and been answered with silence.

'So this is where you come to escape.'

I say it lightly but Bob is serious.

'Come out here to think,' he says.

His eyes are black. Shoulders hunched. He struggles to find words. I cringe at my thoughtlessness. What he is dealing with, Barbara's illness, is inescapable. But I cannot talk about illness and death right now. Too many of my own fears.

I look around the shed from the shelter of the carport then take a big step up to the wooden floor. There is no door to stop the wind from seeping in, no heating to dull the cold. It's like stepping into an icebox.

Bob goes straight to the workbench in front of the window. He is silent and lets me poke around. It's a shabby, spider web encrusted shed with grimy windows. There's little attempt at order. Machinery is scattered everywhere. Sanders, grinders, saws. All huge and expensive looking. The kind that fools you into believing you would be able to rebuild your house if only you had the time. Drills, about three, lie on the bench. Nails, screws, nuts and bolts scattered like shiny confetti. There are hammers and screwdrivers, all sizes, and dusty containers full of little treasures. Ordered boxes and jars sit undisturbed in rows, their contents obscured by years of dust. Everywhere, the underlying smells of paint and turpentine.

Bob stands fiddling with bits of hose near a pile of fresh wood shavings. Trapped under his clothes, Vita wriggles like a restless foetus. From his perch, he can see who goes to and fro on the water, how the weather is building. Who's coming to call.

'Nice spot. See who's arriving. Decide whether you want to come out from hiding or not,' I joke.

He grins. And the shadowy edges of wear disappear from his face. 'Something like that.'

'Has anyone ever done a biography of Dorothea?' I ask, picking up the biggest screwdriver I've ever seen.

He hands me Vita and leaves the shed. Wordless. I'm not sure what to do. Wait? Go? Not for the first time, I think Bob is unfathomable.

After a minute or two, the back door bangs shut. A shadow streaks through the rain. 'Here,' Bob says, pushing a book in a wet plastic shopping bag towards me. 'This is the only book we've found about her life.'

In the bag there's a faded paperback with a drawing of a coquettish looking young woman on the cover. *My Heart, My Country*, by Adrienne Howley.

'Who was Adrienne Howley?' I ask, turning to the back cover to read the blurb.

'She nursed Dorothea for the last eleven years of her life in a hospital in Randwick,' Bob says.

'Is she still alive?'

'I don't know. Good place to start, though. With your search.'

That night I call Sophia in Melbourne. 'Bob needs to talk about death and dying. I don't think I can help him,' I tell her.

'Why not? You know more about it than most people. What are you afraid of?'

I hesitate. 'It's too close to home.'

There's a long sigh. 'We're all gonna die one day, remember? Only a fool fails to get a grip on that.'

'Yeah, but . . .'

'It might help you.'

'I thought *you* might call him, talk to him. You're good at all that stuff,' I say.

'Ah, come on. That won't work. You're right there!'

'But what if I say the wrong thing? Make it all worse? Cause new problems?'

'You won't.'

'Barbara's fading. She looked translucent today.'

'Yes.'

'She can't make it up and down the steps any more. Bob has to drive her. He's got an old ute. Drives it down the track backwards and up the track, frontwards. It's a frightening sight. Does about twenty-five kilometres a year, he says.'

'Yes,' Sophia says. She is not shocked by the news of Barbara.

'Bob says chemo is not a cure. It's just giving her more time.'

'Does Barbara talk about her health?'

'Not really. Not in any way that admits any possibility that she won't survive.'

'How does he handle that?'

'Life goes on as usual. They're getting the painters in soon, to paint the house. I want to help them both but I don't know what to do.'

'Be there for the family. They will be so busy supporting her, they will need support themselves,' Sophia suggests.

'What about finding little goals?'

'What kind?'

'Not tiring, unachievable goals. Just interesting events that can be brought to her door.'

'Go on.'

I hear Sophia settling into the deep chair by her phone. Ready for a long chat. She'll be dressed in her old, navy blue cashmere sweater and orange fleecy-lined trousers, her old dog, Lucy, at her feet. Not much changes around Sophia. She's worked out who she is and what matters.

'Well, she's fascinated by Dorothea Mackellar. Done some pretty good research. There's a biography written by a woman called Adrienne Howley. If she's still alive, I think Barbara would like to meet her. Thought I might try to find her.'

'Hang on a sec.'

The phone clunks and footsteps echo across a bare wooden floor. After a few minutes, Sophia settles back into her chair with a sigh and a whispery shuffling of papers.

'Hmm, I thought so. She's a nun, a Buddhist nun.'

'Who?'

'Adrienne Howley.'

It feels like cymbals clashing, drums rolling, crowds cheering, the universe reeling – all at once. Fate? Coincidence? What does it matter?

'I don't know where she is right now, but I'll make a few calls and let you know,' Sophia says.

It takes a week for Sophia to find Adrienne Howley's phone number. In another of those little twists of fate, it turns out she lives just north of Newcastle, only three hours' drive from

Lovett Bay. Easily manageable for a day's round trip.

'She's written a book you should read,' Sophia tells me. 'It's called *The Naked Buddha*. It's a simple explanation of the life and teachings of Buddha. It's very good.'

'How did a nurse in an old people's nursing home end up writing a biography of Dorothea Mackellar *and* a book explaining Buddhism? What kind of a dame is this?'

Sophia's belly laugh booms down the phone.

'Give her a call and find out.'

'I feel a bit like a fairy godmother granting wishes. Do you?'

'Feels good, huh? Once you stop thinking about yourself all the time, the world opens up again.'

'Gimme a break, Sophia. Permission to whinge just a little.'

'Nah. Now bugger off and get Adrienne organised to meet Barbara.'

'You don't think it will be too much for her? She's pretty fragile.'

'Ask her. But do it before you ring Adrienne.'

It's difficult, when you feel weak and ill, to find the energy to talk to a stranger, to ask questions that reveal the person before you. For Barbara, energy is a precious and finite commodity. Perhaps she has other, more pressing chores, the kind you race to finish when time is limited. Captions on photos in the family album. Letters to children, the kind that when you are no longer a physical presence, they can open and read and feel the comfort of their mother.

I know Barbara is a passionate collector of native Australian plants. I've seen her exquisite collection of pressed native flowers with their names carefully hand-printed below – almost finished but put aside at a time when the future seemed infinite. Did she really have the time for a total stranger to come by to fill in a few details about Dorothea Mackellar?

Bob is in the shed when I walk to the house to tell him about Adrienne. I can see his face through the window, round and full of concentration, bent towards his job. There is a sound like humming over the top of a buzzing machine. He's singing, I think – but, God, he's really tone deaf!

The shed still looks like a madman's hardware sale. In the daylight, I can see broken furniture – chairs, small tables, shelving, stacked in a corner. There's a loft, too, next to the carport, which is used as storage for huge bags stuffed with sails for his boat, he tells me.

'That's my boat down there. *Larrikin*,' he says, pointing out his shed window.

'The one with her backside sticking out of the water? I've gone past it hundreds of times.'

Bob's not fond of my description. 'She's a racing boat. Built to be light and take the weight of people in the rear.'

'I see. Now listen. I've found the writer – well, Sophia's found her, the woman who wrote Mackellar's biography.'

Bob looks shocked. 'Already?'

'Actually, it took longer than we thought. She's a Buddhist nun.'

'*Nun!*'

'Buddhist nun.' I can barely speak. Laughter set to explode – like the puppies just before their morning walk.

'I have never really asked,' I say, looking around, thinking if I had a kitchen in this kind of disarray I would never even toast a slice of bread again, 'what you do?'

'I fix problems.'

'What kind of problems?'

'Engineering problems.'

'And?'

'And what?'

I give up. 'So do you think Barbara would like to meet the nun?'

'She's inside. In bed. Today's not a good day for her.'

'Well, can you ask her at some stage? Today if possible?'

I'm anxious to nail down dates and times. My old journalistic habits have kicked in. Always hammer down the story. Quickly.

He drops a couple of metal tubes and walks towards the house. I'm left standing.

'Come on!' he calls impatiently.

'Oh, right.'

Barbara is asleep in the end bedroom so we tiptoe back along the hallway to the kitchen for a cup of tea.

Bob reaches inside the fridge and pulls out two plates – one with an orange and almond cake, another with a lemon cake. 'There're a few scones here, too,' he says, his eyes smiling but his face serious.

'Overdoing the cooking thing, aren't I?'

He doesn't answer, but cuts a sliver of both cakes and puts the scones back in the fridge, saying: 'The scones will need heating to be any good.'

'Those scones are rocks now. Chuck 'em out.'

'I design and build kilns,' he says, as if there'd never been a break in the conversation in the workshed.

'Is that why Barbara loves pottery? Why there's so much around the house?'

'Brick kilns,' he says. 'Not pottery kilns.'

'Oh.'

Silence. Not comfortable.

'Have you built many?'

'Yeah.'

'Where?'

'Up and down the east coast of Australia.'

'So where does all the pottery around the house come from?'

'Barbara's been collecting Australian pottery from the twenties, thirties and forties for years. Half the collection is still packed in boxes.'

'Is she good at it?'

'Yeah. She's an expert, really.'

We both turn with relief when Barbara opens the kitchen door, looking so tired I feel like holding her up. But she smiles, takes a cup of tea and, when Bob asks, says yes, it would be wonderful if Adrienne Howley could visit.

Bob sees me out the back door.

'There're a couple of points I forgot to mention,' I tell him.

He stops, which I gather is a signal to continue.

'Adrienne is in her seventies.'

He shrugs: 'I can drive her up the hill in the ute.'

'She's also blind.'

'Anything else?'

'Not at this stage.'

'Good.'

I don't know why, but I never doubted for a moment that an elderly, blind, Buddhist nun wouldn't hesitate to climb into a total stranger's car, drive for three hours, then climb on a boat, and clamber up more than eighty steps to sit and talk to a woman dying of cancer about a poet who'd died more than thirty years ago.

16

I'D EXPECTED AN ANSWERING machine, which is usually what you get when you're in a hurry to contact someone, but Adrienne Howley picks up the phone on the second ring. Fate again? After burbling a slightly chaotic explanation of why I'm calling, I hear a long sigh from the other end of the line. Before she can say no, I bulldoze on.

'Could you find time to come here? I'd pick you up and drive you home, but it would be better, if you have the time, to stay overnight. There's a little boat trip, too. Only five minutes. And easy. If you can manage it.'

'*Tarrangaua*,' she almost whispers. 'Oh, I'd love to come. I've always wanted to go back there and I never thought it would happen. Thank you, thank you for asking me.'

And it's as simple as that. All she has to do is arrange for her cat to spend a couple of nights with her local vet while she is away.

'Shall I wear my robes?' she asks just before we complete our arrangements.

'Would you like to?'

'Only if it doesn't disturb anyone.'

'We'd all love it. Be the talk of the bay for months.'

When I ring Bob and tell him to expect the 'blind Buddhist nun', as she inevitably becomes known, the day after tomorrow, he panics: 'It's too quick. We need to think about it a bit.'

His response punches the thrill out of me. Why should there be a delay? What's the problem? I say nothing, though, and hide my disappointment. Maybe Barbara's struggling. For some reason,

I delay calling Adrienne. She was so excited I don't have the heart to tell her the visit has to be postponed.

The following morning, there's a knock at my door. Bob stands there looking as though he's forgotten to comb his hair.

'Barbara's thrilled.'

'So it's on!'

'Yeah.'

In the afternoon, Bob returns with a printout of a map to Adrienne's front door.

'You pick her up. I'll drive her back,' he says.

'That would be fantastic, thank you. You'll like her, Bob, she sounds really great on the phone. Full of life and energy. And she knows the situation with Barbara. It will all be ok.'

I had begun this for Barbara, thinking in some idiotic way that when someone is dying she deserves to have every wish fulfilled. A kind of mad rush to make life film-script perfect because it's what we all dream of and it's never like that in reality. But it was giving me a large dose of happiness, too.

I'd done the same thing for what we all knew would be my husband's last Christmas alive. I'd rushed around madly trying to find everyone's dream gift which, in the case of his daughter Lulu, was a border collie puppy. I eventually found one in country Victoria and arrived home with a stinking, piddling ball of black and white fluff. At the time I thought it was madness but Lulu adored that dog, Bella. She put a new structure in Lulu's life when the framework centred on her father collapsed.

It is the Christmas she remembers with the most fondness: 'The best ever,' Lulu still says, often with her armed draped around Bella's neck. It was worth the effort.

Of course, the one wish that really mattered to Barbara was impossible to arrange.

≈

Finding Adrienne's home is confusing at first. Because there is a large sign announcing Lorn Learning Centre on the front verandah that I *think* belongs to her house. There's nothing about Buddhism. So I sit in the car a moment and check street names and numbers. While I'm fiddling with Bob's directions, the door opens. A woman appears wearing the deep maroon robes of a Tibetan nun. Can't be too many Tibetan nuns in Newcastle, I think.

I scramble from the car and fight with the latch on the front gate. 'Adrienne?' My voice is overloud in the still, tree-lined street.

She nods.

'I'm Susan.' I walk up to her and put out my hand, which is unseen and ignored.

She is small but not frail. Except for her skin. Which is paper thin, the veins blue and close to the surface. Her hands are slim, with freckles to match the ones on her face. Her eyes, the part of her that has almost given up, are bright blue. Although she is well into her seventies and cannot see, she moves quickly and gracefully.

'Come in, come in. I have tea and biscuits, if you like. Or perhaps juice, or iced tea.'

'If you don't mind, we'll get going.' I am anxious to move on. To get back before dark.

I follow her down the wide, dark hallway, her robes rustling like a taffeta ball gown. No lights are on and it is almost dark enough to stumble. But then, Adrienne has no need of light.

'Sorry to be in a rush,' I mutter.

'I'll just put the cat in his cage. The vet is down the street,' she says.

She takes a tidbit from a box and calls gently. When an old grey cat saunters inside she scoops her up, gives her a quick caress around the ears and places her in the cat box. Which makes her very bad-tempered. She throws herself against the bars, splayed like a spatchcock on a grill. Adrienne clucks soothingly until she subsides in a grumpy, furry heap.

'I'll take the cat to the vet, if you like,' I offer.

'Thank you. I am not good at crossing roads.'

'Oh, ok.'

But I'd only wanted to pay for the overnight stay. Hadn't even thought about how blind people manage to cross roads in suburban areas where there are no traffic lights or pedestrian crossings.

On the highway, a light, misty rain blows in random waves. Oncoming cars, with their headlights on full beam, loom out of the grey weather like giant insects.

I want Adrienne to be the source of all wisdom on this trip, to magically show me the path to happiness and contentment. I want to ask her all the questions under the sun and have her give me answers that will guide me for the rest of my life. I'm looking for a good fairy to come along, tap me on the shoulder with her wand and make all the bad bits dissolve into dust, leaving in their wake only joy and happiness. I've always been tempted to hand over responsibility for my life to someone else, maybe because it's a lot easier than growing up. And I've always imbued with magical qualities anyone who chooses a spiritual way of life.

When my husband was ill and the priests wandered down the driveway to see him, I expected them to have all the answers, to whip a quick little miracle out of their prayer books. But they never did. When an old priest who loved a bet and who called my brother for racing tips, rang to say the priests were praying for John, I had a wild hope for a while that the force of good men would prevail and my brother would be spared. But he wasn't. And yet here I am again, hoping against hope that someone will show me the way when I should know by now that I have to find it myself.

Adrienne does not play that game as we sit enveloped in the car. Instead, she tells me about how, as a child, she saw her mother stab her lover in the eye with a pair of scissors. She tells me about being diagnosed with cancer and sailing around the world with a mad sea captain, waiting to die. Five years later she realised her *imminent* death was taking a long time, so she abandoned ship and returned to Australia where she eventually studied Buddhism.

When I ask her why Buddhism, she says with unexpected vehemence, 'Because nothing in my life ever made any sense. I wanted to try to make sense of it all. The meaning of life, if you don't mind the cliche.'

We talk in short bursts on that drive, taking turns in an odd little mental soft-shoe shuffle that, as trust grows, leads us closer and closer to telling the truth about ourselves. I am so intent on our conversation that I get hopelessly lost and go round and round in circles, passing a cemetery about four times before Adrienne leans over to pat my knee: 'I think, dear, we are not moving forward.'

For a second I assume she means spiritually, but it is only my wretched navigation.

'Do you have some sight, then?' I ask. I peer through the rain, struggling to find the right road to Sydney.

'I am what is known as legally blind but I have a little peripheral vision.' She smiles, her face softens and it's easy to see that she's been an extraordinarily beautiful woman. 'I don't miss out on much even though my sight is nearly gone. But I wish I could still read books. I miss being able to read quite dreadfully.'

Her laugh is loud and packed with irony when I ask whether she has found the meaning of life. 'What I have found is the ability to live life in a way that is useful. And that has made some sense of it all.'

When she tells me she works in palliative care, I wonder again at the hand of fate. If Barbara wants to talk about death, Adrienne will know how to handle it. Barbara never discusses her health or the future and I suspect it is because she doesn't want to upset anyone. This is an opportunity for her to open the door.

For a while we are silent, just swooshing through the rain, the wipers thunking rhythmically in slicker and slicker swathes of muck as trucks and passing cars kick up oil from the freeway onto the windscreen. Every so often I glance across at her. She is always in the same position with her hands folded neatly, her back straight, a slight smile on her lips. Only her eyes change – sometimes they are closed, sometimes open.

I want to ask Adrienne a question, but do not know how to begin. It is about right and wrong. Not the easy black and white stuff. I want to understand how you figure out what is harmful – or potentially harmful – behaviour, when wading through the murky wastelands of everyday life. I think I want to know whether cancer is my punishment for every selfish act, every morally wrong choice. I have never asked 'why me?', but I am beginning to ask 'why?'. Cancer has a way of forcing you to look at your life and the way you have lived it. The simple fact of getting older gives you the understanding that whatever you do, whatever actions you take, stay with you forever. How much more peace of mind I would have had if I'd put aside what I believed to be important and instead focused on what mattered.

'Is there a way,' I finally ask Adrienne, 'to learn to make only the right decisions?' I am, of course, thinking about the ex-lover.

'Ah,' she says, a smile playing around her mouth. 'What is right? What is wrong? When it's all added up at the end, how do we know?'

She is silent then, for so long that I stumble into an oversimplified explanation of my enquiry because I feel I cannot mention the ex-lover. 'Am I doing the right thing by Barbara by trying to give her little goals, moments to look forward to, distractions, if you like? Am I making it easier or harder for her?'

'What is your motive?'

'To create hope.'

'That is a good motive.'

'Is that enough?'

'Yes. But of course, often there are many motives in any single decision.'

'I get a surge of hope and confidence when people include me in future plans,' I explain. 'If they believe I have a future, perhaps I do.'

'Do *you* believe you have one?' Adrienne asks.

'Some days I do, some days I don't. Some days a headache can send me into a spiral of anxiety. Is it a brain tumour? A pain in my chest makes me think of secondaries lying in wait. Sometimes, I think feeling hope is a kind of emotional torture because, of course, all it takes is a single badly chosen word or some thought-less remark to shatter it.'

'That's because,' Adrienne said, 'you are trying to find hope in the words and actions of other people. You must have it yourself.'

By the time we reach Church Point, the rain has stopped. I call Bob and he arrives in his boat. Two little tan and white faces stretch their necks to see over the side. The puppies are still too timid to ride the bow of the boat like all the other dogs on Pittwater.

Adrienne steps into the tinny like a teenager and settles in the only passenger seat. The puppies immediately jump all over her and, in seconds, blood is gushing down her arm. I'm appalled and can't think what to do.

'Here,' Bob says, pulling out a handkerchief. He wraps it around the scratch and Adrienne holds it tight.

'My skin is thin – from too many years of being in the sun,' she explains. 'But don't worry, the bleeding will stop soon.'

The water is smooth as a polished floor, the wind almost nonexistent. It's turned into a soft day in shades of grey. Light grey sky, deep grey hills, silver grey sea. We set off for *Tarrangaua* at a slow and easy pace.

'You'll be staying with me,' I tell Adrienne. 'I hope that's ok. Barbara gets tired really quickly.'

She nods and then we are all silent. Adrienne is entranced. She breathes in the sea air as though it is a delicate perfume. She turns her face to the stern to catch the gentle drift of sea spray and closes her eyes, bathed in the physical world.

In their eagerness to be off and running, the puppies leap out of the boat before we're even alongside the pontoon, risking a fall into the watery gap. They are learning to judge rocking surfaces well but the tide is as low as it ever gets and the ramp rises steeply to the shore. They slide on the planks like declawed cats on a slippery bough until they reach the fixed jetty then, with a skip of relief, they roar off into the bush. No amount of calling or the promise of treats can lure them back. Noses to the ground they follow their silent, secret signals and disappear from sight.

'Don't worry about them,' Bob says. 'They'll come back when they're tired.'

'But the phone calls will start.'

'Everyone knows you're trying.'

Adrienne climbs the ramp as though she's been doing it all her life and waits onshore while we tie up the boat. The rain starts to fall lightly again so I thank Bob, grab Adrienne's arm and lead her to my house.

'We'll have dinner at home tonight and then go up to *Tarrangaua* tomorrow morning. Is that ok?'

'Of course, dear.'

'I've invited a couple of friends around to join us. Do you mind? I've told them it's a quick dinner, over early. Bob too, if he feels he can leave Barbara for a while.'

'Sounds lovely.'

Stewart is coming with a visiting friend from our days in New York, a writer who uses a lot of colourful language. I've asked Stewart to tell his friend to hold back the swearwords in front of Adrienne.

'I think you'll enjoy these blokes. They're a lot of fun. By the way, I've got steaks for dinner but if you're vegetarian, I can cook up a frittata.'

'If I were cooking for myself, I would eat vegetarian, but Buddhists must eat whatever is put in front of them – and I love beef!'

Stewart and Kinky arrive at 6.30 pm and Kinky opens the conversation with a few choice words. I'm ready to faint but Adrienne laughs.

'I'm unshockable,' she says when I tell Kinky to ease up. 'And I've read all his books. I'm a big fan. And my son loves his music. He has all his albums.'

Bob comes in looking a little wet and bedraggled, his face crevassed by lines of worry.

'Barbara ok?' I ask.

'Yeah, she's fine. She sent me down here. Told me I needed a bit of new company for a while.'

'But you didn't want to come, did you?'

'Don't like to leave her on her own.'

'She wouldn't have pushed you out the door if she didn't feel ok. Relax for a while. Have a break.'

I push a glass of red wine into his hand and tell him to sit down.

'Dinner's ready. It's going to be an early night.'

During dinner, Stewart is solicitous and polite. Bob is quiet and withdrawn. Kinky is in full flight and debates Adrienne furiously about religion, morality and everyday values. She is in her element.

'So is there life after death?' Kinky asks at one point, his black eyes suddenly hard and flat. Stewart and I know he is baiting Adrienne and I take a breath to leap to save her. But she is quick.

'How many people do you know who have returned from death to tell us what to expect?' she asks.

'None,' Kinky responds.

'So what good does it do to wonder about something we can never know?'

Bob puts his knife and fork together and pushes his chair back from the table. 'Thanks for dinner. I'll head home if you don't mind.'

Bloody insensitive Kinky, I think. Then I realise he probably doesn't know Barbara is dying. I jump up to see Bob to the door.

He turns to Adrienne. 'See you tomorrow. Barbara's really looking forward to meeting you.'

When I open the door, two scruffy wet puppies quivering with happiness dash inside, leaving muddy paw prints all over the floor. They're panting with exhaustion. I dry them off with a towel, check for ticks, and plonk them on their own bed. They stink of wet wool.

Stewart and Kinky get up to leave and by 9.30 pm Adrienne is asleep and the puppies have fallen into an exhausted coma. I lie awake for a long time, listening to Adrienne's breathing.

I've been thinking about studying Buddhism for a while, and Sophia has told me about beginners' classes held every November in Katmandu. I ask myself, that night in early spring, why I want to learn the philosophy. What is my motive? Is it to find a way to become a better person? Is it to find a way to lead a more harmonious life? Or is it because I hope God will grant me a longer life if He sees I am making an effort to be a more compassionate human being? Was I silently bartering for a future with my very nebulous idea of a bigger power? Was self-interested gain the motive or was I really looking for enlightenment?

Without too much mental prodding I realise my motives are unclear. I decide to delay making a decision until I am sure that I am not searching for some kind of quid pro quo from God.

Adrienne and I make our way to *Tarrangaua* around eleven the next morning. Adrienne moves slowly but firmly, never stumbling.

The sky is blue and the bay even bluer. It is high tide and there's just enough swell to send corkscrews of light shimmering from one shore to the other. Everything smells new and fresh after the rain and the earth underfoot is soft. The shrieks of cockatoos rend the air like the grand finale of a bad rock band, and the stairway to *Tarrangaua* is slippery and damp. When I try to hold her arm, though, Adrienne smiles and pulls away.

'I'm quite all right, dear. Quite all right.'

Halfway up the stairs, the cockatoos go berserk, flapping around a towering spotted gum like an army of mad archangels.

'There's a goanna trying to get up the tree,' I tell Adrienne, 'and the birds aren't happy about it.'

'Probably a nest somewhere,' she replies.

The goanna, its black and pale green body blending neatly into the colours of the tree trunk, whips its tail back and forth but it's no match for the frenzied cockatoos that swoop on it in an almost military attack. One, two, three . . . there are eight of them and they each dive-bomb the giant lizard until – defeated – it climbs down the tree to the ground. The birds fall silent. Hunched on branches like white-robed, black-eyed guards, they watch the goanna lumber into the scrub.

The sudden stillness is eerie. The cockatoos' heads are all turned in the direction the goanna has taken, each bright yellow crest clenched in a tight curl like a question mark. Not even the normally irrepressible noisy miners make a sound. Adrienne and I stand, waiting, although we have no idea what for. After a few minutes, the cockatoos calmly fly off. The threat is over. We begin our climb to the house again.

Adrienne lifts her robes to step over a large branch fallen from a spotted gum. Her face twists sideways for a better view. She looks, for the first time, like someone with a disability.

At the top of the winding stairway, where the workshed looms, Adrienne stands still. I don't know what she sees or how clearly, but I will never forget the rapture on her face that morning.

'This was the place she loved best. This is where she always longed to be,' Adrienne says. She means, of course, Dorothea Mackellar.

Bob is at the kitchen door emptying the tea pot into a drain where a whole lot of delicate purple and white native violets bloom happily. He explains that today, Barbara is not well enough to get up. Does Adrienne mind talking to her in the bedroom?

We move down the long hallway, past some of Barbara's early Australian pottery collection, past the photographs of Lovett Bay in the 1800s. Adrienne runs her hand along the bagged walls, then the cupboards, feeling her way, feeling another era, perhaps, in her life.

Barbara sits up in bed in her large, dimly lit bedroom where heavy pink and blue curtains hold back the light from outside and a large cedar chest of drawers dominates one wall. She is glowing pink from her shower and her freshly washed hair is parted to one side and caught back with a pale blue barrette. She looks incredibly young and carefree and her eyes are filled with anticipation.

Adrienne and I sit on two chairs culled from the dining room and Barbara straightens her carefully prepared list of questions. I've brought a tape recorder and we press the button. Bob tiptoes in with tea and puts the mugs on the bedside table where they stay untouched.

'Is the house different?' Barbara asks Adrienne. 'How did you find it when you arrived at the front door?'

Adrienne pulls her chair closer to Barbara and lies her arm on the edge of the bed, as though offering it to Barbara to hold if she wants to.

'It felt a little ghostly, I suppose. But only at first. I felt perhaps *she* was saying, "Oh, you're back again".'

'Did you come here very often?'

'I never came here with Miss Mackellar although I visited the house a couple of times with her permission. She often told me to bring my two sons here for a holiday but she didn't understand that we didn't have the finances for holidays.

'They were quick visits. She was in hospital at the time. Mr

Birch and I came – he was her driver – and once the housekeeper, Mrs Scallwell, came too, just to pick up something she wanted, but mainly to check everything was all right.'

'How did you find it then?'

'It was beautiful.'

'There is very little mention of this house, *Tarrangaua*, anywhere.'

'This was her private place. Here she was out of the public eye altogether. She loved the isolation and was passionate about the bush. She could cook for herself, although she wasn't terribly interested in it, and I remember her telling me about sitting out there on the verandah having a steak and a bit of salad. A kookaburra came along and sat on the rails and if she didn't give him some he would jolly well help himself.'

'That still happens!' Barbara says, laughing. 'There is a legend,' she adds, 'that says Dorothea used to swim across the bay with only a red bathing cap on and that Chips Rafferty, who lived on the other side, would wait with a towel ready to wrap her. There's no mention of Chips in your book but I like the story. It makes Dorothea sound like a free spirit.'

'She was a free spirit, but Chips was a real friend to turn his head in a gentlemanly manner and wrap her in a towel.'

'There has also been talk of a relationship between them?'

'I don't think so,' Adrienne replies after a moment. 'Not from what I know of her.'

'There is a nearby pathway known as Lover's Lane. Do you think there was anyone else around here in whom she had a romantic interest?'

'No, I don't think so. She had friends who came up from Sydney occasionally. But Dorothea was a very private person and she would be very circumspect about anything like that. She had very strong feelings about what constituted good behaviour. Dignity was very important to her. Not a forced dignity, either.

It was a natural dignity, the kind that comes from understanding exactly what is right and wrong, what is dignified or undignified.'

'Did she have much of a sense of humour?'

'Yes, and a quick wit that could be very cutting if anyone tried to put anything over her or tried to take advantage of her.'

'Can I ask why you're so interested in Miss Mackellar?' Adrienne asks. 'Your questions go far beyond what I thought you'd want to talk about.'

'I guess my interest was spurred along by the bushfires when the house, and virtually the history of it, could have burned to the ground. I wanted a record of what had been here and what remained and as soon as I wanted to know more about the house I realised I had to find out more about Dorothea Mackellar. There was so much we didn't know. You are the only direct link we have found to her. How long did you know her?'

'Eleven and a half years, twelve hours a day, six days a week, and she loved to talk. On a good day she never stopped talking. On a bad day, she would be exhausted. Towards the end, she started having little mini-strokes, which tired her out. If anyone said anything that riled her, that could also be exhausting.'

'She loved language, I suppose.'

'There would be certain words that would always affect her. Just the names of some colours would bring tears to her eyes. She thought that "The Colour of Light" was her best poem.'

'She never married and never had any children. Do you think she felt her life had been wasted in any way?'

'No, I think she was quite satisfied. She had done what she could and left something behind her that was worthwhile. She hadn't brought disgrace on her family, or done anything terrible. She never did a horrible thing to anyone. She was not self-satisfied and I don't think she died with any regrets. But there was sadness. At times. She could not mention her brother Keith, who was killed in the Boer War, without tears spilling. Right to the very end.'

Barbara puts her notebook aside, slipping her pen inside the pages so it won't get lost in the folds of the bed linen.

'I have only one more question. A small one, but important to me. What did she wear, do you remember? Were her clothes dark or light? Did she wear hats?'

Adrienne thinks for a while before answering. 'She liked softly coloured clothes as I recall. Yes. And some bright florals. She always wore a bright floral housecoat indoors. I'm not sure about hats. By the time I knew her, she didn't go out much.'

Barbara lies back on her pillow and I leave the room. Disappointed for her. Dorothea looked nothing like her ghost. There is no more mystery, except to wonder whom it was, that Melbourne Cup day, who passed by so whimsically.

Adrienne stays with Barbara and the two of them talk for another hour. Not about Dorothea, Adrienne tells me later. About family, love, dreams and hopes.

By mid November, after the wild spring winds have whipped through Lovett Bay and scattered the last of the bright yellow wattle, chemo is almost a month behind me. Barbara is fading slowly but fighting every step of the way. In her bedroom, where we now have most of our chats, because she rarely leaves the room, she insists she is feeling better and better.

I have a boat, now. One of Bob's sturdy metal crates, which I've named *Tin Can*, and although I'm still too nervous to use it often, just knowing it's waiting at the foot of the garden makes me feel more independent. I ask him if I can buy it after Barbara tells me he is planning to design and build a smaller boat to whiz to and from Church Point.

'Only if you give it a test run first,' he says as I broach the subject early one morning when the ground is golden from puffs of fallen wattle and the first hint of summer has blown in on an aromatic westerly wind.

'Could you give me a couple of lessons, too?'

'Yeah. But there's not much to driving a boat. Five year olds can do it. You'll pick it up in a flash.'

''Course I will.'

The first time we go out we motor slowly because I know that's the best way from my forays with Sophia, but when we hit the open part of the bay, he tells me to push the throttle forward. We race along in an ear-splitting engine roar and I think I'm banging along brilliantly until I look at Bob's wincing face.

'What's wrong?' I shout.

'You're breaking my fucking balls!' he shouts back, his hands cupping his testicles.

'Oh God, sorry.'

I yank the throttle back and he nearly goes through the wind-screen. Oops. Forgot that little lesson with Sophia.

'Sorry.'

He breathes again. White-faced. 'There's a middle speed, you know. There's not just slow and flat out.'

He reaches across and moves the throttle until we're rocking along nicely. 'Right. Now turn back to Lovett Bay.'

I swing the wheel sharply and almost shoot Bob out of his seat. He bumps his head hard against the side window.

'Oh God, I'm so sorry.'

He gets back his balance and looks at me. 'You are the worst learner I've ever experienced. A shocker.'

And we laugh because we both know it's true and Bob's face is transformed. The lines of weariness soften, the tight band of restraint around his mouth relaxes. He looks years younger. There's a hint of larrikin about him, like the name of his boat, and I wonder if he chose it because that's what he knows lurks inside him.

'If you want a boat to race to Palm Beach, this isn't the right one,' Bob says after we agree on a price. 'The engine is a bit tired and if it blows up within a year, I'll refund some of your money.'

'Sounds fair.' To me, the boat feels stable and solid. It suits me beautifully. 'Anyway, I've given up rushing,' I add.

'What you need is practice,' he says. 'Get out every day. On your own.'

He takes a deep breath. Seems to steady himself a bit. 'Have a go at docking,' he adds. 'Do it over and over until you feel the strength of the wind and water.'

'I know about breezes,' I say. 'They can nudge you into the middle of the bay before you start the engine.'

Bob nods. 'You've got to respect the elements. You can't treat them lightly or they'll get you.'

17

NEARLY A MONTH AFTER MY last chemo treatment, the new editor at a magazine I once edited has offered me part-time work and I decide to take it on. I am worried about being home all day with nothing to think about except my health. And I've committed to house renovations. I need the extra money. The plan is to spend three nights a week staying with Pia in her inner city apartment. Bob and Barbara will look after the puppies and I will return home every Thursday night for a three day weekend.

My head is still bald but no-one seems to care. Despite their image, women's mass market magazine offices aren't glamorous places. Everyone works too hard to bother with frilly clothes and high heels but I try, for a day or two, to wind a scarf around my head. Then I stop. I am who I am. And right now, that means bald. With a funny little bump on my crown that looks a bit weird. Too bad. Take me or leave me. There will be no more bending to be someone I am not. Not for a job, a man, a friend or even a life. Somehow, during the last few months, I have finally grown into my skin. The influence of environment or the threat of mortality? Probably a bit of both.

But I have no idea how to handle life beyond chemo. After months of feeling like an alien I am suddenly dumped back into mainstream living. Do I march on as though cancer never invaded my life? Am I cured? Can I behave like everyone else again and eat and drink whatever I like? The truth is, no-one ever gives you the all-clear so the threat of a recurrence means a sense of being constantly on the edge of a precipice.

Physically, I just thought I'd quickly feel ok and bounce back to normal. I wasn't prepared for the tiredness to continue and even escalate for the first few months after the end of chemo. And my concentration is still shot. Two minute spans are about the limit. I don't know if it's chemo, menopause or just the whole damn bang lot of what's happened in the past six months. Bottom line, concentrating from the beginning to the end of a sentence is torture.

After four weeks of struggling to get to the office by nine, struggling to work solidly through the day to 5.30 pm, I am exhausted. Often, I have to crawl under my desk to rest, hoping no-one will see me. The effort of even sitting for long periods is dizzying. One night, I sit at my desk until everyone has long gone because I cannot find the energy to stand and walk out of the building.

Every day, hot flushes pound in and out with their attendant waves of nausea, and they make interviewing people hell. I sit for ten minutes, cool and in control, and then out of nowhere my forehead starts to prickle with heat, my face turns purple, sweat gathers in large droplets under my eyes and bottom lip. Then it gushes in streams down my face, shirt front, back and the backs of my legs. I look wrecked and I feel like I am slowly going mad.

Nearly everyone is kind and understanding. People do their best to help me out. A cold drink, a box of tissues to mop the sweat, a fan turned directly onto my face. I particularly remember Glenn Close, the American actress, when I interviewed her in Far North Queensland on the set of the miniseries *South Pacific.* 'If I break into a sweat,' I told her, 'please don't worry. I had my last chemo treatment a month ago and my body is still adjusting.'

She looked at me closely, a slight woman with flawless skin and clear grey eyes, exuding health, sexuality and intelligence. 'Come inside where it's cooler,' she said. 'Tell me how we can make you as comfortable as possible.'

No fuss. Just cut to the practical. She let me bumble around my questions, never lost patience when I repeated one or two and made me feel like a member of her family. She had the ability to see beyond herself and compassion came easily to her. Which I must say is rare in the Hollywood stars I've interviewed over the years.

But coming home from that assignment, with my right arm encased in a tight elastic bandage to prevent lymphoedema, which is sometimes triggered by long flights, I know I've done a poor job. And I don't have a clue how to prevent it happening again. My mind is like a quagmire, thoughts fracturing before they form. Even worse, I have trouble understanding what people say to me. I hear their words through a kind of slow motion fog.

I have lost, too, the journalistic instinct for the *headline* quote – the sensational sentence everyone latches onto and that catapults a bland interview into hot gossip. Cancer, which threatened my well-being, makes me suddenly protective of other people's welfare. So I self-edit and soften indiscreet words that I know would cause a furore in print. It is a form of professional suicide, but I can't live any other way now.

On a personal level, every simple decision seems to have major ramifications. What kind of takeaway food might do me harm? Is barbecued steak carcinogenic? Will colouring my hair – when it regrows – increase the risk of cancer? What is good for me? What will hurt me? It feels, some days, as though I am wading through a paddock filled with landmines. The cancerous growth has been removed so, *technically*, I am not sick any more. Only I am sick from chemo. But it's not the kind of sickness people can see. There is no gushing nose, no fever, no cough, not even a tummy ache. Only a wave of wretched tasting chemicals in my mouth every so often, and a tiredness that permeates every fibre of my body. I am caught between wanting to push myself harder and being terrified it might hurt me, send me back to the cancer ward. It's a bastard not knowing *why* you've had a disease because it means you have no idea what to do in future to prevent it happening again.

We talk one day, Barbara and I, about having no 'lift'. We mean when you go to step up – off a boat, up some stairs, across a water-course – and there's no strength to make the step. No lift. I've never thought about where the strength to climb out of a boat comes from before. What instruction goes to the brain and is then passed down the body until the right muscles get the message and, poof, like magic you raise yourself to where you want to be? Now I put a foot on the pontoon and nothing happens. The other foot doesn't follow unless I pull myself up with my arms. Instructions aren't getting through from the brain to the muscles. It is shocking and humbling.

One night Pia returns late to her apartment with a group of friends in tow, and the music plays until 3 am. Once I would have joined the party but now I cry from sheer weariness and cannot get up the next morning until an hour after I am supposed to be at the office. But if it isn't the noise of a party disturbing me, it is the sound of drug deals taking place in the laneway alongside the building, the guttural scream of buses climbing the hill outside the front windows. All the scatty, random sounds of a city at night that seem unremarkable when you live in it. When you live far from it, in a place where the soothing slurp of an incoming tide fingering the large rock at the bottom of the garden lulls exquisitely, city noise is like the constant hammering of a headache.

At Pittwater, my tired mind winds down just by sitting for a few moments and watching light play on water. Colours are always changing. Silver dawns, fiery sunrises, hard flat noons when the sun sucks the colour from the trees. And then lush late afternoons when greens turn deeper and deeper until they fade into the black of night. The bay is its own kaleidoscope. Silver, turquoise, lime, blue, gold, orange. Sometimes bloated with water. Sometimes so drained by the pull of the moon, the sea grass lies stranded and bowed until the water rises and it can begin again its silent, underwater ballet.

The smells, too. The dank, briny scent of low tide when the sand lies exposed and wet, almost muddy. The dusty, roasted smell of eucalypts in the heat of a forty degree day. The sugary fragrance of wattles, the musty smell of damp rocks. Then there's the wind. On the coast, there is almost always wind, but each one has a personality, characteristics that tell you where it is coming from without having to look to see which way the bows of the yachts are pointing. A southerly is clean and cool, a northerly clingy and damp. In summer, a hot, parched westerly brings the fear of bushfires until a frisky sea breeze late in the afternoon forces it back the way it came.

On a calm day of soft rain, light and shadow melt restfully. When balloons of purple clouds roll in and thunder bellows, rain pounds down in a shimmering wall and lightning flashes in jagged forks or long, flat sheets. When the sun shines and there's a hint of breeze, the bay glows like the pearly scales of fresh fish and is almost rainbow coloured. Sometimes the wind whisks the water until it is lacy with whitecaps and it is pleasant to simply sit and listen to the way the sounds change with the weather. The song of casuarinas, the taffeta rustle of cabbage palms, their fronds trilling like notes on a piano, the agonised creaking of spotted gums. And occasionally, the snap and crash of a huge branch falling to the ground. It is impossible to disengage from the physical world and I am reminded, over and over, that control is an illusion.

I manage to stagger around the office for three months in what seems like smaller and smaller circles. Then, as the first wispy new fluffs of hair blossom into a full, curly thatch of an entirely new colour – black when I'd been red – I understand I can no longer go on. It is not just the exhaustion. It is the wrenching sadness I feel every time I walk into a tall, dark building, leaving behind the sky and the light of day.

I miss the feel of the breeze on my face. Instead of the sexy tang of sea air, I mingle with the scents of hundreds of strangers that seem to me, in that time of heightened sensitivity, to be awash in an overpowering, synthetic stink. I miss the puppies and their uninhibited joy, their sweet earthy smell. I miss the easy, quiet pace of a community that has become a family. Every moment locked away in an artificial environment feels wasted. As I lie in my thundering city bedroom, I long for the light from a full moon to trickle quietly through my bedroom window instead of the pounding flashes from headlights.

In the city, weather is to be endured. At Lovett Bay, it is better than television, a constant source of movement and change. Is it a day to sling on wet weather gear for a walk, to huddle in bed under feather quilts until the sun reaches the bay? Is it a day when the prevailing wind shucks all the boats with their noses pointing to Scotland Island, or a day when the wind, bad-tempered and erratic, spins them first one way and then another, like confused and cranky two year olds. Is it a day when the bush flattens out in the heat and turns so crisp it crackles underfoot? Or is it a day when the sun strikes molten hot after rain and the earth steams until each breath feels like sipping soup. You fling off shoes, wriggle toes in spongy grass and feel anchored to the land.

Once, a snake, glossy as freshly shined black patent leather, swayed from the tip of its tail just outside the back door, its lipstick red belly a slash of warning. Shy but poisonous. Keep your distance. I hammer down my fear of snakes for long enough to see the beauty of her dance. Then slam the door. Red is often the colour of danger in the bush. Red-bellied black snakes. Red-back spiders. Red glow of bushfires.

A diamond python takes refuge in the vine alongside the back porch where I tip the tea leaves. Gordon's python, perhaps. One day, the tea leaves uncoil and I can't help screaming, even though I know the snake is harmless. But I am not repulsed or deterred from continuing to tip my tea leaves in the same place. It is life. It is exciting in a way that restores the spirit instead of draining it. If my time is to be cut short then every moment must be as good as it gets.

So I resign from my work. Again. I have done it so often now, it holds no fear for me. This time, it does not feel as though I am leaping into nothing, but instead, as though I am grabbing what is most important to me at this stage of my life. At Pia's city apartment, I pack my small suitcase for the last time, put the box, where my new silicone prosthesis spends each night, in a David Jones shopping bag, and drive home through the choking Sydney traffic.

I am about to spend a heap of money renovating the house, I don't have a job, and I feel quite absurdly happy. It seems ridiculous to worry about the future. I don't even know if I have one. The truth is, none of us do. If you can look at that simple fact from the right angle, it is empowering. Fear doesn't mean much when you turn to face it. Just looking at what scares you most makes it smaller, easier to handle. Even, sometimes, downright ludicrous.

I finally stop hedging my bets. In a peculiar way, what I've arrived at is *faith*. Not the religious kind, but the sort that comes from inside yourself.

I slip back into the harmony of Lovett Bay life instantly and time, which I once filled with work, frantic partying or the lover, slows to a manageable pace. There is time to daydream, time to clean the grungy corners of windows and take pleasure in it, time to talk to Barbara on the verandah, time to give to other people. Half an hour slips by watching two little kids in bright yellow life jackets and floppy cotton hats sitting side by side in a boat the size of a bathtub. They are learning to row, and spin in laughing circles until they get the hang of it. It is a privilege, this gift of time, one that cannot be frittered negligently.

I decide to get my growing hair coloured and go back to the hairdresser who was so kind when it was falling out.

'Turn it auburn,' I tell him. 'A good, rich, red-brown colour.'

Four hours later, I emerge fuchsia pink. 'You could guide the ferry in at midnight with your hair,' Bob says when he sees it.

I return to the hairdresser. 'Make it blonde.'

A week later, a friend comes to lunch. 'Interesting shade of green in your hair. Looks good with the purple streaks. Going punk?' she asks.

Back to the hairdresser. 'Plain white will do.'

I return from the washbasin and look in the mirror. My hair is canary yellow.

Col, who fixed Stewart's wine rack nearly six years ago for Fleury's birthday, now owns the wonderful poultry supply shop Caotic Chook next to the hairdresser's. I see his reflection in the mirror. He's in shock.

A few minutes later his wife, Cher, rushes in with a glass of red wine. 'Col thought you might need this,' she says.

Back in Lovett Bay, the boys in the boatshed see me coming and money changes hands.

'You let me down, Susan,' says Veit.

'What do you mean?'

'I tipped black this time. I lost the bet.'

My loyalty to the hairdresser finally ends. I get a number two clip and begin again. Au naturel.

Brigitte rushes in one morning on her way to catch the ferry, bowl of porridge in one hand, spoon in the other, the rest of her city necessities hurled in a bag slung over her back.

'Susan. Susan,' she says. Always the double-barrelled monicker. Eating as she talks.

'Hi, Brigitte. How are you? The boys?'

'Good. Good. Susan! Susan! Do you think you could cook for the Elvina Bay Fire Shed dinner this month? There's no-one to do it.'

'Sure. When is it and how many people?'

'Friday night. There's usually about thirty people.'

'Thirty!'

'Yeah. But you only have to do one course. There's always a dessert competition and four or five people make cakes or pies, or something.'

'Is there a budget?'

'Well, spend as little as possible. The idea is to raise money for the fire brigade.'

She scrapes the sticky edges of her bowl and puts it down on the seat on the back deck. 'I'll pick it up on the way home. So you're ok? You'll do it?' She's rushed and rushing.

'Yeah. But how? Do I cook here or there?'

'Cook everything here and we'll all help to carry it. I can do rice, if you need it. Let me know.'

And she is gone in a swirl of ankle length skirt and shoulder length hair.

On Thursday, when the builders come by via water taxi to discuss plans, I am knee deep in osso buco. The house is filled with smoke from searing the meat and the kitchen is chaotic. My biggest saucepans are scattered all over the kitchen benches and the smell of garlic and lemon fills the air. As usual, I am catering for the Russian army. Thirty people, Brigitte said, so I've raised it to sixty. Just in case. Wouldn't want anyone to go hungry.

I slap cups of tea and slices of lemon cake in front of them and leave them to look around and measure on their own.

'You having a party or something?' one of them asks.

'Nope. Fundraiser for the fire shed.'

'Oh? Is it the first Friday of the month already?'

Late on Friday afternoon, Bob comes to help load the boat. One large cast iron pot and three enormous stainless steel pots are stacked so they won't fall. They weigh a ton each. Or that's what it feels like. Bob carries them uncomplainingly but I can see faint lines of disapproval around his mouth. I've over-catered. We both know it.

'The average portion size per person is 250 grams,' he says, stepping into a rocking boat with the cast iron pot. 'You expecting the entire western foreshore community tonight?'

'Maybe.'

He gives up. I hand over a garbage bag filled with washed lettuce and a large bottle of salad dressing. Then another garbage bag filled with cooked penne I plan to warm in hot water for a minute or two before serving.

'Is there anyone meeting us at the other end?' Bob asks.

'No. I don't think so.'

He sighs. 'Well, at least it's high tide. We can take the boat right in to the sea wall to unload. Means it's not quite so far to carry everything to the fire shed.'

He starts the boat and we chug out of Lovett Bay, going past *Trincomalee* and around the bend into Elvina Bay. The fire shed is on the south side of the bay, near Beashel's Boat Shed. It's a typical fire shed. Weatherboard, cement floor and couple of roller doors. There's a small group of people gathered out front who turn as we approach and wander down to the boat.

'Hi. I'm Lisa.'

'Hi. I'm Alan.'

'Hi. I'm Alan, too.'

'He's Roy,' says Lisa, pointing at a quiet, shy bloke who turns out to be her husband.

They grab saucepans and bags until there's nothing left, and I follow them empty-handed.

From six o'clock onwards, tinnies glide in slowly as though

drawn by a silent bugle call, and men, women, young kids and toddlers stroll, race or stumble past the wheelbarrows lined up along the jetty, towards the fire shed.

'They're to cart the shopping home,' Bob explains, when I ask him what all the wheelbarrows are for.

'They just leave them on the wharf?'

'Yep.'

'No-one nicks them?'

'Nope.'

When the crowd looks big, Roy raises the second roller door and drives the bright, shiny fire engine with its tank and hoses outside onto the grass, just in case the weather turns mean and we need shelter. He is laconic, with a dry sense of humour and makes us all laugh.

Lisa, who is clearly a phenomenal cook and an even better organiser, directs the boys to set up serving tables, haul out piles of mismatched plates and cutlery donated over the years. She slams a load of homemade sausage rolls into the oven to feed the kids, and fills the urn to heat water for the washing up. People pay $7 and get a ticket for dinner, kids run riot and entertain themselves, and it's a great night out. Bottles of wine are opened and glasses filled and there's a quiet exchange of local information. Who will distribute the bags for clean-up day? Who needs hoses for a fire pump? Should there be a fire shed Christmas dinner this year as well as a kids' musical concert? Who'll be Santa Claus? Will there be any back-burning this summer? How's the season looking for bushfires?

'Did you hear about Michelle's dog?' one of the Alans asks when dinner's been served and we're all sitting and eating.

'No, what?'

'Python got her.'

There's a shocked silence.

'Poor Millie,' says someone.

'Oh, she's not dead,' Alan adds. 'Michelle saved her.'

Michelle, who is terrified of snakes, was so incensed when the python began to strangle and crush her tiny chihuahua cross, she didn't stop to think. She grabbed the snake, whacking it until it released the dog.

'Millie immediately bolted down the hill, raced down the jetty and jumped on the ferry at the end of the wharf where she leaped into some woman's lap and refused to move,' Alan continues. 'Impressive, don't you think, that a little dog understood it was the safest place for her?'

Not long afterwards, the python, which is a non-venomous and usually non-aggressive snake, bit Michelle on the ankle when she passed by without seeing it. Do pythons have memories, I wonder?

When everyone's eaten and the desserts have been judged, Lisa looks around. 'Bit left over, isn't there?' she says with a trace of a New Zealand accent. She looks at the bench. Pots are lined up like soldiers, most of them half full.

'Nearly all the salad has gone, though,' I say in defence.

'Hmm. Well, I'd say it's a perfect result. There's a fire shed meeting on Monday night and this will feed everyone.'

She grins and so do I, and we begin loading leftovers into plastic containers to freeze. Whoever happens to be standing near the sink starts the washing up and nearly everyone takes a turn. There's no formal organisation, it just happens in the way things do when everyone is considerate.

'Time to leave?' Bob comes into the kitchen, shoulders hunched as usual, face looking worn. I look at Lisa.

'Yep. Nothing else to do here. Don't worry about taking the pots and pans. I've got to whiz in to Lovett Bay tomorrow and I'll drop them off.'

And she thanks me, and so does everyone else. And they say wonderful things about the food and I feel as though I have been useful. Which is a good feeling. And ok, my ego fluffs a little. But not enough to worry about.

Lisa reimburses me for the food and Bob and I follow the path to the jetty by the light of the moon.

'Will you be coming to the Christmas dinner in a couple of weeks?' Lisa calls.

'Love to,' I yell back. 'Can I do anything?'

'I'll let you know.'

The boys in the boatshed, always friendly and cheerful even on the dankest mornings, are my daily entertainment. Each day I watch big, tired yachts, with peeling paint and a whole marine environment attached to their hulls, get towed in by a small, banged-up tinny and coaxed into a wooden cradle to be lifted from the water. Then the scraping, sanding, painting – a complete makeover, as we'd say in the women's magazine business – begins. It is hard, dirty work but little by little, oysters, mussels, clumps of seaweed and every kind of barnacle, are scraped from the hull. Little chips and indentations are filled, sanded back and smoothed over until, finally, rollers on long poles are used to swish on the paint. A racy, graceful thin line in a contrasting colour is painted around the hull about a foot below deck, giving even the plumpest, most cumbersome boats a youthful lift. Occasionally, a boat gets painted deep burgundy or elegant black. Whatever the colour, the end result is that sad, tired old shells are transformed into confidently beautiful vessels.

At the risk of sounding sentimental, I feel Lovett Bay is having the same effect on me. Layers of emotional baggage are being sifted so I can edit out the lousy episodes and store the finer moments. The last shreds of grief about the boys, the anger with the lover? Tossed out and drowned. I can choose to hang on to old hurts and perhaps blame them for any unhappiness. But why go down that path when it is so much more pleasant to remember the best times and aim, instead, for contentment?

I don't know if I would have arrived at all these conclusions in the course of time or whether being ill hastened the process. Whatever the answer, whenever I make a wish (on a falling star, on the first cherry of the season, on any number of rites instilled by my mother that I haven't been able to shake off and perhaps never will), it is always the same. *Give me health and I will take care of the happiness myself.*

Much later, when I have nestled into the unhurried tempo of a life that revolves around weather and whim instead of deadlines and schedules, I learn my Little Gairie Beach shack buddy, Tony, is seriously ill.

'Come and stay for a while,' I tell him when I visit him in hospital where he's having chemo and radiation therapy for oesophageal cancer. 'Come directly to me. Don't even go home for a day or two.'

He is weak and tired and I know what is squirming around his mind.

'Come to Lovett Bay and let me feed you up,' I continue. 'We'll pretend we're at the shack.'

'Your house,' he says to me with a raised eyebrow and curled lip, his face as pale as the hospital pillow under his head, 'is exactly the same as the shack except it has running water and a dishwasher. I,' he adds like a politician delivering a speech, 'reminded you about the best parts of your childhood at *my* shack and you went off and found a shack of your own.'

And I realise he is right. When my brother and I were still young enough to be at primary school, rare family holidays usually meant a trip to Phillip Island, where we stayed in a wobbly shack built from bits of wood nailed to a frame. The shack belonged to my grandfather's sister, Auntie Mert, and her husband, Uncle Albert. Uncle Albert was famous in the family for his aversion to work.

'Come and help with breakfast, Albert,' Auntie Mert would say.

'Just wait till I light my pipe,' he'd reply.

'We need some wood for the fire, Bert.'

'Just wait till I light my pipe.'

My mother says it was always 'just wait till I light my pipe' and my dad tipped that when the angel Gabriel told him to come on in through the pearly gates, Albert would pause and drawl, 'Just wait till I light my pipe.'

The thing was, though, that Uncle Albert found his passion at this little shack on Phillip Island. Auntie Mert always went fossicking for beautiful shells, which were everywhere in those days. She collected so many Uncle Albert started playing with them until he created wonderful designs. Then he set his works of shell art in concrete and panelled the side and front fence. People eventually came from miles around to see it. Overseas visitors often sent him shells from distant corners of the world to add to his collection.

'Found his niche,' my mother said. 'Took him a long time. But that can happen. Only the lucky ones *know exactly* what they want to do. Never forget Mert, though. She was a worker. Didn't even make five feet and she could swing an axe like a man. Don't think she ever sat down. Not that I saw, anyway.'

I wondered, when she told me this story, whether my mother lived in an era when *characters* were revered instead of reviled, when to be *odd* meant individual and special, not mad. Was hers an era when conditions were so strenuous there was neither the time nor desire to pluck away at the frailties of people who did not conform?

Before Auntie Mert and Uncle Albert fixed up the shack and sold it at a profit, the roof was tin and the kitchen had a single kerosene burner in one corner. There was a cupboard with a curtain to hide a couple of pots and a few chipped plates. Dishes were washed outside under the tap at the base of the water tank. When the wind blew, which it does most of the time on this bleak island off the coast of Victoria, there were so many gaps in the walls my skirt would kick up as I sat at the kitchen table.

When it rained, which it did nearly as often as it blew, every bucket, bowl, dish and cup was put into action to catch the leaks. Once, when it poured nonstop for seven days, my mother taught my brother, and a friend he'd brought along, to knit.

'The friend's dad was appalled,' my mother told me years later. 'You just weren't supposed to teach boys stuff like sewing and knitting. But I couldn't think what else to do with the lot of you. It didn't stop raining until the day we left for home.'

There was a dunny out the back and a cold water shower outside. Swimming was supposed to keep you clean. The shower was just to rinse off the salt water. At night we lit hurricane lamps because there was no electricity and the house was filled with the permanent pong of kerosene mingled with the smell of the sea. Smells that, when I strike them now, race me back in time. Come to think of it, they were the same smells that wafted through Tony's Little Gairie Beach shack. Perhaps that's why I instantly loved it there.

Just after sunset each night at that funny little shell house, often even in mid-summer, we'd wrap ourselves up in coats and scarves and rush across the road to the beach to watch the penguins. There were hundreds of these shy little black and white birds that looked like they were surfing in on the waves to attend a formal dinner party. They'd hit the beach, look around timidly and, if the timing seemed right, waddle up to their burrows in the sand dunes. Mostly, the only people there to watch this wonderful spectacle were my parents and my brother and I. We considered it a crowd if there were five or six strangers.

After the penguin parade (as it is still called, although I understand there are now reserved seats and tourist buses at the site) we'd scamper home to a dinner of bread, butter, raspberry jam and cream. There may have been a sausage or a chop as well, of course, but all I remember from those carefree days in that funny old shack is the richness of the butter and cream. The thick, soft slices of fresh white bread. And the wonder of ruby red raspberry jam made by the farmer's wife down the road.

My mother would let me eat till I groaned because I had a sparrow's appetite as a child and usually ate so little she used to sneak raw eggs into my morning chocolate drink. Once, she tried to reinvent the magic of bread and butter and raspberry jam with cream when we were at home in the barracks of Bonegilla. But it tasted wet and slimy and I turned away from the plate.

In Auntie Mert's and Uncle Albert's shack, no-one ever told us to pick up our clothes, wash our hands or say our prayers. And my father didn't drink much because it was a fair distance to the pub, which meant my mother relaxed and came shell hunting with us. We valued cowries above all, with their exotic leopard spots, and put them to our ears to hear the sea.

'Here, Possie,' my brother would say, 'listen hard. Can you hear mermaids singing?'

I sniffed because I was just starting to question Santa Claus and fairytales and I thought my brother was setting me up. But I heard their song so when he grabbed my hand and pulled me along to the rockpools at low tide, I followed happily.

'What are we looking for?'

'Seahorses!'

'Horses don't live in the sea.'

'These do.'

I imagined great beasts with fins and gills and stamping hooves shaped like fish tails, so I wasn't prepared for the delicate little creature he pointed out.

'It's too small to be a horse,' I grumped, disappointed.

'But in the water, it has the strength of ten horses,' he said. 'And look! Starfish!'

I leaned closer to the rockpool and saw a teaming saltwater city. Tiny fish, shells with worms peeking out, crabs, and those magical seahorses and starfish.

'It's a fairyland,' my brother told me.

And for a while, I believed in fairytales all over again.

That shack was paradise and Tony, also a country kid, probably had one just like it in his childhood too. Perhaps that's why he fell in love with the crumbling hut at Little Gairie Beach when he returned to Australia from the glittering social whirl of London. He could be himself. No airs and graces, as the old saying goes.

In his hospital bed, Tony plucks the edges of his sheet, mulling over my offer of a bed and home care.

'So come home with me. Please. I'd love it,' I say.

He hesitates a second longer. 'Yes,' he says finally, and for a moment he grins in that wicked, naughty little boy way he had before illness thinned his hair and turned his skin the same grey as an old man's stubble.

For the first day or two at Lovett Bay, I let him rest in bed but he cannot settle his mind, worrying about the debris of his life. His business, the people who depend on him and, of course, his health. Because I think it may amuse and divert him from his problems if only for a moment or two, I suggest he spends a little time each day watching events unfold at the boatshed. 'You'll be constantly entertained,' I promise. So he sits in his navy and white kimono, sartorial and impossibly attractive despite his illness, working on a tapestry of sunflowers and looking up from time to time to see what's happening at the boatshed.

It happens to be the day Ken's wooden sailing boat, *Sylphine*, the one he sails in the Woody Point races, is to go back in the water after a long time in the slip. Toby and Dave are there on their barge, the *Laurel Mae*, to gently drop the boat into the water. It all goes according to plan. Except it lands in the water upside down, sinking so quickly the boatshed blokes don't have time to turn it upright. It goes straight to the bottom. Which gives everyone such a shock, they just stand and look for a full minute or so. Then it's bedlam. Ken races in and gets into a wetsuit. He and one of the boys, who's already in a wetsuit, dive deep, come up for air, discuss options, dive again and so on, until there's a plan. Eventually, the boat is brought up and righted, no damage done.

By the end of the whole event, Tony has tears running down his cheeks from laughing silently, too sore in his chest and throat from radiation to actually make a sound. 'This is a good place for me to be right now,' he says, still shaking with repressed laughter. And because he's been a theatrical and literary agent for most of his life, he adds: 'What do you think they'll come up with for an encore?'

He dies in hospital two months later. His wake is held at Little Gairie Beach and we all trek there to bid him goodbye. It's a still, perfectly bright day and the sea is flat as a sheet of glass. As we gather on the rocks at the seashore to toast Tony's colourful life, his sister puts down her glass of wine to say a few words. Out of nothing and nowhere, a wave rushes in, snatches the wine and roars back out to sea. It is behaviour so quintessentially Tony, we all gasp.

'He may be dead,' someone says, 'but he isn't gone!'

The sea remains flat for the rest of the speeches.

Not long after the sinking of the *Sylphine* and Tony's death, the staff at the boatshed drops to one.

'Where's the other fella gone?' I ask Ken.

'Got another job,' he replies shortly.

Still curious, I ask Veit what happened to him.

Veit stifles a laugh. 'Got cross with a boat surveyor. Threw him off the dock.'

'Never seemed the volatile sort to me. Goes to show you never can tell.'

'Quiet as a lamb mostly,' Veit agreed.

18

OUT OF THE BLUE, Bob rings and suggests a walk.

'Where to?' I ask, not quite understanding why he's asking me along.

'What about up to Flagstaff?'

'Where on earth is that?'

'I'll show you.'

We set off in the late morning. Bob is dressed defensively in long sleeves, trousers tucked into socks, a hat and boots. I wear a short-sleeved T-shirt and long trousers.

'I should have told you to wear long sleeves,' Bob says as we walk alongside the creek, heading west. 'The bush can get prickly.'

I shrug. I am feeling well and strong, as I always do until I try to do any physical work. I'm not sure why, but I can never remember I am still recovering until I hit a wall of exhaustion. Which means, of course, that perhaps I won't be able to complete the entire walk.

'What's Flagstaff?'

'You'll see.'

Just past the last house and near the mouth of the estuary, there's a thicket of short, stubby, baby cabbage palms, with thorns that rip deep into your skin if you brush too close. We bend almost double and clamber through a natural tunnel between the plants, trying not to touch them, but it's impossible. When we emerge into less dense scrub on the other side, there are pinpricks of blood on both my arms.

'I hope you know the way. Looks like nothing but scrub to me,' I say, rubbing spit on my scratches.

'This is an old walk, quite famous once, and there's a path here. We just have to find it,' Bob replies.

The walk, Bob explains, was built in 1895, when it was part of a grand scheme to make this area of Pittwater a fabulous national park on the same scale as Yellowstone National Park in the United States. There used to be a stone pathway, about four feet wide, leading from the ferry wharf along the shoreline. There was a shed, a kind of shelter, with a tank to collect fresh rainwater run-off from the roof, too. People came in droves to boil their billy and have a picnic here.

A bit further on, after we've crossed a creek bed, he stops and points at some old footings in a clearing. 'That's all that remains of the shed.'

'Bit of a hike to get here from Sydney. It's a wonder they bothered,' I mutter.

'Lot of them came for the wildflowers. The land was thick with them in spring. Quite beautiful.'

'S'pose they picked the lot and there are none left now.'

'No, they're around. But not as many. Back then the landscape was covered with flowers. Wax flowers, flannel flowers, all sorts of boronia. Ask Barbara about them when we get back.'

The bush is lush after heavy spring rains and the undergrowth is thick and ferocious. Prickly Moses cuts my cheeks. When I grab the wire thin leaves of a grass tree, my palm begins to bleed. Why, I wonder silently, am I enjoying this so much? And the answer rockets back: because I'm in the bush and I love it and it's a challenge.

Bob climbs steadily towards the escarpment. The track is barely defined or non-existent. A couple of times we are forced to retrace our steps after we follow what turns out to be a wallaby track, not the old pathway.

'How do you know where we're going?' I ask.

Bob doesn't answer and we trudge on.

'See this,' Bob says, kneeling to brush away dead leaves and dirt. He reveals three perfect, man-made sandstone steps. A few paces further on, he points out a dozen or so similar steps. 'This is the old path. We're going the right way.'

We push through big patches of that bloody merciless prickly Moses, step over fallen trees and hold back overhanging branches to stop them whipping our faces. There will be ticks, I think, and then chide myself for being wimpy. Ticks are a fact of life on Pittwater, like snakes and spiders, and you either learn to deal with them or you move on. There's no way I'm moving on.

We continue climbing through bush that changes from dense rainforest to rocky escarpment. We go past xanthorrhoeas with their grassy skirts and long spikes, Christmas bush ready to break into masses of delicate red and yellow star-shaped flowers. There's pale mauve grevilleas with tendrils that turn back on themselves to pollinate, deep purple hardenbergia and, at our feet, cheery blue-faced daisies called brachycome. Barbara, I realise, has been subtly teaching me to recognise the plants of Lovett Bay, nudging me towards a greater understanding of the bush without making a fuss. But I look around and there are so many other plants that I cannot name and it fills me with shame. This is my backyard now and I still know so little about it. It is an ugly ignorance.

Nearer the summit, where the vegetation thins into straggly stands of banksias and low growing escarpment shrubs, there's a large, dark cave.

'Is this where we're aiming for?' I ask Bob. Sweat is rolling down my face, the back of my T-shirt is stuck to my skin. Bob hasn't even worked up a glow.

'Nope. Just a bit further. We're nearly there, though.'

My nose is running horribly. After sniffing a while longer, I finally stretch my T-shirt and blow my nose on the sleeve.

'Sorry about that. Hope you don't mind. Sick of sniffing,' I say.

He reaches into his pocket and brings out a whitish handker-chief. 'Here,' he says, handing it to me. 'You should have asked. Barbara has the same problem. Why do you think there are boxes of tissues all over the house?'

'Barbara was right, you know, all those months ago,' I say, blowing my nose again. 'She told me the bush would seduce me and I'd give up the idea of white rose hedges and beds of pretty English annuals.'

Bob laughs. 'My wife always seems to know more than the rest of us.'

'How much further?'

'Not far. A couple more turns and we're there.'

Closer to the top, the vegetation changes dramatically. The soil is sandy and loose and stands of gnarled old banksias grip tightly to the side of the hill. They look like they're on fire with large orange and yellow flower cones, thick as dunny brushes. Small steps are chipped into a couple of rocky outcrops and then the track veers left. Ahead, there's a long, shadowy sandstone cave with a wooden table and bench seat. The overhang is pockmarked with erosion, the air cool. It smells musty, like an old wardrobe that hasn't been opened for years.

'God. How long has this been here?' I ask.

Stupid question. Millions of years probably. But the table and seat? Ten years or maybe one hundred years? There are initials and dates carved into the table top from the twenties to the late nineties and I trace them with my fingertip. (A few years later, when I visit the lookout, the table has collapsed and I discover two names, Donald and Quartermain, and the date, 1/12/10, are carved underneath, presumably by the blokes – or perhaps a single bloke called Donald Quartermain – who built the table.) At the front of the cave there's a hook hanging over a circle of stones, where once the billy hung to boil water for tea. I find out later that there used to be a tank to collect water that ran down the rock face.

I want to sit and absorb the cave but Bob seems uneasy, pacing in one spot, unable to sit down. 'Let's get to the top,' he says. 'It's not far at all, a few more steps.'

We move through straggly banksias and lots more prickly Moses. By now, both my arms are badly scratched and bleeding lightly. I think about lymphoedema, wonder briefly if I'll have to give up bushwalks. But that's no way to live. I just have to remember to bring antiseptic ointment at all times. Adapt instead of withdraw.

We emerge at the top of the escarpment where the wind is strong and cool. The landscape tumbles roughly below, spilling, jutting, jabbing. Boats sit on the water like giant seagulls, and jetties finger their way along the shorelines like badly spaced teeth. Scotland Island floats alone. I see the toe between Lovett and Elvina Bays. In the distance, a narrow neck of land separates one side of Mona Vale from the Pacific Ocean, which is a thin band of pale blue in the distance. Closer, there's the roof of my house, the roof of the boatshed. On the other side of the bay I can see the farmhouse a family called the Olivers built when they settled here in the 1800s. Where we stand, there's an old iron and wooden seat that's probably been here as long as the table. Eventually, I sit on it and stare all the way to the Pacific Ocean, not moving even when little black ants start to crawl over me.

After a while, I realise Bob is still nervy. 'Are you ever going to sit?' I ask.

'Barbara is getting worse,' he replies.

'That's what happens, Bob. You can't change that. Short of a miracle, there will be more bad days than good from now on.'

He turns away, but not before I see tears in his eyes. His shoulders are gathered up around his head and his arms hang rigidly by his sides, fists clenched.

'But what can I do?' he asks. 'What should I do?'

I realise then that the reason we've walked to this place high on a hill is to talk about Barbara. He knows my husband and brother died, understands I am aware of what lies ahead for him. He wants to know what to expect, how to be prepared, how to care for the woman he loves and whom he's been married to for thirty-five years, had four children with, retired with, and had all the usual ups and downs with.

'I don't know what's right or wrong,' I tell him. 'I only know what I failed to do when I had the chance. I can tell you that your own life has to be put on hold, that you will have to set aside your work and the anger you must feel at what is happening. Barbara comes first. Everything now is about her welfare and conjuring up every bit of happiness possible.'

'But she wants to go on with painting the house,' Bob says, frustration exploding in every word. 'We put it off when she was diagnosed, and now I think it's madness. The house will be a mess, the fumes will knock her around.'

'Paint the house. It's what she wants. You can both stay with me until the fumes fade.'

He looks at me incredulously. 'Why would you do that?'

'Why did you and Barbara care for the puppies, help me every day?'

He sits, at last, on the seat, tension oozing out of him in long, flat ribbons. 'Barbara hates the idea of hospital. She wants to stay home,' he says.

'That's fine while she is still able to get up and walk around,' I respond. 'But one day she won't be able to get out of bed at all. And you will need help to care for her properly.'

'I have the help,' he replies. 'Our children will come, when it's time. One of them is a nurse.'

'When Sophia cared for her mother and sister, she brought in the equipment she knew they would need long before it was required, so that when the critical moment came, when they really needed it, they didn't have to wait.'

'Equipment?'

'The wheelchair. The bedpan.'

'Yeah. I guess it has to come to that, doesn't it?'

'It usually does.'

We linger in silence on the big rock where a flag flew on special days one hundred years ago. The guy rope anchors and the central cavity for the flagpole are still there – the reason the lookout is called Flagstaff. So long ago. So many people who were young and full of dreams, now dead. What on earth is it all about?

I turn to Bob. 'What do you think it's all about?' I ask.

'I don't know,' he says, instantly understanding what I mean. 'But all you can do when the pressure is on is try to survive.'

He stands up, ready to head home. 'Not many people remember this pathway,' he says, closing the subject on death.

We begin walking back along an even rougher route that takes us past two dams built nearly a century ago when food was grown here to supply Sydney in the early days of settlement.

I have never thought much about the history of European settlement or the history of this land. My generation was taught English history at school, as though it was the only history that really counted. Will future generations have more respect than we did for this fragile country? Are they being taught about how every plant regenerates differently? Sometimes from bushfire. Sometimes from smoke. Sometimes from seeds falling in autumn, sometimes from tubers. Or will they go on to trash it like we did out of ignorance and greed? Mostly ignorance, though. This is a land like no other and I am only now, at my age, beginning to understand a little of it.

≈

The house painting goes ahead in a frenzy of drop sheets, ladders and singing painters wearing splattered overalls. 'They're Italian,' Bob says, as though that automatically explains the singing.

Bob and Barbara move into my still unrenovated house, for a short stay – just while their bedroom is being worked on. For me, it is a wonderful time. Every night there is a team to cook for, which gives me a central purpose. Every day Barbara rests and Bob disappears to his workshed, returning on the dot of twelve for lunch, then vanishing again until about five or six o'clock. Unless I am out and Barbara is alone. Then he sits on the sofa closest to where Barbara rests. While he sketches ideas for whatever problem he is working on, he can also hear her breathing.

Bob, it turns out, can do almost anything. Fix taps. Build houses. Design boats. Fix engines. Even repair appliances. He is an engineer with a licence to do electrical and plumbing work. He fixes a leak I didn't even know I had in the bathroom. Gets the exhaust fan working over the stove. Rips apart an iron I planned to throw out, orders a new part, and gets it going again. Give Bob a broken hose and he'll return with a new watering system.

I see his mind whirring constantly. When he's tongue-tied, I realise it's because his words can't keep pace with his thoughts. When he is silent, he is observing, assessing, storing information, thinking. He is not frightened of the kind of responsibility that means making hard decisions. Perhaps because he knows he is compassionate. And he is clear about what is important. He does not need applause to make him feel big. Only the knowledge he has given his best. He is, I understand one day, one of the few grown-ups I have ever met.

I am often gone for part of the day, seeing one doctor or another, trying to rebuild my strength and, to be honest, seeking constant reassurance that the cancer has not returned. I usually come home in the afternoon, crash for a couple of hours, and then brew my evil tasting concoctions. Do they help? I don't know. Once I ask Sophia how much of illness – of cancer – is mind over matter.

'Well, Buddhist monks have pretty good minds. They meditate, live peacefully, eat simple food and don't smoke or drink. They still die of cancer.'

Right. *I am strong and my body is strong.* Or is it all in the lap of the gods, after all?

On the first Tuesday morning of Bob and Barbara's stay, I leave home early for an appointment but the phone rings when I am halfway to the city.

'Barbara can't get out of bed,' Bob says. 'What should I do?'

Without asking any questions, I turn the car around and head home, alarmed by the sound of panic in his voice. On the water taxi I explain what's happening to the driver, Geoff.

'If we call you,' I say, 'come quickly. Barbara is ill.'

Because we are a community, nothing else needs to be said. Everyone has known about her cancer for months.

I race up Ken's jetty and run up the steps to the house. At home, Barbara lies in bed, happy and smiling. For a moment, I can't understand the panic. She is pale, as usual, but looks quite relaxed.

'I'll get up in a minute,' she says.

Bob grabs my elbow and takes me outside. 'She's been saying that since eight o'clock this morning. If she could get up, she would. Today's the day for another chemo treatment.' Barbara would never skip those little bolts of poison that she felt were extending her life.

Bob goes up the hill to his house to call her doctor. Then he rings me, so Barbara can't hear what he says.

'They say to get an ambulance and get her to hospital.'

'How do we do that?'

'I'll take care of it. You stay with Barbara.'

When you live in water-access-only areas, the Water Police become your water ambulance. They are based in McCarrs Creek, only minutes away, and generally know the community well enough to have a list of who's pregnant, who's sick and who's dying. The Water Police then call an ambulance, and when everyone is assembled at the police office at the marina, the police and the ambulance staff both come over in the police launch to fetch the patient.

The police arrive wearing their practical navy overalls with the ambulance attendants and their gear. A stretcher, little suitcases, even oxygen. Once again, Barbara tells everyone she is fine and she'll get up in a few minutes. Half an hour later, the stretcher is brought alongside the bed and she is gently moved onto it.

'I'm not bedridden, you know,' she says emphatically. But her eyes are filled with tears and all we can do is hold her hand and nod.

They carry her down the steps, those lovely young men with open faces and strong bodies, and place her in the boat so gently Barbara feels no pain. Then they cast off, with Bob on board, and move slowly across the water.

I gather the puppies and go inside. Memories of my husband and brother, of the nightmare rushes to hospital with an infected bone flap in the skull after brain surgery, of seizures, of more surgery as the tumours grew rapidly, yammer in my mind.

I want to run from all this. I don't want to go through it all again, the sense of helplessness, the drawn-out wait for death, the grief that grinds through every day even while a loved one is still alive. Grief that leaves you without the strength to feel, for a little while after they die, anything but relief. And when the relief fades and the final reality of death seeps in, you're left with huge waves of pure, lonely grief and it's all you can do to keep standing.

≈

I call in to see Barbara in hospital with a huge bunch of hydrangeas gathered from the old garden behind my house. Once the doctor lived there, and then new houses were built until the last one burned down in the 1994 fires and it's never been rebuilt. Only the stone chimney remains, sticking straight up like an ancient monument. And a few of the toughest old-fashioned plants. Canna lilies, wisteria, magnolias and, in spring, daffodils and snowflakes.

The hydrangeas give the barren hospital room a lift but it is a bleak place. Hard to bear when the elegant verandah of *Tarrangaua* beckons with its views of a teeming outside world.

'I want to be at home,' Barbara says.

'I'd want to be home, too,' I reply, holding her hand for a moment.

There are three other people in her room, wheezing, coughing, leaking life at the same rate as plastic pouches of fluid are being pumped into them. Better by far to hear the music of the bush and the water.

Barbara has no tubes hanging from her arm but she can barely move. Her body is closing down slowly.

'Can you cope if Barbara comes home?' I ask Bob after I return to Lovett Bay that evening. 'It's a huge job. Relentless. A bit like having a baby. It's utter dependence we're talking about. Hard stuff.'

'We'll manage,' he says. And he quietly explains he's been ready for this situation since long before our chat on Flagstaff. Without any fuss, he's planned each stage of Barbara's care with love tempered by the hard edges of reality. He will care for her while she can still get out of bed and for as long as she can get by with oral painkillers. As her health breaks down even further, their children will be called on. First Kelly, an experienced intensive care nurse. When two people are no longer enough, Meg, an engineer, will come.

'Three of us can handle it,' Bob says.

'Four,' I say. 'Let me help where I can.'

As soon as Barbara returns home, the community kicks in gently. Debbie from Frog Hollow brings Thursday night desserts. Ann from Little Lovett Bay comes to read on Wednesday evenings or an occasional afternoon when Bob has to go out. I call in for chats, loaded with cakes or a stew or a giant frittata. Veit, from the boatshed, carries the food up the steps and occasionally stays to eat some of it.

Somewhere amongst all the visits, Dolce scoffs some rat poison hidden in peanut butter and Bob and I rush to the vet to get her stomach pumped. Barbara lets Vita onto her bed while we are gone and cuddles her until we return a couple of hours later.

Barbara talks as though one day she will be well and makes us all feel that perhaps there will be a miracle. As each week unfolds, there are new dramas and problems, but mostly the transition from being unwell to invalid is smooth and dignified.

One day, despite Barbara's ravaging illness, one of the neighbours calls in to see her to try to drum up support to put pressure on me to get rid of the puppies, which I still don't have completely under control.

'I love all God's creatures,' Barbara says, putting an end to the discussion.

'Bloody social engineers,' I rage when Barbara tells me what's happened. My rage is with the neighbour, for her selfishness when Barbara is so ill. But I also feel threatened. My puppies are my anchors, part of the reason I get up, go walking, and remember to eat. They are my family.

Not long afterwards, the puppies flush a dying wallaby out of the bush onto the sand flats where it collapses. The puppies circle it, yipping hysterically, trying to get at its throat. Up the hill, Brigitte, who is pregnant, is watching through binoculars and crying even more hysterically. Her two little boys are distraught.

'Jesus, what's going on?' I ask, unaware at this stage of what's happening on the sand flats.

Pia is staying for a few days and we go onto the deck to take a look.

'Oh shit,' I say.

I rush out and grab Veit from the boatshed, telling Pia to get up to Brigitte's house to shake her out of her hysteria. 'And take those bloody binoculars off her. And take the kids some cake.'

Veit and I run for the wallaby and grab a puppy each.

'Wait here while I lock the puppies inside,' I tell him.

I tramp through the wet sand, a puppy under each arm, and chuck them into the shower stall, pulling the screen closed. They won't escape from there. Then I grab antiseptic and scissors and cotton wool in case the wallaby is hurt. When I return, Veit is sitting next to the animal, stroking its shoulder.

'It's nearly dead,' he says. 'But not from the puppies. It's old. Look. There are beetles crawling all over it and it has sores everywhere.'

The puppies have nipped an ear and we bathe it. Then Veit lifts the wallaby and carries it into the bush, lying it down on a bed of leaves to die in peace. When we return to the house, I tell him to strip and throw his clothes into the washing machine. He can wear some old trackie daks of mine until his gear is clean and dry. He jumps into the shower with the puppies and it takes half an hour to scrub away the smell of decay and get rid of all the insects on their bodies.

'Thanks, Veit,' I say, when he emerges smelling of soap and shampoo. 'Thanks.'

He shrugs. Says he wouldn't mind a cup of tea. 'And do you have any of that lemon cake?'

I smile. 'Sure I do.'

Pia returns looking pleased with herself. 'All calm up there now,' she says, dusting her hands.

When Veit has gone, I put the puppies on their leads and Pia and I go up to *Tarrangaua* to see Barbara. I'm distraught about the whole episode. Wonder what I should do. I figure Bob and Barbara will have the answer. To my horror, I sit by her bed and burst into tears.

'God. I'm so sorry,' I say. 'This is appalling.'

Barbara smiles and pats my hand. 'Tell me what's wrong,' she says.

And I blurt it all out. Ashamed of burdening her with triviality compared to a life that's shutting down. And yet unable to stop myself.

'Talk to Bob about it,' she says. 'He'll know what to do.'

'Barbara, I am so sorry. What an awful performance.'

'Don't mind a bit. Quite good to have a person behave normally around me.'

And I am suddenly aware that despite the loads of morphine, she knows exactly what is happening. She doesn't miss a nuance.

Bob is waiting for me in the kitchen. By now, he knows the story and all the details. We are, after all, a small community and Pia, a great storyteller, has filled him in on the details.

'What do you think I should do?' I ask.

He looks at the floor and says nothing.

'Do you have any ideas?'

'Only one,' he replies, 'and you won't like it.'

'What?' I ask defensively.

'Find a new home for one of the puppies. Together, they're a pack. Alone, they become a pet,' he says.

'No way! Absolutely no way!'

I storm into the sitting room and tell Pia I'm going home. With the puppies. Her eyes open wider but she says nothing.

'Lovely cup of tea thanks, Robert,' she says, getting up to follow me. 'So it's fishing tomorrow, is it?'

Bob nods. 'On the incoming tide. I'll give you a call,' he says.

Outside, I explode. 'Fishing! How can you think about fishing?'

'Oh, get over it,' Pia says, not unkindly. 'It will all blow over in a couple of days. Come fishing. At least the puppies won't be able to get into any mischief on the boat.'

She's wrong, of course. First they eat all the bait. Then when Bob hauls in a big octopus, red with fury and fear, they hunt it around the boat until it scrambles up Pia's leg. She's torn between laughing and screaming until Bob yanks it off, its little suction cups popping as he pulls each tentacle loose.

'This will make terrific new bait,' he says happily.

I burst into tears. 'You can't kill it! Octopuses are great mothers, you know. They're really maternal. She may have babies waiting for her to come home.'

Bob starts to look trapped. He looks at the octopus, which is going redder and redder, then chucks it overboard just as Pia catches a fish.

'Should I whack it on the head?' she asks, pleased with herself.

Before he can answer, the puppies leap for the wriggling fish and land in the tackle box. Hooks, sinkers and all sorts of paraphernalia go flying.

Bob takes the hook out and tosses the fish back in the water. 'Leatherjacket. Too small to get much meat off.'

He starts the engine. 'Let's call it a day, shall we? Looks like a storm might be coming in.'

Pia and I look up. The sky is spotless.

At the pontoon, we invite Bob in for a drink. He shakes his head. 'Think I'll go home. Give Kelly a break.'

'Is there anything we can do?' Pia and I ask, almost in unison.

'Nothing anyone can do, is there?' He turns towards the steps, three fishing rods and a tackle box in his hands. He looks beaten.

'Think it was all a bit much for him. On top of everything else,' I say.

Pia gives me a hard look. 'Who told you octopuses are great mothers?' she demands.

'Barbara.'

'Oh.'

About three months after I quit my job, the news editor calls and asks me if I'm well enough to take on a little work from home and it suits me magnificently. Write. Rest. Reread. Focus ten times harder than I ever had to, but sit at my desk until the job is done. One or two stories a month and a little income starts to dribble in again. And I can see the sky from my desk. Feel the weather as it changes.

Bob invites me to join his crew, sailing on his boat, *Larrikin*, for the Woody Point twilight races on Wednesday evening, and I jump at the chance. The Woody Point yacht club is a local institution, created about twenty-five years ago by a group of 'social drinkers with a boating problem'. Not one of the original members even owned a yacht. It is not a swish yacht club. It is not even a very organised yacht club. Basically, you can sail anything that floats and if you want to protest about someone else's behaviour in the race, your protest has to be delivered to the commodore along with a slab of beer. No slab, no protest. By the time everyone finishes the slab, no-one remembers what the problem was in the first place.

'Don't expect much comfort,' Bob says as we head for *Larrikin*'s mooring.

'What! No sofas or fridges?'

Bob looks at me to see if I am being critical so I keep my expression neutral.

'It's about weight, you see. When you're racing, you want as little weight as possible. But we've got a toilet. If that's any help.'

. 'Big decision, was it, to allow a toilet? Bit of weight there?'

He thinks I'm being serious.

'Yeah. Blokes are ok about peeing over the side but girls like a toilet. Knew I'd never get Barbara on the boat without one.'

Larrikin is a racing yacht, the kind that is all about speed and wind and testosterone. There is no femininity here at all, just winches, rigging and enough hardware on the deck to make it difficult to know where to put your feet. It is as cheeky as its name, with a stern that sits half out of the water as though she is always on her mark, ready to fly off with the slightest puff of wind.

The first time I sail on *Larrikin*, it's a sauna of an evening, thick and still. There's five of us on board but only three skilled sailors. I'm a novice and I've brought a friend who's never been on a boat before. We're trapped amongst nearly thirty boats stalled at the start line. There's not enough breeze to fill a handkerchief and we're all slopping around pushing away from each other with our feet. Being on a yacht when there's no wind is like running out of petrol on a freeway. There's not a thing you can do and nowhere to go. To ease the boredom, people are jumping overboard for a swim. Or else having a beer. Or both.

There are still about ten people swimming off the stern of their boats when movement trickles across the water like a gentle breath blown over the top of a hot cup of tea. By the time we all register the change in the weather, a hard and fast wind has blown up out of nowhere and black clouds are boiling over Bayview, in the south. People are yanked on board and the race is underway. The ones that are swimming too far from their boats to make it back are hauled onto *Perceverance*, the start boat, to sit out the race.

'Jesus! Where did this come from?' I call.

'Concentrate. Just concentrate,' yells Bob.

The boat is knocked hard and we all go flying while Bob struggles to control the tiller. There's noise everywhere. The howling wind, sails cracking loud and sharp like whips, stuff crashing around the cabin. Bob's yelling instructions, Nick, Konrad and I are struggling to control the sails.

'Get back there,' Bob tells my friend, pointing at the stern, 'and stay there.'

She stumbles back, grabbing anything fixed to keep her balance, and we race straight up the middle of Pittwater at a forty-five degree angle. At Stokes Point we set for a tack around the marker buoy as a gust hits the boat and the headsail gets wrapped around the mast. Bob is as white as the sails. Konrad skittles forward on all fours like a monkey and tries to unlock the sail. We're heading into a bay where hundreds of boats are moored and we've got no control. About thirty feet from disaster, Konrad manages to untangle the sail and Bob regains control. We round up to chase the fleet across to Portuguese Beach. It's the kind of race that can put you off sailing forever.

The home leg is a hard beat with tack after tack, until it feels like our arms will fall off from pulling sheets (ropes) and winding on sails. Halfway home, the clouds split open and thunder and lightning ignite the sky. Rain pelts down in big, round balls and it's impossible to see through the squall. There's a heavy fog of rain and foam.

When we're about two hundred feet from the finish, the wind drops to a breeze, a vivid red sunset breaks through the clouds and, behind us, the sails of other boats are ghostly in the lilac light. The sound of the boat moving through the water returns to a quiet slush. Out of nowhere little black heads pop out of the water.

'Penguins!' shouts my friend. 'They're lucky, aren't they?'

They dip and dive, quacking with a joy that's contagious, and we all start to laugh. Then, when we look behind us, we see we've won the race.

'God, it's good to be alive,' Bob exults.

Back on the mooring, we pack the boat roughly and jump in the tinny to go to the dock. As we walk up the jetty, my friend turns to me with the light of excitement still in her eyes. 'That was the best fun I've ever had,' she enthuses.

I look at her in disbelief. And then I understand. She thought it was a typical sail. She had no idea what was going on.

'It *was* pretty good,' Bob says. And he means it. He looks radiant.

'Bit too adventurous for me,' I mutter.

'Gotta have a challenge every now and then,' he adds. 'That's what sailing's all about.'

'Do you know where we came?' Konrad asks.

'We won,' Bob says. 'Barbara won't be happy with that. It'll increase our handicap.'

We troop up the hill and give Barbara a detailed report. 'It makes me feel part of it,' she tells me when I ask her if she's really interested or simply being polite. 'It makes me feel as though I'm out there on the water with you all.'

Christmas unfolds in steamy, overcast days, leaving me feeling like a hot reduction. Mildew blossoms in the closets and settles on shoes, turning them the same mottled green as the spotted gums outside. The faint mossy smell of constantly damp furniture fills the house. On the deck, a film of green mould clings to rails and chairs, the grass grows overnight. It is an indolent time, when too much effort results in too much discomfort to be worth it. It seems incredible to think I've been at Lovett Bay for nearly a year and my second Pittwater Christmas is approaching. So much has changed. So much has happened. And my view of the world will never be the same.

I start making the puddings in the weeks leading up to Christmas Day, to give them time to mature. The kitchen fills with the sweet, boozy smell of dried fruit soaking in brandy. And every time I see someone new arrive at the boatshed, I fly down with the bowl and demand they have a stir and make a wish.

The boys in the boatshed, who are like family now, grab the wooden spoon every time I call in.

'Is there a limit to the numbers of wishes?' Veit asks, his long arms lifting and turning the mixture carefully. 'Or should I repeat the same one every time I stir the pudding?'

His question stalls me for a moment. Why do we always say make *a* wish? Why not make *some wishes*? Why shouldn't we be able to make as many wishes as there is time for?

'Nope! There's no limit. Go for it!' I tell him.

In the final days of the second millennium, we are a small group of about twelve. There's Pia and her father Bill, my mother, Marty and Witch, and a few others. We initiate a tradition of bringing together separate family celebrations around the bays, for pudding. And because I am the only person who makes her pudding from scratch, it is decided the *Tin Shed* in Lovett Bay will be the place to gather.

At 7 am on Christmas Day, Pia gets up to light the Weber for the turkey. It is indicative of Pia's attitude to cooking that she first consults the barbecue book and then counts the exact number of heat beads recommended to cook a ten kilo turkey. She counts them out carefully until there are just four left in the bag.

'Chuck 'em in,' I insist.

'It says forty-two beads, not forty-six!' she says firmly.

'Four won't make a difference.'

'If you were meant to use four more, the directions would have said so.'

She has a point and she's a perfectionist. But it's too late. I've thrown in the extra beads and lit the fire starters. Pia throws up her hands, resigning from the future of the turkey.

Marty and Witch bring prawns, we crack champagne and eat them on the pontoon at the foot of the garden. It's a hot summer's day with the humidity in the high nineties and we cool our feet by hanging them over the side in the water. Except for Marty. He doesn't take his shoes off.

'There are sharks, you know,' he says.

'Yes, Marty, we know. But we'll see them coming. Get your shoes off!'

'Ooooh, well, I don't think so.'

'Jesus, Marty, death's been stalking you for years and he's getting closer all the time. Don't you want to live a little dangerously before the grim reaper gets you?' As I say it, I realise with a jolt that I am feeling strong enough to joke about death.

Marty pretends to think for a while, his cheeks rosy pink with health. 'I see no reason to tempt fate,' he says finally, and turns to go back to the house. 'I'll keep an eye on the turkey.' But we all know he's going for a snooze between courses.

The turkey, when it is pulled from the barbecue kettle, is magnificent. A big, fat, golden bird glistening with juice and tender as a young chicken.

Pia gives me an accusing look. 'Seems all right, even though we didn't follow the directions *precisely*!' I get the feeling she might have lynched me if the bird had burned.

It's after 4 pm by the time we've waded through the turkey and ham. The Towlers Bay contingent arrives, wearing silly party hats and sillier grins, and our numbers swell to about twenty-four.

Pudding is served, we all search madly for threepences and sixpences, and then, when there are only about eight of us left, we climb those eighty-eight steps and lurch into Barbara's bedroom, where we sing carols until our throats hurt.

When we can sing no longer, Marty stands framed by the window that looks out on the dry-stone wall that was built when Dorothea Mackellar wandered alone through the corridors of the house. He recites Longfellow's 'Highwayman'. It seems that no-one moves.

The house plans are finally approved by council just before Christmas and a starting date of April is set for the builders. I agonise over spending the money and ask sensible, steady Bob if I am being stupid.

'It's not the best investment you can make but you won't lose money,' he says.

I hold my breath and sign the contracts. All or nothing. As usual.

One morning after taking Barbara a dish of what I hoped would prove utterly beguiling – a gentle, old-fashioned tuna mornay that might soothe a tender stomach – I mention a meeting with the builders.

'I think Bob should be there,' Barbara says firmly.

'Absolutely not,' I reply. 'You've all got enough to do. Please don't even mention it to him.'

'Men tend to listen to other men. That doesn't mean you can't handle it all. You can. But it will be easier if Bob is there. I've only got one bit of advice about the whole undertaking. Never think that you're stupid. If there's something that doesn't feel right, mention it.'

The builders arrive at 2 pm. Bob arrives five minutes later.

'Go home,' I tell him, closing the door in his face.

'Barbara insisted,' he replies, quite unruffled, pushing the door back open. He comes in and helps himself to a cup of tea.

I give up and we all sit down to go through the nitty gritty of money. I keep reminding myself not to sweat the small stuff but it's amazing how hard it is to hold on to thoughts like that when you feel stronger and stronger and you begin to think your life might have a bit of distance in it after all. 'Watch it!' I tell myself silently. 'Don't forget what matters.' Cancer, I suspect, is going to keep me honest with myself forever.

Phil arrives with his bobcat, the builders lob up with their brawn and we are, at last, underway. Even the sun shines briefly and the rain holds off while the new foundation poles are buried. At the end of the day, the front yard is a mess, mud is piled high everywhere and all Gordon's careful plantings have been trampled. It looks like a war zone and I wonder what I have started, how it will all end.

At night, I study the plans intently, trying to visualise the final result. Every so often I find myself looking at the drawings back to front and my stomach gives a flip of fear. Maybe I'm building a total horror and I won't have a clue until it's too late. About three weeks into the project, I notice, for the first time, six heavily inked black dots on the upper storey floor plan.

'What are these?' I ask the builder.

'Poles for the supporting beams.'

'But they're right in the middle of the house.'

'That's how they'll be able to support the beams,' he says, giving me the impression he thinks I'm slow-witted.

'But I don't want them there! I want that all open and free.'

'They're there to keep the roof up. Without them the house will cave in,' he insists.

Duh! Should I feel stupid? No, bugger it. I don't want them and I know I won't be able to live with them: 'If I have to have them, you can stop work now. I am not having six bloody great poles in the middle of the floor! What a joke. Am I supposed to have tables made to fit around the poles?'

'Most houses on the Pittwater have them,' the builder says, getting terse.

'Not this one!'

The builder leaves. The boys look everywhere but at me. They are used to lemon cakes and cups of tea, big bowls of soup, resurrected leftovers from dinner the night before. Any problems are sorted out 'man-to-man' with Bob, although I am always there.

Half an hour later, the builder calls. There is, apparently, a way around the pole problem after all. Reinforced steel beams. Harder for the builders, of course, and that is the crux of the issue.

'Great,' I say, putting down the phone with exaggerated gentleness.

Knowledge is everything. I'd seen a magazine photograph of a house with a vast open space between beams, giving uninterrupted views. I knew it could be done, but not how. I had no idea what was involved but if I hadn't seen that picture I would probably have given in.

By mid-February, Bob's second daughter, Meg, takes leave from work to help her father and Kelly care for Barbara. Barbara needs round the clock attention so the hub of the house moves from the kitchen and verandah to the bedroom. It's Bob's way of keeping Barbara in the loop of family life, family decisions and family fun for as long as possible.

On an unseasonally hot Saturday night in late March, I come home from a dinner party at Michael's on Scotland Island at about 1 am. Bob is waiting on the pontoon in the moonlight. I know as soon as I see him that something's wrong.

'What's happened?' I ask.

'Can you come up the hill?' he says quietly. 'Barbara has died.'

He leads the way up that long, long stairway on a night so bright there is no need for a torch. Occasionally, the thump of a startled kangaroo jolts the stillness. Once or twice, the low moan of an owl floats across the bay.

Meg and Kelly are sitting around the table on the verandah in the cane armchairs. Nicole, Barbara's youngest child and now with two children of her own, is with them. She arrived a couple of days earlier after Bob called her to let her know Barbara was battling.

Scott, their only son, is on his way from the United States but won't arrive until morning.

Their faces are pale in the night, but the talk is loud and there is laughter as the kids talk about 'Mum'. The day the budgie died and she hid it in the freezer to bury after the kids went to school. She forgot about it until one of the kids pulled it out thinking it was an icy pole. The day the back of the station wagon flew open and the bassinet nearly rolled out the back. Baby and all. The way the galah she rescued furiously and consistently attacked her even though she'd saved his life.

I leave them reminiscing and go to the bedroom where Barbara lies still, her hands folded neatly, the top sheet turned down and tucked in. I thank her for her friendship and say farewell. I do not ask why her and why not me. They are questions I will never ask again. What is, is.

At 5 am, the nervous energy of despair worn out, the kids file off to bed and I go home. In the morning, the undertakers arrive.

I will never forget standing on the lawn at *Tarrangaua* that bright Sunday morning as the Water Police boat, carrying Barbara and her family, made its way towards Church Point. Meg still in her pyjamas, Kelly looking out to sea, Nicole leaning against her dad. Scott, whom Bob collected from the airport earlier, stood with his hand on the stretcher. Barbara, I think, was a lucky woman. She'd been surrounded by love until the last and was able to die in the home and environment she loved best. She'd chosen her terms for death and her family had made it possible.

In the afternoon, a small fleet of tinnies noses into the bay. As if in agreement, they travel as slowly and quietly as possible, their wakes streaking the bay with plumes of white. Friends climb the steps to the house. They stand on the verandah and tell stories about Barbara. After a long time, they make their way home, their boats slipping through the still waters of Lovett Bay in gentle ceremony.

A week after the funeral, we learn we've won the Woody Point yacht race series. Bob stands to make a speech on the sloping concrete of the Lovett Bay boatshed where the end of season Annual General Meeting is traditionally held.

For a moment, he cannot speak. Then he raises the heavy wooden trophy high and says: 'For Barbara.'

19

THERE IS A GREAT LOSS AMIDST our little enclave. Barbara was a wise, intelligent woman who steered and supported our lives in subtle ways. Now, there is no-one to run to, to ask 'What is that bird called?' 'Is this a weed or a rare and precious plant?' 'What tree should I plant next to the house?' No-one to idle away an hour or two over a cup of tea and a slice of cake, talking about subjects that once would have seemed insignificant but now enrich each day.

'The glossy black cockatoos are back' she said one afternoon. 'Casuarinas must have nuts.'

And her words turned my walks into an expedition in search of these magnificent big birds with a slash of vivid red under their tails. When I discovered them one exhilarating morning, alerted by the sound of nuts being loudly cracked and the low burble of an almost human-sounding conversation, I stood and watched and tried to remember what Barbara had told me about them.

'Shy,' she'd said. 'Rare and endangered in this area because their habitats are under threat.'

Then I rushed to tell her I'd seen them and she gave me a loose-leaf folder filled with information she'd collected which I took home to read to better understand the birds.

'How's the little fungi forest going at the turn by the big spotted gum?' she asked another time.

And I became her eyes and feet and searched beyond the bound-aries of the track to find her fungi forest. When I found it hidden in a damp, dark gully, a mass of tiered, pale brown mushrooms crenellated like an ancient castle, it felt like a grand achievement.

'The fungi forest is thriving,' I reported back.

'Ah, good. It's such a fragile thing.'

In her unique way, Barbara pushed me to see and understand detail when I'd made a career of skimming the surface. And it meant my life, which was now mostly confined to Lovett Bay when once I'd strutted the world, did not feel diminished. It seemed, in fact, fuller than it had ever been.

One day I said to her that I realised people were wrong when they said we don't have distinct seasons here.

When I see the escarpment foaming with pale pink wax flowers and deep pink boronia, I know it's spring. When the angophoras fizz, we're moving into summer. When the spotted gums disrobe and white ants hatch by the zillions, it's summer. By autumn, the sandflies have given up altogether, mozzies are on the wane, and the leopard moths are whirring along the tracks like frantic helicopters. The midges arrive in autumn, too, so it pays to keep your mouth closed when you're walking. In winter, the westerlies turn clean and cold and lose their toastiness. Seasons don't need to be marked by bare trees or snow on the ground. There's a million signs of change if you look for them.

Barbara smiled at me when I told her all this. It was a small smile but a little smug, as though she felt she'd accomplished what she set out to do.

'So many people forget to open their eyes as they walk around,' she said.

And I am glad I remembered to thank her for opening mine.

In the weeks after Barbara's death, Bob and I fall into a routine. I cook and he brings the wine. The house up the hill is lonely, the memories of Barbara's presence too vivid and raw for solitary evenings. By coming to my home, he avoids those early hours of the evening that seem emptiest – the times he and Barbara would have a pre-dinner drink and prepare dinner together, discuss the day's events, tally what the children were up to, plan the following day.

As winter sets its course, the renovations move into high gear. Living in a house that's being ripped apart and resurrected in different stages feels like living in a derelict building and I have given up trying to keep life clean and tidy. Mid-June, the front wall comes down, the deck is ripped up and the cold whooshes through the gaps in the tarpaulin the builder puts up each night to block the hole. It's freezing. Stewart and Fleury offer their house in Towlers Bay and I gratefully accept.

'That's silly,' Bob says when I explain I'll be moving for a while. 'There's plenty of space at *Tarrangaua*.'

'People will talk,' I reply.

'Let them. This concerns only you and me. And anyway, I don't want to have to get in the boat every night to come to dinner at Towlers Bay. They're probably talking already,' he adds with a smile. 'That's what happens in small communities.'

So I move up the hill for the next few weeks, with the puppies of course, who are so used to being there they settle immediately. Bob gives me my own areas, turning one bedroom into my office, and emptying the closet in the spare bedroom. But I never feel completely at ease. It is not my space. After years of being my mother's *gypsy* daughter, I have finally found where I want to set my table each night. I don't want to feel as though I'm camping any more.

Bob builds a roaring fire every evening and we sit in front of it on different sides of the coffee table. He works, sketching ideas. I read. When I jump up and rush outside into the chill of the verandah to cool a hot flush, he gets so used to it, he doesn't even look up. I prepare huge meals and fat begins to cling to my bones. My energy levels lift a little and work gets easier.

Without being conscious of it, my panic attacks fade away and I walk with dogged routine every morning through the national park, as I did when I first came here what seems like so many years ago for Fleury's birthday party.

Often I meet neighbours on the track. Maureen from Towlers Bay with her old border collie. Caroline from Little Lovett with a sweet-natured cattle dog cross called Figaro. Tim and Leisa with Ponzer. And usually on his own, strolling as though the world is his for the asking, gorgeous Obi, the itinerant labrador. He wags his tail madly and greets me like a long-lost best friend. Sometimes he turns and joins Dolce, Vita and me. At other times the huge, boofy blonde dog continues on his way alone.

Over time, I learn Caroline has had two types of cancer, the first striking when she was in her early twenties, the second, in her early forties. 'I survived the first diagnosis so I never doubted for a moment that I wouldn't survive the second time,' she says as we talk on our walk. She is tall and slim, with a beautiful smile and a sharp mind.

'I thought I was going to die,' I reply.

Because we have been through similar crises we understand the unspoken subplot of many of our conversations.

'Got a shocker of a pain in my knees,' I say one morning as we push ourselves to walk faster and faster up 'heart attack hill'.

She stops immediately and turns to me because she knows what I am *really* asking is whether I should worry about it. Any bone pain could be a symptom of the dreaded *secondaries*, cancer spreading to the bone.

'Both of them?' she asks.

'Yeah.'

'Arthritis, perhaps?'

And the fear, nearly always irrational, is sponged away.

Sometimes Bob comes with me on my walks and points out what is all around that I never much noticed until, from her bed, Barbara opened my eyes. The exquisite little white flowers, fringed like Victorian lampshades, of the blueberry ash trees in Towlers Bay. The vibrant yellow flowering tips of geebungs. I love the word *geebung* so much, I ponder whether I'll name my house *Geebung* once the renovations are finished. *GEEBUNG*. Sounds joyful, with hints of amazement in it. And casual. Nothing grand and Latin about it at all.

If Bob and I walk early enough in the morning, when the earth is damp and the trees are still glossy with dew, the sunlight strikes massive spider webs spanning the track. They are more than six feet wide, and if they are not high enough, we have to duck low to avoid getting tangled in the sticky, gossamer threads.

'They're golden orbs,' Bob explains, pointing to a large spider covered in golden hairs, with black, orange and yellow stripes on its legs. 'There's the male. See? He's tiny compared to her. Smaller than the nail on your little finger.'

'Do they bite?'

'No. Not unless they're cornered, but they're not poisonous. Mostly, if they're frightened, they shake their web. Trying to scare us off, I think.'

He reaches near a spider to show me what happens and the web vibrates, shimmering in the thin morning light like a huge, golden jewel. When he takes his finger away, the web settles into stillness once more. By the end of autumn, the track is thick with webs and it's like wandering through a strange, ephemeral kingdom.

One late afternoon, after a restless day, the sky is a mass of rainbows. More than I have ever seen at one time. A double rainbow stretches from the Elvina Bay side of the escarpment bang into the middle of Lovett Bay.

'I know exactly where to dig for the pot of gold,' I tell Bob as we look at the sight from his verandah.

He smiles, but his eyes are wet and I know he is thinking it is a sight Barbara would have cherished.

Without even noticing, I start adding Bob's washing to my own. And on days when I go off to do a story, Bob cooks dinner. Barbecued lamb chops, with the tails crisped. Four vegetables at least, of course. And once, a roast of pork with the crackling salty and crunchy. We ate every delicious bit of it. Ox tail stew is his favourite but because he is a man who likes balance, he makes it infrequently so it remains a treat.

We always sit at the dining room table with the fire burning in the background, and as we relax with each other, we begin to talk and talk. There is so much to sift through, in the months following someone's death. In the talking, it's as though an old skin is shed and a new one slowly acquired. The memories, once recounted out loud, are filed and stored making room, eventually, for a future.

If the nights are filled with talk, the days are consumed by watching my house creep closer to completion. Every day there are decisions to make. Should a window on the stairwell be much deeper? Should we put a window on the wall facing a lightwell? Is the ceiling high enough in the middle area? Should the kitchen bench, now sticking out into the main room like an overgrown thumb, be cut back? Should I finish the downstairs area instead of just getting it to lock-up stage? I've had plans drawn but I don't really need the space so I've told the builders just to enclose the area.

Sun is already spilling through the clerestory windows at the back of the house and there is a grand sweep of space that gives the feeling that the building is suspended above the water.

I begin asking about completion dates. Will it be finished by late spring? I visualise furniture in place, where to hang paintings. But deadlines for completion come and go, so often the way when you've a water access property and at the mercy of tides and weather. If the beginning of the renovation seemed to storm ahead, the end is dragging on in miniscule increments. I feel increasingly frustrated as weeks fly by. I wait for the corrugated iron specialists to arrive and clad the outside walls. The man who is making the stairs is running behind schedule. The fireplace is the wrong size. I remind myself that I have learned not to sweat the small details and that a glitch here or there is unimportant. They are little hitches, not life-threatening events. But I am impatient. I want my own home. Finally, it is time for the painters and the floor sanders to begin the final touches. Almost there!

One night, over a bottle of red, Bob tells me again that one way to solve the on-going problem of the puppies running off when given the slightest chance is to find one of them a new home. 'Please think about it,' he says. 'Right now, you have two dogs that add up to less than one because they are loyal first to each other, and only sometimes to you. If there is just one dog, all the dynamics change. You become leader of the pack and have some control.'

In my heart, I know he's right. But the thought of choosing is intolerable. I delay for weeks until a dead bandicoot turns up on the lawn. I can only assume the puppies hunted it down. One puppy must go.

'How can I choose, though?' I ask Bob. 'It's like deciding which child you love best.'

I delay making the decision for as long as I can but when I find a good home, it is crunch time. In the end, the decision-making is easy. Vita must be the one to go. She is the hunter, the ringleader. Beautiful, wilful, the animal who sleeps only lightly and keeps her distance on the bed. Who, when she picks up a scent, cannot be distracted from it.

When I pass Vita to her new owner at the Church Point ferry wharf, I am quite calm.

'She has two meals a day for another month and then you can cut it to one meal a day,' I say. 'She loves cheese and goes mad for bacon. But she's not greedy. She only eats as much as she wants and leaves the rest.'

'She'll be fine,' says my friend, holding her up to his face. Vita covers him with tiny licks, her little pink tongue darting in and out.

Will he learn quickly that she only does that when she's frightened or nervous? Will he learn to soothe her fears with a tummy rub? Then I shut down these thoughts. *I am strong and my body and mind are strong.* This way, the puppies will both survive. If they stay here together, one day they'll find the fox baits in the national park and that will be the end.

'You'll be wonderful for each other,' I say, waving goodbye and reversing the boat away from the wharf before turning back to Lovett Bay.

Bob is waiting at the dock with Dolce when I return and he puts her in my arms.

'Do you think she senses Vita is gone?'

Bob shakes his head. 'You're not going to like this, but she already seems pretty happy to be an only child.'

'Tonight will be the test. She's never spent a night away from Vita before.'

'Maybe. But I reckon she won't miss a beat. Vita was the leader of the pack. Now *she's* king pin.'

Bob looks at me closely. 'How are you coping?'

'Fine. Absolutely fine.'

That night, I jam my finger in a cupboard door and although the pain is slight, I sob and sob. Every past grief erupts and I feel like my world is caving in around me.

Bob hands me a cognac, which I gulp down. He brings another.

'I am so sick of bloody loss,' I say between sobs. 'Oh God, sorry. Sorry about Barbara. That's real loss. I know that. But Jesus. When's it going to end?'

'Never,' Bob says. 'Because that's the way life is.'

But I keep crying until I fall asleep on the sofa. When I wake in the morning, Bob's put a cover over me and Dolce is curled in the crook of my legs.

'Hey, little puppy. There's just you and me now.'

My face feels like a football, my eyes are claggy. Dolce doesn't stir.

'Do you miss your little sister?' I ask her.

Her eyes don't open. When I rub her ears, she stretches happily and sighs loudly. But her eyes stay closed. This is not a dog that's unhappy. This is a dog that thinks she's won the lottery.

A few days later, when there's still no sign of any moping, I decide to rename her.

'I can't have a dog called Dolce without a Vita to follow,' I explain to Bob.

He shrugs.

It takes a few weeks, but eventually, by a kind of osmosis, she is named Chip Chop from all the times I've called her chubby chops for the fluffy whiskers around her cheeks. And life becomes much simpler, as Bob said it would.

I love staying with Bob and he is thoughtful in every way, but I am always a guest, mindful of keeping someone else's sense of order. I long to be in my own home, leave dishes in the sink and stay up all night playing music. Mostly, though, I want to be surrounded by my own past. All I have to do is look at a rug from Samarkand and I see my brother, young, gorgeous, on the eve of his wedding to Dolly.

I bought the rug as their wedding present in the 1970s, when I was on the almost obligatory pilgrimage overland from London to Katmandu. After haggling for two days, I finally paid $100. It wasn't until we were leaving town that I discovered the rug trader had fleeced me. The rough kilim was worth about $25, another trader told me. For $100, he went on to tell me, I could have bought a beautiful, soft silk and wool rug. It was the roughness I liked, I told him. And he shook his head as if to say he would never understand foreigners.

When I gave the kilim to my brother, Dolly, whom I was meeting for the first time, explained bluntly that they preferred silk rugs, thank you. When I thought about it, my brother was always immaculate, had superb taste, looked gorgeous and was a perfectionist. I was the messy, disorganised one who always got back to the office from lunch with splashes of spaghetti sauce on a white shirt. After Dolly rejected the gift, I bought them a couple of incredibly expensive Japanese carved ivory *netsuke* representing gambling. For luck. As I recall, my brother went on a historic losing streak and eventually sold them or put them away. He never told me exactly what he'd done.

I kept the rug, now with holes chewed in it by various puppies, because it reminds me of those events as no photograph could do. Kept too, my big heavy table that every removalist has cursed, because when I am alone I can conjure up a memorable dinner or two and feel cheered by the images. I've kept some wineglasses that are a bugger to wash but were given to me by my brother. They stand alongside the delicate Limoges dessert plates my mother brought back from Paris and gave to me on the day she said, 'I don't think I'll be giving many more dinner parties.' The day I realise she is getting old and the fight goes out of me (and her!) and a new tenderness creeps into our relationship.

Other things too. A potato peeler that works brilliantly, white bed linen I lugged home from New York that I spray with lavender water before I iron. They crunch fragrantly, the way real linen does, and have a heavenly scratchiness. The big, cast iron pot I carried from Paris.

Odd, I think, as I pack away stuff so the builders can paint the walls and sand the floors, that I have so few framed photographs. So I go looking for old envelopes stuffed with prints and sift through them for a moment or two. Then I put them away again. They trigger a flash of mad hope that if I pick up the phone and dial the right numbers, perhaps my brother will answer. Then, when reason surges in again, it brings with it the old, familiar anger of loss. No, it's better to stay away from photos for a while longer.

To make the house empty enough for the floor sanders and the painters, furniture is stacked in piles outside in the yard, wrapped in plastic and tarpaulins. Every time it rains, I cross my fingers there isn't a leak caused by a little rat-like marsupial called an antechinus. They love plastic – especially yellow plastic – and chew the tops off olive oil bottles and jars of mustard. I saw my first antechinus at Bob's house. Bob had caught it in a trap in the pantry, where all the yellow tops had been chewed to bits. One of his daughters took the trap to Barbara's bedroom for her to identify it. There's a rodent hierarchy in the bush, it turns out.

'Bush rats are ok,' Barbara told us. 'Antechinus are very ok. But rattus rattus are a no-no. You can tell the difference by their tails. Bush rats have hairy tails about the length of their body. Antechinus have short, hairy tails. Rattus rattus have long, hairless tails.'

When Bob's daughter opened the trap for Barbara to take a look, it leapt out of the trap and onto the bed, paused and looked her straight in the eye, cheeky, arrogant, as if to ask what *she* was doing in *his* house.

'Antechinus,' Barbara said, unperturbed while the rest of us screamed and hopped from foot to foot (why do we do that?). 'Leave it alone.'

And off it scooted.

Cute or not, I would prefer them to leave the plastic that protects my furniture intact.

It is my habit, every evening after the workmen have gone home, to do a tour of the house, getting a feel for how it will be to live in it. One afternoon I arrive a little early, just in time to see one of the painters, the older, more arrogant one, slapping a second coat of high-gloss white paint on the bathroom door. Gordon Andrews' fabulous painting of a bright red rooster has been oblit-erated. I had told them *not* to touch the door. Now it is white.

'Oh, sorry, love,' he says, casually. 'Do you want me to see if I can get the white off? It's a bit late, and I don't think it will work, but I'll give it a go.'

Visions of an extra week spent trying to restore the rooster flash through my mind, so I shrug and tell him 'no'. But I am incensed. I've already destroyed a lot of Gordon's touches in the frenzy of putting my own stamp on the place, and only quite late into the changes realise I am destroying some lovely, quirky work. Why do I always go like a bull at a gate? Why don't I ever try to understand what's there before I rip it out? Why don't I see what's under my nose until it's too late?

Still angry and upset, I go into the bathroom to remove the mirror over the basin for the painters. So it takes me a couple of seconds to notice what is behind the mirror. In a few black lines, Gordon has drawn an irreverent self-portrait, full of humour and life.

I whirl on the painters. 'Touch that, and you will both be dead!'

The portrait is there now, hidden behind the mirror. A secret. Gordon's little joke. He may have sold the place, but his presence will remain.

Later, I wonder if he drew the picture after I asked him, in the days just after I agreed to buy the house, to leave one little piece of his art behind.

'I don't care what you leave, Gordon,' I told him. 'An old card, an old invitation, a postcard – anything. Just a bit of you to leave in the house.'

Looking back, he was remarkably restrained in his response. I mean, the whole house was a reflection of his creativity. Everywhere you looked, there were the most stunning little nuances. How crass I'd been and how polite he was not to point it out. Which must have been hard. Gordon was not renowned for being overly polite.

When I moved in, I never found what I thought was his end of the bargain – no postcard, not even a 'welcome and good luck' note. The portrait, I believe, was Gordon's subtle fulfilment of our bargain.

After about five weeks, when I've decided the painters will probably live with me forever, they pack up and leave. I pay the final part of the bill. The renovation is over. The house is mine again. The freshly sanded and polished floors gleam like a golden lake, and the walls are flat expanses of pure white.

'It doesn't need a stick of furniture,' I say to Bob when he arrives with a bottle of champagne to toast the future. 'The bay comes right into the house and gives it life. And art. And warmth. And . . . it's great, isn't it?'

He pops the cork and fills two glasses. Then we wander out onto the new deck and lean on the rail where there is no longer a groove and a little ledge to rest an elbow and a glass.

'I didn't expect to feel so nostalgic about Gordon's quirky details,' I murmur.

'Don't have any regrets,' Bob says, holding up his glass to clink with mine. 'Before the renovations, it was essentially Gordon's house. His style, ideas and way of life. But he doesn't live here any more. You do. You've made this your own home and it's great. So here's to health and happiness.'

'How come you always say the right thing?' I ask.

Bob smiles and refills our glasses.

'How come?' I ask again when he doesn't reply.

'Don't think I should answer. It's best to quit while you're ahead.'

We're silent for a long time. The view is too gobsmackingly brilliant to disrupt.

'I've cooked dinner,' he says when it feels like an hour has passed. 'But it's easy to transport. Would you like me to bring it here?'

'Would you really *do* that?'

'I get the feeling you don't want to leave.'

'You're right. It's hard to explain. I feel like I've found where I belong and it's such a lovely, secure feeling I don't want to let it go.'

'I'll bring dinner. You find a couple of chairs and a table. I'll be back soon.'

The furniture has been brought inside and piled in a tight little square in the middle of the floor. After pacing around it for a minute or two, I give up. If I move anything the whole shebang will topple.

I find a couple of cushions in a cupboard and sling them on the floor with a candle between them. We dine on Bob's lamb curry, finish the champagne and leave the washing up for the morning. Chip Chop and I spend our last night at *Tarrangaua* and I wake at dawn to rush down the hill to begin restoring order.

When I open the back door and look through the house to the bay and the ancient escarpment, I feel every hard earned penny spent was worth it. My house embraces the water, the trees, the sky, and the whole great big, bloody glorious outdoors. My front yard stretches into the sitting room, my backyard comes into the kitchen. It's peaceful, spectacular, wonderful. This is a building that doesn't try to compete with its surroundings. No house, no matter how beautiful, ever could here. Of course there is bare earth all around, huge piles of it where the bobcat has made way for the building. It is rough and ragged and the work to get it into shape will be hard. But I don't care. I am quite simply overjoyed by *my home*. It is, without doubt, the most beautiful home I've ever owned – well, actually, the house is not beautiful. It is still a simple tin shed. But the way it incorporates its environment makes it sensational.

I remember, a long time ago when I was a young reporter in New York, I lived in a shoebox apartment. If I looked out the window I could see what the woman in her kitchen on the other side of the street was making for dinner. New York was claustrophobic to a country kid like me and I knew I'd never cope unless I found a home with a garden and space. I checked the real estate ads every week and eventually hit gold.

The property was in Long Island City, in Queens – one stop on the subway from Manhattan and two stops from my office, closer than where I currently lived. I braved the unknown suburbs and discovered a mostly bleak, industrial area not far from the 59th Street bridge. Hidden amongst grimy streets lined with glittering hookers and pimps in broad brimmed fur hats was a block of beautiful old brownstone houses.

The apartment consisted of two whole floors with wood burning fireplaces in every room and views over a garden. It was a massive, elegant space with a large marble entry hall, ceiling roses and cornices. And the rent was reasonable because in those days, it wasn't trendy to live anywhere but Manhattan.

When I moved in I thought I would never live in a more beautiful space again. It is nearly thirty years since those days – and I have finally bettered it. With a soaring heart, I begin arranging belongings. Bob helps me to move furniture around and saws off the kitchen bench that sticks too far into the room. Every so often I stop and look at my new world and hours drift by. I feel like the luckiest woman alive.

We have returned to our old routine of dining at my home most nights. Bob arrives around 6 pm. If it is cold, he lights the fire.

Then he watches the television news while I cook dinner. He calls me if he thinks there's a story that will interest me. When the news ends, he turns off the television and puts on music. Which is the signal to open the wine. It is a routine that brings the pleasure of certainty. It is casual and familiar and makes no demands of either of us. But I am aware that his support is smoothing my life in many ways.

Somehow he is always at the pontoon when I get home and he helps me tie the boat and schlep the shopping up to the house. He notices when the petrol is low and a full tank appears just before I plan to take it to be refilled. One day I return from an assignment and find him stacking timber offcuts neatly for next winter's kindling. 'Had a couple of empty hours,' he says when I thank him. Which makes it no big deal. So I bake him a cake to have for morning and afternoon tea. And often I pack leftovers from dinner that he can warm for his lunch the next day.

Sometimes he insists on taking me out to dinner to give me a break, he says, from the kitchen. After a while he stops suggesting restaurants because he realises I would rather eat on the deck and watch night slicken the bay. I like to tune in to the evening sounds of weary kookaburras, ill-humoured cockatoos, noisy miners, parrots, sometimes a whipbird.

Often, a deep brown wallaby, her chest the same rusty colour as the local stones and with a joey in her pouch, hops across the front lawn. If we move or make a noise, she stops and inclines her head quizzically, her front paws held loosely as though she is unde-cided about her next move. She is wild and beautiful and her joey, wide-eyed and curious.

If the evening is spectacular and the fish are jumping, Bob sets up the steel tub from an old washing machine by the edge of the water and we light a fire. We take down camp chairs, fishing rods, a table, hurricane lamp, a couple of torches, and a big, black, cast iron pot filled with meat and vegetables to cook over the fire.

'Don't have much faith in me as a fisherman,' Bob says, looking at the pot.

'Just covering all the bases.'

The fire brings out the neighbours.

Before long, there's a party. Well, not a party. A get-together. Everyone contributes something – wine, food, wood – and when a fish is caught, cleaned and cooked within minutes, we share it. We sit there late, with the fire throwing shadows across our faces and toasting our toes.

'I'd like to sleep out here,' I tell Bob. 'I don't want this to end.'

'Ever been camping?' he asks.

'Not really. We stayed in a caravan once when I was a kid. Dad kept hitting his head on the top of the door, even after we tied a hanky there to remind him to duck. Went home the next day after he drew blood.'

'Not a good start.'

I get into the habit of calling Bob from Mona Vale on my way home, to ask if he would like me to pick anything up. Mostly, all he ever asks for is a newspaper. Occasionally a bottle of milk. By now, there is not much we don't know about each other. He tolerates my mood swings, triggered by days of incessant hot flushes. I agree to pack a wound on his bottom for a couple of weeks so he can check out of hospital earlier than recommended. Wadding the bandage into a deep cut hurts him like hell, which makes it a terrible job until I visualise his backside as a leg of lamb and pretend I am inserting cloves of garlic into it. When I tell him my method, he laughs so hard he cries.

'You wouldn't be this rough with a leg of lamb, would you?' he asks.

I slap his rump by way of an answer.

He is never critical of my more eccentric excesses but tries to influence me to use reason before plunging in. His quiet caution saves me from a couple of big mistakes. He talks about his life and his children, his love of sailing and his need of a challenge. I tell him about the lover.

'What did you get out of it?' he asks, genuinely puzzled.

'Nothing noble. Nothing worthwhile. Only respite, for a while, from grief. Then it turned into a grief of its own.'

'Are you glad it is ended?'

'Yes. It was a form of madness. I look back and wonder how I allowed it to happen.'

'It's in the past and it is always better to look forward,' he says.

There is a track, now, that runs from *Tarrangaua* to the back of my house. 'Sick and tired of going up and down all those bloody steps,' Bob explains when he asks me to come and look at the new pathway he's cut. He's wearing goggles and protective clothing and there's a lethal, sharp-toothed blade on the machine he's carrying. I follow him up the hill behind my house.

'So now we have a back track?'

'It's not a new track. Once it was known as Lover's Lane.'

'Oh, Barbara's Lover's Lane. So this is where it was.'

He's slashed bracken and overhanging boughs are trimmed to English garden perfection.

'Found the footings of the old caretaker's cottage,' Bob says. 'Come and have a look.'

We walk along the cut path to where he points out eight brick pillars forming a rectangle. The cottage must have been small. One or two rooms, perhaps.

'Barbara's research shows that the vegetable garden to supply the house used to be here, too,' he adds. 'Mind you, the footings might have been for a tank stand. I'm not sure.'

Nearly forty years later, the land has returned to thin scrub with straggly, quick growing wattles that spring up to give more tender plants protection until they establish. The soil looks mean and sandy, too barren to support even a crop of carrots.

'Wonder how they got anything to grow here. Poor soil, hungry wallabies, lyrebirds and brush turkeys that scratch worse than a coop full of hens.'

'There's an old story that rum was the main crop in the early days of the colony,' Bob says. 'Pittwater was a good place to hide a still or two. Or three. And there were plenty of secluded little coves for smugglers to lie low in.'

We walk the length of the track to where it ends near Bob's workshed. It's an easy trek, not steep enough even to increase our heart rate.

'Adrienne Howley says there was never a romance between Dorothea and the doctor. Bit sad, really, that he cut this path to her door and she had no time for him.'

'Dorothea lived a lonely life, I think,' Bob replies.

'Are you lonely, Bob?' I ask. And then I realise it's a dumb question. 'Of course you are. Sorry. Silly question.'

'Are you?'

'Yes. Often. But I enjoy our friendship. It's the best part of my life right now.'

Bob pulls his goggles back on but I put a hand on the machine. 'Give it a rest. Come and have a cup of tea.'

He shakes his head. 'Nope. Thanks. Want to get this done today. I'll drop by when I'm finished. What's for dinner? Should I bring a bottle of red or white?'

Chip Chop spends her time between the two houses, reluctant to give up her chaise longue on Bob's verandah where she can see who's coming and going and where she feels queen of the bay. At my home, older, bigger Cinny, Ken and Jan's German pointer, is fiercely territorial and sools her off with gnashing teeth and low-bellied growls whenever she wanders too close to the boatshed. So *Tarrangaua* is a bit of a refuge for Chip Chop.

When Cinny starts to wander up the steps to extend her domain, Bob gets protective. 'Go on! Get home! Get home!' he shouts, chasing Cinny down the steps. And I love what his actions reveal about his loyalties.

Summer steams in and I join Bob's crew on *Larrikin* for Woody Point sailing again. Every Wednesday at 5.30 pm, even in a gale or a storm, the crew meets at his dock.

Nick and Ann from Little Lovett, who sailed here from England when their children were young, are regulars. Ann, who read to Barbara every Wednesday evening during her illness, sits with me up the back of the boat. And we chat while the boys tack and winch and bleed an extra puff of boat speed from the wind.

It is old-fashioned girl stuff about the best fruit at the market, the last book we read, how the children are faring. I realise this kind of talk is a new skill for me and it's such a blessed relief after years of *shop* talk. This is the kind of conversation I never had time for once, may even have felt embarrassed to engage in as a younger woman. Now I do not care about the political correctness of saying out loud that *this* is *boys' work* and *that* is *girls' work*. I live without any agenda except my own conscience. Another gift that cancer has given me? Or is it because I no longer have to function in the workplace and have nothing to lose? Either way, it's a privilege.

This year, the weather is frightful every Wednesday evening for weeks. There are strong winds, rain, crackling storms and lots of frothy whitecaps, even in the bays. The weather is too rough to take Chip Chop on board and week after week she mewls plaintively, running along the shore, trying to keep pace with the boat.

One Wednesday, Nick breaks. He leaps back into the tinny, charges for the shore, scoops her up and returns to the yacht.

'Here, Ann,' he says, plonking the dog in his wife's lap. 'You look after her.' Shy, polite, stoic Nick, who never raises his voice, not even to shout a warning, embarrassed to abruptness to disguise his gentleness.

'Yes dear,' she says, looking at me and winking.

But it's a rough race in strong winds. The boat heels uncomfortably and the dog clings to Ann in fear. When we return to shore at the end of the race, she's the first off the tinny. We call her back to see what she'll do and I swear she shakes her head to say *no way*. For the next two or three weeks, she's nowhere around when we set off to sail. Smart dog.

We begin our regular, post race dinners at one house or another. The talk is invariably about who cut off whom, who couldn't sail in a teacup, who doesn't know the rules, who's done the handicapping for the year (universally unappreciated).

About the fifth Wednesday into the series, it is a filthy evening. We march out in full wet weather gear – overalls, jackets with hoods – and flounder through the race. The power of the weather is awesome. Boats are knocked hard, the wind is frenzied. The rope that controls the mainsail keeps jamming, which means we heel badly before I can loosen it. We slip and slide on a wet deck. One careless movement and we're overboard. Water races into the cockpit and sloshes around our feet. Our bums are frigid and wet, our fingers stiff with cold. The boat has never felt more vulnerable. The noise is ferocious. By the finish, one or two boats have been blown aground, and many are limping home, sails reefed to almost handkerchiefs.

'I can't believe I'm going to say this,' I tell Bob, 'but that was the most excruciatingly good fun!'

He laughs. 'Told you you'd get to like the challenge of a tough sail more than a doddle in the evening breeze.'

'Well, I still like a doddle. But I know a bit more about sailing now. I'm feeling more confident. And so much stronger. Every day, so much stronger.'

He pats me on the shoulder and continues packing up the boat.

Dinner is at Stewart's house in Towlers Bay. Bob and I set off in his boat from Lovett Bay in heavy, stinging rain. The water is rougher than I've ever seen it in the bays so we motor slowly. The boat coasts on the crest of waves, then falls into the dip. Corkscrewing with the clash of wind and tide. Water breaks over the bow and seeps in from all directions, trickling down our necks, soaking our clothes underneath our slickers, wetting our feet.

We arrive cold, damp, and childishly excited in the way you are after you've done something really difficult and it's safely over. We race up the steps to the house and the blazing fire, carrying an apple cake, two bottles of wine and a jug of custard. Inside, we peel off layers of stinky wet clothes and grab a glass of wine. The house smells reassuringly of curry.

'This is Anne and John,' Stewart says, introducing us to a couple we've never seen before. 'They've just sailed in from Newcastle for a few days, on their way to Tasmania. They're moored in Towlers Bay.'

'Are you from Newcastle?' I ask Anne.

'Good lord, no. I'm from Sweden and John is from England. We're both retired and we just keep sailing around the world.'

She is very tall and very thin and talks with a Scandinavian lilt. It turns out she's a doctor and John was once an advertising guru. She is wearing a beautiful, almost formal dress with an exquisite lace collar and cuffs. I cannot help telling her how lovely she looks.

'I made the dress,' she says. 'I have a sewing machine on board. And I crocheted the lace. There's not much to do when the wind drops and you're stuck for a few days in the middle of the ocean.'

'How long have you known Stewart?'

'Oh, about an hour. He swung by our boat and asked us if we'd like to join him for a curry. And we thought, what a lovely idea. It was miserable on the boat. Where's your famous hot, dry Australian weather?'

'Well, it's gotta rain sometimes.'

Stewart calls us to the table. There are about a dozen people, an average size dinner party for Pittwater.

'Do you *always* get invited to dinner so casually wherever you travel?' I ask as we all sit down.

'Pretty much. Water and boats bring people together no matter what language they speak. Maybe it's because we know you can never trust the elements, and one day we might need help. I think that creates a bond between sailors.'

Stewart puts a couple of ladles in two big pots of curry and we all help ourselves. It's hot, spicy and perfectly cooked.

'Thought you knocked the marker but I didn't see you go round it again,' Stewart says to needle Bob.

'Stewart, we were lucky to *find* the marker in that weather. But we didn't knock it.'

The blokes rehash the race for an hour or so and by the time dessert is served, the weather has calmed to a shiny stillness. The moon rises, full and creamy, and sends a yellow glow across Towlers Bay. It has turned into a still, perfect night.

Bob and I head home, slightly tipsy. Behind us, a snowy swathe stretches and melts into the water.

'Aren't we lucky? All this beauty,' I whisper, trying not to disturb the peace.

Bob nods. The boat is moving slowly enough to swim beside.

At Woody Point, the long finger of land covered in young spotted gums that separates Towlers Bay from Little Lovett Bay, Bob slows the boat and cuts the engine. I look across at him, not under-standing what is going on, and he leans forward and kisses me.

I feel a rush of tenderness for this man I have come to love and respect. Two words that rarely come together. And yet when they do, how much greater the possibility of lasting passion, because there is trust and knowledge *before* chemistry intrudes and explodes all reason.

'I am no great prize,' I tell him that night on the boat.

'I think you are.'

'I have one breast.'

'One is enough.'

'I don't know how long I will live, maybe months, maybe years.'

'I could walk under a bus tomorrow.'

'I am a risk.'

'Not to me.'

The relationship with Bob unfolds slowly and evenly, without drama or misunderstanding. Well, mostly. But then a little drama here and there never hurt anyone.

We are both old enough to know what we want from each other and secure enough to articulate it instead of retreating to silent, festering corners. We have neither the pride nor ego of youth so we don't compete but try, instead, to complement each other. And there is love. Intensely physical, intensely satisfying and jammed with joy.

After a while, instead of trying to hide the scar on my chest, I turn on the bedside light and ask him to look closely at it.

'It is ugly,' I say, pointing at the jagged edges.

'Yes. It is. But it is part of you and therefore beautiful.'

'Why do you love me?' I ask time after time, seeking reassurance because I cannot believe a man who could choose anyone has chosen me. What do I have to offer? Neither youth, nor a fancy job. Just one breast and a risky future.

He never answers this question and I let it lie until one day his silence stings and I invoke the name of his wife to make him take notice of my need: 'I can never replace Barbara. I am not like her.'

And he turns to me. '*Replace* is a terrible word,' he says. 'People can never be *replaced*. I don't want you to be a *replacement*! I came to love you for who you are. You alone.'

And I leap on his words, looking for phrases to sustain me when I feel insecure, as we do in a new relationship.

'So who am I, this person you love?'

But he grins because he sees my trap. 'You are . . . you.'

Exasperated, I demand more. 'Explain to me! I need to hear words.'

'I'm not good with words. They're difficult for me. Don't I show how I love you every day in the things that I do for you?'

And I am finally silenced.

I have used words all my life to create a desired effect so I should know that words can be empty. Actions, as the old cliche goes, speak louder than words. That's Bob's maxim. But then I think about the way he uses words, sometimes hesitantly, sometimes in a rush, always sparsely, and I understand he is wonderful with words because he doesn't use them to achieve a result. He only ever says what he means.

Eventually I make *Poule avec sa mique*. Col, from the upmarket poultry shop, painstakingly bones the chooks for me. But when Bob goes in to the shop to pick up our order, Col waits, arms folded, rocking back and forth on his heels, clearly not happy.

'Mate,' Col says. 'Mate, do me a favour, will ya?'

'Sure. What?' Bob asks.

'Burn the bloody recipe book where this mick pool business came from, will ya?'

On another occasion, Col delivers a box of spatchcocks late one Friday night when Bob and I are in our sunken bath with its floor to ceiling windows. When Col can't find us upstairs, he wanders onto the downstairs deck and sees us in the bath.

'Looks good, mate,' he says, leaning against the window, ready for a long chat.

Bob is laughing loudly. I'm trying to cover whatever bit of me I think is most vulnerable, which makes Bob laugh even more.

'Havin' a good time, are ya?'

'Great!' Bob says.

'Yeah. Looks good. Any room for me?'

'Of course,' Bob says. 'Get your clothes off. Come on in.'

'Might just do that. Water looks good and hot.'

I finally find my voice. 'Go upstairs and drop off the spatchcocks. There's a beer in the fridge. We'll be up in a minute.'

'Right then. Ah, leave the water in for me will ya. I love a bath!'

He disappears and Bob and I collapse with laughter.

'I wouldn't want to live anywhere else in the world, would you?' I ask, because I am sure of his answer.

Bob raises his eyebrows, which is a sign that he's thinking hard. 'We'll move,' he says finally, and my face must look whacked. 'But only if we find something better.'

'Bastard! Had me going there for a second.'

'Yeah. Felt good.'

Not long after, Bob moves in, first with his tool kit, then with his clothes, and so do the white cockatoos. They want my tender new lemons on the trees I planted only days after I bought the house when I was full of doubt and worry and with my father's words ringing in my head: 'A house is not a home until it has a lemon tree.' So I planted two trees, just to be sure. And after Tony died, I added a lime tree. Whenever I walk past it, I think of him. 'Gin and tonic, please, dear. Lime not lemon, if you don't mind.'

Ken, who has a lemon tree in his backyard, told me I'd never get any fruit. Told me the soil was too poor. But I carried in bag after bag of manure until the soil turned dark chocolate and I see him look across at my luscious fruit sometimes, and scratch his head.

When the tree is white with cockatoos heavy enough to break young branches, I rush outside and chase them off. But one very early morning, when I'm just out of the shower, I glance outside and see lemons scattered all over the ground. The tree is thick with cockatoos taking a single bite and then dropping the fruit to pluck another.

'Get off, you bastards,' I shriek, racing out stark naked with nothing but a hastily grabbed tea towel to flick at them. 'Get away.'

Enraged, I pick up the damaged fruit and throw it at them where they hover in nearby gum trees, waiting for me to tire.

Jack walks past and says, 'Good morning. Real buggers, aren't they?' he adds.

'What can I do about them?' I wail.

'Not much.'

And then I realise I'm standing there without a stitch on. 'Oh Jesus,' I say, looking down.

'What's the matter?' asks Jack, puzzled.

'Nothing.'

And I flee inside.

Just as winter begins to cut short the days and the sun moves north, changing the pattern of light on the house, Bob leaves for a five day business trip to Melbourne. I pack little containers of fresh and dried fruit, fill a thermos with strong coffee, and make sandwiches to eat during the long drive. I am irrationally terrified that something will happen to him, that I will never see him again. That he, like my husband and brother, will be snatched away.

'Ring me often,' I plead. 'I want to know you're ok.'

'All right. But stop worrying. I've done this trip hundreds of times.'

'Yeah, but ring me anyway.'

Late morning, the phone rings. 'Next time,' Bob says emphatically, 'don't put in so many prunes!'

That night he rings from his youngest daughter's home and we talk each other to sleep. Love doesn't change much, no matter how old you are.

While he's away, I attack all the jobs I've been putting off. Piles of ironing, cleaning the fridge and washing the windows. But chores don't fill the gap and the days and nights balloon emptily.

On the day he is due home, I shop in Mona Vale for groceries to make a special welcome home dinner. At the fruit market, I am pondering the flowers when an arm slips around my waist. I know who it is immediately from the scent. Tangy as sunbaked skin after swimming in salt water. No claggy colognes for Bob. Sometimes, when he's sitting at his desk and I'm passing by, I'll bend and kiss the back of his neck just so I can inhale what smells to me like summer.

I kiss him hello, ridiculously happy to see him, grabbing a couple of bunches of flowers to hide my pleasure.

'Those flowers are awful,' Bob says. 'Put them back.'

'They're fine.' I put them in the trolley.

He takes them out and returns them to the buckets. 'No. I really don't like them.'

His behaviour is so out of character I shrug and let it go. We climb into our separate cars and go home.

We pull in to the commuter dock to unload at the same time and he leaps out of his car, rushes to his boot and brings out a big, fat bunch of beautiful white lilies. His face, so often serious, is gloriously smug. 'These,' he says, 'are better flowers.'

That night, after a dinner of baby roast lamb followed by lemon pancakes, we snuggle on the sofa while he tells me about his trip. The fire is warm, the house feels full again and something suspiciously like contentment oozes cosily.

'What would you say,' Bob murmurs, swirling wine in his glass and looking at it intently, 'if I asked you to marry me?'

'Why don't you ask me and find out, you dope?'

He looks at me for a second and then glances away quickly. 'Well, will you?'

'Will I what?'

'Marry me!'

'*When*?'

And we start laughing.

'But,' I say, serious, 'if your children don't like the idea, we won't go ahead. Ok? We don't need the formality of marriage. Not if it's going to cause problems.'

Bob dials his kids. They are incredibly kind, wish us luck, and tell us it is wonderful news. Which must be difficult for them. Then Bob rings Barbara's mother in Melbourne.

'Oh yes,' she says calmly, 'Barbara told me it would probably happen.'

Barbara's incredible generosity of spirit. And her love for Bob. She loved him enough to want him to be happy after she died. A rare woman.

What's the best way to explain how I felt that evening? I was happy, of course, and cherished, which is so critical. But mostly I felt settled in my mind and spirit. No more searching, no more restlessness, no more trying to find a place to set down roots. I was fifty years old, and instead of doors slamming in my face they were swinging wide open.

'There's just one thing,' I say to Bob.

'What's that?'

'I do not want to move from my house. Can you live here, instead of *Tarrangaua*?'

'I think I could live anywhere with you.'

'Actually, there's one other thing.'

Bob looks at me nervously. 'Yes?' he asks.

'You know that glorious old wreck in the bay, the old barge with the turned-up tail?'

'Ye-e-s?'

'Do you think we could restore it? I've always wanted to bring her back to glory.'

'No.'

It's said with such finality, I can't think of anything to say.

'That's the kind of project,' he adds, 'that makes contented couples end up divorced!'

'Bit soon for a divorce. We're not even married yet. Might as well let the idea go, then?'

'Good.'

How do I explain the relationship with Bob? As I write this, it feels as though we have been together for forty years instead of, by the year 2005, four. Bob is my friend and our friendship is deep, forged in times that neither of us wants to remember but that we can never forget.

I feel comfortable whingeing about aches and pains when once I would have hidden what seemed like evidence of aging, and I don't bother with stretchy fabrics and sexy shoes any more. 'I like what's underneath the clothes,' he says when I ask if he cares that I wear jeans and clumpy workboots now. I have put on weight and I like it because I am fit and healthy and that's all that matters.

I wake each day to a man who cares deeply about my happiness and does whatever he can to ensure it. It is said that in relationships, some of us are gardeners and others the gardens. Bob, of course, is a gardener. What I love most, though, is the way he notices. If I am tired after a long trip, the next time we have to travel a long way, he invents a reason to stop halfway to rest. He never once makes me feel like a liability or a nuisance. If he says he will be somewhere at a certain time, he is there. This is a man who somehow never gets caught up at the office, never gets waylaid at the pub by a bloke he hasn't seen for years.

This is a man who puts himself between you and a cranky bison (which he did on a trip through Yellowstone National Park), this is a man who will chop parsley for two hundred people because you ask him to. This is a man who brings the dog when he picks you up after day surgery, even though he has to leap across three boats at the commuter dock, holding the dog in his arms, to reach the dock. But he does it because he knows the dog gives you joy.

This is a man who studies people and quietly creates opportunities for them to follow their dreams. This is a man who is tough but not afraid to be soft, a man who understands quite clearly the difference between right and wrong and, even if it costs him, will resist doing harm.

The greatest bliss is that when he says something, it is the truth. Even if it's not what I want to hear. Which means, of course, that the trust is absolute. And that is the greatest of all gifts.

20

WE ARE MARRIED IN THE middle of Lovett Bay on Perce's lovely old restored, navy boat, *Perceverance*, which is also the Woody Point start boat. It's a splendidly sunny day in mid-winter. A day so unseasonally warm, there is no need for jackets even on the water where the breeze is often stronger and colder. Jack, our neighbour up the hill, fills the ferry wharf with fronds of fern so we walk through a delicate green arbor to climb on board, dogs and all (Chip Chop, Obi who always mysteriously knows when there's a party on, and my stepdaughter's dog, Bella), to meet the marriage celebrant.

We anchor in the heart of Lovett Bay and after a glass or two of champagne, Bob and I stand together and slightly red-cheeked with nerves, answer the questions until the celebrant announces us man and wife. My mother, with rings weighing down every finger on both hands and dressed to the hilt, looks suspiciously like there is a tear in her sharp, old eyes. Earlier, she'd followed me in to the walk-in wardrobe, insisting she fasten the buttons on my velvet top, *like a proper mother-of-the-bride*, she said. When Paul and I married, we sneaked off to the registry office, denying her the chance to play the role.

Pittwater shines as we putt putt around the crumbly shores for an hour or two, with beautiful yachts under billowing white sails passing and people waving, and shouting good luck. We sip champagne and watch an occasional sea eagle take to the sky. After we sign the documents, we return to the house down the hill, the *Tin Shed*, where we live and where Sophia waits with a lunch prepared earlier. The table is set with the good silver cutlery, I've pulled out the crystal glasses. There are flowers everywhere. One huge bunch delivered earlier by Stacky.

'There's not a strelitzia left in the bay,' he announced proudly. 'Picked the lot. Happiness always, you two.'

Even my mother, who always sets a brilliant party table, approves. We feast on cold seafood and roasted spatchcocks and finish with a wicked cake layered with dark chocolate and meringue. Long after everyone has gone to bed, Bob and I, with Chip Chop sleeping between us on the sofa, look into the flames of the fire, holding hands. It is a day to hang on to for as long as possible.

'Happy?' he asks.

'I have never been happier in my life.'

And he sighs, as though he's done a good job.

The following night we decorate the pathway from the ferry wharf to the house with candles in paper bags. We fill the bottom of the bags with sand to hold them steadfast and stop them from setting alight. Their glow is festive and it feels like we're following a magical pathway to a carnival where coloured lights necklace the front deck. On the lawn, fires in old washing machine drums warm the cold night air and out the back, Gordon's old dinghy is filled with ice and booze. Lisa from Elvina Bay, now a wonderful friend, has prepared enough food to still even my paranoia about not having enough, and we invite what feels like the whole of Pittwater to help us celebrate. I dance barefoot until my feet bleed.

21

FOR OUR HONEYMOON, we set off from Sydney in Bessie, Bob's ten-year-old burgundy coloured, much dented (mostly by me on city streets) 4WD. We're going camping. Our destination is Cape York.

I insist on taking camp stretchers, down filled pillows with white pillow cases, white sheets and four camp ovens. I pack plenty of wine glasses (plastic? Never!), white table linen and candlesticks. I am filled with romantic ideas of beautiful candlelit suppers, cocktails at sunset. I have no idea of how camping actually works. Bob is grim-faced but jams it all into Bessie without saying a word. Bob has been camping all his life. It was the only way he could afford to take his family on regular holidays. For him, it flows naturally. For me, the romance quickly fades and it becomes a gruelling process of putting up house and then taking it down the next morning. Of getting a kitchen organised and dismantling it. Of packing and unpacking. I can never remember where the torch, spatula, loo paper, or whatever, is.

My breaking point comes as we set up camp on the banks of the Jardine River in Far North Queensland. To get there, we've rattled along corrugated red dirt roads, plunged through creeks, winched a fallen tree that was blocking the track and churned through deep drifts of sand, slipping and sliding, almost crashing into trees. It has been a day filled with fright. As I set up those silly camp stretchers I insisted on taking, I jam a finger on the side of my body where infection is a great risk. I am covered in sand fly bites, filthy, hot, frightened of the saltwater crocodiles that cruise in vivid view from our tent and just plain exhausted. I cry and cry.

'This isn't working for you, is it?' Bob asks, dabbing antiseptic on my bleeding finger. I look down at my unspeakably filthy feet, black from walking through old campfire dust and cannot respond. 'We'll get you on a plane from Cape York. We'll leave tomorrow.'

Every fibre of me wants nothing more than to get on that plane. But it means Bob will have to drive home alone, 4000 kilometres, along jaw-shattering and hazardous roads. Challenging enough with two of you, downright depressing alone. This is a turning point for me in many ways. I cannot let him go on alone. We are partners, through good and bad. With that decision, I find myself letting go of worry about danger, dirt, heat and discomfort. All that matters is Bob's safety. And my commitment to him shifts from starry-eyed to steadfast.

I now understand that camping holidays are an achievement, a daily set of new challenges that stretch the mind and body, and emotions. At home, routines are safe and fixed and designed for easy comfort: Arrive, turn on a light, a tap, a stove, flop on a couch. With each new camp, though, home is built from scratch and there is no such thing as 'too tired'. If you are 'too tired' to pitch camp at the end of a long day's driving along rainbow coloured dirt tracks, there is nowhere to sleep, nothing to eat. Physical boundaries are pushed to the limits. But if it is exhausting at first, each day fitness levels improve. The aches and pains from unfamiliar exercise diminish, new muscles appear in my arms, and my stomach feels suddenly flatter.

As my body changes, so too, do the frames of everyday life. It's bedtime not long after the sun goes down. There is no electric light to read by, no television to invade our lives. The birds wake you in the dove-grey light of pre-dawn. What would seem like punishment at home, becomes privilege in the bush. Every sunrise is a brilliant daily performance, every new campsite a home with a strikingly different view – hills the colour of wild salmon, silver deserts with soils that range from ochre to black, turquoise oceans, creeks the colour of old gold. After a while, we develop little idio-syncrasies. Bob combs his hair every day even though it is quickly blown by the wind through the open car window. I clean my shoes even though they are instantly dusty when I put them on.

I eventually realise that this kind of travel is not about ticking the boxes ('been there, done that'), it's what you learn about your-self and your partner that is the gift. Most extraordinary of all is the shock you feel when you look in the mirror for the first time in weeks. Who is that middle-aged woman staring back at you? Because, of course, you feel young again. Adventurous, capable and physically challenged. The hammering of biological clocks is non-existent in the middle of nowhere. How you *feel* becomes, for once, the true measure of age.

Most of our camps are bush camps. What that means is no taps, no showers, no electricity, no dunnies (as they are universally referred to), no anything. But there's nearly always a river just metres away so clear I can see the catfish bottom feeding; shade from snowy ghost gums, pure and elegant in the morning sun and night skies so lustrous they make city lights seem dim and dirty. I learn, over days and weeks, to revel in the illicit freedom of being able to pee wherever and whenever I want. On the long, empty stretches of road, no-one sits cross-legged until a proper loo is reached (it may be days away!). You stop, squat by the car wheel (or in the middle of the road if you want to!) and that's it. If a rogue vehicle happens along at an inappropriate moment, no-one gives a damn.

One night I wander from the campfire, flicking the torch around, looking for a good spot to pee. The earth flashes with tiny, bright lights. Thousands of spiders' eyes glow like a river of diamonds and I calmly move on to another area of ground when once I would have screamed. Hours slip by watching a pair of pure white herons soar like the Concorde, ducking and weaving in a magical courting ballet. One morning, six black cockatoos fly over us, their red tails flashing like airborne sirens and in the evening, when the thermals grow powerful, hundreds of kites spiral heavenwards, silhouetted by a sinking, orange sun. Some nights, we build up the campfire and sit into the late, dark hours, listening to fish jumping and the occasional hoot of an owl.

At one camp, Bob goes fishing on an incoming tide, armed with live bait caught earlier in the day. I stand near him with my *croc* stick (useless, I know, in the event of a crocodile attack but it gives me comfort). I wear a headlamp torch (like a miner's) and scour the shore for unwanted company. We've been told about the over sociable fella around the bend who measures eighteen feet. We do not want to be introduced. As Bob whoops with the sound of success – a large bite on his line – I casually ask him what the two shiny red lights are further down our sandy bank.

'I think,' he tells me, casually dropping his rod, 'it's a fuckin' croc!' With that, we both high-tail it to higher ground and sink into a reviving glass of wine, grins on our faces and feeling wondrously alive.

Temperatures get searingly hot, insect life lethal. So daily rituals are quickly pared back to a minimum. Routines are simplified to a degree that would seem impossible at home. If it seems spartan at first, it soon feels quite liberating. One wash a day from a bucket of water, standing naked in an isolated camp site, with your partner washing your back. Going to bed with sandy feet is what I now call 'clean' dirt, the kind that comes from sand and dust, not grease and grime.

A single hot plate over a fire is ample for creating the most sumptuous meals, making a mockery of my collection of pots and pans at home. Often I turn to Bob and say: 'How good is this?' And he smiles just a little, looks into the flames of a campfire and nods. The ritzy array of expensive condiments I stocked up with soon taste over-complicated and is passed on to other campers. A little garlic, a little onion, a touch of chili or salt and pepper, and food tastes simple and pure. On good camps, we eat fish freshly caught by Bob – a smutty grunta, a bream, a mango jack. A much-coveted barramundi is undersized and lives again as Bob throws it back. Usually, though, it's chops, steak, whatever fresh produce we can pick up along the way. As a last resort, we open a can, usually of borlotti beans, or beetroot, or corn.

Most mornings, the campfire is still warm and it takes just a few dried leaves and twigs to get it blazing. The old, blackened billy goes on, the smell of wood burning fills the air, and the prospect of a hot cuppa in an enamel mug holds more thrill than a five-course dinner at the best restaurant in town. One day, on a rough, isolated track, we pull off the road for an easy lunch of salami on crackers, with tomatoes, cucumber and cheese. As we drop the tail gate one corner of Bessie slowly sinks.

'AARRRRRH!' Bob storms, spinning in one spot. It is our third flat for the trip. The red earth, as fragile as pie crust, is covered in three-cornered jacks and needle-sharp spinifex so 'ARRRRH!' goes on for quite a long time.

After weeks of being with your partner twenty-four hours a day, with virtually no privacy, outside entertainment or relief, I suspect only committed relationships survive intact. Time and again, we are each revealed at our weakest in situations where there is nothing to hide behind, no door to slam shut. Some-where along the way, I watch a couple in their seventies roll up their inflatable mattress together – he at one end, she at the other, squeezing the air out to pack it as tightly as possible. As they meet in the middle, the old woman surrenders her grip on the mattress and cups her hands around her partner's face, kissing him gently on the mouth. He smiles and gives her a gruff, loud kiss in return. It is an image that will stay in my mind forever, one I hope Bob and I will replicate as we continue our safaris into the next two decades.

We pamper ourselves just once – a bath and a flushing dunny in a ritzy motel. At first, the relief from our spartan regime is exquisite. But at night, when we draw the curtains, the bedroom seems tight and confined. When I wake in the hours before dawn, there is nothing but blackness.

'I miss the stars,' I tell Bob in the morning. And the next night as I lie in bed, I ask: 'Where is the moon?' When I thoughtlessly tip my tea dregs over the balcony, camping style, and douse a passing young couple, Bob smiles.

'Why don't we move on?' he suggests.

On the last night of our trip, we pitch camp in five minutes and have our first uncooked dinner of thick slices of Kassler with salad and tinned baby beetroot (too buggered to go searching for wood in the dusk). We sink into bed covered in red dust.

'I think,' I mutter to Bob before falling into a deep, dreamless sleep, 'I achieved a personal best today.'

'Hmm,' he responds, faking interest.

'I have worn the same shorts for eight days in a row.'

But he is already asleep.

EPILOGUE

I STARTED WRITING THIS book down the hill in the *Tin Shed* (I never did get around to renaming my house *Geebung*), where Bob and I lived when we returned from our honeymoon. Now, as I finish it, I sit in the room that was once Dorothea Mackellar's bedroom in the pale yellow house on the high, rough hill, looking through a forest of towering spotted gums across Pittwater to Scotland Island. We swapped houses because I couldn't bear watching Bob run up to his shed whenever he wanted a tool, or whenever he wanted to fix something. I guess we *really* moved so Bob could get his shed back. I thought it would be a terrible wrench to pack up my life again, but it was easy. Home is where Bob is. And Chip Chop.

Almost two years have passed since we first carried lots of boxes and armchairs along the back track – or Lover's Lane, as Barbara called it, and I now know why. I drink abstemiously these days – a glass of champagne to celebrate, a good red on a winter night.

Pia has moved to a coastal town in northern New South Wales, where she works hard for charity and the local community. She's built herself a gloriously glamorous house and turned into an awesome cook. She's even been known to deviate from a recipe. Only slightly, of course.

Lulu has a lovely, gentle, funny partner and they've been living together for a few years. Bella still drops twigs in your lap, but she's grey around the muzzle and her black fur is turning brown. In her heart, though, she still thinks she's a puppy and if we let her, she'd join the dog race in a flash. But we hold her back. She's too old. Obi has a new family and wanders much less now he is more settled.

My stepdaughter, Suzi, has a child of her own, a wonderfully smiley little boy with huge blue eyes and a passion for olives. She asked me to be godmother and it's a role I relish. Now that she and her partner live in Sydney, we see each other as often as we can. They are splendid parents.

Our little ghetto in Lovett Bay has changed quite a lot since I moved here. Ken and Jan have sold the Lovett Bay Boatshed to Michael and Marybeth, a fantastic family with big, generous hearts who work hard and meticulously and are building a fine reputation. Ric and Robyn have settled into the house next door to the *Tin Shed* and are great friends.

The people who live in the *Tin Shed*, John and Terese, are a vibrant, engaging couple and wonderful to be around. And up the hill behind the *Tin Shed*, Jack and Brigitte have three boys instead of two. As the Buddhists say, change cannot be halted.

At first when we moved into *Tarrangaua*, I wanted to plant grand native gardens and tame the bush. But every time I visualised borders or clusters of ordered shrubs, I found them unappealing and dull. One day, the thought occurred to me that there was no way I could improve on nature. So it was better by far to let the burrawangs and xanthorrhoeas, the acacias, banksias and casuarinas, find their own places to set down roots. They are, after all, more suited to this rugged terrain than any strays I might bring in, native or not. In any case, wallabies seem to have developed the most exotic tastes and soon devoured the few shrubs I planted in my first wave of creativity. So I am content, now, with a lemon and lime tree, and a few white magnolias in the courtyard at the back of the house. Barbara, I think, would be pleased with that.

The first Easter we lived here, we held an art exhibition of linocuts of Pittwater scenes and Pittwater's wonderfully quirky boatsheds by Katie Clemson, a friend. (Some of the boatsheds appear in this book.) To open it, we invited Australian author Di Morrissey, who grew up in a house just beyond Frog Hollow. In her evocative speech, Di talked about the day she met Dorothea Mackellar. She was nine years old and a lonely child, living here at a time when there were few weekenders and even fewer full-timers.

'Dorothea, or Miss Mackellar — she was only ever known as Miss Mackellar — asked me what I was doing,' Di explained, standing in the long, beamed sitting room in a misty pink suit, her bright blonde hair piled high on her head. 'I told her I was looking for fairies.'

Dorothea asked Di: 'Have you found any? May I help you?'

'And so we set off looking for fairies together,' Di continues. 'After a little while, when we returned to the house after hunting unsuccessfully, Dorothea asked me what I wanted to be when I grew up.

'"I want to be a writer," I told her, wide-eyed and innocent of her fame.

'"Do you?" she replied. "Well, I write a little, too. Would you like me to recite a poem I've written?"

'"Oh yes, please," I said.

'Dorothea, in her lilting voice with its trace of a Scottish burr, began "The love of field and coppice" and did not stop until she'd recited every verse of her iconic poem, "My Country".

'When she finished, she smiled at me and I looked at her gravely and said with surprise in my voice: "You know, that was really *quite* good."'

After her speech to open the art exhibition ended, I asked Di what Dorothea Mackellar wore the day she met her.

'A long, dark dress and a hat, I think. Yes, that was it. A rather dull coloured dress, navy or black, in a heavy fabric. The hat was quite big. Straw, I think.'

So Barbara's fleeting glimpse of a woman in a dark dress and straw hat, the roaming wraith, was laid to rest. I wish Barbara had been able to hear Di's words.

Our life here is rich in all the ways that count. Rich in love, in family and friends, in community life, rich simply because we are able to live in such a stimulating and accessible physical world. When I look back, I realise many of the times I thought were so tough that I might not recover taught me instead what I needed to know and understand to grow stronger. They led me, eventually, to more joy than I ever thought existed. I guess what I learned above all else was to never give up, and to accept change instead of using it as a means to escape the hard episodes.

It is now six years since I was diagnosed with breast cancer and the great big crashing fear of those first days of diagnosis and chemo has abated. I know it will always be there in some form although I do not think about cancer often, only if I find myself worrying about small problems and need reminding that life is finite.

As I write, it is raining, which is a blessing because we've had drought for four years and the bush is powdery and brittle. The lack of water has brought shy lyrebirds to the garden looking for food. Wallabies, skittish and unapproachable in good seasons, wait at the back door, swaying with hunger, for a few scraps. I find I cannot begrudge them food, even if it means letting them decimate the lemon tree and strip the herb garden until the plants give up and wither.

The drought has been so mean even the kookaburras laugh less and brush turkeys that usually flee hysterically at the approach of a human simply fly to a high branch and hover until you go indoors. Then they scrounge desperately once again. The desire to survive makes heroes of most of us, I think, as I watch them.

As I write today, though, Lovett Bay is grey, like the sky. Every so often, when heavy black clouds roll in thickly, I cannot see beyond the trees. That's when I feel like I am sitting high above the world in my private paradise. Chip Chop sleeps at my feet under the table and waits impatiently until we go for our afternoon walk when the bush is alive. She still can't be trusted not to run off occasionally so I take her on the lead and she is used to it now.

Each day here holds some surprise. A goanna on the lawn or marauding the eggs in the chook shed, a python slithering along the hallway, a cheeky antechinus making a nest in the piano. Not a moment is empty or idle. There is not a day when I don't give a silent thank you for being alive.

And of course, there is Bob.

ACKNOWLEDGEMENTS

Thanks to the great, big, fabulous Pittwater community who make my life richer in every way, every day. Thanks, too, for letting me write about you all with such good grace, humour and generosity of spirit. Apologies too, if my memory has failed me here and there. When there is so much wonderfulness, moments can blur a little despite the best intentions. Thanks to Caroline Adams, my friend, dog walking partner and brilliant agent, who not only nursed this project from a vague idea to the finish, but whose sage and canny advice made the process one of lighthearted fun – tempered by a cool eye for the details. My mother, Esther, deserves a special thank you for not flinching from my exposure of some of her more memorable times. Her response, when she read the manuscript, was typically to the point. 'Don't change a word. And thank God you didn't turn me into a wimp.' Thanks to Peter Martin who kindly assessed the 'cringe' moments in the manuscript and made wise recommendations about potential family sensitivities. Thanks to Maggie Tabberer, a fabulous, compassionate and earthy dame who is an inspiration to us all, and who made time to read *Salvation Creek* despite a hectic schedule. Thanks for the kind words, Maggie. And thanks also to William McInnes, a great actor, terrific writer and best of all, a lovely, laconic bloke who knows who he is and never loses sight of what matters in life, for his support. Thanks to the whole team at Random House but especially Fiona Henderson, Katie Stackhouse (whose uncle is

Stacky — an amazing coincidence), and book editor Jo Jarrah, whose eye and ear saved me time and again. Thanks too, to Bob's children, who have shown me nothing but warmth and kindness even when it must have been incredibly tough for them. Then there is Bob . . . who quietly encouraged, endlessly supported and finally cajoled, until the manuscript was finished. 'Have a go,' he said when I muttered vaguely about doing a booklet on Pittwater. 'You've got to take a risk sometimes.' Under Bob's coaching, I finally understood the nobility of trying instead of fearing failure. A recipe for life, really, isn't it? For the rest, I hope the book manages to express my gratitude to family, friends and colleagues who stuck around for the down times as well as the up. Thank you. You are all the very best.

ABOUT THE AUTHOR

Susan Duncan spent her childhood in country Victoria where her father was supply officer for Bonegilla Migrant Camp. The first full sentence she uttered, according to her mother, was 'Mama mia, my tooter's kaput!' Fractured English, German and Italian picked up from happily running wild around the camp.

When she was nine, the family moved to Melton, near Melbourne, to run a country pub. She was never taught to pull a beer because her father didn't believe in women behind the bar, but she learned the words to just about every sing-a-long song from World War I onwards and will still launch into 'Danny Boy' with the least encouragement.

After completing her secondary education at Clyde, Woodend, a girls' boarding school where there was as much emphasis on teaching good manners as maths, she quickly quit university to take up a journalism cadetship on a trade fashion magazine before joining *The Sun* newspaper in Melbourne.

After a twenty-five year career that spanned radio, newspaper and magazines, including editing two of Australia's top-selling women's magazines, she woke up one morning and chucked in her job. The decision to drop out came after the deaths of her husband and brother within three days of each other.

She thought abandoning the rat race would be easy: find a country cottage in a small town and follow a different path. But without a family or a job to define her idea of herself, she struggled to understand who she was and where she belonged. Grief, loneliness and being needy blurred even the sharpest line between understanding what was right . . . or very wrong. For a while, she was headed for disaster. Then she took a chance and risked everything on one last role of the dice.

By every rule in the book, it was a gamble that should have failed. And it nearly did. But somehow, out of the terrible mess she'd created, she found a wondrous new world and *an unexpected life*. She also discovered that not only is it *never* all over until the last breath fades away, it quite simply gets better and better. All you have to do is . . . survive.

LEMON CAKE RECIPE

2 lemons
200 g castor sugar
250 g self-raising flour
pinch of salt
1 level teaspoon baking powder
250 g softened, unsalted butter
4 large eggs, very fresh

Syrup
150 g castor sugar
juice of 1 lemon

Preheat oven to 160°C. Grease and flour an 18 cm non-stick round cake tin. Zest both lemons and juice one of them (or you can use just one lemon for a less lemony result). Pulverise zest with castor sugar in a food processor. Sift flour with salt and baking powder and add with butter and eggs to food processor. Process until smooth. Tip into tin and smooth top. Bake for around 30–35 minutes or until cooked.

It is very important the butter is soft but not warm or wet. Cool, soft butter is best. It is also most important to process the mixture until the sugar granules disappear. (Smooth DOES mean smooth.)

To make the syrup, mix sugar with lemon juice. Turn hot cake onto a serving dish, and either leave the flat bottom on top, or turn right way if you prefer, spoon syrup over. (You can either melt the sugar and lemon juice over a low heat or simply combine the two and stir to a paste. I stir to a paste and then smooth it over the cake. It forms a very crackly, delicious topping.)

Finish the cake by putting a flower (a gardenia, a sprig of lemon blossom, a camellia – whatever is in season) in the centre. Ann, a friend from Lovett Bay, once surrounded a cake with those delicate white flowers of the potato vine (*Solanum jasmi-noides*) and it looked quite beautiful.

Another trick is never to overcook. The cake will go dry quite quickly if it's overdone. Keep pressing the top lightly and when it's just slightly firm, it's done.

Eat straight out of the oven. Or, if you allow it to cool, stir some icing sugar into double cream and add a little passionfruit pulp. (Not too much or the cream will be too runny.) Serve alongside cake. Or, if you are making cupcakes, slice top off cake and fill with cream mixture. Replace top. YUM!

This cake recipe is bulletproof. It can be doubled (add one extra egg and an extra 25 g butter but don't increase the amount of baking powder); it makes fabulous cupcakes and mini cupcakes; and it can be frozen and microwaved to refresh. I have microwaved cupcakes left in a container on the kitchen bench for two weeks (went away and forgot about them) and they revived deliciously.

If refreshing in microwave, 10 seconds per cupcake or slice will do it. Frozen cakes take a little longer.

If you want to use a loaf tin, the cake will take about an hour to cook. Usually, you can smell when it's just about ready to pull out of the oven. Buttery, eggy, heavenly scents waft through the house. Perfect with a cuppa!

Happy eating!

If you loved *Salvation Creek*, don't miss *The House*, the beautifully written sequel that continues Susan's story.

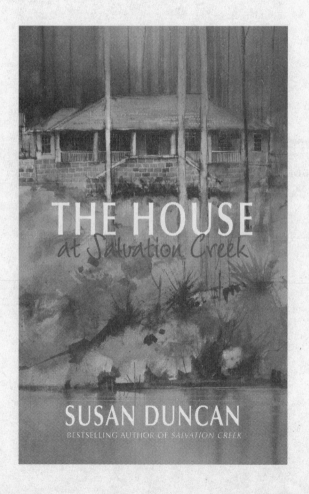

THE HOUSE
at Salvation Creek

SUSAN DUNCAN

BESTSELLING AUTHOR OF *SALVATION CREEK*